THE LIFE AND LETTERS OF WILLIAM LISLE BOWLES

THE LIFE AND LETTERS OF
William Lisle Bowles
Poet and Parson
1762–1850

Robert Moody

Christopher Kent
March 2010

First published in the United Kingdom in 2009
by The Hobnob Press, PO Box 1838, East Knoyle, Salisbury, SP3 6FA
www.hobnobpress.co.uk

British Library Cataloguing in Publication Data
A catalogue record for this book is available from the British Library

ISBN 978-1-906978-02-0

Typeset in Scala 11/12.5pt. Typesetting and origination by John Chandler
Printed by Lightning Source

Contents

Illustrations will be found between pages 192 and 193

Acknowledgements

The author is indebted to the following institutions in the United States of America who have kindly supplied copies of letters in their custody: the State University of New Jersey, New Brunswick, Harvard University (Houghton Library), Princeton University (Department of Rare Books and Special Collections), Huntingdon Library, Art Collection and Botanical Gardens, San Marino, California, the University of Michigan (William L. Clements Library), New York Public Library (the Carl H. Pforzheimer Collection of Shelley and His Circle), Yale University (Beinecke Rare Books and Manuscript Library Services, Special Collections), Bryn Mawr College Library (Seymour Adelman Collection), Rice University, Houston, Texas (Fondren Library), the University of Texas at Austin (Harry Ransom Center) and the University of Tennessee (Hoskins Library).

The following institutions in the United Kingdom have also supplied copies of documents and correspondence held by them: Bath Public Library, Lambeth Palace Library, the Bodleian Library, University of Oxford, the Royal College of Surgeons of England, the National Library of Scotland (John Murray Archive), the British Library (Fox Talbot Museum/Lacock Abbey Collection), Northamptonshire Record Office, Keswick Museum and Art Gallery, Wiltshire and Swindon Archives, Chippenham and the Wiltshire Archaeological and Natural History Society, Devizes.

The author wishes to express his gratitude to the staff of all these bodies who have been unfailing in their kindness in assisting him in his endeavours to see as many as possible of the surviving letters written both to and by Bowles.

Thanks are also due to Miss Suzanne Eward, Librarian and Keeper of the Muniments of Salisbury Cathedral, for allowing the author to consult the Cathedral Chapter Act Books and for bringing to his attention the existence in the Cathedral Library of the portrait of Bowles, here reproduced by kind permission of the Dean and Chapter.

Introduction

If at the end of the eighteenth century any educated person had been asked whether he or she had heard of William Lisle Bowles the answer would surely have been a resounding 'But, of course!' Bowles's *Fourteen Sonnets Written During a Tour* were a runaway success and were universally admired. To the young Samuel Taylor Coleridge the author of the sonnets was 'the exquisite Bowles', William Wordsworth was stopped in his tracks by his reading of them and Charles Lamb had 'no higher idea of heaven' than to hear Coleridge reciting one of Bowles's sonnets.

Throughout his long life Bowles continued to write large amounts of poetry and to enjoy considerable success both as a poet and the writer of many books and pamphlets. His fame outlived him for a short period and in 1855 the Rev. George Gilfillan included an account of Bowles's life in the second of two volumes of his poetical works. In this memoir Gilfillan asserted that 'the events of this gentleman's private and professional life were of no particular interest'. This may well have been true in 1855 but it is to be hoped that the events of his life will be of interest to a reader in the twenty-first century. Some seventy years were to pass before another attempt was made to give an account of his life. In 1926 Garland Greever's *A Wiltshire Parson and his Friends*, while a considerable volume of his correspondence is reproduced, the account of his life is far from comprehensive and fails to convey the wide variety of Bowles's works and achievements. Finally, extensive research by Doreen Slatter resulted in two papers appearing in the *Wiltshire Archaeological and Natural History Magazine* in 1993 and 1996. The first of these, 'The Revd William Lisle Bowles (1762–1850): the Need for a Re-appraisal', ended with the hope that 'someone will fill out the work done by Greever and show that Bowles was a much more considerable figure than has been acknowledged' and the second, 'William Lisle Bowles: The Making of the Bard of Bremhill', concluded with the assertion that 'work could still be done, however, to expand and explain in greater detail the interest of Bowles' career and to identify more of his friends'.

These were the challenges that persuaded me that the time had come to produce as detailed an account as possible of Bowles's life. In an effort to achieve this, I have been able to examine several hundred letters written by and to him and to include extracts from many of them, thus enabling the reader to 'hear', as it were, the true Bowles in all his moods.

It has not been my intention to attempt to pass any judgement on the merits of Bowles's very large poetic output. The opinion of those qualified to do so is that some of the early sonnets are indeed of the highest quality, and therefore I have quoted three of them in full. A perusal of Gilfillan's work, in which almost all of Bowles's poetical works are printed, will enable the reader to discover the quality of much of the remainder of his poetry.

Chapter 1
1762–1795

William Lisle Bowles was born on 24 September 1762 and baptised on the following day at King's Sutton in Northamptonshire, the eldest son of Dr William Thomas Bowles, the vicar there, and Bridget, daughter and co-heiress of Richard Grey DD, Archdeacon of Bedford. His paternal grandparents were Thomas, vicar of Brackley, also in Northamptonshire, and his wife Elizabeth, daughter of William Lisle, Member of Parliament for Brackley, from whom his second forename was derived.

In 1769, through the influence of his father-in-law, who was a friend of the patron, Bowles's father was presented to the living of Uphill with Brean in Somerset some 20 miles south-west of Bristol. Many years later Bowles graphically described the journey 'from the borders of Northamptonshire to the shores of the Severn' and in particular the small procession that set out from the Angel Inn in Bristol's Redcliffe Street on the afternoon of 8 May on the final stage of their long journey. In the leading chaise were young Bowles with his parents and one of his sisters, and in the second were two brothers and three young sisters with a nurse-maid and a more elderly maid-servant. Both carriages followed 'a rustic lad, in yellow and blue livery, something between a footman and a jockey . . . on a black scampering pony, enquiring, in an accent scarcely understood, the road to Uphill in Somersetshire'.[1] Both the chaises were laden with boxes containing books and such other household effects as could be conveyed with the family to its new home. However, before the party could set forth on the last stage of the journey from Northamptonshire a search was made for young Billy, as Bowles was then called, who had wandered off unnoticed, attracted by the sound of the bells pealing from the tower of the church of St Mary Redcliffe. Doubtless the seven-year-old boy, resplendent in 'a new white hat, the crown encompassed with a stripe of gold lace, in a sky-blue jacket and a neat pair of <u>Banbury-fair</u> boots', did not long escape the notice of the anxious searchers.

On the way to Uphill the travellers passed through Brockley Coombe, where they paused while Bowles was taken by the hand of his father and led, in silence, to the top of the hill from which a panoramic view of the surrounding country, with the River Severn and the Welsh hills in the far distance, could be enjoyed. So impressed was young Bowles that he thereafter attributed to this, his first view of the Somerset countryside, his 'earliest associations of poetry with picturesque scenery'.

Their destination was a village described not many years later as 'consisting of a few cottages, occupied by fishermen and labourers . . . at the conflux of the River Axe with the Bristol Channel'.[2] The small Norman church of St Nicholas, which comprised a nave and chancel surmounted by a central tower, situated entirely on its own on a small precipitous hill overlooking the river Axe, and the parsonage house were almost certainly the only buildings of any size or consequence in the Rev. William Bowles's somewhat bleak new parish. The family's new home probably provided limited accommodation for the new rector and his wife with their seven children and three servants, and was later said to be a 'snug parsonage, thickly covered with rose, jasmine, myrtles, and vines, and mantled with festoons of various plants; its russet-thatched roof relieved by luxuriant masses of foliage – a true picture of English home scenery, which in the wide world for comfort and tranquillity is not surpassed'.

Bowles himself was later to describe their new home as being 'In a most retired situation, as forlorn as a solitary parish near a desolate coast could be'.[3] However, it is likely that Bowles spent most of his childhood not at Uphill but many miles away at Shaftesbury in Dorset in Barton Hill House,[4] which had belonged to his father's uncle, Matthew Bowles, an attorney-at-law, who had died in 1768. By the terms of his will the whole of his estate, including Barton Hill House, was to be held by his trustees subject to a number of life interests, and it must have been known that eventually all his property would pass to Bowles's father. As a consequence it is likely that, until this occurred, he made annual payments to the trustees of his uncle's will to enable him to occupy the house that would provide him and his family with considerably more accommodation than the parsonage in Somerset. Further, in Shaftesbury and the surrounding countryside the family would also have found many more congenial friends and acquaintances than in and around the tiny village on the shore of the Severn estuary.

It is not known for certain where Bowles received his early schooling, although he later wrote that he learnt the first rudiments of his education from a parson by the name of Norman, who wrote to his father from Bleadon, a village not far from Uphill, probably in 1769 when Bowles would have been about seven years old:

Master Bowles appears <u>already</u> to have acquired, under his incomparable master, a Fund of Learning and Humour, visible in his representation of Sir Tobit; and if the <u>blossoms</u> are so fair at his early age, what unparalleled <u>fruit</u> may we not hope for, when he is <u>got</u> on top of Parnassus?[5] A prospect Grand enough to make so dull a mortal as your humble servant proud![6]

Billy's father thought his young son's early talent so prodigious that when he returned home from the Rev. Mr Norman's house he made him turn *Joe Miller's Selected Jests* into verse, and whenever company came he was made to recite his translation before the visitors.[7]

Very little is known about his childhood in the town where the family of Bowles had lived for very many years. Certainly, when his eight-year-old younger sister Mary died in 1773 her body was buried not in the church at Uphill but in the parish church of the Holy Trinity in Shaftesbury,[8] where Bowles's ninety-four-year-old great-great-grandfather, another William Bowles, had been buried in 1717.

In quite unexpected places in his later writings Bowles relates incidents from his youth. For instance, in his history of Bremhill, the village in Wiltshire that was to be his home for most of his adult life, having regaled the reader with his views on campanology he cannot resist adding that:

> when quite a boy, the writer, as soon as he heard the bells of one of the churches at Shaftesbury, stole away from his father's house, and in very short time was in a corner of the belfry. No one took any notice of him except occasionally he had a kind word from one of the gentlemen who have already been mentioned who always rung the first or treble bell of the peal, amonst the rustics in the bellfry. But I recollect most vividly some verses in large letters on the wall, opposite to the place which I always chose as my seat, and on looking back to that period, now my old, accomplished, kind, and benevolent friend is in his grave, I have been half-disposed to think, that not only my love of steeple music, but my love of poetry, if not musical rhythm, took its first unnoticed origin from these verses.[9]

Although it has been said that he attended a school in Shaftesbury, while still a small boy Bowles would certainly have been taught Latin, and probably Greek, by his father who, with his mother, took steps to prepare him for his entry to the school at Winchester where his father's eighty-year-old uncle, another William Bowles, was a Fellow, and the poet and literary critic Dr Joseph Warton[10] had been headmaster since

1766. Bowles later recalled some details of this preparation and of his interview at the school:

> I recollect, previously to my being admitted a 'scholar' on Wykeham's foundation, the great pains my mother took me in teaching me to sing correctly the 100th psalm. Every morning I went through this long lesson. I had mastered, with the help of my father, the <u>shortest</u> ode of Horace; and I was now sent off to Winchester, being persuaded that I could at least <u>sing</u>, if I could not <u>construe</u>! To the election-chamber, on the solemn day, I was admitted, with anxious looks and beating heart. There sat, in large white wigs and in black gowns, the wardens of the New College, of Winchester, the '<u>posters</u>' so called, two examining fellows annually selected from New College, the headmaster of Winchester school, all in dreadful array before me. The first question was, 'Can you sing?' The usual answer is, 'yes', and nothing more is said; but having been so well prepared, and taking heart, I answered, 'yes, <u>a little</u>!' and, fearing my powers should not be duly estimated, instantly began, 'All people that'. The warden of New College, Dr. Oglander,[11] said, smilingly, 'That is enough, boy!' but having begun, I was not so easily repressed, for I went on, louder than before, 'that on earth do dwell;' at length I observed all faces gathering blackness, and I retired, murmuring in an under tone, 'with one accord', when I was received by the boys waiting in the outer room with a shout of laughter and a knock in the mouth, which did not, at that time, tend to convince me of the advantages of public education.[12]

Bowles was one of seventeen boys who were duly elected scholars in 1775. However, as there could only be a total of seventy scholars at any one time, he was not admitted to the school until 25 March 1776 when a vacancy occurred. Aged thirteen, he would have found himself in the somewhat uncomfortable position of being the only scholar who entered the school at that time. He was doubtless relieved when a further six new boys joined him as scholars early in September. His fellows were by no means all perfect pupils. As an example, Thomas Wright, who was admitted four months after Bowles, although older than him, was removed in 1778 for 'riot in the streets and assaulting William Moody', probably a fellow scholar of that name.[13]

Bowles later described one of his journeys from Shaftesbury to Winchester:

> Every boy in the school had a whip, and a <u>pair</u> of boots, which they were particularly fond of displaying – comparing the cost, workmanship, neatness &c. The Author was sent from Shaftesbury, on a little pony,

with a servant, <u>not</u> with a pair of <u>new boots</u> but <u>ingloriously</u> in a <u>pair of worsted boot-stockings</u>, which, my father observed, would keep my understockings from the dirt, as well as the <u>best pair of boots</u> in Shaftesbury! I said nothing, but <u>woefully</u> proceeded thus to equip myself, having a <u>guinea</u> as pocket-money.

In my equestrian character, with a heavy heart, I set out to <u>cross</u> the downs to Salisbury, under conscious humiliation at my equipment, the odious <u>boot-stockings</u>! In passing over the downs, as I was not seen by any one, I bore up tolerably well, but deigned not a syllable to the servant, who assured me, in vain, that <u>boot-stockings</u>, in summer, were just as good as <u>boots</u>. I was, as is expressively called in Wiltshire, 'stomachy!'.[14]

The moment I dismounted, at the White Hart,[15] I had determined to make <u>my escape</u>, and never return to school or home. I had a guinea in my pocket: I set out from the inn 'on my forlorn hope' . . .

By the farther end of the Close, just in the corner, was a handsome shoe and boot shop . . . As good luck would have it, a tempting pair of <u>new boots</u>, which I thought would fit me, hung at the door. I walked backwards and forwards for twenty minutes, first looking at the boots, then feeling my money – then looking again at the boots. At last I went boldly into the shop, and said to the shopman, 'What is the price of <u>these boots</u>?' 'The price of these boots, young gentleman, is just twenty shillings!' I had a guinea in my pocket, so that if I bought them, I should have <u>one</u> shilling, with which to go to school; and that was almost as bad as wearing <u>boot-stockings</u>!

Needless to say, Bowles bought the boots, and:

Was just <u>strutting</u> out of the shop, when I spied the inglorious stockings. I took them up with some loftiness of scorn, threw them into the canal,[16] with other <u>inglorious</u> substances, till they were completely out of sight; and then returned, with <u>one shilling</u>, and my new boots to the Inn.[17]

Many years later Bowles related:

Removed to Winchester School, and rising before the other boys as junior of the chamber, at five o'clock in summer, and as soon as it was light in winter, I had no English book to read, at the dim window, but Ken's manual,[18] consisting of prayers and admonitions, composed when he was a Fellow of the college, for the use of the scholars of that foundation.[19]

Stories of the boys' ill behaviour during Warton's headmastership have been much exaggerated, although the serious rebellion of 1793 was undoubtedly the cause of his eventual retirement. His ill-deserved reputation as a lax disciplinarian has overshadowed his success in encouraging those of his pupils who displayed poetic inclinations, and Bowles, together with his contemporary, Thomas Russell,[20] can be numbered among them. Bowles must surely have read Warton's *An Essay on the Writings of Pope* as well as *Poems on Several Occasions, by the Reverend Mr Thomas Warton*. In this volume appear poems written not only by Warton's late father but also by Warton himself and by his younger brother Thomas,[21] later professor of poetry at Oxford and poet laureate. It has been said that Warton transmitted to his pupil 'his very moderate estimate of the poetry and character of Pope',[22] an opinion that was later to be developed by Bowles with perhaps unexpected consequences.

Bowles later described how his great-uncle, William Bowles, who had been a Fellow at Winchester since 1725, would regularly ask him to dinner on Sunday and that:

> After dinner, I had one glass of wine from a bottle, out of which, at 84 years of age, he indulged himself with Three! One glass of wine allotted to me and a shilling with it, were always accompanied with a health, which he never omitted, and, at the age I have mentioned, I have seen him repeat it with tears in his eyes: it was the following

> To the Three Score Ten
> May God make them Happy Men[23]

During his final year at Winchester Bowles was captain of the school, and he regarded his old master with such affection that following Warton's death in 1800 he wrote a monody in his honour. It seems that Warton impressed on his scholars the need to find inspiration for their poetry in nature, and in the verses composed after Warton's death Bowles declares that he 'bade my silent heart rejoice and wake to love of nature'.[24]

It seems that at some stage in his youth Bowles was sent abroad, as many years later the Irish poet Thomas Moore[25] recorded in his journal that Bowles on one occasion gave an account of his education at Strasbourg, although, apart from the fact that he learnt French fortification and that his knowledge of the French language was less than perfect, nothing else is known about this episode in his early life.

Although he was senior on the roll to enter New College, Oxford, to which, as a Wykehamist he would have been expected to proceed, there were no vacancies in 1781,[26] and so instead, the nineteen-year-old Bowles was elected a scholar of Trinity College, Oxford, doubtless owing to the presence there of the senior fellow Thomas Warton, his old master's brother. One of Bowles's earliest poems, 'On Leaving Winchester School. Written in the Year 1782', was composed at this time. In it he anticipated returning to his *alma mater*, when he would 'think upon the joys that crowned my stripling years'.[27]

In 1781 there had appeared the third volume of Warton's *History of English Poetry from the Close of the Eleventh Century to the Commencement of the Eighteenth Century*. Although it has been said that Warton did not take his tutorial obligations particularly seriously, three friends, Henry Headley[28] and William Benwell[29] together with Bowles, nevertheless soon attracted the attention of Warton, who gave them every encouragement. It was not long before Bowles produced evidence of his considerable abilities by winning the Chancellor's Latin verse prize for his poem 'Calpe obsessa, or, The siege of Gibraltar'. It was later said to be in 'the collection of Oxford Prize Poems published by Mr Valpy' and 'a composition of extraordinary merit and classical beauty for so young a writer'.[30] One of the unsuccessful contenders for the prize was Charles Abbott,[31] later Lord Tenterden and Lord Chief Justice. In 1785 Bowles was awarded a Cobden exhibition granted to a Trinity man from Winchester and in the following year he graduated. However, as his exhibition did not expire until 1789 he continued to reside intermittently in college for two or three years. At least one of his prolonged absences was caused by the sudden death of his father in 1786 at the age of forty-nine at Barton Hill House.[32] He lies buried in Shaftesbury where, in Holy Trinity Church, a tablet was erected to his memory.[33] From his father Bowles inherited Barton Hill House, although his mother continued to live in the house until her death.

While at Oxford Bowles paid his first visit to London, with the intention of hearing the works of Handel performed in Westminster Abbey. He had very little money, and therefore had no alternative but to travel from Oxford to London by night on the outside of a stage-coach that left at 10p.m. His much later account of his arrival and sojourn in the metropolis tells us more about the young Bowles at this time:

> I arrived at the Bedford coffee-house, Covent-garden, about nine o'clock in the morning. Young men then wore their hair clubbed behind, and filled with powder and pomatum, in an appendage which was called 'a pig-tail' . . .

As soon as possible, after some refreshment, I sent for the friseur de l'Hotel. It seemed as if I arrived at the mansion of the muses, for the different bed rooms were marked with the names of Melpomene, Clio, Thalia, &c. Clio was alloted to me; but *le voici*, the friseur! Willing on such an occasion to shew I was not a mere academical bumpkin, I told him my hair must be dressed quite in the mode; the consequence of the order was, I had a whole pound of pomatum, with layers of powder worked into my <u>metropolitan pig-tail</u>, ('vanity of vanities,' saith the preacher!) and so tightly was the graceful appendage stuck to my poll, that I could scarcely <u>shut my</u> eyes, much less move my <u>head</u>.

I had already purchased my ticket for the first performance at the Abbey; which was to commence in about three quarters of an hour. Having had no rest, I thought I would lie down for some little time, but as my hair was *en queue* I lay on my back, lest any part of my curls in front should discompose. I held my ticket in one hand, and for fear of dozing told the waiter to be sure to call me, (as I had travelled all night from Oxford,) in time for the music at the Abbey, which he engaged to do.[34]

Needless to say, the waiter failed to call him and when Bowles awoke he discovered that the performance had finished four hours before. However, the next day he arrived at the Abbey in time to hear the funeral anthem that had been composed by Handel and sung at the burial of Queen Caroline.

Among Bowles's contemporaries at Oxford were a number of young men 'of literary taste and talent', as he described them. With him at Trinity were, as well as Henry Headley and William Benwell, Henry Kett,[35] James Dallaway,[36] Josiah Dornford[37] and George Richards[38] – all young men whose various achievements were to secure them a place in the *Dictionary of National Biography* and who, with Bowles, doubtless formed a group of like-minded men. Bowles's fellow Wykehamist Thomas Russell was elected to New College in 1780 but died in 1788. After his death his *Sonnets and Miscellaneous Poems* were published, and the assertion has been made that, with Bowles, he 'may claim an important place in the revival of the sonnet in England'.[39]

At some point during his final year at Oxford it is said that Bowles fell in love with a niece of the lawyer Samuel Romilly,[40] but his wish to marry her was thwarted, probably because of his lack of means. As a consequence, although he had incurred debts at Oxford amounting to the considerable sum of £70,[41] he decided to seek consolation, probably in 1785, by embarking on a tour to the north of England and Scotland, following which his sonnet 'To the River Tweed' was published anonymously in November in the *Gentleman's Magazine*.[42] Later, perhaps in the summer of 1787, Bowles undertook an extended journey to Antwerp and Switzerland. It was during this expedition that he composed a number of sonnets, beginning with one written on landing at Ostend on 21 July 1787 and including another while in Ostend on the following day. On his return to England he decided to write them down, with a view to seeking their eventual publication and, if possible, repaying his debts.

It was now necessary for Bowles to earn a living, however modest. It was natural for him to follow in the footsteps of his father and grandfather by entering the church. In 1788 he was ordained deacon[43] and appointed by Dr Charles Wake[44] to be his curate at East Knoyle, a small village with about 800 inhabitants[45] in the south-western corner of Wiltshire and some 4 miles from Shaftesbury, where Bowles's mother was still living following the death of her husband. His stipend was a modest £40 a year.[46] Wake, who had been rector at East Knoyle since 1746, was a widower, having lost two wives; the second, Bathshua, second daughter of William Beckford[47] of Fonthill, had died in 1777. His sister Magdalen was the recently widowed wife of Bowles's kinsman, another William Bowles, a canon of Salisbury Cathedral. Not only did Wake have this close connection to a member of the Bowles family, but Bowles was returning to a part of Wiltshire where his name was well known: his great-grandfather, Matthew Bowles, who died in 1742, and his great-uncle, William Bowles, fellow of Winchester, who died only seven years before Bowles's arrival in East Knoyle, had both been rectors of nearby Donhead St Andrew.

Bowles himself was later to assert that both of his parents were descended from old and much-respected families, and that his father was 'of an ancient family in the county of Wiltshire'. Certainly, so far as his Bowles ancestors are concerned, their right to bear arms was duly confirmed when Henry St George,[48] Richmond Herald, and Sampson Lennard,[49] Bluemantle Pursuivant, carried out their Wiltshire Visitation in 1623.[50]

Probably because no suitable house was available, Bowles did not make his home in East Knoyle as one would have expected, but in Donhead St Mary, a small village some 4 miles away.

As Wake was also rector of Fonthill Bishop, and, more importantly, a prebendary of Westminster, it is certain that it fell to Bowles to perform most of the duties expected of the rector and his curate. In his replies to Bishop Shute Barrington's[51] Visitation Queries, given just five years before Bowles became curate, Wake declared that divine service was performed in both the morning and afternoon on Sundays, with a sermon being preached at the morning service and with the holy sacrament of the Lord's Supper being administered four times a year.[52] The church in which Bowles would have officiated was, and still is, notable for the elaborate decorated plasterwork in the chancel that depicts scenes from the Old and New Testaments and was designed by Christopher Wren's father,[53] who was rector from 1632 and lost the living during the Civil War, with the plasterwork being held against him at his subsequent trial.

Having spent much of his childhood and youth at Barton Hill House in Shaftesbury, it is certain that Bowles would have been acquainted with members of most of the leading families residing within easy reach of Shaftesbury and in particular those living in the south-western corner of Wiltshire and in the neighbourhood of East Knoyle and Donhead. In Donhead St Andrew was Ferne, the estate of the Grove family, occupied by the thirty-year-old Thomas Grove,[54] his wife Charlotte and their four young children, and in Donhead St Mary John Kneller[55] owned Donhead Hall when Bowles arrived in 1788. The rector of Donhead St Andrew was Dr John Benett,[56] whose elder brother Thomas Benett[57] owned the nearby Pythouse estate, and at Clouds in East Knoyle lived James Still,[58] whose son James Charles was to marry Charlotte, one of Wake's daughters. It is very likely that Bowles had already met and so would have been instantly accepted by all these families.

In 1788 Bowles learned of the death of his friend Henry Headley, who died on 15 November at the age of twenty-three. Headley was a poet of considerable promise who, two years earlier, had produced *Poems and Other Pieces by Henry Headley* and in 1787 his best-known work – *Select Beauties of English Poetry, with Remarks*. Headley's death moved Bowles to compose *Verses to the Memory of Henry Headley, of Norwich*. These, together with a sonnet later entitled 'To Poverty', both stated to be by 'Mr Bowles', were published in the *Gentleman's Magazine* of December 1788.[59] These are the first of Bowles's work bearing his name, apart from his Prize Poem written while at Oxford, to appear in print.

The success of seeing his work published in the *Gentleman's Magazine* must surely have persuaded Bowles that the time had come to attempt to have printed and published some of the sonnets he had written following his tours of the north of England and Europe. It is likely that in the autumn or early winter of 1788, on a journey to Oxford, the twenty-six-year-old Bowles stopped in Bath and called on Richard Cruttwell,[60] a printer and publisher and proprietor of the *Bath Chronicle*. As Bowles later recalled:

I had three times knocked at this amiable printer's door, whose kind smile I still recollect; and, at last, with much hesitation, ventured to unfold my message: it was to enquire whether he would give anything for 'Fourteen Sonnets', to be published with or without the name. He at once declined the purchase, and informed me he doubted very much whether the publication would repay the expense of printing, which would come to about five pounds. It was at last determined <u>one hundred copies</u>, in quarto, should be published as a kind of 'forlorn hope;' and these 'Fourteen Sonnets' I left to their fate, and thought no more of getting <u>rich</u> by poetry! In fact, I owed the most I ever owed at Oxford, at this time, namely seventy pounds; and knowing my father's large family and trying circumstances, and those of my poor mother, I shrunk from asking more money when I left home, and went back with a heavy heart to Oxford, under the conscious weight, that my poetic scheme failing, I had no means of paying Parsons, the mercer's, bill![61]

In either January or February 1789 the sonnets appeared under the title of *Fourteen Sonnets, Elegiac and Descriptive, written during a Tour*, being printed in Bath by R. Cruttwell and sold by Charles Dilly[62] in London. The advertisement at the beginning of the slim booklet of fifteen pages declared:

The following Sonnets, (or whatever they may be called) were found in a Traveller's Memorandum-Book. They were selected from amongst many others, chiefly of the same. The Editor has ventured to lay a few of them before the Publick, as he hopes there may be some Readers to whom they may not be entirely unacceptable.

It is likely that Cruttwell sent one or two copies to Bowles, who was doubtless delighted to see his sonnets in print but not so pleased, perhaps, to notice that pages 6, 7 and 8 had been misnumbered 14, 15 and 16!

Almost fifty years later Bowles was to relate:

I confined myself to fourteen lines, because fourteen lines seemed best adapted to unity of sentiment. I thought nothing about the strict Italian model; the verses naturally flowed in unpremeditated harmony, as my ear directed, but the slightest inspection will prove they were far from being mere elegiac couplets.[63]

The poems, which were issued anonymously, soon attracted attention, being mentioned in the March number of the *Analytical*

Review where the sonnet 'Written at Bamborough Castle' was reprinted. However, this review was far from favourable and must has caused Bowles some annoyance: 'The author of these Sonnets evidentally endeavoured to imitate Mrs Charlotte Smith's little elegant compositions; they are certainly very inferior, yet their simple unaffected style gives them some claim to praise.'[64] Further, they were noticed by the *Monthly Review; or Literary Journal*:

> These sonnets, as the Advertisement informs us, were found in a traveller's memorandum-book; but they are not the Sonnets of a traveller who was glad to pick up any lame and hobbling muse to beguile the tedious way, and who wrote, like Sir Richard Blackmore,[65] to the rumbling of his chariot wheels. They have some poetic merit, and the admirers of the plaintive Petrarch, and his English imitator, Mrs Charlotte Smith[66] of Bignor Park, will peruse several of them with pleasure. As a sample we give the 6th sonnet, *To Evening*.

This sonnet is then printed in full, with the reviewer adding: 'These two concluding lines are beautiful.'[67] So that the present reader may understand what it was that so impressed the reviewer, the sonnet is here reproduced:

> Evening! As slow thy placid shades descend.
> Veiling with gentlest hush the landscape still,
> The lonely battlement, the farthest hill
> And wood, I think of those who have no friend;
> Who now, perhaps, by melancholy led.
> From the broad blaze of day, where pleasure flaunts,
> Retiring, wander to the ring-dove's haunts
> Unseen; and watch the tints that o'er thy bed
> Hang lively; oft to musing Fancy's eye
> Presenting fairy vales, where the tired mind
> Might rest beyond the murmurs of man kind,
> Nor hear the hourly moans of misery!
> Alas for man! that Hope's fair views the while
> Should smile like you, and perish as they smile!

Imagine Bowles's surprise and delight, therefore, when he received a letter from Cruttwell telling him that all copies of the sonnets had been sold,[68] and that had he printed five hundred copies he had no doubt that they also would have been sold. As a result Bowles and Cruttwell probably met when seven further sonnets were selected to be published with the original fourteen. On 14 May it was announced in the *Bath Chronicle* that the volume was 'in the Press, and speedily will be published'[69] and on 21 May the paper announced that it would be published 'on Friday next'.[70] And so it was that five hundred copies of *Sonnets Written Chiefly on Picturesque Spots, During a Tour* were duly printed and published on 29 May, with Bowles now being named as the author. The advertisement, written by Bowles, tells the reader a little more of how the sonnets came to be written:

> The following Trifles were chiefly suggested by some Picturesque Objects which presented themselves to the Author in a Tour to the Northern Parts of this Island, and on the Continent. They were before committed too hastily to the Press; but the favourable Reception which they experienced, has induced him to revise them, and, with the Addition of a few more, to make them less unworthy of the Publick Eye.
>
> It having been said that these Pieces were written in Imitation of the little Poems of Mrs Smyth,[71] the Author hopes he may be exused adding, that many of them were written prior to Mrs Smyth's Publication. He is conscious of their great Inferiority to those beautiful and elegant Compositions; but, such as they are, they were certainly written from his own Feelings.

In the July number of the *Monthly Review* appeared a notice of the second edition, which was followed in 1794 by the publishing of 750 copies of *Sonnets (Third Edition) with Other Poems*, consisting of twenty-seven sonnets and thirteen other poems.

It would be surprising if Bowles were not astonished, if not a little flattered, to hear that in the *St James's Chronicle* in May 1793 appeared a *Sonnet addressed to the Rev. W.L. Bowles* written by the young poet Mary Locke,[72] containing the lines:

> Pour, pour again, sweet Bard, thy wonted strains,
> Soft let them breathe on Sorrow's list'ning ear:
> For who like thee so tenderly complains,
> Stealing from Pity's eye the ready tear?
> Resume thy lyre, and with a master's hand
> Awake its chords, that now neglected lie; . . .

Bowles was never afraid to alter the words of a poem once written if, on a reprinting or republication of it, he thought improvements could be made. So it was that his sonnet 'To the Tweed', which first appeared in the *Gentleman's Magazine* in 1785 when Bowles was barely twenty three years old, re-appeared as one of the famous *Fourteen Sonnets*, but with only ten of the original fourteen lines remaining unaltered in the 1794 edition. The travelling sonneteer is addressing the River Tweed, and in the original version:

Pauses with fond delay thy shores to greet;
The waving branches on thy banks that bend,
E'n now a soft and soothing charm bestow,
And the lone murmurs of thy wave below
Seem to his ear the pity of a friend.

But by 1794:

Delighted turns they beauteous scenes to greet.
The waving branches that romantick bend
O'er thy tall banks, a soothing charm bestow;
The murmurs of thy wand'ring wave below
Seem to his ear the pity of a friend.

No doubt the instant success of *Fourteen Sonnets* encouraged Bowles to attempt to publish more of his work. They were followed in 1789 by *Verses to John Howard, F.R.S.*[73] *on his State of Prisons and Lazarettos*. These verses, dedicated to Bowles's old master Dr Warton as 'a small testimony of respect and gratitude', were printed in Bath by Cruttwell and sold by C. Dilly in London and C. Rann in Oxford. In the following year appeared *The Grave of Howard, A Poem* printed in Salisbury by Edward Easton.[74] In this poem Bowles pays tribute to the work of the prison reformer John Howard, who died in January 1790 and lies buried in southern Russia where he had been investigating the state of Russian military hospitals. At the same time his *Verses on the Benevolent Institution of the Philanthropic Society, for protecting the children of Vagrants and Criminals* were printed in Bath by Cruttwell for the benefit of the Society, which had been instituted in 1788. In the following year appeared ten pages of a reflection on the French Revolution entitled *A Poetical Address to the Right Honourable Edmund Burke*[75] as well as *Elegy, written at the Hot-Wells, Bristol, Addressed to the Revd William Howley*.[76] Howley,[77] later Bishop of London and then Archbishop of Canterbury, had been one of Bowles's friends at Winchester, where he twice won the prize for English verse.

In 1791 *Monody, written at Matlock, October 1791* appeared. This volume contained three poems –the 'Monody', 'The African' and 'On Leaving a Place of Residence'. By this time no educated person in the country could have been unaware of the sufferings of the thousands of slaves being transported in British ships from West Africa to the West Indies, nor of the general opinion that the slave trade, with all its attendant evils, should be abolished. Hundreds of tracts and poems describing the plight of the slaves and urging abolition were being published, and so, in writing and publishing 'The African', Bowles was doing no more than might be expected from a thinking clergyman. 'The Dying Slave' was another poignant product of Bowles's imagination, in which he urges the slave:

> Fear not now the tyrant's power,
> Past is his insulting hour;
> Mark no more the sulen trait
> On slavery's brow of scorn and hate;[78]

The writer of a letter that appeared in the *Gentleman's Magazine* in 1791 expressed such an excessively favourable opinion of the sonnets that even Bowles may have considered it to be not entirely justified:

> I never, Sir, so much wished for the eloquence of an Addison, as I do at this moment, that my persuasions might carry with them a kind of authoritative influence, in recommending to the notice of the world the Sonnets of the Rev. Mr Bowles, which, not to speak in the rhapsody of blind adoration, but in the coolness of deliberate criticism, I esteem the productions of the greatest genius since the days of GRAY . . . the *harmony* of his *verse*, the *dignified simplicity* of his *expression*, and the *sublimity* and *pathos* of his *ideas*, are perfectly original and utterly inimitable . . .[79]

Bowles would doubtless have been pleased to see his name included in *A List of Living English Poets, with Biographical Notes regarding them* published in the *Gentleman's Magazine* in 1792. However, he would have been surprised to learn that the author of the list believed him to be 'a native of London', gratified that in most of his sonnets and other poems 'there is pathos, a fancy, a melancholy, and moral turn, that are highly pleasing', but not so pleased that the writer of the list considered that there was 'throughout by far too much laxity and carelessness'.[80]

A copy of *Fourteen Sonnets* came to the attention of a boy at Christ's Hospital by the name of Samuel Taylor Coleridge.[81] The slim book was given to him by a schoolfellow, Thomas Middleton[82] (later Bishop of Calcutta), and made such an impression that, being unable to afford to buy a copy himself, within eighteen months he had made over forty transcriptions to present to his friends. It is widely accepted that it was his admiration of Bowles's work that persuaded Coleridge to turn his attention from metaphysics to poetry, and in his *Biographia Literaria* (1817) he refers to 'the genial influence of a style of poetry, so tender, and yet so manly, so natural and real, and yet so dignified, and harmonious, as the sonnets, etc of Mr Bowles',[83] and remarks that 'The reader must make himself acquainted with the general style of composition that was at that time deemed poetry, in order to understand and account for the effect produced on me by the Sonnets, the Monody at Matlock, and the Hope, of Mr Bowles.'[84]

Coleridge's admiration for Bowles's work appears to have known no bounds. For instance, in February 1792 he wrote to Mary Evans, a schoolfellow's sister with whom he had fallen in love: 'as compensation for the above rhymes . . . in my next letter I will send you some delicious poetry lately published by the exquisite Bowles'.[85] In the same year Coleridge's fellow undergraduate at Cambridge, Christopher Wordsworth[86] (youngest brother of the poet), noted that, after a long literary discussion, 'Coleridge talked Greek, Max. Tyrius he told us, and spouted out of Bowles'.[87]

An even more enduring tribute was paid by Coleridge to Bowles when, much later, in the opening lines of his sonnet 'Samuel Taylor Coleridge to William Lisle Bowles', he declares:

> My Heart has thanked thee, Bowles! For those soft strains,
> Whose sadness soothes me like the murmuring
> Of wild bees in the sunny showers of Spring!

Certainly Bowles's early sonnets are considered to be his finest poetical works. In the opinion of Dr William Hunt: 'The simplicity and earnestness of Bowles had all the charm of novelty and contrast. His pensive tenderness, delicate fancy, refined taste, and, above all, his power to harmonise the moods of nature with those of the mind, were his chief merits.'[88]

The eleventh sonnet in the original collection of fourteen sonnets, written at Ostend on 22 July 1787, affords an example of what it was that appealed so strongly to the first readers of it; and, perhaps, explains why, two centuries later, it was included in *What Sweeter Music*, an anthology of poems on music:

> How sweet the tuneful bells' responsive peal!
> As when, at opening morn, the fragrant breeze
> Breathes on the trembling sense of wan disease,
> So piercing to my heart their force I feel!

And hark! With lessening cadence now they fall,
And now, along a white and level tide,
They fling their melancholy music wide,
Bidding me many a tender thought recall
Of summer-days, and those delightful years,
When by my native streams, in life's fair prime.
The mournful magic of their mingling chime
First wak'd my wond'ring childhood into tears!
But seeming now, when all those days are o'er,
The sounds of joy, once heard, are heard no more.[89]

The extent to which Coleridge was influenced by the work of
Bowles has been meticulously analysed by Norman Fruman in his
Coleridge, The Damaged Archangel.[90] Perhaps the most striking example
is to be found in Coleridge's use of the last six lines of Bowles's *Monody
on Henry Headley*. Bowles wrote:

I, alas! remain
To mourn the hours of youth (yet mourn in vain)
That fled neglected, – Wisely thou has trod
The better path: and that High Meed, which God
Ordained for Virtue from the dust,
Shall bless thy labours, spirit! Pure and just.

The first lines of a poem written by Coleridge while still at
Cambridge, and published many years later in 1836, read:

– I yet remain
To mourn the hours of youth (yet mourn in vain)
That fled neglected: wisely thou has trod
The better path – and that high meed which God
Assigned to virtue, tow'ring from the dust.
Shall wait thy rising, Spirit pure and just!

Bowles would surely have been aware of this and, recognising
Coleridge's genius, perhaps did not disapprove. Indeed, Bowles himself
was later to be influenced by Coleridge. In the words of Fruman:

Keeping in mind how extensive were his borrowings from Bowles, we
are in a better position to understand Coleridge's delight, when, in later
years, he came upon a line of his own in one of Bowles's poems. '[It]
gave me great pleasure,' he wrote, 'from the thought, what pride & joy

I should have had at the time of writing it, if I had supposed it possible that Bowles would have adopted it'.[91]

Other scholars have noted the influence of Bowles in Coleridge's work. There is evidence that, while an undergraduate at Cambridge, Coleridge had read his 'African Slave', echoes of which appear in Coleridge's 'Slave Trade Ode', which won him the Browne Medal for the best Greek ode in imitation of Sappho.[92]

Not only Coleridge but also Wordsworth,[93] Southey[94] and Lamb[95] were deeply impressed by their first readings of Bowles's sonnets, and as a consequence it has been said that 'Bowles can be seen as a founding figure of English Romanticism'.[96]

Some years later Wordsworth told the editor of *Recollections of the Table-Talk of Samuel Rogers*: 'When Bowles's Sonnets first appeared, – a thin 4to pamphlet, entitled *Fourteen Sonnets*, – I bought them in a walk through London with my dear brother, who was afterwards drowned at sea.'[97]

It is more likely that it was the second, rather than the first, edition of the sonnets that so impressed him. Wordsworth was walking on one of the bridges crossing the River Thames when he began reading a volume of Bowles's sonnets, and was so captivated by them that he stopped and would not continue until he had read the whole book.[98] Southey, also, was deeply moved by the sonnets. Having read the third edition in 1794, he and a friend named Robert Lovell[99] called on Richard Cruttwell, Bowles's Bath printer, spoke highly of the sonnets and arranged with Cruttwell to have some of their own poems published in the same type and form.[100] Many years later, in the preface to his own *Poetical Works*, Southey wrote that 'I am conscious also of having derived much benefit at one time from Cowper and more from Bowles . . .'.[101] Lamb, too, thought highly of Bowles's early work and acknowledged that he had 'no higher idea of heaven' than to hear Coleridge reciting 'one of Bowles's sweetest sonnets . . .'.[102]

His sonnet number VIII, 'To the River Itchin, Near Winton', is a typical example of Bowles's early work, and a reading of it perhaps helps to explain why young men who in due course would produce poetry of far greater merit than anything Bowles could ever hope to achieve were so full of admiration:

Itchin, when I behold thy banks again,
Thy crumbling margin, and thy silver breast,
On which the self-same tints still seem to rest,
Why feels my heart the shivering sense of pain?
Is it – that many a summer's day has past

Since, in life's morn, I carol'd on thy side?
Is it – that oft, since then, my heart has sigh'd,
As Youth, and Hope's delusive gleams, flew fast?
Is it that those, who circled on thy shore,
Companions of my youth, now meet no more?
Whate'er the cause, upon thy banks I bend
Sorrowing, yet feel such solace at my heart,
As at the meeting of some long-lost friend,
From whom, in happier hours, we wept to part.[103]

Sonnet number XIII, entitled 'TIME' in the first edition and later 'Influence of Time on Grief', is another of Bowles's early sonnets that has attracted the admiration of critics over the years. It was chosen by Sir Arthur Quiller-Couch[104] to be included in *The Oxford Book of English Verse 1250–1918*:

O TIME! Who know'st a lenient hand to lay
Softest on sorrow's wound, and slowly thence
(Lulling to sad repose the weary sense)
The faint pang stealest unperceived away;
On thee I rest my only hope at last,
And think, when thou hast dried the bitter tear
That flows in vain o'er all my soul held dear,
I may look back on every sorrow past,
And meet life's peaceful evening with a smile:
As some lone bird, at day's departing hour,
Sings in the sunbeam, of the transient shower
Forgetful, though its wings are wet the while:-
Yet ah! How much must this poor heart endure,
Which hopes from thee, and thee alone, a cure!

In July 1794, when the third edition of *Fourteen Sonnets* appeared, it was scrutinised by Coleridge, who wrote to Henry Martin:

I sent for Bowles's Works, while at Oxford – how was I shocked – Every omission and every alteration disgusts Taste & mangles Sensibility. Surely some Oxford Toad has been squatting at the Poet's Ear, and spitting into it cold Venom of Dullness. It is not Bowles – He is still the same (the added Poems prove it) – descriptive, dignified, tender, sublime. The Sonnets added are exquisite – Abbe Thule are marked beauties – and the little Poem at Southampton is a Diamond – in whatever light you place it, it reflects beauty and splendor. The 'Shakespear' is sadly unequal to the rest – yet in whose Poems, excepting those of Bowles, would it not have been excellent.[105]

In December Coleridge was regaling Charles Lamb with recitations from Bowles, who must surely have been flattered to find himself named as one of the twelve 'Eminent Contemporaries' (including Joseph Priestley,[106] Edmund Burke and Lafayette[107]) who were the subjects of Coleridge's sonnets that began to appear in the *Morning Chronicle* at this time.[108] In 1796 Coleridge put together a small collection of sonnets (without a title but for convenience called *Sonnets by Various Writers*) and in the opening paragraph he explains: 'I have selected the following Sonnets from various authors for the purpose of binding them up with the Sonnets of the Rev. W.L. Bowles'. Three sonnets by Lamb were included in the collection, and it has been said that they 'are chiefly remarkable as reflecting the diction and the graceful melancholy of William Lisle Bowles whose sonnets had in a singular degree influenced both Lamb and Coleridge while they were still at Christ's Hospital'.[109]

It was at this time that Coleridge copied Bowles's *Verses on the Death of Henry Headley* into his hymn-book as a source of inspiration.[110] Further, in the same year he bound up a selection of his own sonnets with the fourth edition of Bowles's and sent them to Mrs Thelwall,[111] declaring in a note on the flyleaf of the Bowles volume: 'This volume . . . has given me more pleasure, and done my heart more good, than all the other books I ever read, excepting my Bible.'[112] And in the 1797 edition of his own poetry, one of the sections is headed 'Sonnets, Attempted in the Manner of the Rev. W.L. Bowles'. If imitation is the sincerest form of flattery, then this dedication must surely represent an extraordinary tribute from one of England's greatest poets to the Wiltshire curate.

Bowles always enjoyed an excellent and friendly relationship with his printer Richard Cruttwell and, if the following anecdote is to be believed, with Cruttwell's journeymen printers as well. A printer who served his apprenticeship in the office of the *Bath Herald* related many years later that he could recollect hearing, in the early part of his apprenticeship, other printers talking:

> . . . of Mr Bowles and his manners when correcting his proofs . . . how he would walk about the office sometimes puzzled for a word to suit his rhyme or measure, when he would appeal to the journeyman printer for the same, and frequently receive and adopt the suggestion of the workman.[113]

As has been seen, at the end of 1794 the third edition of the sonnets entitled *The Poems of the Rev. W.L. Bowles AM late of Trinity College Oxford including Sonnets and several other Poems, never before published* . . . appeared, printed by Richard Cruttwell in Bath and sold by E.C. Collins in Salisbury and Charles Dilly, the famous London bookseller. As Collins was the proprietor of the *Salisbury and Winchester Journal* he made sure that an advertisement appeared in the newspaper on 12 January declaring the volume 'This day is published priced at 3s'.[114] The fourth and fifth editions followed in 1796. This great success doubtless persuaded Bowles to bring more of his work to the public's notice and so, in 1796, first and second editions of *Elegiac Stanzas, written during sickness at Bath, December 1795* as well as *Hope, an allegorical sketch, on recovering slowly from sickness* were placed before a doubtless eager readership. It is clear from these works that Bowles had recently been unwell and in the advertisement printed as a preface to *Hope* . . . he writes: 'The descriptive part was suggested by the scenery on the banks of the Southampton River, where the Author occasionally took his morning walks in the beginning of May, after tedious and melancholy confinement.' Further, the work was inscribed to 'The Most Reverend William,[115] Archbishop of York, in gratitude for Kindness and Civilities experienced from him during Sickness'. In the advertisement he also shows how anxious he is to accept constructive criticisms of his work:

> The Author takes this opportunity of expressing his regret that the second Edition of his prior little Poem (written in sickness) should have appeared, before he could avail himself of the judicious suggestions of the Critical Review respecting the strict sense of the word Contentment.
>
> He will always be happy to pay attention to observations which are conveyed in the language of candour and liberality.

Having read the *Elegiac Stanzas* Charles Lamb wrote to Coleridge on 8 June:

> Why the poem is alone sufficient to redeem the character of the age we live in from the imputation of degenerating in Poetry, were no such beings extant as Burns,[116] Bowles, Cowper[117] and --- fill up the blank how you please, I say nothing . . . I will not notice in this tedious (to you) manner verses which have been so long delightful to me and of which you already know my opinion of. Of this kind are Bowles, Priestly, and that most exquisite and most Bowles-like of all, the 19th Effusion . . . Are you acquainted with Bowles? I see, by his last Elegy (written at Bath) you are near neighbours.[118]

Coleridge was in two minds about *Hope*. In December 1796 he wrote to John Thelwall: 'Bowles (the bard of my idolatry) has written a poem lately without plan – or meaning – but the component parts are divine. It is entitled – Hope, an allegorical sketch. I will copy two of the Stanzas which must be particularly interesting to you.' He then transcribes the two stanzas and adds: 'The last line is indeed exquisite.'[119]

In October 1796 Charles Lamb wrote to Coleridge and asked: 'Have you seen Bowles's new poem on 'Hope'? What character does it bear? Has he exhausted his stores of tender plaintiveness? Or is he the same in this last as in all his former pieces?'[120]

On 14 November Lamb refers to Bowles's influence on Coleridge by writing in effusive terms:

> . . . Coleridge, I love you for dedicating your poetry to Bowles. Genius of the sacred fountain of tears, it was he who led you through all this valley of weeping, showed you the dark green yew trees, and the willow shades, where, by the fall of the waters you might indulge an uncomplaining melancholy, a delicious regret for the past, or weave fine visions of that awful future.[121]

At this time Coleridge was certainly besotted with Bowles's poetry. Lamb knew this well and on 10 December wrote to him: 'Burns was the god of my idolatry, as Bowles of yours. I am jealous of your fraternising with Bowles, when I think you relish him more than Burns or my old favourite, Cowper'.[122] However, Lamb's enthusiam soon waned, and in 1798 in a letter to Robert Lloyd he writes of 'the race of sonnet writers & complainers, Bowless & Charlotte Smiths, & all that tribe, who can see no joys but what are past, and fill peoples' heads with notions of the Unsatisfying nature of Earthly comforts'.[123]

In April 1795 Richard Brinsley Sheridan,[124] by now a successful playwright and Member of Parliament, married as his second wife Esther Jane, daughter of Newton Ogle,[125] Dean of Winchester, and then spent much of the time at his father-in-law's house near Southampton. Frequent boating parties were arranged, and Bowles often enjoyed sailing in a small cutter called the *Phaedria* after the magic boat in the Fairy Queen. He was inspired to write a poem that was much admired by Sheridan.[126] Others in these parties were his old schoolfriend William Howley, later to become Bishop of London and Archbishop of Canterbury, and Joseph Richardson,[127] the poet and author and later one of the proprietors of the *Morning Post*. One of the poems written by Bowles and inspired by his visits to Southampton Water was entitled 'Southampton Castle'; it was inscribed to the Marquis of Lansdowne[128] who had built a magnificent house overlooking the river and the Isle of Wight.

One day, probably early in 1796, Bowles was dining in Sheridan's house in London. He later related:

> Sheridan asked me if I knew any young man of poetical genius who would furnish a good Tragedy for Drury Lane. I instantly said – having just read his Poems, published at this time but unknown to the general reader, – 'Coleridge! If any body can write a fine Tragedy in the present day, Coleridge can!' Coleridge was personally unknown to me; I had never seen him, and spoke, <u>not</u> on account of any of his Sonnets, which might have disposed me to be partial, but from the tone of expressive pathos, in other parts of the Poems.
>
> Sheridan, however, who had never heard the name, said Kindly, 'Will you write to him, from me?' 'Yes'. I wrote; . . .[129]

Soon after this, Coleridge, who by now was living at Nether Stowey in the Quantocks in Somerset, wrote to Bowles, sending him some 'accompanying trifles' – perhaps an advance copy of a new edition of his poems which was published in the following July. He also wrote:

> The plan I have sketched for my tragedy is too chaotic to be transmitted at present – but immediately I understand it myself, I will submit it to you: and feel greatly obliged to you for permission to do it. It is 'romantic and wild and somewhat terrible' – and I shall have Siddons[130] and Kemble[131] in mind.

In this letter, while rejoicing in Bowles's 'new edition' – doubtless of *Fourteen Sonnets* – Coleridge then proceeded to mention alterations to one of the sonnets that did not meet with his approval, and somewhat ominously concludes: 'I could write a great deal about your late alterations, but will not detain you any more.'[132]

Early in the summer, while in Gloucester, Bowles met and had a conversation with William Linley,[133] the author and composer who had returned to England from India in the previous year and had begun a working relationship with his brother-in-law Sheridan, who, as well as being a dramatist and Member of Parliament, was also manager of the Drury Lane theatre. It is likely that Bowles invited Linley to visit him at Donhead, as on 23 July Linley, who was enjoying the female company at Cowley Place, the house in which he was staying, wrote to Bowles to say that he would prolong his visit until 14 August but would 'the day after bend my course to Donhead by the conveyance you pointed out to me at

Gloster'. In this letter he wrote:

> A worthy baronet in the neighbourhood claims acquaintance with you,
> vizt [tear] Stafford Northcote.[134] He has a charming estate contiguous to
> Cowley.
>   Your poems are the order of the day here. In truth I know not
> where they are not so. One of the Miss Barings – and I think the prettiest
> – was reading the sonnet to Hope this morning, and I happened to say
> I was going to pay a visit to the author soon. 'Bless me!' (Half a dozen at
> a time). 'Do you know Mr Bowles? I should like to be acquainted with
> him, of all things!' Happy dog, groaned I. – I am afraid of disgracing
> you, Bowles, but I should like to set some of your words to music. I tried
> once, but could not then please myself. Adieu!'[135]

Coleridge was determined to visit Bowles, whom he had never
met, to seek his opinion on his proposed tragedy. He wrote in December
1796 to John Thelwell[136] saying: 'I never <u>saw</u> him but once; and when I
was a boy & in Salisbury <u>market place</u>'.[137] In June of the following year
Coleridge wrote to John Prior Estlin:[138]

> . . . I shall have quite finished my Tragedy in a day or two: & then I mean
> to walk to Bowles, the poet, to read it to him & have his criticisms – and
> then, accordingly as he advises, I shall transmit the play to Sheridan, or
> go to London & have a personal interview with him . . . When I arrive at
> Bowles's I will write again – giving you a minute account of the bard . . .'[139]

Sadly, no letter giving Coleridge's impression of Bowles at their
first meeting appears to have survived.
    At the beginning of September 1797 Coleridge did indeed visit
Bowles at Donhead, bringing with him the nearly completed tragedy
called *Osorio*.[140] Perhaps he also brought with him his translation into
English of the Latin inscription written by Bowles and appearing on
the memorial to Richard Camplin[141] in Nether Stowey church – unless
his translation was one of the 'accompanying trifles' referred to in his
earlier letter. Bowles's lines and Coleridge's translation appear in many
editions of Coleridge's works.
    Later in the year, in October, Coleridge sent a copy of his tragedy
to Bowles, requesting him to forward it to Sheridan. Also enclosed was a
'little volume' – perhaps the 1797 edition of his *Poems* – for transmission
to Sheridan at the same time.[142] In the same letter he asked to see a copy
of Bowles's *Spirit and Progress of Discovery* before it is printed, promising
to 'shew it to no human being, except my wife'.[143]

Chapter 2
1796–1804

In the midst of all this literary activity Bowles was carrying out his duties as curate at East Knoyle, although it was not until 1792 that he was ordained priest[1] – and so until then he would not have been authorised to preside at the sacrament of the Lord's Supper. However, it is likely that he would have officiated at most of the baptisms and funerals of his parishioners, and certainly until Dr Wake died in 1796, when a younger man was appointed in his place. Between 1789 and 1795 the average number of baptisms in each year was twenty-seven and the average number of burials was sixteen, although 1790 was a year during which an exceptionally high twenty-seven deaths were recorded. The average number of marriages celebrated at East Knoyle each year during the first seven years of Bowles's curacy was eleven, so it is likely that not many weeks passed without Bowles being called upon to officiate at one or other of these rites of passage.

He lived from the time of his arrival in 1788 not in East Knoyle but in a house near the church in Donhead St Mary, some 5 miles away, later called Burltons.[2] In 1793 he paid £800 to purchase a house in Donhead St Mary, probably the same property and described in the deed of conveyance[3] as being then in his possession and occupation. Also conveyed to Bowles were several fields and a tenanted cottage. After Bowles had moved from the house it was much extended, and in 1829 was described as 'a small mansion' when Lord Arundell[4] and Sir Richard Colt Hoare[5] mentioned it in their *Modern History of South Wiltshire*. In 1792 Bowles caused a Latin inscription to be placed on an urn in the garden of the house[6] – an activity to be much repeated by him in later years.

As soon as he had arrived in East Knoyle as curate he would, of course, have become acquainted with Harriet, one of the daughters of the rector, Dr Wake; and after a while he began to court her. A poem written by Bowles on 26 October 1791 and entitled 'Absence' was surely written with Harriet in mind, when she was in London and he in Wiltshire:

How shall I cheat the heavy hours, of thee
Deprived, of thy kind looks and converse sweet,
Now that the waving grove the dark storms beat,
And wintry winds sad sounding o'er the lea,
Scatter the sallow leaf! I would believe,
Thou, at this hour, with tearful tenderness
Dost muse on absent images, and press
In thought my hand, and say: Oh do not grieve,
Friend of my heart! At wayward fortune's power;
One day we shall be happy, and each hour
Of pain forget, cheered by the summer ray.
These thoughts beguile my sorrow for thy loss,
And, as the aged pines their dark heads toss,
Oft steal the sense of solitude away.
So am I sadly soothed, yet do I cast
A wishful glance upon the seasons past,
And think how different was the happy tide,
When thou, with looks of love, wert by my side.

It is no surprise to discover that Wake did not look with any favour on the pretensions of his curate – a man with a modest income, or so he thought, and no immediate prospect of any preferment. It is certain that Wake had made this very clear to Bowles, who was making every effort to secure a living that would produce an income sufficient to enable him to maintain Harriet in such a manner as would satisfy her father. It can be deduced from a letter written by Harriet to Bowles at the end of October 1792 that Bowles had written to Wake telling him that he was going to Bristol to see an attorney about the possible purchase of a living, and while he was in Bristol Harriet wrote:

I am able to write to you in much better spirits than I imagin'd I should. My father returned to Knoyle Monday to dinner. I was with Charlotte when he arriv'd but it was so bad a day I did not the least expect to see him before Tuesday. I was sent for immediately and when I appear'd before him I was so exceedingly agitated that I had some difficulty to speak to him. – perhaps he perceiv'd. I was distress'd for he did not enter on the subject that was uppermost on my mind till the evening he then enquir'd if I had seen you and beg'd to be inform'd of every particular he said a thousand affectionate things to encourage me to speak my whole mind to him and I did venture to tell him what I have already confess'd to you.
He alarmed me more than I can describe by saying that he was convinc'd my affection for him was so great that I should not hesitate

to give up all idea of you if he was to tell me the happiness of his life depended upon my doing it. This was so unexpected that the tears came in my eyes and I could make no reply. Your letter he receiv'd Tuesday morning and was very much pleas'd with it. I know he wishes to talk with you and I have every reason to suppose that his consent will not be withheld if you succeed in the business you are upon. My father intends leaving Knoyle the 8th of next month. You will be here on Sunday I hope. I shall not put my name to this letter for perhaps it might not reach Bristol before you have left it. Believe me ever yours.[7]

As a prebendary of Westminster, as well as being rector of St Margaret's, Westminster, the widower Wake would be expected to spend a considerable part of each year in London living in the Little Cloisters near the Abbey with his unmarried daughters, and so it was that early in November 1792 he left East Knoyle with Harriet to spend some months away from his parish. Upon returning to Knoyle, Bowles wrote to Harriet expressing his sorrow at not seeing her before he left for Bristol and asking her to let him know as soon as she arrived safely in London. He knew that various people were conspiring to prevent any engagement with her and he warned in his letter, 'I am afraid certain persons will be busy about what they have no concern in, in your absence from Salisbury, but I cannot say what I would wish about this matter at present.'

As soon as Harriet arrived in London she wrote:

I am this instant arriv'd and have had a most melancholy journey you must be prepar'd to hear something that I fear will give you pain. I only hope it will not shock you so much as it did me. I will not distress you by relating what I have suffer'd since last I saw you I have been use'd I am sorry to say ungenerously. My Father has commanded me not to write to you but how can I forebare doing it. I find my aunt Bowles[8] is the person who has set him against you. She has hear'd many things to your disadvantage and has persuaded my father that I would be very unhappy if I was to leave him even supposing you had a large income. How strange it is they will not allow me to judge for myself. I am told you are so changeable that it is impossible for you to be long attach'd to any one. I cannot believe it of you. It is requir'd of me to give you up but that I never will do . . . Do write to me. I will watch the coming in of the post. Saturday morning I shall expect to receive a letter from you. I hope to get it without being found out I must run the risque for I want to know what you think of this matter . . .

Harriet would indeed have received from Bowles on Saturday an exceedingly long letter, beginning:

> I am greatly distress'd at what you tell me. But I think you are deceived as to the author & I believe there is <u>another person</u> at the bottom of all this who would spare no pains to set your father against me & that your Aunt Bowles is made the <u>ostensible</u> person & perhaps deceived herself . . . I know that not one of them can bring a <u>single thing</u> against me, or prove any one action of my whole life that I should be asham'd to avow. As to the <u>changeableness</u> of my affections I hope I need not say more than I have done already to you – Who are they, that, without any knowledge of me, without a shaddow of proof, without even the slightest acquaintance, without so much as knowing me by sight (for I don't know that I ever saw your Aunt Bowles) should stand up and judge me, say exactly what my disposition is, say what my <u>heart</u> is <u>made</u> of, & assert that you could not be happy with such a person as myself! . . . I shall with great anxiety expect another letter & I hope in God to hear that you are happier . . . I should not think it advisable to enter into a correspondence if you have <u>promis'd</u> your father that you <u>would not</u> . . . Let me know if by any means I might have half an hour's conversation with you. If it can possibly be contriv'd I will come to Town directly. I would give the world to see you and consult with you.

On Monday Harriet responded by writing a letter that must have been very difficult for her to compose. During the course of this very long epistle she says:

> I have been told something about you which I confess has made me uneasy, do not be displeas'd with me for saying so. I never could mention it when with you though it was often in my thoughts, and I am almost inclin'd now not to tell it you, yet I wish you to know what I allude to, for it is a kind of thing I could not speak of to your face. I must write it, or you will never know what I mean. I cannot tell you all that has been said to me about this matter. I have been inform'd that when you are from home, it is suppos'd greatest part of your time is pass'd with vicious Women, this is the chief thing, I believe alleged against you by my Aunt Bowles. My Father spoke of it to me when at Salisbury, and assur'd me that I must not expect to be happy with a person who would most probably prefer others to me, this is what I meant by saying that I had heard you was of a changeable disposition. But I assure you all this has made very little impression on me . . . It is impossible to say how much I wish to see you. I do not know how it

can be manag'd unless I was to meet you in Harry the seventh Chapel. The people about the Abbey are not aquainted with you by sight, so I do not think we should run much risque of being found out. I cannot see you in the street because it would appear embarassing for me to go out without a servant, but there would be nothing odd in my going to see the waxworks in the Abbey. I cannot think of any other way of seeing you, perhaps you will not approve this plan. I have not much opinion of it myself when I reconsider the matter, but if I meet you any where I must run the risque of being discovered . . .

On the following day Bowles wrote back to Harriet, telling her that he had received a very civil letter from her father and was thinking of writing to him and speaking very firmly, 'for his conduct has been very wrong to me. As you have not promis'd that you would not write, let me know what you think. I shall wait with anxiety.' In her response, written the next day in less than five minutes in order to catch the post, Harriet tells Bowles to act as he thinks proper as 'your judgement is better than mine', and in his reply he outlines what he will say in a letter to her father – but he says he will not write the letter until the following Monday, to give her time to say whether or not it meets with her approval. In her letter written on Saturday Harriet gives her approval, except that she thinks it better for Bowles not to say anything about her being forbidden to write to him. Bowles replies to Harriet that he is sure that he would be given notice to quit his curacy but he 'didn't consider this a moment'. He continues:

I fear your next letter but pray write (if but a line) immediately to let me know the worst – & whether my letter has irritated him – I fear I have spoken too plain but it can't be helped now . . . I suppose you know I have given up all thought of the living. I now think it would have been very imprudent & I have since heard good news from the Bishop of Durham[9] which may prevent my trying to purchase preferment until something very advantageous should offer – let the worst come to the worst. I think we could make up between us about three hundred a year independent of anybody – If this could be contriv'd with the chance of a living from the Archbishop or Bishop of Durham and what I may have after the death of my mother, perhaps it would be be[st] to settle at once, at least if your father continues to use you unkindly. I imagine that I shall have eventually five or six thousand pounds – tho I cannot tell exactly not knowing how my mother will leave her fortune. I have at present about three thousand of my own . . .

Harriet's next letter merely told Bowles that her father had received his letter but had not disclosed the contents to her; he was proposing to write to Dr and Mrs Dobson in Salisbury, presumably to seek their advice. Bowles replied at once in his customary affectionate way, imploring Harriet to write 'the <u>moment</u> you hear from Salisbury'. Although no reply had been received from the Dobsons, Harriet's next letter followed immediately, as (she says) Bowles would worry if she failed to do so, telling him that her father's conduct had entirely changed. He was now 'kind and affectionate and behaved to me the same as formerly'. In the meantime Bowles had met and dined with Dr Dobson, who told him that he had received Dr Wake's letter but said little else about it. Bowles now thought of coming up to London, and wrote another letter to Wake who replied, as Bowles reported in a letter to Harriet, that:

> This consent was <u>conditional</u>; that I had <u>no income</u> & therefore on that account only he must be consider'd as having given a negative; . . . he has <u>consulted with no one</u>; his objections were not from any <u>one</u> cause, but from many, which at first he did not consider; he acted <u>precipitably</u> & was sorry that he had.

Early in December Bowles wrote to Harriet to tell her that he would be in London the next day, planned to stay for ten days and would, of course, wish to see her. He stayed at the Bedford Coffee House in Covent Garden, and it is to this address that Harriet's next letter is sent. How could they meet? Harriet did not think that there would be any harm in conversing in the Park – 'my father's servant will be with me if we meet any of my acquaintances'. She suggests walking in the Green Park after breakfast. However, they failed to meet, and several notes passed between the two, in one of which Harriet writes that she will be in 'Hide [sic] Park' by two and 'shall walk under the wallnut trees in the same place where I walk'd with you last year'. They did eventually meet in the park, but their planned meeting the next day failed to materialise, with Bowles writing to 'My dearest Love' in some desperation to say that 'I walk'd exactly in the same place where I met you yesterday – it was five minutes more than half past eleven when I got there. I walked till twelve & then took it for granted I should see you in the College Garden, but I found both doors lock'd.'

It seems that they did manage to meet on more than one occasion without Dr Wake's knowledge. In one note Harriet writes: 'I suppose you had not time to come into the College garden today. I write to inform you that the box at Covent Garden is taken in my name and is the fourth from the stage. I hope I shall see you tonight.'

Bowles did not reply immediately to Dr Wake's letter, but took a great deal of trouble in composing it and in consulting a number of people on its wording. Preserved with the letters written by the lovers is what must be a draft of Bowles's lengthy reply, in the course of which he stresses that it was not true that he had no income; that he could 'settle three thousand pounds at least on Harriet tomorrow'; and that if what he must receive from his parents' wills was added, as well as the chance, if not certainty, of preferment, he hoped it would not be thought a 'bad foundation for us to build on'. On the same day that this letter was sent Bowles wrote to Harriet:

My dearest Love

I wish to write to you by the same post that I have written to your father, tho I have time to say very little, only to desire you will let me hear from you immediately to let me know in what manner your father took what I have said to him. – There is now I fear little chance of reconciliation. We must be determined – there can be no other way – I have written very decisively to him, but what I said had the entire approbation of all whom I consulted – the Stills, Helyars etc. It is happy for us that almost all your father's friends & relations consider that we are in the right.
It would not be proper I think to come to Town immediately but it will be necessary for me to see you before long, having much to consult you about. God knows how much I wish for that pleasure. You will be surprised to hear that I din'd & slept at Wishford yesterday – Mrs J was very civil – Magdalene¹⁰ was there who appears very well – I have not time to say more, having taken almost all morning in writing and copying the letter to your father. – I will write again the moment I hear from you.
Believe me ever with the greatest affection
Yours W.L. Bowles

By the New Year Bowles was back in Donhead, and as soon as he arrived home on 7 January he wrote to Harriet to tell her that he had left London at 10 o'clock on Saturday, arriving at Salisbury by eleven o'clock that night, where he stayed until the following morning. From there he rode on horseback 'very fast to get to Knoyle by Church-time arriving just before eleven'. He thought 'you should tell your father what day I left Town, as he might think I neglect his Church which perhaps he would be glad to find'. He also writes:

I will write to you again the moment I hear from the Attorney in London about the Chaplaincy – I am amusing myself by planting trees & pulling down Hedges & when you come to see Mrs Benet[11] in the summer, I hope to shew [you] my retreat in a little order.

In several letters written over the following weeks much is said about the possible, but ultimately unsuccessful, purchase of a regimental chaplaincy. Harriet must have heard rumours that Bowles was to leave Donhead as he was soon writing to say:

Who can have told you I was going to leave Donhead – there is no other place in the County I can go to, & if I were to go, I must pay the house rent, or let it, as I took it for a term of years. I suspect this report might have originally come from the same quarter with many other lies – It might have been said to make you fancy that as I should soon leave this County, I should soon forget you.

During February he let Harriet know that he had received:

the offer of another chaplaincy in the light horse for fourteen hundred pounds but [as] war is now absolutely determin'd on, it requires on [all] accounts, more consideration than it would if I purchas'd it in time of peace – I have not been two days from home a long while, except the beginning of the week to Bath where I went on account of a Publication I have in hand there but which, perhaps, from indolence I may never finish.

Towards the end of February Bowles had a nocturnal adventure that he felt he should relate to Harriet:

Coming from a Gentleman's house, at about eleven o'clock at night, I got a fall from my horse in the middle of the Chase,[12] I was very near being oblig'd to take up my lodging in the downs, or under a tree, as I knew not a step of the road, which at all times is difficult. I was going to Mr Caplain's to sleep & we set out together from the place where we din'd – But as I stay'd behind & got my fall, we some how or other lost each other, & I had a very uncomfortable prospect – my horse was gone & have seen nothing of him since – I had wandered about nearly an hour & a half, when by good luck I saw a cottage, where for a little money, I got a conducter & came to Mr Caplain's between two & three in morning . . . so much for one night's adventure which was the most unpleasant I ever met with.

Harriet delivered a stern rebuke for such conduct. She wrote:

> I wish you would oblige me by not riding about in the dark, what an
> escape you had why did you not sleep where you din'd? Was it absolutely
> necessary you should go to Mr Caplain's that night; pray do not run such
> a risque in future; only imagine what I should have suffer'd if I had
> heard that some dreadful accident had happen'd to the friend I most
> value, which might have been the case, you were certainly very fortunate
> to escape unhurt, did your horse stumble with you? If so I shall not be
> sorry you have lost him.

At the beginning of March Bowles wrote to tell Harriet that his
horse was discovered four days later 'very sociably feeding among the
deer with his saddle on'. He also let her know in each of his letters how
his mother, who was suffering from increasing ill health, was faring.
Harriet herself had also been ill, and was clearly suffering from some
unknown ailment. In one letter she wrote:

> Mr John Still[13] has din'd with us twice, the first day he was here, my
> father before him and Mr Peter Still[14] at Dinner ask'd why I did not
> advise you to apply to the Archbishop for the living of Knoyle after him.
> He spoke it in [illegible] I believe nobody heard him but me and I made
> no answer . . . I have suffer'd a great deal of pain from the rheumatism
> since you heard from me. I have been confin'd to the house this whole
> week.

Harriet told Bowles that she had gone to see a play with her sister
Magdalene but later was so unwell that 'I did not get up till four o'clock'.
She had heard from her sister Charlotte that Bowles was going to a
music party at Clouds, the home of the Still family, and wished that she
could have been there with him.

It is clear that by the middle of March Dr Wake was beginning
to look more favourably upon Bowles's pretentions and in one letter
Harriet wrote:

> I am inclin'd to hope my father may be brought round again, if he is left
> to judge for himself. He has mention'd you lately and one day when I
> ask'd him for his snuff box he told me he was sure you would dislike my
> smelling it if you saw me.

In a letter postmarked 23 March and addressed to 'My Dear
Friend', Harriet wrote, 'If my father keeps his resolution of leaving the

Cloysters the latter end of May, I shall be at Knoyle in eight weeks time', and concludes by signing herself 'Ever yours most affectionately'.

However, Harriet's hopes of once again being back in East Knoyle were never to be fulfilled. In the April number of the *Gentleman's Magazine* the following melancholy notice appeared among the announcements of deaths: 'In her 25th year Miss Wake, daughter of the Rev. Dr. Wake of Knoyle in Wilts. This amiable and beautiful young lady was on the eve of marriage but a putrid fever put a period to her life in a very few days.'[15] There is no indication in the last letters written by Harriet to her lover very shortly before her untimely death, probably from typhus, that her father had given his consent to their marriage, so one can deduce, perhaps, that when his daughter was stricken by a fatal illness Dr Wake relented at last and signified his agreement to their union. It is not known whether Bowles travelled to London to see Harriet before she died, nor how he came to terms with what must have been a bitter blow. What is clear is that little is known about Bowles's activities over the next few years, with his muse apparently deserting him and nothing being published in his name. With the ageing Dr Wake spending many months of the year in London and when in East Knoyle probably relying on his curate to perform most of his duties, it is likely that Bowles spent most of the time in the country occupying himself with parochial activities.

In April 1794 a county meeting was held in Devizes, as a result of which it was resolved that a subscription be opened to meet the cost of augmenting the Wiltshire militia by 400 men and supplying equipment to them all, with a view to assisting in securing the internal defence of the country against the threatening French.[16] During the course of the summer long lists of the names of those who subscribed, with the amounts given, appeared in the *Salisbury and Winchester Journal*, and eventually – and rather belatedly – Bowles's name appeared in a short list published in September.[17] He is named at giving the somewhat modest sum of 3 guineas, with Dr Wake donating a rather more generous £10. In the same number of the newspaper appeared a list of some three hundred hopeful investors in what was to become the Southampton and Salisbury Navigation Co., the intention being to construct a canal that would enable shipping to sail from Salisbury to the sea. It is clear that Bowles was willing to speculate a good deal more of his own money in this venture, and he joined many others in subscribing the very considerable sum of £100, all of which he doubtless lost when, a few years later, the enterprise failed and the company was forced into liquidation.

In 1795 preferment at last came his way when he was presented to the living of Chicklade, some 7 miles north of Donhead and worth £230 per annum. However, he failed to take up residence there and continued to live at his house in Donhead, paying a small stipend to a curate to carry out his priestly duties at Chicklade. By this time he was also being noticed by those in the higher ranks of the church, and on Friday 7 August 1795 he preached a sermon in Salisbury Cathedral at the triennial visitation of the bishop of the diocese; the sermon was then printed and published by James Easton[18] in Salisbury.[19] He had to wait six years before being invited to preach a sermon in St Paul's Cathedral, at the anniversary meeting of the Sons of the Clergy. This sermon, preached on 7 May 1801, was duly printed in London by Ann Rivington and sold by F. and C. Rivington[20] and by Cadell and Davies.[21] As has been seen, towards the end of 1795 Bowles was suffering from some sort of illness that gave rise to his *Elegiac Stanzas written during sickness at Bath, December 1795*. In these verses Bowles clearly makes reference to his lost love when he considers the 'consoling phantasies that spring from the thick gloom' that touch his heart:

> Was it the voice of thee, my buried friend?
> Was it the whispered vow of fathful love?
> Do I in ***** green shades thy steps attend,
> And hear the high pines murmur thus above?
>
> 'Twas not thy voice, my buried friend! – O no;
> 'Twas not, O *****, the murmer of thy trees;
> But at the thought I feel my bosom glow,
> And woo the dream whose air-drawn shadows please.

It is likely that the asterisks hide the words 'Knoyle's' and 'Knoyle', where, of course, he first met and courted Harriet Wake.

In September 1796 Bowles's friend William Benwell, from his Oxford days, died of a fever contracted while ministering to sick villagers – just ten weeks after his marriage. Bowles was moved to write 'Lines on the Death of the Reverend William Benwell'. These were published in the *Bath Chronicle* and reached a wider audience when in the following year the *Gentleman's Magazine* published a letter from 'Academicus', in which he requested 'Mr Urban' (John Murray,[22] the proprietor of the magazine) to add to the notice of Benwell's death and character that had already been published:

. . . the following Sonnet written by an intimate friend and fellow-collegian of the deceased, the ingenious author of 'Sonnets, and other Poems', the third edition of which was elegantly printed by Cruttwell, at Bath, in 1794 and has since published 'Elegiac Stanzas, written during Sickness at Bath, December 1795;' and 'Hope, an allegorical Sketch, on recovering slowly from Sickness, 1796' . . .

Then follows the poem with the suggestion that:

In Mr Bowles's above mentioned performance, intituled [sic], 'Hope', he seems to allude to his departed friend in the three concluding lines of his 14th stanza addressed to Love:

' – If some true and tender heart there be,
On which, through every chance, thy soul might trust,
Death comes with his fell dart, and smites it to the dust'

They have, at least, been so applied by
ACADEMICUS.[23]

History does not relate whether Bowles was indeed intending to allude to Benwell's death as 'Academicus' supposes.

In 1796 there appeared in *Lounger's Common Place Book* an article[24] on Bowles's old schoolfriend Thomas Russell, whose promising career as a poet was cut short by his early death at the age of twenty-six in 1788. It is thought that it may have been written by Bowles, who was clearly an intimate friend of Russell.

On 30 October 1796 Dr Charles Wake died at the age of seventy-five and was buried at East Knoyle, where his gravestone records not only his own death but also that of his first wife at the age of thirty-two and his second at the age of forty. He had been the incumbent of Knoyle for fifty years.

The departure of Wake paved the way for Bowles to begin corresponding with Harriet's sister Magdalene. In January of the following year, while at Winchester on his way to London, he wrote to her to let her know that he would be staying in London until the end of the month and that her post to him should be sent to the Prince of Wales Coffee House in Conduit Street. Doubtless she wrote to him there. Any hope that Bowles might be offered the extremely valuable living of East Knoyle following Dr Wake's death was soon dashed, when John Ogle,[25] one of the sons of the Dean of Winchester, Dr Newton Ogle, all of whom were good friends of his, came to Donhead to stay with Bowles so that he could look at the parsonage house at Knoyle and see whether it would be suitable for his occupation. However, Bowles wrote to Magdalene to tell her not to take too much notice until 'the business is settled', as he put it. He also told her that in a day or two he was going to London with the Dean to 'see the Bishop'– probably the Bishop of Winchester who was patron of the living – and that he looked forward to have 'another tete a tete' at Donhead soon.

The death of Wake also paved the way for preferment in the church at last to come Bowles's way. The pluralist Wake was not only a canon of Westminster and rector of St Margaret's, Westminster, and East Knoyle but also rector of nearby Fonthill Gifford, Fonthill Bishop and Berwick St Leonard. John Still, the brother of Wake's son-in-law James Still, was rector of Dumbleton, a small village near the Gloucestershire/ Worcestershire boundary, and it is likely that before Wake's death it had been decided that he would succeed him as rector of Fonthill. In that event he was to resign the living of Dumbleton, worth £345 a year, to enable it to be offered to Bowles, and it is probable that this possibility had already been mentioned to the patron of the living, Lord Somers.[26] Early in 1797 Bowles was again writing to Magdalene:

> I have the offer of another living from Mr Markham, son to the Archbishop,[27] it is tenable with Dumbleton & about 130 pounds clear – but I must live there, as his chief object in offering it to me was to have been near him, as his own living is close to it – it is about a mile from the great road into the north near Tadcaster & not far from the Archbishop's, who seems very much to wish me to take it – I am doubtful however about it, & shall not determine till I have seen the House. Markham and myself leave Town on Wednesday next, to go & look at it & if I like it I am to be presented to it immediately.
>
> The only thing that makes me hesitate, is, its being so far from my connexions – J. Ogle is certain to have Knoyle – it was this day settled between the Bishop & the dean – so you may make your self perfectly easy about any dilapidations[28] – If I do not take the living, I am to have the curacy at Knoyle at a reduced [?] stipend & not much duty as Ogle will certainly make it his residence . . .

A day or two later he wrote again to Magdalene from Yorkshire:

> I have relinquished the idea of taking the living in this county as the House is very bad & would cost a good deal to make it habitable – I hope to be at Knoyle next Sunday but it is a long way from this place & I am not certain of a place this evening in the Coach – It is most probable the

Dean[29] & J. Ogle will accompany me, as I have wrote to request they should meet me at Salisbury, & he is coming to be presented. – I need not say how much I wish to see you, & how glad I am to hear you are well – I trust you will, before you go to Town, stay some days at Donhead.

I write this from the Archbishop's Palace which is about 6 miles from the Living. Markham wishes me so much to accept: in this respect it might have been pleasant, as the family always live here in the summer and the neighbourhood is very good.

I met Calcot[30] at the Archbishop's & heard the <u>compositions</u> sung beautifully. I went to Lambeth, but the A.B. was gone into the Country, so I wrote him a note to thank him about Knoyle & that I was going into Yorkshire with Mr Markham who had offered me a small living . . .

Why Bowles should be 'thanking the Archbishop of Canterbury about Knoyle' is not clear when there was no question of the living being presented to him. On the next day Bowles wrote again to Magdalene from Bishopsthorpe[31] to say that his mother was so 'bad' that he had to put off the Dean and Ogle from coming to Donhead but that they still would 'most probably be at Knoyle on Sunday for J. Ogle to read in'.

It seems that at this time Bowles was going hither and thither in pursuit of a good living in the church and also advising Magdalene on the investment of some of her fortune, for at the beginning of March he wrote to her:

I return'd here yesterday from Chichester, but have not seen Lord Egremont,[32] as he was call'd up to Town upon the business of the Bank, the day before I came – Of course nothing is concluded about the particular occasion of my journey.[33] . . . You will direct to Donhead as I shall be at home for certain Tuesday – & let me know whether you have done anything about the <u>stocks</u>. Notwithstanding the present alarm, I still think it is the best thing which can be done...

In March Bowles wrote to her from London:

. . . I have been to Lambeth this morning & was very kindly receiv'd. The Archbishop told me he would let nothing slip which he thought worth giving me, but, at the same time, thought I could not do better than accept Dumbleton – My friend Miss Markham[34] is going to be married to young Lord Mansfield[35] with twenty thousand a year – I hope very much I shall get all my business concluded so as to be at Knoyle Sunday next & as you complained that some time ago I express'd no wish about seeing you, believe I do now most earnestly wish for that pleasure & that I am

ever my dear M –
Yours very affectionately
Wm. L. Bowles

The news from Portsmouth of today of the most dreadful nature –
the sailors have rose upon their officers Admiral Colpoys[36] has been
executed[37] – the French are at sea & our fleet refuse to meet them – God
knows what will be the end!

In speaking to the Archbishop of Canterbury, it is more than likely
that Bowles ventured to reminded him that he had made a promise to
his mother that when the living of Bremhill, near Calne in Wiltshire,
became vacant it would be offered to him.

On 12 March Bowles wrote to Magdalene with a full account of his
mother's failing health and telling her that he had 'just sent to Bath for
some of the waters, hoping they may have some effect towards creating
appetite' and that in this situation he could say 'nothing about coming to
Town or any other plans'. On the 14th Bowles wrote again to Magdalene,
letting her know about his mother's condition and commenting at
length on the ramifications of the dilapidations of the parsonage house
at Knoyle that were being calculated and negotiated following the change
of incumbent. On the 26th a very brief note from Bowles to Magdalene
told her that his mother had died at last 'perfectly composed and free
from pain'. She was later buried with Bowles's father in Holy Trinity
Church in Shaftesbury.

In the following month Bowles wrote to Magdalene advising her
on the investment of some of her money, and told her that he and his
brother and sisters were executors of their mother's will and that her
estate (except her furniture that had been given to him) would amount
to £6000 or £7000 and their father's estate (in which their mother had
had a life interest) to perhaps £9000 or £10,000. Soon afterwards he
wrote again about a possible visit of Magdalene to Donhead, and told her
that he would be in London at the beginning or in the middle of May to
see Lord Somers about the living of Dumbleton, which was now vacant
following the resignation of John Still. Bowles had been at Oxford with
John,[38] the son and heir of Lord Somers, and so it is more than likely
that after leaving university they had kept in touch with each other, as a
result of which Lord Somers might more easily have been persuaded to
offer the living to his son's friend.

There is nothing in the surviving correspondence between
Bowles and Magdalene to suggest that they would soon wed and so it is
something of a surprise to learn that on 29 May 1797, in the church at

East Knoyle, the thirty-five-year-old Bowles and Magdalene entered into what was to be an apparently very happy, if childless, marriage that was to last for almost forty-seven years.

Two days before Bowles's wedding day it was announced in the *Salisbury and Winchester Journal* that Lord Somers had presented him to the rectory of Dumbleton.[39] It is likely that Bowles had already resigned the rectory of Chicklade to enable that living to be held by John Still jointly with Fonthill Gifford. Bowles never took up residence at Dumbleton but continued to live at Donhead, doing occasional duty as curate to John Ogle, the new rector, and doubtless paying a small stipend to a curate to perform his priestly duty at Dumbleton.

Before his mother's death Bowles had sold Barton Hill House, which had been, when he was not at the parsonage house in Uphill, his childhood home and was left to him in his father's will. It was with particular sadness that he parted with his old family home, and he gave vent to these feelings in a poem entitled 'On Leaving a Place of Residence', which begins with the lines:

> If I could bid thee, pleasant shade, farewell
> Without a sigh, within whose circling bow'rs
> My stripling prime was pass'd, and happiest hours,
> Dead were I to the sympathies that swell
> The human breast . . .

In this poem he surmised that his father would have hoped that he would continue to live in the house and nurture the gardens and grounds; he continues:

> These thoughts, my father, ev'ry spot endear:
> And, whilst I think, with self-accusing pain,
> A stranger shall possess the lov'd domain,
> In each low wind I seem thy voice to hear . . .[40]

In 1801 Richard Gough[41] composed *Verses addressed to the Rev. William Lisle Bowles*, in the course of which he asks:

> Wilt though, O Bowles, if Shaston be that place
> 'Where in this hard world thou hast happiest been'
> A picture furnish with poetic grace?[42]

On Christmas Day 1798 the readers of the *Salisbury and Winchester Journal* would have learned that 'In the Press and speedily will be published "St Michael's Mount" A Poem by the Rev. William Lisle Bowles.'[43] Publication was not quite as speedy as had been expected, as it was not until May that another advertisement appeared, announcing that 'In a few days will be published St Michael's Mount, a Poem, by the same author'[44] and again, much later, in September that 'This day is published, price 2s, Ornamented with a Beautiful Vignette, St Michael's Mount, A Poem by the Rev. William Lisle Bowles.'[45] A week later the same advertisement appeared, with the price now being stated as 2s 6d! *St Michael's Mount, a poem written in Cornwall, 1797* was eventually published as well as, also at the end of 1798, a sixth edition of Bowles's sonnets and *Coombe Ellen, a Poem, written in Radnorshire, September. 1798*, composed after a visit to Cwm Elan, the estate near Rhayader that had been purchased by Bowles's friend Thomas Grove of Ferne in 1792. In March 1798 Bowles had preached a sermon in Salisbury Cathedral before the assize judges on the Western circuit who had just arrived in the city. The sermon was duly printed and published in May.[46]

It was in 1798 that John Britton,[47] who had yet to achieve fame as an antiquary and topographer, first met Bowles; he later described him as being at that time 'a gay and handsome young man, then flushed with the fame arising from praises by Coleridge and by many other poets and professed critics'.[48] His fame was such that in 1798 there appeared in the *European Magazine* a sonnet entitled 'To the Memory of a Poor tho' Virtuous Woman, attempted in the manner of the celebrated Mr Bowles'[49] and a few years later in the same magazine a poem by Thomas Enort Smith, 'To Mr Bowles, on reading his two Volumes of Sonnets, and other Poems', included the lines:

> Bard of the pensive song, whose sweet-strung lyre
> Each melting softness joins to richest tones
> Struck from the chords of true poetic fire,
> Thy sovereign melody each bosom owns . . .[50]

A poem written in 1798 called 'For A Garden-seat at Home' hints at visits by the rich and famous to Bowles's comparatively humble home at Donhead, to his sadness over Harriet Wake's death, to nearby Wardour Castle, the magnificent seat of Lord Arundell, and even that the ability to paint should be added to the list of his other talents:

> Oh, no; I would not leave thee, my sweet home,
> Decked with the mantling woodbine and the rose,
> And slender woods that the still scene inclose,
> For yon magnificent and ample dome

That glitters in my sight! Yet I can praise
Thee, Arundel, who, shunning the thronged ways
Of glittering vice, silently dost dispense
The blessings of retired munificence.
Me, a sequestered cottage, on the verge
Of thy outstretched domain, delights; and here
I wind my walks, and sometime drop a tear
O'er Harriet's urn, scarce wishing to emerge
Into the troubled ocean of that life,
Where all is turbulence, and toil, and strife.
Calm roll the seasons o'er my shaded niche;
I dip the brush, or touch the tuneful string,
Or hear at eve the unscared blackbirds sing;
Enough if, from their loftier sphere, the rich
Deign my abode to visit, and the poor
Depart not, cold and hungry, from my door.

During the last decade of the eighteenth century the clergy of the Established Church were becoming increasingly alarmed at the rapid increase in the number of meeting houses being established by Protestant dissenters – and in particular by Independents or Congregationalists, Methodists and Baptists. Indeed from 1797 to 1799 in the diocese of Salisbury no fewer than 115 dissenters' meeting houses were registered with the Diocesan Registry and the Clerks of the Peace of Wiltshire and Berkshire.[51] In 1798 a young curate named William Mogg Bowen published his *Appeal to the People, on the Alleged Causes of the Dissenters' Separation from the Established Church*, and in August the Bishop of Salisbury[52] during his triennial visitation pointed out the 'great expediency and necessity of exertions from the parochial clergy' to 'prevent the delusions to which the lower classes of the people, especially in the villages' were exposed because of 'the increased activity of dissenters of various denominations, and the great number of licensed preachers registered in the course of last year'.[53]

This brought forth a rash of pamphlets commencing with *A Letter to the Bishop of Salisbury, on his late charge to the Clergy of his Diocese* by Henry Wansey,[54] who, having retired from business as a Salisbury clothier, now spent most of his time in travelling and antiquarian research, having been elected a fellow of the Society of Antiquaries in 1789. He wrote under the pseudonym of 'A Dissenter', but it seems that no one was in doubt as to his identity, and nearly all of the authors of the ensuing eleven pamphlets in what became known as the 'Wanseyan Controversy' likewise attempted to conceal their identity by adopting pseudonyms.

Bowles always had some sympathy for orthodox dissenters but was particularly averse to what at the time were called 'ranting village preachers' and to Rational Nonconformists such as Unitarians. In October his *A Rowland for an Oliver, addressed to Mr Wansey, on his Letter to the Bishop of Salisbury* was published by James Easton in Salisbury and F. & C. Rivington and John Hatchard[55] in London, and advertised for sale in the *Salisbury and Winchester Journal*. Two further pamphlets were written by him in 1798 bearing the overpoweringly verbose titles of *The Dissenter Done Over; or the Woeful Lamentation of Mr H. W. A Wiltshire Clothier; setting forth How the Clergy of this Realm, all dressed in fiery Scarlet, have attacked with Mastiff, Guns and Pistols, the poor Lamb-like and inoffensive Dissenters, Describing also The dreadful Vicar of Scarborough, with a Turban on his Head, and the Koran in his Hand, crying, Fee, faw, fum'. – The whole Faithfully translated from the inimitable Production of the same Mr H. W. ; and set to the Tune of 'The Taylor Done Over'* and *A True Account of the Deplorable Malady of H---y W----y, a Wiltshire Clothier; Shewing How he mistook a Barber for a Clergyman in a red Coat; and a Lancet, with which it was attempted to bleed him, for a Scymitar, Being An Epistle From his Cook-maid, Doll Dish-clout, to Mrs Bacon, the Tallow-chandler's Wife* – this pamphlet also being advertised for sale in the *Salisbury and Winchester Journal* in November.[56]

In the following year Bowles, now writing as 'A By-Stander', produced his fourth and final contribution to the controversy, the sixty-three-page booklet entitled *Fair Play is a Jewel: or, the Language and Conduct of the Discussers Discussed: in which the case is fairly stated respecting the Bishop of Salisbury's Late Charge, and Mr Wansey's Letter: The Illiberal Charges brought against the Clergy are repelled; and the Pretentions of Some, among Dissenters, to Exclusive Wisdom and Charity, are examined: Occasioned by a Pamphlet, entitled 'Rights of Discussion'*. This was published by Easton in Salisbury, Rivington and Hatchard in London, T. Baker in Southampton and in Bath by the printer and publisher of Bowles's first sonnets, Richard Cruttwell.

Bowles's stance in the controversy has been admirably summarised by David Jeremy in his paper 'A Local Crisis between Establishment and Nonconformity: the Salisbury Village Preaching Controversy, 1798–1799'. He writes:

> . . . In descending to malicious ridicule with two sets of Grub-street verses (one, *The Dissenter Done Over*, a parody of Wansey's *Letter;* the other, *A True Account*, a caricature of Wansey himself), Bowles directed attention to the clothier's abhorrence of violence . . .
>
> In denigrating Wansey, Bowles sought to associate him with the extremists favouring the French Revolution. His parting shot in

A Rowland for an Oliver inferred Wansey's sympathy for the London Corresponding Society with a rather devastating pun: 'If I might add a little advice with respect to Authorship, I would just whisper to you two words: *Ne sutor ultra crepidam*: which signifieth, *Stick to the Spinning Jenny.*' Plautus's tag, 'let the shoemaker stick to his last', must have recalled the radical shoemaker Thomas Hardy . . . In so vilifying Wansey, Bowles's object must have been to create the spectre of a Protestant Vinegar Hill . . . Also in his last tract of the controversy the Orthodox Dissenters, but not the Methodist 'ranters' were defended by Bowles. He denied that their motives were political; referring to Malham's *Broom*[57] he asserted, 'These improper and intolerant expressions, the majority of the clergy would not avow, any more than the respectable part of the Dissenters would avow Mr W.'s absurd abuse, and many other intolerant sentiments, avowed by some of their society, against the church'. Bowles described Kingsbury[58] as 'an amiable and venerable man, and, in this respect, Malham's *Broom* 'an injudious attack'. Bowles, judging by the fact that no cleric challenged him, appears to have put forward the views of the majority of the clergy of the diocese in *A Rowland for an Oliver*, his only completely serious pamphlet.[59]

By 1798 the whole of the country was galvanising itself into action in the face of the threat of invasion posed by Napoleon Bonaparte. Large numbers of associations of armed volunteers had been formed in the confident expectation of being able to repel the French Jacobins, who were now being portrayed as ruthless monsters. It seems that even some of the clergy were being tempted to join the associations and had to be restrained by the archbishops from doing so. Although Bowles may not have been among them, he certainly wished to do his patriotic duty, and in 1799 Rivingtons published in London his *A Discourse delivered to the Military Associations for the Town and District of Shaftesbury, on Monday, Dec. 3, 1798, and published at the Request of the Mayor, and Officers of the respective Corps*. In 1797 the Tory politician George Canning[60] had founded what was to become the highly successful *Anti-Jacobin Review and Magazine* in which, in the March 1799 number, it was declared that:

In his address Mr B. attempts to prove that the Armed Associations of this country are *as justifiable from the tenor and spirit of Christianity, as those laws are which punish the robber and the murderer* . . . Mr B's is a respectable discourse for the purpose, and we doubt not, from the circumstances which give rise to its publication, it was heard with the attention it merits.[61]

News of Nelson's great victory over the French at the battle of the Nile reached London on 1 October 1798 and Bowles soon put pen to paper by writing the intensely patriotic *Song of the Battle of the Nile, published for the Benefit of the Widows and Children of the Brave Men who fell on that memorable Day, and humbly inscribed to the Gentlemen of the Committee*, published in 1799 and printed for T. Cadell, jun. and W. Davies, in the Strand and C. Dilly,[62] in the Poultry. Needless to say this poem met with the enthusiastic approval of the *Anti-Jacobin*: 'This bard is entitled to more than *critical* commendation for the benevolence of his purpose, and the harmony of his strains. True piety is ever accompanied with humility and modesty; and this happy union is not less striking in the poet himself than in the hero he celebrates . . .'[63]

The report of Bowles's discourse and the publication of his *Song of the Nile* probably persuaded the editor of the *Anti-Jacobin*, John Gifford,[64] to ask Bowles to review two of Richard Polwhele's[65] recently published poems, *The Old English Gentleman* . . . and *Sketches in Verse* . . ., and his reviews duly appeared in the June number of the *Anti-Jacobin*.[66]

The example set by Bowles, to publish a work with the profits to be devoted to charitable purposes, was followed by Sheridan when, either during or soon after 1799, his 'List of rules and regulations for a Piscatory Party in commemoration of Isaac Walton' included Rule 8 that reads: 'it is resolved in humble imitation of the example set by the Revd. W.L. Bowles that in case any copies of the said Fresh-water Log book should be sold the profits shall be applied to Benefit the Widows and Orphans of deceased Fishermen'.[67]

It may be recalled that while at Oxford Bowles had won the Chancellor's Latin verse prize for his poem 'Calpe obsessa, or, The siege of Gibraltar'. Now, in 1799, Bowles himself recited the poem in the Theatre in Oxford on Commemoration Day.[68]

During the years of Bowles's curacy at East Knoyle little of note appears to have occurred in the neighbourhood, although on 22 September 1799 the burial in the churchyard of a young boy named Robert Elliot was the sequel to an astonishing and tragic occurrence in the church. On the day after his burial it was reported:

> On Friday Mr Whitmarsh took the inquest at East Knoyle on the body of Robert Elliot, a boy aged ten years, who was found hanged in one of the bell-ropes in the belfry adjoining the church. It is singular that a man was tolling the bell for a funeral at the time the accident happened, but he being a lunatic and dumb, it was impossible to get any information

from him; and a man working in the church swore he did not cease tolling the knell for a moment. Verdict: accidental Death.[69]

Among the literary figures with whom Bowles became acquainted on his visits to London at this time was Samuel Rogers,[70] the wealthy poet, at whose breakfast parties he would have met many of the most influential men of letters and the arts of his day. Bowles and Rogers commenced a friendship that was to last for many years. In the summer of 1800 Rogers wrote from London to Bowles in Donhead:

> I cannot tell you how I thank you for your kind invitation. Believe me, I shall accept it very gladly whenever it is in my power. One hour's conversation with you, where you are now, would be worth all I can ever see of you amid the smoke and stir of this dim spot.[71]

Some time later, in an undated letter, Rogers wrote:

> I am very, very sorry that we have not met. Can you breakfast with me to-morrow? If so, pray do and pray say you will – or <u>when</u> you can. I am just now at Holland House, but will come at a moment's notice, whenever I may have a chance of seeing you and will let Moore know, who wishes much to meet you.[72]

The man named Moore is almost certainly Thomas Moore, the Irish poet, later to become a near neighbour of Bowles in Wiltshire and from whose journals a delightful and intimate picture of Bowles's character can be gleaned.

The demand for copies of Bowles's sonnets continued unabated. In 1798 Nathan Drake[73] in his *Literary Hours: or Sketches Critical and Narrative* had praised both Charlotte Smith and Bowles for their success with their sonnets by 'assuming the elegiac measure', and so it is no surprise to learn that a seventh edition of the sonnets was published in 1800 as well as a reissue of the sixth edition, with the allegorical sketch 'Hope' added.

Bowles was an enthusiastic musician, playing the violin, 'cello and flute with reasonable proficiency and delighting in listening to music being performed whenever he was able to do so. He also turned his hand to composition. A letter written to him by Sheridan, in about 1801, suggests that he was anxious to see performed one or more glees that he had written. 'Tom' referred to in the letter is Sheridan's son[74] and Knyvett[75] is the musician who, with others, had revived the Vocal Concerts at the Hanover Square Rooms:

I have spoken to Tom who says you are too late for this year, as all glees have been presented some time, but that for another year all you have to do is to send whatever you wish to be presented to Knyvett, and it is certain of taking its fair chance. I am particularly disappointed at this, as I shall not now be at liberty to sing the glee which after all I *stole*, and which I think quite beautiful, but which upon my honor I have shewn to nobody, nor will I without your express permission . . . Pray give my best regards to Mrs Bowles.[76]

Bowles's wish to see his work in this field become more widely known came to fruition in 1802 when 'Come to these scenes of peace. A glee for three voices' was published and a few years later, in 1808, when 'Adieu thou darling of my heart; a Duett Composed & Dedicated to Miss A'Court by The Revd Willm. L. Bowles' was printed by Preston[77] in London for James and Henry Banks,[78] the Salisbury musical instrument makers and music sellers. The music is written in the key of F major and the words are of an extremely sentimental nature:

Adieu thou darling of my heart whom never more these Eyes shall view
Yet once again before we part nymph of my Soul again adieu
Yet one more kiss, that kiss the last that I can ask or thou can'st give
Tho' on my lips it die too fast shall ever in remembrance live.[79]

The Miss A'Court to whom Bowles dedicated the duet was probably Caroline, fourth daughter of Sir William Pierce Ashe à Court and his second wife Letitia, daughter of Henry Wyndham of Salisbury.

By this time Coleridge had recovered from his extreme enthusiasm for Bowles's poetry, and on 26 August wrote to his friend William Sotheby,[80] the author and translator: '. . . I well remember, that after reading your Welch Tour, Southey observed to me, that you, I, & himself had all done ourselves harm by suffering our admiration of Bowles to bubble up too often on the surface of our Poems'.[81] In an earlier letter to Sotheby he even refers to Bowles's 'execrable Translation' of one of Dean Ogle's poems,[82] although he is charitable enough to say that he was 'confident that Bowles goodnaturedly translated it in a hurry, merely to give him an excuse for printing the admirable original'.[83]

Shortly after this Coleridge wrote again to Sotheby, and his words echo the sentiments of many later critics of Bowles's poetry:

. . . The truth is – Bowles has indeed the <u>sensibility</u> of a poet: but he has not the <u>Passion</u> of a great Poet. His latter Writings all want <u>native</u> Passion – Milton here and there supplies him with the appearance of it – but he has no native Passion because he is not a Thinker – & has probably weakened his Intellect by the haunting Fear of becoming extravagant . . .[84]

Despite this criticism, almost certainly unknown to Bowles, his prolific pen continued to keep the printers and publishers busy. In 1798 Switzerland had been occupied by the French and the sufferings of the people inspired Bowles to write *The Sorrows of Switzerland: a poem*, inscribed to Mrs William Douglas, a native of Switzerland, and published in 1801. Many editions of his sonnets and poems followed, with *The Picture: verses written in London, May 28,1803, suggested by a magnificent landscape of Rubens, in possession of Sir George Beaumont* being published in 1803.

Beaumont was a patron of the arts and a landscape painter, of whom it has been said that 'his social position, wealth, and cultivation secured for him a distinguished position as a ruler of taste'.[85] His wife Margaret was the daughter of John Willes[86] of Astrop, a hamlet some 3 miles from Bowles's birthplace, King's Sutton, and it was he who had presented to Bowles's father the living of Uphill and Brean. Bowles paid elegant tribute to this fact in the inscription at the commencement of *The Picture* by stating that the verses were inscribed to Lady Beaumont:

> Not so much on account of the kindness and hospitality he has himself experienced from her ladyship and Sir George, as that he has an opportunity of making a small return of gratitude for the greatest obligation conferred by her family upon one who lives not to thank them – his *father* who was preferred to the livings of Uphill and Brean, Somerset, by John Willes esq.[87]

It is thought that it was a syndicate of London publishers who requested Bowles to produce an edition of Alexander Pope's[88] works, with a commentary on his life, and it is certain that by 1801 he had begun to give serious thought to the undertaking. By the end of the year he had contacted the publisher William Davies of the firm of Cadell and Davies and had probably arranged with him that he would be sent a copy of all of Pope's works, as on 10 January 1802 Bowles wrote to him:

> I came home a day or two ago but having received nothing from you either Pope or the other books. I write to request you will let me know as

soon as possible your plan about the Edition. I have made myself better acquainted with what ought to be done, & consider'd the subject with some attention . . . I shall stipulate nothing about the price, leaving it entirely to arbitration when the whole is finished.[89]

After apologising for the delay in replying to Bowles's letter – a 'very afflicting domestic loss' was the reason – Davies responded by writing just a week later:

. . . We detained the copy of Pope's Works that had been prepared for you, in the Hopes of procuring Dr Vincent's Nearchus[90] to send with it, but in this we have failed for the present, and therefore Pope is sent without it and we hope has come to your Hands with this. With regard to the Notes of former Editors, we are anxious to submit wholly to your Decision, what shall be restored, what retained, and what rejected indeed we hope you will favour our Edition with a good many additional notes, &c and perhaps some short prefatory Account of what you have done. In short, dear Sir, with whatever you are so good as to do for us, we are sure we shall be perfectly satisfied – and as to the Remuneration, we never, for a moment, thought of offering you less than a hundred guineas, and if, on Completion of the Business, it is found that this Sum is inadequate, we hold ourselves bound to make such moderate Addition thereto as might be thought right.

  On Inquiry of the Printers respecting the Dramatic Poem, we find that only one Sheet had been printed, and the Matter of another composed – More had been composed but as the proofs were never returned, all beyond the second sheet was distributed again.[91]

It is clear that Bowles had been in correspondence about publishing a new volume of poetry, as later in the year Bowles wrote to Cadell and Davies:

Mr Bowles respects to Messrs Cadell & Davies, & if agreeable to them he would leave the price for the vol: to be fix'd by any person conversant in such business – suppose Mr Edwards – this however as they please – Mr B. is entirely ignorant of what may be the value – He thinks however that another small vol: of 150 pages would sell as well as the preceding, but he should not think of publishing it himself, or of offering to any other bookseller, till he had offer'd it to the proprietors of Switzerland – as Switzerland would not answer by itself & it might [illegible] them to publish a vol: without it.

P.S. I have return'd the proof & will send some other things shortly to be added. As soon as Cyrus is printed let the <u>whole</u> of it be sent to me. I would cancel the <u>dedication</u> – if it <u>is not too late.</u>

  Mr Davies will let me know what he thinks about my proposal – or whether he would like to make any other himself – as Switzerland cannot be included till this is determined.[92]

The volume was duly published, with the printers' account for the Cadell and Davies dated April 1802 reading:

	£		d
To printing Cyrus a Drama by W. Bowles			
1st Sheet 500 copies Small 8vo	I	15	–
3 sheets compound only	3	3	–
Corrections by the Author	I	I	–
	£5	19	–[93]

He may have looked to some of his friends for assistance in preparing his edition of Pope's works, as in a letter, perhaps written in 1803, Samuel Rogers wrote to Bowles:

> After some reflection I think it best to send the volumes to you. In a thing of such importance I must not hesitate and I know you will take care of them . . . You will bring these volumes back with you in the Spring, for I cannot tell you how I value them.[94]

In the early months of 1803 Bowles was seriously ill, and in a later comment on his poem called 'Stoke's Bay', written in April, Bowles writes that 'The Author at the time slowly recovering from a severe illness; and cannot omit this opportunity of expressing his gratitude to Mr James North of Bath and to his brother Dr Henry Bowles,[95] physician on the staff to the military hospital at Forton, near Gosport'.[96]

  In the coming years Bowles's sonnets would be found in a variety of anthologies. One of the earliest was George Henderson's *Petrarca: A Selection of Sonnets from Various Authors with an Introductory Dissertation on the Origin and Structure of the Sonnet.* In this collection, published in London in 1803, six of Bowles's sonnets appeared.

By May 1803 Britain was at war with Napoleon Bonaparte and there was every expectation that the country would soon be invaded. Patriotic fervour abounded and, using his literary and musical talents, Bowles was determined to play his part. Towards the end of August a concert and balls were held in the Council Chamber in the city during the Salisbury Race Meeting. The *Salisbury and Winchester Journal* reported:

The second Act of the Concert was chiefly selected from L'Allegro and Il Penseroso ending with the 'Briton's March to Glory' a New Song and Chorus. The Words and Music of this animated Appeal are both by the Rev. Mr Bowles. One of the Stanzas was assigned to Mrs Second, who sang it with exquisite taste and feeling. Indeed, the whole performance gave complete satisfaction to near 300 auditors.

The newspaper than printed all five verses of the song, the first of which conveys a flavour of the whole:

Britons, awake to Glory,
Arm, arm, arm;
Your wives, your Children implore ye!
Lift high the avenging sword.
Be 'Our King and Country' the word,
While we sweep
To the deep,
At a blow,
All the pride of the insolent Foe.[97]

In the following number of the newspaper, under the heading 'MUSIC', it was announced:

This day is published 'The Briton's March to Glory' a New Song, written, composed and dedicated to Lord Hutchinson by the Rev. W.L. Bowles. As sung by Mrs Second and all the principal Singers at the Salisbury Race Concert.
    Printed and sold by Preston, No 97 The Strand and Messrs Banks, Salisbury.[98]

Lord Hutchinson of Alexandria[99] was the hero of the military campaign in Egypt and so a very suitable person to receive the dedication. That it was printed and sold by William Preston[100] in London is an indication of the popular response that was expected. In the words of Colin Pedley:

The rhetorical appeal of Bowles's song was widely used and disseminated in patriotic prints and in new magazines, such as the *Loyalist* and the *Anti-Gallican*, both begun in August 1803 on a weekly basis, with the same purpose 'to rouse and animate the British Nation during the present important Crisis' (the *Loyalist*) and 'to excite the Martial Ardour of the People against Bonaparte and his perfidious designs' (the *Anti-Gallican*).

Magazines such as the *British Critic* had a subheading of 'Invasion' in their miscellaneous review section. The *Bath Chronicle*, 4 August 1803, had also reprinted patriotic lines from Bowles's new poem 'The Picture'. The popularity and effectiveness of Bowles's new song is evidenced by its being repeated at the Bath Harmonic Society's concert on 23 February 1804, as reported nationally in the *Morning Chronicle* and the *Courier* of 2 March 1804.[101]

While as a clergyman it would not have been possible for Bowles to enlist in one of the many volunteer regiments, he did become chaplain to the West Wilts Regiment of Volunteers, and when in April of the following year, 800 men of the regiment received their colours on Hindon Down before commencing a period of training, he addressed the assembled company as 'Freemen in Arms' and concluded his 'Exordium', as the newspaper report termed his speech, by declaiming, 'It only remains to me to offer my fervent prayers that the Almighty Disposer of events will crown your efforts with success.'[102]

It is possible that in 1804, when he was in London, Bowles met the Prince of Wales,[103] as in May it was announced that Bowles had been appointed his chaplain.[104] Some time after this Bowles asked Sheridan, who acted as the Princes's personal adviser, to approach him to ask whether Bowles might dedicate his forthcoming *The Spirit of Discovery; or, the Conquest of the Ocean. A poem, in five books* . . . to him. In October Sheridan, while at Carlton House, wrote to Bowles:

> I received yours this morning being luckily in town, as is also the Prince for a few days. I have this moment seen him, and most graciously will receive your dedication. I certainly should wish you to present your morocco yourself, but I must apprise you of his motions. Upon your question of the manner of dedicating I will write a few lines to-morrow or next day . . .[105]

The Spirit of Discovery, Bowles's longest poem, was published at the end of the year with the dedication duly appearing on the title page, and Bowles described as 'Chaplain to His Royal Highness the Prince of Wales' – a title probably conferred on a whim by the Prince and, so far as is known, involving no duties whatsoever.

Although Bowles was doubtless gratified to receive royal recognition, the death of his thirty-nine-year-old brother Henry, an army doctor who died on board the *Swiftsure* man-of-war in 1804, must have caused him great sadness.

Following the death of his mother, Bowles and his brother Charles became lords of the manor of Barton Hartshorn in Buckinghamshire a small village very close to the Oxfordshire border. The manor had been purchased by their ancestor Thomas Lisle in about 1629 and eventually passed by descent to their father, who by his will directed that the manor should be held by his widow during her life and on her death should pass to Bowles and his brother as tenants in common. Annexed to the manor were the rectory and the advowson of the benefice.[106]

On his mother's death a moderate amount of capital had passed to Bowles, thus augmenting to some degree the income he was already receiving. However, further preferment in the church was surely never far from his mind. He knew from his mother that he would almost certainly in due course be offered the living of Bremhill, near Calne in north Wiltshire, and this is probably why he had always been reluctant to accept any living other than that of Dumbleton where his residence was not expected. Further, she doubtless told him the reason why this valuable living would one day be his. After his ordination John Moore,[107] later Archbishop of Canterbury, had secured his appointment as tutor to the younger sons of the 3rd Duke of Marlborough[108] through the influence of Bowles's grandfather. As this paved the way to his further advancement in the church, Moore promised Bowles's mother that when the living of Bremhill became vacant he would present it to her son. However, it was not until 1804 that the incumbent, the Rev. Nathaniel Hume, eventually died at the age of seventy-two. Garland Greever, in his *A Wiltshire Parson and his Friends*, recounts the events that nearly led to Bowles's hopes being dashed:

> His chief hope of preferment lay in the friendship of Archbishop Moore, who long since had contracted obligations to Bowles's maternal grandfather. Through Bowles's mother an arrangement was made with Moore whereby Bowles was to have the living at Bremhill in north Wiltshire as soon as it became vacant. But the incumbent held on year after year, and meanwhile Bowles saw little of Moore. When the living at last became vacant, the Bishop of Salisbury sent a servant to Bowles to urge that he present himself at Lambeth without an hour's delay.

Nathaniel Hume died on 28 April, and as he was also Precentor of Salisbury Cathedral the Bishop would very quickly have heard of his death.

> Bowles and his wife set off at once and travelled all night. When they arrived at Lambeth, they found that the archbishop, whose memory was

failing, had forgotten his promise and was about to bestow the position upon some other applicant. The repetition of the words 'Biddy Grey', the maiden name of Bowles's mother, brought back to Moore a sense of his obligations, and he requested Bowles to wait in London until the arrangements were completed. Bowles waited far beyond the necessary period, then ventured to call on the archbishop again. He learned that the appointment was his, but that he failed to notify Moore of his London address.'[109]

As a result, in May 1804 Bowles was duly collated to the vicarage of Bremhill. Earlier in the year Bowles's income had increased when the Bishop of Salisbury had bestowed on him the prebend of Stratford in Salisbury Cathedral, vacant following the death of Dr Newton Ogle, Dean of Winchester,[110] to whom Bowles had dedicated the edition of his sonnets published in 1794. At last, therefore, advancement in the church had arrived and a new chapter in his life was to begin.

Chapter 3
1805–1818

The new parson who arrived at Bremhill early in 1805 to assume his duties was not, therefore, an unknown clergyman from an obscure parish some 30 miles away near the Dorset border in the south-western corner of Wiltshire, but a poet whose sonnets were admired throughout the country and whose poetry had been published in many editions during the previous five years. Further, he was already acquainted with the 2nd Marquis of Lansdowne whose seat, Bowood, was within walking distance of Bremhill.

The living was considered to be a good one. In a description of Wiltshire published in 1814 it was described in this way: 'The living here is an endowed vicarage having great tithes. It is very valuable, but would have been still more so but for an Act of Parliament passed in 1775, which fixes the rate of tithe at five shillings per acre.'[1] Bremhill was a rural parish of some 6000 acres and with a population of about 1300 souls.[2] The 2nd Marquis of Lansdowne was the owner of most of the land, with the farms generally consisting of between 150 and 200 acres. The parsonage that was to be Bowles's home for many years to come was a seventeenth-century house with a fifteenth-century core; it was of quite a moderate size with just a drawing room, dining room and study with the usual domestic offices on the ground floor. His predecessor, Nathaniel Hume, had been living in the house for a very considerable time, and shortly after his death a schedule of dilapidations[3] was prepared claiming that £207 17s 7d was required to be paid by his executors to put the house, stables, barns, malthouse and fences, as well as the chancel of the church, in good order. The house was later to be transformed by Bowles, and the gardens, extending to about 2 acres, were to be embellished with every conceivable form of bower, grotto, cascade and hermitage – not to mention urns, seats and inscriptions. It is likely that Bowles began work on it very soon after he and his wife Magdalene moved into the parsonage, as within six years of their arrival the 3rd Marquis of Lansdowne,[4] who succeeded to the title and estates in 1809, described the garden as one of the prettiest spots in the county – and within ten years it was celebrated enough to be described in great detail in the *Gentleman's Magazine*. In a poem written at the parsonage in Bremhill in September 1808, Bowles invites his readers to 'Come, and where these runnels fall, Listen to my madrigal!'[5], indicating that within a very few years the waterworks that were to be such a feature of the gardens were in place.

It is almost certain that Bowles employed Josiah Lane[6] of Tisbury, who had created grottoes at Wardour Castle and Fonthill, as well as at Bowood, to undertake similar work in the garden at Bremhill. In 1810 Lord Lansdowne wrote to Bowles:

> I shall not forget what you mention respecting Lane, whenever I have occasion to do any thing to the rock work at Bowood. At present there is so much essential repair wanted there, and I have also so much on my hands in London, that I shall delay doing anything that is not indispensible [*sic*], till I am able to reside in Wiltshire, particularly in the ornamental department, which I can only judge and direct upon the spot. I perfectly remember Lane who is an excellent executive workman, altho' if I am not mistaken, his haste requires sometimes the active superintendence of his employer, as you may perhaps have found at Bremhill. Your garden there is certainly one of the prettiest spots in the county . . .[7]

Bowles's income from the living of Bremhill as well as from Dumbleton was supplemented by that derived from the prebend of Stratford in Salisbury Cathedral. However, in 1805 he exchanged this prebend for that called *Major Pars Altaris*, a prebend enjoying an insignificant income; and so it seems strange that this exchange should have been made. Nevertheless, with the addition of the interest on the capital inherited from his parents, Bowles was now enjoying a comfortable income that gave him the means to carry out considerable additions and improvements to his parsonage as well as to create his notable garden.

Very soon after he arrived in Bremhill Bowles made the acquaintance of a young man named Bryan Waller Procter,[8] an old Harrovian who was articled to the Calne attorney Nathaniel Atherton. Procter, who was later to achieve fame as a poet and essayist writing under the pseudonym of Barry Cornwall, recalled meeting Bowles in 1805 and 1806. He writes:

> I frequently went to see him at his parsonage, and joined him (my flute with his violoncello) in practising duets. He knew much more about music than I did, and appeared to be a certain though not very

rapid performer. A schoolfellow of mine, when at H
me Mr Bowles's Sonnets, which I greatly admired; a·
very ready, perhaps not a little proud, to join the rᵉ
harmonious interludes. As far as our acquaintance wenι, .
a player of the violoncello; for I never heard him speak of his sᴏι.
or refer to poetry on any occasion . . . Mr Bowles had a blunt, almost a
rough manner, which did not quite answer my preconceived (immature)
idea of a poet. I had imagined that I should see a melancholy man,
pressed down by love disappointed, and solemn with internal trouble;
I found a cheerful married man, with no symptom of weakness or
sentiment about him. He had a pretty garden at his Bremhill parsonage,
where he erected a hermitage, and was unwise enough to endow it
with a multitude of inscriptions; at which his neighbours were fond of
laughing, as instances of affectation. For myself, I never saw anything
affected or fantastic in this gentleman. His wife was a lady, tall, and of
good manners; not ill adapted to a poet who had previously exhausted all
his sorrows in song.[9]

It is certain that Bowles's new parishioners looked to him for
help in their dealings with the 2nd Marquis of Lansdowne, who did
not live at Bowood but in the Gothic-style castle that he had built near
Southampton. As an example, he wrote to Bowles from London on 10
January 1806, the day after the public funeral of Nelson in St Paul's
Cathedral:

I have received your obliging letter appraizing me that Mr Thomas
Marriott [?] of whom you have reason to think wishes to become my
tenant for a small farm in your neighbourhood. I have every wish to
pay deference to your recommendation and will write to say that I wish
Mr Marriott should have the ground provided always he be inclined
to give as much rent for it as another person may be found inclined
to pay, whatever that may be. And now having answered you upon
the matter of business allow me to ask you for a copy of the lines you
wrote upon the death of Lord Nelson which struck me very much when I
read them in I know not what Newspaper, which I cannot find. I am the
more interested in the subject as I am endeavouring to get a Monument
erected in Dublin by public subscription dedicated to his memory on
rather a magnificent plan[10] though I did not attend the melancholy
[illegible] of yesterday.[11]

The lines that had so impressed Lord Lansdowne were undoubtedly
Bowles's short poem of four verses entitled *Dirge of Nelson*.[12]

Another casualty of the battle of Trafalgar was Bowles's old friend from Donhead, John Cooke, who was killed in action while in command of the *Bellerophon*. Bowles was moved to write a poem 'Death of Captain Cooke', in which he quotes Cooke's dying words: 'Let me die in peace'.[13] Bowles kept in touch with Cooke's widow, and a few years later, in 1810, Harriet Grove[14] recorded in her diary that on 9 October 'Went to Pythouse, called on our way on Mrs Cooke.' There she met Bowles's sister Sarah Burlton with Sarah's daughter and her husband Charles Benett (Magdalene's cousin), and Bowles himself, whom Harriet found 'very entertaining'.[15]

Since the end of the eighteenth century Sir Richard Colt Hoare of Stourhead, assisted by William Cunnington[16] and others, had been opening numerous barrows in Wiltshire and was in the habit of inviting his friends who had a particular interest in the history of the county to observe the excavations. In *The Ancient History of South Wiltshire*, published in 1812, Colt Hoare relates what occurred when a barrow at Fovant was being opened:

> The opening of this Barrow was attended by so many awful circumstances, and gave birth to so beautiful and truly descriptive a Poem by my friend the Rev. William Lisle Bowles who attended the operations that it will ever be remembered both with horror and pleasure by those who were present. During the tremendous storm of thunder and lightning by which my friend and companion Mr Fenton, my surveyor Mr Philip Crocker[17] etc etc were surprized, our only place of refuge was the barrow, which had been excavated to a considerable depth; the lightning flashed upon our spades and iron instruments, and large flints poured down upon us from the summit of the barrow so abundantly and so forcibly that we were obliged to quit the hiding place.[18]

In reviewing Colt Hoare's work, the *Gentleman's Magazine* thought that 'they seem to have had an ample recompense for their alarm by the receipt of the following beautiful Poem, which Mr Bowles, who quitted the antiquarian party that evening, forwarded to them on the following morning'.[19] There followed the inevitable piece of dramatic poetry that Bowles was capable of writing at a moment's notice! Some years later, in 1823, in a letter written to Colt Hoare, Bowles rather appropriately told him that 'my Antiquarianship always turns to Poetry!'[20]

It is certain that as soon as he arrived in Bremhill, if not before, Bowles began collecting material for his contribution towards a projected history of 'modern' Wiltshire that was being proposed by Sir

Richard Colt Hoare as a successor, as it were, to his *Ancient History of South Wiltshire*. In 1928 a volume of manuscript collections relating to Wiltshire, all in Bowles's handwriting and dated from 1804 onwards, together with another manuscript collection consisting of about 450 pages (in the hand of a copyist but with notes by Bowles), was offered for sale.[21]

In 1806 a pamphlet was published, printed by Baker and Fletcher in Southampton and containing three poems written by Bowles – 'Bowden Hill', written in June 1806 and dedicated to the Marchioness of Lansdowne, 'The Banks of the Wye', written in the following month and dedicated to Miss Morrison, and 'Cadland, Southampton River', written in September 1806 and dedicated to Andrew Drummond. At a time when plurality was still widely accepted and, indeed, expected, Bowles proudly describes himself on the title page as 'Rector of Dumbleton, Gloucestershire; Bremhill, Wilts; Prebendary of Sarum and Chaplain to H.R.H. the Prince of Wales'.

It is probable that nothing else was published at this time because he was busily employed in the completion of his preparation for the publication in 1806 of *The Works of Alexander Pope, Esq., in verse and prose . . .*, a ten volume work that had been commissioned by a syndicate of publishers and for which Bowles was paid £300.[22] As well as reproducing and editing Pope's work, Bowles was critical of Pope's character, both moral and poetical, and it was this that was to cause such controversy in the years to come.

It was Bowles's practice to visit London each year in the summer, when he would be sure to meet old friends and, in particular, to visit the annual exhibition of paintings at the Royal Academy. A poem entitled 'Exhibition, 1807' enables one to learn which paintings on show in that year caught his attention, and which met with his approval. Wilkie's[23] *Blind Fidler*, Turner's[24] *Morning*, and Callcott's[25] *Market Day* as well as his friend Sir George Beaumont's[26] *Keswick* clearly pleased him. His criticism of de Loutherbourg's[27] *Scene in France* was couched in very plain terms when he wrote:

Artist, I own thy genius; but the touch
May be too restless, and the glare too much:
And sure none ever saw a landscape shine,
Basking in beams of such a sun as thine,
But felt a fervid dew upon his phiz,
And panting cried, O Lord, how hot it is![28]

The painting that Bowles could not fail to mention was West's[29] famous *Death of Nelson*, which caused a sensation when first exhibited in the painter's house.

In 1807 Bowles received from his fellow poet Frank Sayers[30] a copy of his collected poems. Having abandoned a career in medicine, in 1790 his *Dramatic Sketches in Northern Mythology* appeared, and this set him on the path of a literary career. It seems that Sayers sent a copy of his poetry to a number of fellow writers, including Walter Scott, who also acknowledged a copy of the collected poems in June 1807.[31] In acknowledging receipt of his copy in November, Bowles wrote:

> I beg leave to thank you most cordially for the volume of poems you were so kind as to transmit by my friend W. Linley. Of course I was no stranger to the name of Sayers, nor to the northern Dramatic Sketches which I have read with increased pleasure. To the first poem, the descent of Frea, no words from me could do justice. The wildness of the circumstance and characters, the novelty and sublimity of the imagery, the rich and appropriate diction, and the unity and simplicity of the conduct, in my opinion place it far above anything in Gray.[32] The Giant-Killer is perfectly original, and in its way inimitable. And the sonnet on Uncle Joe is a most exellent burlesque of affected simplicity, which is to me far more offensive in writing, than any other affectation. If anything should bring you towards Bath, I hope I need not say how happy I should be to receive you at Bremhill, and am with greatest respect,
> Sir
> Your obliged humble Servant[33]

While working on his critique of Pope, Bowles continued to write large quantities of poetry, little of which matched the quality of his early sonnets and most of which has been dismissed by modern critics as decidedly second rate. Certainly this could be said of much of the content of *Poems, (Never before Published) written chiefly at Bremhill, in Wiltshire*, published by Cadell and Davies in the Strand and by Cruttwell in Bath in 1809. One of these poems, entitled 'The Sylph of Summer; or Air' contains a singular 'Digression, on the Loss of a Brother' and includes the lines:

> THOU TOO DIDST PERISH! – As the South-West Blows,
> They bones, perhaps, now whiten on the coast
> Of ALGARVA. I, meantime, these shades
> Of village solitude (Hoping, erewhile,

To welcome thee, from many a toil restor'd)
Still deck, and now the empty urn alone
I meet, where, swaying in the summer gale,
Willow whispers in my evening walk.

Bowles was referring to his brother Henry, who died on-board ship off the coast of Portugal some five years before, and the empty urn is a reference to the urn that he had placed in the garden at Bremhill bearing the inscription '*M.S. Henrici Bowles, qui ad Calpen, febre ibi exitiali grassante, publice missus, ipse miserrime periit – 1804. fratri posuit.*' In 1809, in his *English Bards and Scotch Reviewers*, in which more is said about Bowles than about Wordsworth or Coleridge, Lord Byron[34] was the first to publicly criticise and even make gentle fun of Bowles's work and of his critique of Alexander Pope. In it he includes the lines:

As for the smaller fry, who swarm in shoals
From silly Hafiz[35] to simple Bowles.

He also describes Bowles as 'The maudlin prince of mournful sonneteers. And art thou not their prince, harmonious Bowles!' and contrives to belittle his sonnets as being suitable for only very young people by declaring 'Delightful Bowles! Still blessing and still blest, All love thy strain, but children like it best.' [36] He later writes:

'Awake a louder and a loftier strain',
Such as none heard before, or will again!

Byron adds:

'Awake a louder and a loftier strain' is the first line in Bowles's 'Spirit of Discovery'; a very spirited and pretty dwarf-epic. Among other exquisite lines we have the following
–'A kiss
    Stole on the list'ning silence, never yet
Here heard; they trembled even as if the power,'
&c &c
    That is, the woods of Madeira trembled to a kiss: very much astonished, as well they might be, at such a phenomenon.[37]

And later he writes:

Nor this alone; but pausing on the road,
The bard sighs forth a gentle episode;
And gravely tells – attend, each beauteous miss!–
When first Madeira trembled to a kiss[38]

To these lines Byron adds a note that they allude to the story of two
lovers 'who performed the kiss above mentioned, that startled the woods
of Madeira'.[39]

Byron's friend John Cam Hobhouse[40] also supplied some lines:

Stick to thy sonnets, man! – at least they sell.
Or take the only path that open lies
For modern worthies who would hope to rise:
Fix on some well-known name, and, bit by bit,
Pare off the merits of his worth and wit:
On each alike employ the critic's knife,
And when a comment fails, prefix a life;
Hint certain failings, faults before unknown,
Review forgotten lies, and add your own;
Let no disease, let no misfortune 'scape
And print, if luckily deformed, his shape:
Thus shall the world, quite undeceived at last,
Cleave to their present wits, and quit their past;
Bards once revered no more with favour view,
But give their modern sonateers their due;
Thus with the dead may living merit cope,
Thus Bowles may triumph o'er the shades of Pope

Hobhouse's contribution was omitted from the second edition of
English Bards and Scotch Reviewers published in the following year, as later
Byron was to say: 'I am grieved to say that, in reading over those lines,
I repent of their having so far fallen short of what I meant to express
upon the subject of his edition of Pope's works'.[41] He did, however, in
the second edition retain the lines 'Stick to thy sonnets, man! – at least
they sell' and also implied that Bowles was the worst of Pope's critics:
that in writing of his private life he raked 'from each ancient dunghill
every pearl' and 'let all the scandals of a former age Perch on thy pen,
and flutter o'er thy page'![42]

The second edition of *English Bards and Scotch Reviewers* includes
Byron's revised and final version of his lines on Bowles and his works,
and reads:

Hail, Sympathy! Thy soft idea brings
A thousand visions of a thousand things,
And shows, still whimpering through three score of years,
The maudlin prince of mournful sonneteers.
And art thou not their prince, harmonious Bowles!
Thou first, great oracle of tender souls?
Whether thou sing'st with equal ease, and grief,
The fall of empires, or a yellow leaf;
Whether thy muse most lamentably tells
What merry sounds proceed from Oxford bells
Or, still in bells delighting, finds a friend
In every chime that jingled from Ostend;[43]
Ah! How much juster were thy muse's hap,
If to thy bells thou would'st but add a cap!
Delightful Bowles! Still blessing and still blest,
All love thy strain, but children like it best.
'Tis thine, with gentle Little's[44] moral song,
To soothe the mania of the amorous throng!
With thee our nursery damsels shed their tears,
Ere miss as yet completes her infant years:
But in her teens thy whining powers are vain;
She quits poor Bowles for Little's purer strain.
Now to soft themes thou scornest to confine
The lofty numbers of a harp like thine;
'Awake a louder and a loftier strain',[45]
Such as none heard before, or will again!
Where all Discoveries jumbled from the flood,
Since first the leaky ark reposed in mud,
By more or less are sung in every book,
From Captain Noah down to Captain Cook.
Nor this alone; but, pausing on the road,
The bard sighs forth a gentle episode:
And gravely tells – attend, each beauteous miss!–
When first Madeira trembled to a kiss.
Bowles! In thy memory let this precept dwell,
Stick to thy sonnets, man! – at least they sell.
But if some new-born whim, or larger bribe,
Prompt thy crude brain, and claim thee for a scribe;
If chance some bard, though once by dunces fear'd,
Now, prone in dust, can only be revered;
If Pope, whose fame and genius, from the first,
Have foil'd the best of critics, needs the worst,

Do thou essay; each fault, each failing scan;
The first of poets was, alas! but man.
Rake from each ancient dunghill every pearl,
Consult Lord Fanny[46], and confide in Curll;[47]
Let all the scandals of a former age
Perch on thy pen, and flutter o'er the page;
Affect a candour which thou canst not feel,
Clothe envy in the garb of honest zeal;
Write, as if St John's soul could still inspire,
And do from hate what Mallet[48] did for hire.
Oh! hadst thou lived in that congenial time,
To rave with Dennis,[49] and with Ralph[50] to rhyme;
Throng'd with the rest around his living head,
Not raised thy hoof against the lion dead;
A meet reward had crown'd thy glorious gains,
And link'd thee to the Dunciad[51] for thy pains.

Bowles was doubtless continually irritated by his name being associated with the trembling woods of Madeira. In 1816 in a review of *Hypocracy – A Satire* mention is made that 'the walls of St Mary's trembled at the unusual sound' brought forth the comment 'as Mr Bowles informs did the woods of Madeira at the first kiss performed in them by his pair of lovers'.[52]

In the following year, in writing to John Murray the publisher, Byron brought up yet again the misunderstanding about whether it was the lovers or the woods in Bowles's *Spirit of Discovery* that had 'trembled to a kiss', and Bowles's later conversation with him about the matter that had caused him such anguish. Byron wrote:

> It [the conversation] did not occur 'soon after publication' &c but in 1812 – three good years after – I recollect nothing of 'seriousness' now as the company were going into another room – he said to me that all his friends had bothered him crying out 'Eh Bowles how come you to make the woods of Madeira tremble to a kiss' whereas it was not the woods but the lovers who trembled – though I see no great reason why they should either. – I have had no opportunity of restoring the 'trembling' to its right owners … Bowles was courteous and civilised enough & so was I too I hope.[53]

Bowles cannot have failed to have read or been made aware of the disparaging references to him and his work in Byron's *English Bards and Scotch Reviewers*, but decided, perhaps wisely, not to embark on a public debate with him – at least, not at the present time.

Byron had some further fun at Bowles's expense when, in his 'Hints from Horace' written in March 1811, he includes the lines:

> For you, Young Bard! Whom luckless fate may lead
> To tremble on the nod of all who read,
> Ere your first score of cantos Time unrolls,
>
> Beware – for God's sake, don't begin like Bowles!
> 'Awake a louder and a loftier strain!'
>
> And pray, what follows from his boiling brain?
> He sinks to Southey's level in a trice,
> Whose Epic Mountains never fail in mice.

'Awake a loud and loftier strain' was, it may be recalled, the first line of Bowles's *Spirit of Discovery*, which Byron had thought, perhaps ironically, one of its 'exquisite lines'!

In 1808 the second edition of *Bath Characters or Sketches from Life* by Peter Paul Pallet was published in London. This volume of satirical dialogues was in fact written by Richard Warner,[54] the curate of St James's Church in Bath, and all the characters were thinly disguised representations of well-known Bath residents. Warner describes a fictional conversation between 'Bow-wow' (the Rev. Mr Bowen, minister of St Margaret's Chapel) and 'Resin' (Signor Rauzzini, Director of the Concert):

> 'I'll give you a song to cheer our spirits, my boy . . . the stewards indeed refused it, because it was *too free*, forsooth, for the women . . . I'll be sworn it would have made ten times more *fun* than the namby-pamby lines of *Billy Sonnet* (the *poet-laureate* of the club), which he *fitted up* for the occasion.'[55]

It was widely accepted that 'Billy Sonnet' was, of course, William Bowles (or Billy as he was known as a boy).

It is clear that Bowles was on easy and visiting terms with the 2nd Marquis of Lansdowne and that in November 1808 paid him a visit at Southampton Castle, as on the 19th the Marquis wrote to Bowles:

> . . . I did not see the beautiful lines you addressed to Harriett until after you had left this [place]. I think them profoundly impressive and they were very much admired by Lady Londonderry to whom I sent them as

she is a bettter judge.

Adieu make my respects to Mrs Bowles. All here join in good wishes.[56]

However, in the following year the 2nd Marquis died and was succeeded by his half-brother, Henry, as 3rd Marquis and 4th Earl of Kerry. He had been Member of Parliament for Cambridge University from 1806 until 1807 and for Camelford from 1807 until 1809, when he succeeded to the peerage. A man of great talent, at the age of twenty-five he found himself Chancellor of the Exchequer and in 1807 leader of the opposition. He and his wife, Louisa Emma, daughter of the Earl of Ilchester,[57] quickly established a very close and friendly relationship with Bowles and his wife, despite the great difference in social rank between the master of Bowood and the Bremhill parson.

Bowles would have discovered very soon after arriving in Bremhill that in the hamlet of Tytherton situated in his parish was a community of Moravians who had been settled there since the early eighteenth century, and he soon established cordial relations with the minister, Lewis Renatus West. West had a large family and, as Bowles later recorded, 'as the whole family were proficient in music, a <u>monthly</u> concert was established at the parsonage'.[58] Many years later, in writing to Edward Phillips in Melksham, he mentioned that 'All the Wests din'd here yesterday & we had excellent music – I hope you will come over, the next concert which is the first Monday in every month . . .'[59]

To copy poems into scrap or manuscript books was a favourite and seemly occupation for young ladies at this time. The first pieces of poetry copied into an album kept by a young lady named Elizabeth Charter were memorial stanzas by Bowles and Robert Southey, 'To the Memory of Emma Frances Peachey[60] who died on the island of Madeira, 1809', with Bowles's contribution being headed 'E.F.P. aet 25, 1809'.[61]

In each year between 1809 and 1812 various poems by Bowles appeared in the *Gentleman's Magazine*. One entitled 'The Winds'[62] was followed in 1810 by a poem 'On reading "Fragments by a young Lady lately deceased" Miss Elizabeth Smith'[63] and in 1810 by verses spoken in the Theatre at Oxford on the installation of Lord Grenville[64] as Chancellor of the University.[65] The first two of these poems had been included in *Poems (never before Published) Written Chiefly at Bremhill* that appeared in1809 and were dedicated to 'The Right Honourable the Countess of Cork and Orrery[66] . . . in token of respect and esteem.' Among the verses included in this volume is one entitled 'Melodies of Remembrance', which commences:

Ah, no! forgive the vain, intruding thought
And let me, * * * *, + love thee as I ought.
Love thee with warmth no language can express
With ecstasy, subdued by tenderness![67]

And at the end of the poem 'The reader may place any name he likes, with the exception of Chloe, Delia or Dorothy!' The girls' names in this mischievous footnote were perhaps unfashionable names that Bowles would not like to see inserted in these passionate lines.

In 1812 there appeared in the *Gentleman's Magazine*: 'In the following Lines, copied from the Bath Chronicle, we think we trace the Muse of that elegant Poet, W. Lisle Bowles. Lines written at Weston-super-Mare, August 5th, 1812.'[68] In this poem Bowles stretched poetic and artistic licence to the limit by asking, 'Was it but yesterday I heard the roar of these white-coursing waves, and trod this shore, a young and playful child, but yesterday?' It is not often that 'white-coursing waves' can be heard in the upper reaches of the Bristol Channel – although to a child, who would have seen little, if anything, of the sea, perhaps they appeared so.

It is likely that by 1811 Bowles had decided to write a long narrative poem, something that he had not done before. It was to be the story of an Indian who was abducted from his home by the Spaniards and then found himself fighting against his own people. At a crucial point in the battle he turns against the Spaniards, as a result of which they are defeated. Bowles decided to seek a publisher who would publish it without his name as author being disclosed. One of the reasons that he later revealed was that he was attempting the poem 'in a versification, to which I have been least accustomed, which, to my ear, is most uncongenial, and which is, in itself, the most difficult'.[69] But perhaps he wanted to see whether his work was of sufficient merit to sell without it being known that the author was a celebrated poet whose work would sell, whatever its quality might be.

Bowles decided to approach William Miller,[70] the most popular publisher in London, and on 14 June 1812 wrote:

Mr Bowles presents his compliments to Mr Miller and informs him that he has receiv'd Sir Richard Hoare's beautiful and splendid work[71] very safe.

Having had the pleasure of seeing Mr Miller in town, and knowing his great respecability as a publisher, Mr Bowles is tempted to lay before him a project which he has had some time in view.

It is this. Mr Bowles has finished a rather considerable poem, which for particular reasons he wishes to have publish'd without his name, and for the same reason not to have his usual publisher, that the author might not be suspected.

In preference, therefore, to any one in London, Mr Bowles applies to Mr Miller, to know whether he would consent to become a publisher of a poem upon the following terms –

Only four hundred copies to be printed, without a name. The publisher to be at all the expense, and of course to be entitled to all the profit, if any, of the first impression.

Should the poem go off with sufficient success, then the publisher to have a power of printing as far as fifteen hundred, with Mr Bowles' name, upon terms hereafter to be agreed on, but the author to retain the copy right.

If Mr Miller shall have his hands full, or is averse to publish for Mr Bowles on these terms, Mr Bowles implicitly trusts that what has been said may be an entire secret.

Mr Bowles thinks it right for Mr Miller's information to state that the poem consists of about 250 lines each book – would make a handsome small octavo volume. Is a story founded on historical fact and related to the great political circumstances of the Spanish in America, which in some degree gives it a special interest as connected with the existing war in Spain.

If Mr Miller thinks that Mr Bowles has said worth his attention, Mr B will write more fully, as soon as he hears from Mr Miller. & when Mr Miller has turn'd the matter in his mind, Mr B would be oblig'd to him for an answer.

If Mr Miller should think an impression of four hundred too few for any chance of profit, Mr Bowles would not object to the impression being five hundred, but not more, for the sake of another edition with the author's name & preface.

Mr Bowles would have no objection to send the first book to Mr Miller, but he wishes at present the subject to be a secret, as well as the name.

The poem was written at the express solicitation of Mr Rogers, Mr Bowles having never attempted a poem of the kind, and Mr Rogers flattering him that he should succeed. Mr Rogers (of St James' Place) is therefore the only living person to whom the circumstance is known.[72]

What Bowles did not know was that in May of 1812 Miller had sold his house, 50 Albemarle Street, and all his copyrights to John Murray, the publisher of the *Quarterly Review*, established by him in 1809 as a

Tory rival to the Whig *Edinburgh Review*. Upon receipt of Bowles's letter Miller sought his permission to pass it on to Murray, who, on 24 June, wrote to Bowles:

> Mr Miller, in consequence of your permission, has done me the favor of communicating to me your letter upon the subject of a confidential publication of a new poem. This I shall have much pleasure in undertaking upon the following conditions, which will, I trust, meet your approbation.
>
> That the First Edition consisting of five hundred copies shall be printed at Mr Murray's sole expense and risque and that Mr Murray shall be entitled to the whole profit, if any, upon this First Edition – this Edition to be published without the author's name.
>
> Should the First Edition go off with sufficient success, then Mr Murray shall have the power of printing any number not exceeding fifteen hundred (unless a greater impression may be hereafter mutually agreed upon) at the sole cost and risque of Mr Murray, and that of such edition the author shall be entitled to one half of such profit, if any, as shall arise after the sale of the impression. The copyrights to remain the property of the author, whose name shall appear in this Second Edition.
>
> I have extended the first impression to five hundred copies, as no smaller number would do more than pay the expenses. The condition respecting the second impression involves a remuneration which will not be thought too great for the risque of both.
>
> Mr Miller communicated to me the anxieties expressed in your second letter, to which I can only offer an insurance of the most honourable secrecy. It may be time to begin printing in December or January and to bring out the poem in February or March when the town is full.
>
> I beg the favour of your opinion upon the terms I have taken the liberty of proposing.[73]

On 26 June Bowles wrote to Murray accepting his terms, asking for about a dozen copies for himself and suggesting 'whether it would not be advisable to wait for the publication of Mr Scott's[74] and Mr Southey's next poems. It would not answer for a poem of six books to come out nearly at the same time with theirs. This, however, is left for Mr Murray's determination'.[75]

Bowles doubtless spent the summer and autumn months completing the poem, and on 14 December wrote again to Murray:

> Mr Bowles has sent the first book of the poem, concerning which he wrote to Mr Murray in the summer. The other books are all completely

finish'd but the first is the only one Mr B has had copied out fair – Mr Bowles does not think it necessary to send the title of the poem, at present, & thinks it had better be delay'd till the whole is printed –

There are seven books, of about 300 lines each, except the first which is more – This is now sent, in case Mr Murray should think it right to begin printing immediately – Mr Murray will have the goodness to say whether it is received & when it will be put to press, as Mr B thinks the best way would be to send the remainder of the poem, by the post, written out, as wanted. If this is put to press immediately, Mr B will send another book the next week, & so on, every Monday. [76]

In December Murray asked to be told the title of the poem and Bowles responded:

Mr Bowles presents his compliments to Mr Murray. The title of the poem is
    Lautaro, or
        The Avenger of his Country

Mr Bowles confidently trusts that he may rely upon Mr Murray's concealment of the author's name which is not known to his most intimate friends. One person only, who suggested the circumstance, knows any thing of the intention. This is Mr Rogers, of St James's Place.

Mr B. more particularly wishes the publication by himself should be kept a secret from any persons connected with the writers of the Quarterly Review . . .[77]

Murray was clearly concerned that sales would be adversely affected by the lack of an author's name, and so in December he wrote to Bowles:

I beg leave to assure you of my resolution to preserve, most faithfully, your secret.

It is very desirable in announcing a work, particularly a poem, without an author's name, to be a little explanatory of the subject, because it must be, at first, by that alone that strangers may be tempted to send for it, and therefore I would be glad to receive by return of post, such particulars of the subject (which you think it prudent to communicate) as may be likely to interest the public – that is to say, if you feel with me the propriety and advantage of a more detailed announcement. With your name to it any thing would be sufficiently attractive, but without a name some attraction must be created.

Do I read rightly Lautaro?[78]

On Christmas Eve Bowles wrote a long letter to Murray with an account of the narrative of the poem.[79]

The opinion of Samuel Rogers was sought on the manuscript of the poem, and in February of the following year Bowles wrote to Rogers suggesting various alterations and saying:

> If you approve, get the lines inserted in the place. It will come in the second sheet, so there is full time and pray hurry Murray. If you borrow the first book of the poem from Murray, which is copied out very fair, you can insert the passage in five minutes, before it comes to the compositor's hands . . .[80]

It is clear that Bowles was becoming frustrated at the delay in seeing his poem published. It was now almost a year since terms had been agreed with Murray, and so in April Bowles wrote to him:

> When I requested you to shew a sheet, after it was printed, to Mr Rogers and Lord Byron, it was under the idea that it would not possibly make a delay of more than a day's post. It certainly would not be advisable if it must prevent the poem being publish'd at the only season when it seems to me there is a fair opening.
>
> I am now going from home for a week, so that I cannot have a sheet before next Saturday, but if one is ready on Tuesday next I shall get it on Wednesday if you will direct it to me at John Benett's Esq.,[81] Pythouse, near Shaftesbury, Dorset.
>
> If you have spoken to Lord Byron, I think you had better tell him that I feel a confidence in him. I wish we could persuade [him] to write about twenty lines as an introduction to the sixth book, allusive to present circumstances, the battle of Salamanca, and the annihilation of the French invading army in Russia. Besides, he owes, as he will acknowledge, some amends to me for quoting me as the author of some nonsense, which, he now knows, I never wrote, at least with the interpretation put on it. We had an explanation on this subject, and he acknowledg'd how wrong he had been very ingenuously. This is entre nous.[82]

By the same year the movement to repeal the laws that had been enacted for the security of the Protestant religion was gathering momentum. Those who were determined to oppose any measure that might lead to Catholic emancipation began organising meetings, with a view to petitions being submitted to both Houses of Parliament praying that there should be no alterations to the existing laws. A meeting of freeholders was arranged to be held in Devizes, the market town not far from Bremhill, at the end of January and Lord Lansdowne was anxious that Bowles should attend the meeting. He was therefore disappointed that Bowles would be away from home and staying in Reading with his friend Archdeacon Robert Nares[83] at the time of the meeting. He therefore wrote to Bowles:

> Many thanks for your letter. Your absence from Wiltshire is unfortunate at such a moment, but I hope we may prevail upon you to accompany the D. of Somerset,[84] Lord Holland,[85] [and] myself from Reading, as we shall have a place for you, and can with perfect convenience bring you back to Reading on our return; and really your countenance and presence, particularly as Mr Douglas and Mr A [illegible] will be absent, is important to the cause of liberality and common sense, and we shall be lucky in the presence of your company.[86]

Bowles duly complied with Lord Lansdowne's request and was one of the many 'gentlemen of rank and property' who attended the meeting held at the end of January.[87] Lord Lansdowne and Lord Holland[88] addressed the meeting at very great length, both attempting to show that the fears of those who opposed the granting of relief to Roman Catholics were unfounded.

In August 1813 Bowles received a letter from his old school-fellow William Howley, by now a canon of Christ Church, Oxford, the incumbent of several church livings and regius professor of divinity at Oxford. He wrote:

> Dear Bowles
>
> Knowing your regard for me I am sure you will rejoice to hear that I am to be the new Bishop of what see I cannot yet tell.
> With best regards to Mrs B
> Dear Bowles
> Affly yrs
> W. Howley[89]

In reply, Bowles asked to be told when the identity of the bishopric could be revealed. A week later Howley replied: 'I tell you because you desired to hear – but it is not a subject of congratulation but rather fills me with apprehension. I am most unexpectedly nominated to the see of London. With many thanks for your most kind letter.'[90]

In October Samuel Rogers was staying at Bowood, and in a letter to his sister Sarah paints a vivid picture of Bowles at this time:

Bowles has dined and slept here twice, and I have twice breakfasted with him. He lives about three miles off (the walk is a very pleasant one) in a very pretty vicarage by the side of a very pretty church. His windows look over a fine valley, and in front appears the white horse cut on the downs, which has a very singular and pretty effect, as indeed it has at Bowood, through a vista in the pleasure grounds. Yesterday, I went to his church, and he was very anxious to exhibit his choir to advantage. He has a violincello, a bassoon and a hautboy. The first is his own, and the transportation of it to and from the church across the church-yard and among the congregation (not in its case) makes an odd appearance. He seems amazingly respected there, notwithstanding his odd manners. He came out of church in his surplice, but without a hat, having left it in the reading-desk, and there he stood, till the clerk, who had more wits about him, came running after him with it. The band sit in the gallery, and none of the congregation below join, except the parson, who sat singing very loud in his desk, to the trial of my nerves. They sang three very long Psalms and the responses (Mason's) to the Commandments. I have promised to go next Sunday, if I am still here, as he did not preach yesterday, though he read prayers – Douglas,[91] the Chancellor of Salisbury (the late Bishop's[92] son, and as odd a fellow as his friend Bowles), having preached for him. We set out together after church on horseback to visit a Moravian establishment, but could not make much progress – Douglas, a very tall and pompous-looking man on a tall horse, stopping his horse all the way to gather blackberries. Mme. de Stael[93] makes a bustle here, but, having arrived only yesterday, we have as yet had no shawl dance, and no recitations . . .[94]

In June 1813 Germaine de Stael had arrived in England. During her life it was said that there were three political powers in Europe – Britain, Russia and Madame de Stael – and so as soon as she arrived in London she was feted by politicians of all parties, was presented to the Queen and other members of the Royal Family and 'aroused vivid curiosity wherever she went'.[95] She was invited by Lord Lansdowne to Bowood where, she later recalled, 'I saw the most wonderful group of enlightened men that England, and therefore the world has to offer'.[96] Lord Lansdowne wrote a brief note to Bowles: 'I think you have expressed some curiosity to see Madame de Stael. Will you come and dine with her Friday. We can give you a bed if you like'.[97]

The authoress Maria Edgeworth,[98] when staying at Bowood in 1818, heard an account of Bowles's meeting with Madame de Stael and retold it to when writing to her stepmother:

> In riding to Bowood that day, he fell from his horse and sprained his shoulder, but still came on. Lord Lansdowne, willing to show him to advantage, alluded to this in presenting him before dinner to Madame de Stael. He is a simple country-curate-looking man and rather blunt, and when Madame de Stael in the midst of the listening circle in the drawing room began to compliment him and herself upon the exertion he had made to come to see her, he replied: 'Oh, ma'am, say no more, for I would have done a great deal more to see so great a curiosity!' Lord Lansdowne says it is impossible to describe the <u>shock</u> in Madame de Stael's face – the breathless astonishment and the total change produced in her opinion of the man. She afterwards said to Lord Lansdowne, who had told her he was a simple country clergyman, 'Je vois bien que n'st qu'n simple cure qui n'a pas le sens commun, quoique grand poete.' She never forgot it. Two years afterwards she spoke of it to Lord Lansdowne at Geneva, and wondered how it was possible that *un tel homme* could exist.[99]

However, Madame de Stael was a great admirer of Bowles's sonnets and translated his 'Hotwells Elegy' into French.[100] It is probable that after this rather inauspicious meeting he invited her to Bremhill to see his garden, where he gave her a copy of one of his books, as a few days later she wrote him a note: 'Thousand thanks for your kindness, my dear sir. If I hear an anthem, I'll pray for you. Poetry and religion are re-united in you, as they must be always. My best compliments to Mrs Bowles.'[101]

Lord Lansdowne was later to re-establish at Bowood the library and collection of pictures that had been dissipated by his half-brother, and his interest in *objets d'art* was the cause of an addition to the contents of the parsonage when, in August 1814, he wrote to Bowles:

> I have just had some imitations made of the best form of Etruscan vases in the Museum for the library here, and as they have succeeded entirely and are very perfect imitations of the originals, I will beg your acceptance of one of them in the hope that you will for my sake find a corner for it in your parsonage . . .[102]

As can be seen from this letter, Lord Lansdowne and Bowles were on the friendliest of terms, and the same can be said for Lady Lansdowne and Bowles's wife Magdalene. As the wife of the rector, Magdalene would have been expected to undertake all manner of good works in the parish and it is clear from the correspondence that passed between them that they were both closely involved in the running of the school in Bremhill established by Lady Lansdowne. For instance, in March 1815 Lady Lansdowne wrote to her from London:

> I am very happy to find that success has crowned your labors and that a woman has been found to chaperonne Anne. I have desired Mrs Broad to write by today's post to the woman who has charge of the furniture which was prepared for the school house to have it sent there immediately and also to desire Savory [?] to pay her weekly as you recommended – and as I conclude her wardrobe is not very rich, I must beg you will order what will make her look decent and give a sufficient change of linnen, and desire it to be placed to my account at Calne.[103]

Over the succeeding years the two friends were in constant touch with each other over the running of the school. It seems that Anne was not a great success as a schoolmistress, and several years later Lady Lansdowne was writing to 'My dear Mrs Bowles':

> I am very much obliged to you for your communication about Anne. She is determined to lessen our regrets at losing her by persevering in her artful line of conduct until the end. It is extremely kind of you to intend remaining at home to receive our new mistress. Her beginning well is of so much consequence to her future good conduct that I feel quite confident, as you so kindly undertake setting her off, in her final success . . .[104]

Some seventy children were taught in the school. A Sunday school had also been established by Bowles, in which about fifty boys received instruction, with a separate Sunday school under the supervision of Magdalene teaching some fifty girls.[105]

In 1813 Bowles's poem, now entitled *The Missionary* rather than *Lautaro, or The Avenger of his Country* as the author had originally proposed, was at last published anonymously, and was an instant success. Byron wrote to Thomas Moore:

Mr Bowles has no reason to 'succumb' but to Mr Bowles. As a poet, the author of 'The Missionary' may compete with the foremost of his contemporaries. Let it be recollected, that all my previous opinions of Bowles's poetry were <u>written</u> long before the publication of his last and best poem; and that a poet's <u>last</u> poem should be his best, is his highest praise. But, however, he may duly and honourably rank with his living rivals . . .[106]

However, *The Missionary* did not meet with universal approval. In writing to Murray in December about a second edition, Bowles says:

In consequence, I verily believe, of my name being known, I have seen an illiberal notice taken both of me and the poem in a satirical [?] publication. Inform me, if you know or have heard, the name of the writer, as I think I ought to take some notice of it in the preface to this edition.[107]

Bowles was probably referring to *The Modern Dunciad, a Satire* (1814), in which appear the words 'While Bowles exists, can satire want a dunce?'[108] In writing to Bowles in December about the number of copies to be printed in the second edition Murray reassures him:

I entreat you not to heed the contemptible article upon your book to which you allude and of which I know nothing but your notice of it. You have the most gratifying praise in the judicious and flattering criticisms which were made upon the work before the author was known and you should not allow the spite of some low fellow – I make no doubt the author is – to diminish one jot of the satisfaction to which you are so honourable entitled. [109]

In April 1814 the abdication of Napoleon caused widespread rejoicing. Bowles hastened to mark the happy occasion by erecting a commemorative obelisk in the garden of the parsonage. However, Napoleon's return from Elba in the following year doubtless caused Bowles to realise that the erection of such a monument was a little premature, but one imagines he felt vindicated by the eventual and final defeat of the French at Waterloo on 18 June in the following year. Bowles decided that he should attempt to raise money to assist the widows and orphans of the victims of the battle, and so on Sunday 20 August 1815 it was reported that he:

Preached a sermon and a collection was made for the benefit of the widows and orphans of the brave men who fell at the memorable Battle

of Waterloo. During the service, two pieces of beautiful music w
appropriate words from the pen of the Rev. Mr Bowles were sung, und\
the direction of Mr Coombes of Chippenham by ladies and gentlemen.
present . . . the church was overflowing, and the powerful arguments
and truly pathetic eloquence of the preacher deeply affected the hearts of
all present. A very liberal subscription followed on the occasion.[110]

Some of the 'words from the pen of the Rev. Mr Bowles' were
undoubtedly contained in the intensely patriotic 'Hymn for Music, after
the Battle of Waterloo', which began:

> Perish, Almighty Justice cried,
> And struck the avenging blow,
> And Europe shouts from side to side,
> The tyrant is laid low![111]

In February 1815 Bowles wrote to Robert Southey, principally to
seek his opinion on *The Missionary*. From Bath he wrote:

> . . . I can with sincerity say, there does not exist a person who has a higher
> sense than myself of your great talents, steadily & consistently, & nobly
> employ'd & [illegible] to extend the knowledge, delight the [illegible] &
> improve the heart – Praise from a person so distinguish'd must indeed
> be grateful & far more than compensate for, any coldness & harshness I
> may have receiv'd in other quarters.
>
> Having been so long familiar with your name & writings, I already
> feel as if upon a literary subject I were writing to a friend, & might I
> take the liberty of asking you a few questions, relative to an anonymous
> poem, which I took the liberty of begging your acceptance of some time
> ago – It was called the 'Missionary', it was publish'd anonymously for
> reasons you might 'wot of' – in short I believe those who prais'd it so
> highly in the Monthly Review for April 1814 would have spoken very
> differently had it been publish'd with my name.
>
> I am now going to publish a second edition of it, with my name; in
> consequence of which, as it might encounter various foes, if I could have
> your opinion about one or two things in it, I should feel more satisfied
> – Perhaps you might have it somewhere by you & casting your eye a
> moment over it, you could judge whether the ideas I have encourag'd
> myself to submit to you are just.

Bowles then proceeds to set out a number of alterations that might
be made and seeks Southey's opinion on them. In a postscript he writes:

Peachey[112] tells me you sometimes come into this part of the Country
– my residence is sixteen miles from here, in the Chippenham Road to
London – I need not say if you and Mrs Southey should ever come this
way, how much Mrs Bowles & myself should be gratified if it might be
convenient to you to make Bremhill your accessible Residence while in
the south of England. P.S. Coleridge, of course, you are aware, is now in
our neighbourhood.[113]

Soon after, on 21 February, Southey replied:

Murray kept your secret well, when I expressed to him my admiration of
the Missionary, and asked to whom I was indebted for what has given me
so much pleasure. I could be angry with myself for not having discovered
you, – but it never occurred to me that a name should be supprest which
would have carried with it so sure a recommendation to so wide a circle
of readers; – and I thought you had been well versed in Spanish, which
the author of the Missionary seemed not to be, by the manner in which
Campeador is accented: – It should be Campĕădor.

   The alteration of which you do me the honour to ask my opinion,
will certainly add much interest to the poem . . .

   I thought you were versed in Spanish literature, because the
solemn and impressive opening of your ode upon the Battle of the Nile
very much resembles that of one of the finest poems in the Spanish
language – Herrera's Ode upon the Battle of Lepanto.

   Whenever I may be travelling westward (or rather southward) it
will give me great pleasure to halt awhile with you: – but my ties with
that part of England are much loosened . . .

   And now, dear sir, farewell. I am indebted to you for many hours
of deep enjoyment, and for great improvement in our common art, – for
your poems came into my hands when I was nineteen and I fed upon
them . . .[114]

In 1809 Bowles had been one of the subscribers to Coleridge's
short-lived newspaper, the Friend, and must have been pleased in the
autumn of 1814 to find him now lodging at Ashley near Box with his
old friend John Morgan and his family. However, Coleridge was now
in a deeply depressive state and seriously addicted to opium. After
visiting Bowles at the parsonage in October 1814, Coleridge's entry in
his notebook reveals his state of mind at that time:

Oct 23rd/Bremmell – Church Bell tolling – from 1. to 5. ad libitum

Superstition, who pays 6d an hour – /
Revd. W.L. Bowles's. – Sweet place.[115]

Early in 1815, with his state of health much improved, the Morgans
and Coleridge decided to move from Ashley to the market town of
Calne. From here, Coleridge was able to travel quite easily to Bremhill
to visit Bowles and to Bowood, where Lord Lansdowne had invited him
to feel free to use his library. It is certain that at this time Coleridge saw
a good deal of Bowles, from whom he and the Morgans often borrowed
a horse.[116] The two poets doubtless borrowed books from each other. On
one occasion, when Bowles wished to consult one of Coleridge's books,
he was told that it had already been lent to Dr Brabant of Devizes, who
in 1815 received a letter from Coleridge which included: 'Mr Bowles has
been wishing to take some extracts from 'Field's Church',[117] but do not
send it back unless you have satisfied yourself with it'.[118]

Coleridge was now looking for a new publisher and sought
advice from Bowles, who suggested that he should approach Byron for
a recommendation. In a letter to Byron, Coleridge writes: 'Your weight
in society and the splendour of your name would, I am convinced, (and
so is Mr Bowles, who in truth suggested this application . . .) treble the
amount of their [the prospective publishers] offer . . .'.[119]

In May 1815 final preparations for a second edition of *The
Missionary* were in hand. Writing to Samuel Rogers in this month,
Coleridge told him:

Mr Bowles leaves Bremhill on Monday next for town. The being so
near him has been a source of constant gratification to me. He has
an improved edition of his 'Missionary' in the press, and a volume of
sermons worthy of a calm-minded clergyman, and which will, I trust,
contribute to counteract the poison of Fanaticism, by way of preventative
antidote; for the already diseased are incurable . . .[120]

When writing to Murray on 30 May 1815, Bowles generously
suggests: 'As only five hundred copies are printed, I shall not think
of taking any share myself should there be a profit on sale, but would
request four and twenty copies for some private friends who probably
would not purchase . . .'[121]

A second edition of *The Missionary* was duly published, with a
third following in 1816. The initial success was not repeated, however.
When writing to Lord Byron on 18 February 1817, Murray told him 'The
Missionary sold very well until the Author put his name to it – & then
it stopped.'[122] The somewhat obsequious dedication of the later editions

to Lord Lansdowne was worded in such a way that it is clear that Bowles was expecting criticism of his work:

My dear Lord

When this poem appeared without a name, your Lordship was among those, who favoured it with approbation.

Such testimony, and that of others, whose praise I might well be proud of, will be a consolation to me, should it, now my name has been avowed, have to encounter severer criticism; and in truth, flattering as its reception has been, I am not unconscious how many things are wanting to render it worthy of your Lordship's sanction, and the public eye.

But, whatever may be its fate, if it be gratifying to me to reflect on the testimony of such approbation as it has already received; I hope I may be allowed to say, without vanity, it must be much more so, to have the honour of liberal intercourse in private life with those who are no less illustrious for talent than station, and are at the same time distinguished by every domestic and social virtue.

In dedicating *The Missionary* to Lord Lansdowne, Bowles addressed him 'My dear Lord' as he would when addressing a private letter to him. Eyebrows were raised at this form of address, and this caused Bowles to write to his friend Samuel Rogers in the summer of the following year:

Lawyer Williams, the barrister, a friend of Horner's, has been here, since I came home, and has excited some anxiety in my mind by saying that, according to strict etiquette, I should not have said in my dedication 'My dear Lord', but only 'My Lord'. I am sorry if I have done wrong; you will witness for me that it was unintentional, as it was my common mode of address, and I thought to have done otherwise would have affected formality; but he seems to think that, what might be proper in private, might not be so before the public.

Had I, contrary to my general usage, addressed Lord Lansdowne as 'My Lord', it might also appear that I spoke as less independent than I have always been, and always shall be. Dallaway[123] ought to have addressed the Duke of Norfolk, or Crabbe[124] his patron, the Duke of Rutland, so, – but I have no patron, nor want one, though I never forget the most trifling kindness I have ever received in the common intercourse of life; and I do not see, in my situation, why I should use different language in public, from what I use in private, to any man living; at the same time there is no one who would less willingly violate the common etiquette of cultivated society . . .

So no more from yours ever,
W.L.B.

Do write and tell me what I am to think of the public news – ecrivez. You
will seriously oblige me if you will let me know whether all is right about
the Dedication, and, if you have had time to look over my corrections
and additions, I shall find it an additional favour if you will give me your
opinion with respect to the conception and execution of what has been
added to the 'Missionary' . . .[125]

It is unlikely that Lord Lansdowne gave a moment's thought to a
matter that was clearly causing Bowles so much trouble!

In Bowles's letter to Murray written from Reading in May 1815,
doubtless while Bowles was staying with his friend Archdeacon Nares,
he continues:

I am finishing some sermons to plain people, with a preface giving a
statement of the occasions. They will be entitled, 'Sermons on the
Doctrines, and Dispositions of Christians . . .'. They are now printing in
Bath, but I hope you will allow me the honour of your name as London
publisher. I would also hope you would not object to be book-seller and
publisher to a kind of historical work, of the same small size, on the
aberrations from the plain sense of the Bible in all ages.[126]

The 156-page book of sermons was soon published and entitled
*Sermons on some important points respecting the faith, the feelings, the spirit,
and the disposition of Christians; preached before a Country Congregation. To
which are added small hymns for charity schools*. Richard Cruttell in Bath
was the printer, and probably the son of Richard Crutwell, the printer and
publisher of Bowles's very first sonnets who had died in 1799. Murray's
name duly appeared as publisher. It is likely that it was also at this time
that a small pamphlet was printed and published in Calne by W. Baily
by 'A Minister of the Church of Christ', with Bowles's name appearing
merely on the last page.[127] This was another religious tract, bearing the
title *A Few Plain Words for the Bible, and a Word on the Prayer-Book, and
the Spirit; addressed to all Sober, Thinking, and Independent Christians*.

When writing to Murray at the end of 1814, Bowles asked, 'Have
you seen an account of my residence here in the Gentleman's Magazine
for September? If not, procure it, and I need not say how happy I should
be at any time to shew you that parsonage and this part of the county
of Wilts'.[128] This account reveals in extraordinary detail the layout of
the garden and the eccentric way in which Bowles provided edifying

poetry at various stategic points for the enjoyment of the visitor. Robert Southey was to write that: 'The garden is ornamented, in his way, with a jet fountain, something like a hermitage, an obelisk, a cross, and some inscriptions. Two swans, who answer to the names of Snowdrop and Lily, have a pond to themselves, and if not duly fed they march to Mrs Bowles's window.'[129]

The whole concept has been roundly ridiculed by later generations and has been recently described as 'a deliberate throwback to the 1740s when the third-rate poet William Shenstone[130] was laying out a poetic-picturesque two-mile circuit around his gentleman's farmhouse, The Leasows, in north Worcestershire'.[131] However, a reading of the description of the garden and of the associated poetry conveys a very clear picture of how Bowles took his inspiration from nature, and plainly saw nothing odd in embellishing his garden in this way. The account was written in the form of a letter addressed to 'Mr Urban', the proprietor of the *Gentleman's Magazine,* and was written by 'A.N.' – probably Bowles's friend Archdeacon Robert Nares, at whose rectory in Reading Bowles had been staying in the previous year. Having briefly described the church and parsonage house and the surrounding countryside, the writer turns his attention to the garden:

A garden of about two acres spreads itself immediately before the house, always a beautiful spot, now embellished by the taste, and immortalized by the verses, of the owner. As it is not of sufficient extent to fatigue either you, or me, or your Readers, let me take you, Mr Urban, by the hand and conduct you round the garden. Should you wish to exchange the narrative for the reality, The Reverend Poet will, I doubt not, be happy to conduct you in person.

Turning to the left from the house, you go through a rustic arch, which leads to the Eastern view. The objects here are pleasing, but not distinct; and coming to a handsome tree, you naturally turn to contemplate it. Looking to the West, the whole extent of Bowood immediately meets the eye. In allusion to which you will find the following elegant inscription affixed:

When in they sight another's vast domain
Spreads its long line of woods, dost thou complain?
Nay, rather thank the God that plac'd thy state
Above the lowly, but beneath the great:
And still his name with gratitude revere
Who bless'd the Sabbath oft thy leisure here.
Deus nobis haec otia fecit. W.L.B.

These lines evidently express the feelings of the Poet himself, but may be applied by others according to their circumstances. A few steps further stands a small, neat obelisk of stone, with no other inscription than ANNO PACIS 1814. W.L.B.P. It might be wished it were something higher; and if the Peace continues, perhaps it may grow. You now enter a plot of decorated garden, not actually divided from the rest of the ground, but distinguished from it by mere interference of art – small flower borders, trellis-work arbours, a fountain perpetually playing, encompassed by rock-work. Here, over a rural seat, we read the following lines:

> Rest, Stranger, in this decorated scene,
> That hangs its beds of flowers, its slopes of green:
> So from the walks of life the weeds remove,
> But fix thy better hopes on scenes above.

For the Cold-bath, where the little rill falls into it, the following verses are destined:

> Mark, where, above the small cascade,
> Quiver th' uncertain light and shade:
> Such shadows human hopes supply,
> That tremble restles, and then die.
> Stranger, thoughtful tread the cave –
> No light is fix'd but that beyond the grave.

Proceeding directly up the slope from this place, you meet with a root-house Hermitage, with a rude stone table, a wooden chair, a small sun-dial on a fragment of a twisted column, and a rustic-cross, which St Bruno, the Hermit,[132] is supposed to have inscribed:

> He who counted all as loss
> Save Peace, and Silence, and the Cross.
> BRUNO.

On the front of the Hermitage, and near the dial, are these:

> To mark life's few and fleeting hours,
> I plac'd the dial 'midst the flowers,
> Which one by one came forth and died,
> Still withering round its ancient side;
> Mortal, let the sight impart

Its pensive moral to thy heart!
BRUNO.

You now pass through a completely embowered filbert-walk to a large pond, into which, at the upper end, falls a pleasing cascade. The pond is terminated by another rural seat, in which these lines are written

QUIETI ET MUSUS
Be thine Retirement's peaceful joys,
And a life that makes no noise;
Save when Fancy, musing long,
Wakes her desultory song;
Sounding to the vacant ear
Like the rill that murmurs near.

On a gentle ascent, above the cascade, is a funereal urn, embowered in shade, to the memory of the Author's brother, Dr Bowles, who fell a sacrifice, at Gibraltar, to the duties of his profession. The pedestal is thus inscribed:

M.S.
HENRICUS BOWLES, M.D.
Qui ad Calpen
Febre ibi exitiali grassante,
Ut opem miseris praestaret,
Publice missus,
Ipse miserrime periit
Anno 1804, aet. 39
Fratri optimo moerens P.
W.L.B.

From this place, by a winding and shady walk, you are re-conducted to the house, and terminate this short, but classical tour, by again enjoying the natural beauties of the scene.

I should not, perhaps, introduce the verses of any other writer with those of Mr Bowles; but the following, being written up in pencil, on the subject of the place itself, may be at least read with indulgence:

TO THE REV. W.L.B
Here dwell delighted! By these airs inspir'd,
Write where they breathe, secure to be admir'd;
Raise here thy voice, exert thy tuneful skill,

And give to Britain one more famous Hill:
So, when the praise of her poetic race
Recording Verse or History shall trace
BREMHILL shall seem, what Pindus was so long,
Not theme alone, but SACRED HOME OF SONG.

Who will not wish that the Poet may long enjoy the place, and the Place the Poet, so worthy of each other?[133]

Bowles delighted to show his garden to many visitors who, despite their private reservations, doubtless expressed to him their pleasure at what they saw. However, Thomas Moore confided to his journal that 'he had frittered away its beauty with grottos, hermitages, and Shenstonian inscriptions'![134]

The parsonage house itself had also been transformed by Bowles who gave it, as described by Nikolaus Pevsner, 'a generous Gothic trim'.[135] The Rev. John Skinner[136] was one of the antiquaries who met annually at Stourhead at the invitation of Sir Richard Colt Hoare to carry out research in the library there and to discuss matters of mutual interest. He records in his journal in 1819 that on one occasion, when Hoare was constructing a sarcophagus in the churchyard of Stourton, he met him there, and Hoare:

> . . . explained to me what kind of sarcophagus it was to be, also mentioned that he had taken the design of the edifice in a great measure from the porch at the Parsonage House at Bremhill, which is of course paying a great compliment to Bowles's taste. Should he survive Sir Richard, I do not know a fitter person to write his epitaph, but I hope that finale will be far distant.[137]

In June 1814 the recently widowed poet George Crabbe was inducted to the rectory of Trowbridge, some 12 miles from Bremhill, and in February of the following year met Bowles for the first time. It seems that Crabbe and Bowles and his wife were to meet in Bath, and perhaps did so for a short time, but then Crabbe appears to have committed some sort of breach of social etiquette and as a result felt that he had acted in an unforgiveable fashion towards Bowles and Magdalene. As a consequence, in a long letter written on 19 February, after expressing satisfaction that 'our distance is not so great as to forbid my reasonable hope of seeing you and Mrs Bowles at this parsonage', he continues:

Have the goodness to say everything grateful to Mrs Bowles and accept my best thanks yourself for the good-humoured forgiveness I received from you both. It has almost reconciled me to my offence, which however I must thus far extenuate as to assure you that I was taken by surprise and had not due time for recollection.[138]

It seems that Bowles was determined to introduce Crabbe to Lord Lansdowne and his circle of distinguished friends at Bowood, and had arranged for him to be entertained in the great house there. Crabbe alludes to this in a letter written to Bowles in July, but is still deeply ashamed at his conduct in Bath some five months before:

Your kindness distresses me; innocent as in fact I am, I nevertheless feel as if I had occasioned you (and that wifully) trouble and disappointment. I was greatly mortified at Bath, where I soon heard that you sought me, though not till some days after, in whose company it was that you did me this honour.

Heaven knows, my dear sir, the pleasure that I should promise myself in such company as you mention and at such place, but I doubt the possibility of being so gratified . . . Be assured, dear sir, of this, that I shall not <u>easily</u> relinquish the pleasure of joining your party and I wish very much to thank the Marquis of Lansdowne for the honour he does me. The Marchioness I may hope to see at some future time . . .[139]

In August Crabbe wrote to Elizabeth Charter, telling her that he was well acquainted with Bowles and had been trying to read his *Missionary* 'as it ought to be read, for it is in many places very tender and beautiful'.[140] In November he wrote to let her know that he had seen Bowles at Bowood and that he was 'a good and pleasant Man and his Verses are like him – not so good Verses as I conceive he is a Man though'.[141] As well as introducing Crabbe to Lord Lansdowne, Bowles was instrumental in arranging for Crabbe to meet Samuel Hoare, at whose house in Hampstead he would later stay on his annual visits to London.[142]

In a letter written to Southey when a third edition of *The Missionary* was being considered, Bowles sought Southey's opinion and also made an unexpected suggestion to him. He wrote to him at the end of December:

I am hesitating to trouble you, but as there is no living man of whose genius I think so highly & on whose judgment I should so implicitly rely, I am induc'd to request your opinion – I am now printing a third Edition of my last poem, & as I want to make it as unobjectionable as possible, I should indeed esteem it as a great obligation & kindness if you would point out to me what you think its chief fault – whether any part requires expansion & whether you think the story of Cid taken from your translation had better be in the body of the work, as it was at first, or separate as it is now in the appendix.

I wish to make an apology about the Quarterly Review but I was led to do so, if I have done wrong in consequence of Peachey telling me you express'd an intention of giving an article on it.

I had an earnest desire to see the Lakes of Cumberland this summer when I might have had an opportunity of being further acquainted with you & particularly as Sir George[143] seem'd anxious I should come whilst he was there – but the duties of a very large parish, & the anxiety naturally calling [?] on a clergyman, endeavouring earnestly & laboriously to do his duty, prevents me – Have you seen a most insolent, audacious & malignant libel, upon us all, without any exception, call'd the Legend of the Cushion by a profess'd Calvinist, who calls himself a Christian, without exhibiting one particle of the Spirit of Christianity? I have often thought what a powerful [?] aid you might render to those who sincerely wish to grant unbounded & unquestioned rights of conscience extended to all yet think it hard that they should be vilified by those who so loudly claim what they will not grant.

Would you pardon me, if I were to ask as a friend deeply interested in your welfare, whether no thought ever occur'd to you, of entering into the Church? I should not ever have adventured to ask you this, if it had not been for a passage in your letter, respecting wordly concerns which I could not read without being affected. – If my thoughts to which I allude, might sometimes arise I am perfectly sure, I could make the way easy to you, by one word to the Bishop of London, who, I know, respects you as much as myself – and I have no doubt, in my own mind, of what, would & must follow.

I sincerely entreat your forgiveness if what I have said may be displeasing but assure you it only arises from an interest your letter excited in me & from a passing thought of what advantage it would be, in this moment of peril if the Church to which I am proud to belong possess'd such talents on her side – I have printed some discourses for my own people, but have not the courage to publish them tho many judges have spoken well of them – If I have an opportunity I will send a volume to you & I am [illegible] – pray do not mention what I have written.[144]

The 'worldly concerns' referred to were mentioned in the letter written by Southey to Bowles earlier in the year in which he wrote that he ought to have been settled by that time in the west of England but it had been his lot 'to be twice disinherited by near relations'.

In November Coleridge wrote that Bowles was 'about to publish, at least is composing, a Reply to some Answer to the Velvet Cushion'.[145] *The Velvet Cushion*, written by John William Cunningham,[146] the evangelical vicar of Harrow, and published in 1814, gave an account of the various parties in the Church of England since the Reformation. Although Bowles would doubtless have enjoyed writing a detailed reply, nothing was published.

In January Bowles received Southey's reply to the long letter written to him at the end of December:

> You ask me a difficult question when you desire me to say what are the faults of your poem. Well as I was acquainted with it I read it once more to see if the perusal would enable me to discover them, and in truth I do not see how you can improve it by any alterations.

Southey then makes a number of suggestions and continues:

> I could not feel otherwise than gratified and obliged by the latter part of your letter. My habits, feelings and inclinations would long since have induced me to enter the church if the terms of admission had not presented an insuperable bar ... I shall read your discourses with much interest; – Murray is frequently sending parcels to me, and they may come thro that channel. I hope Sir George Beaumont will succeed in tempting you to visit this beautiful country, where you may even find hints for Chilese [*sic*] landscape. The grandest sights which I have ever beheld, or can ever hope to behold, have been from the summit of Skiddaw, – which I have within an easy morning's walk.[147]

There is no evidence that Bowles ever travelled to visit Southey. However, it is certain that he did have it in mind to make a tour to the Lake District and Garland Greever, the editor of *A Wiltshire Parson and His Friends . . .*, states that among Bowles's papers 'is a scrap-book containing, in his hand, a list of places through which he would pass "to the lakes"'. Lady Lansdowne had also heard that Bowles was thinking of an expedition out of Wiltshire, one cannot be sure whether at this time or later, but in an undated letter to Magdalene she writes:

> I am quite surprised to hear of Mr Bowles's spirited intentions. I hope he will keep to them as I think you will have much pleasure in your tour. As for him, I think the pleasures and pains will be so nicely balanced that I do not know which will prevail.[148]

The 'pains' referred to here were undoubtedly the extreme and increasing nervousness that Bowles was to experience when faced with any unusual or unfamiliar surroundings, and which certainly prevailed in preventing any prolonged journeys being undertaken.

The success of *The Missionary* probably persuaded Bowles to approach Murray, this time with a suggestion that he might publish a volume of his sermons:

> As General Peachey is going from here tomorrow, I have requested him to convey to you a small volume – I have not <u>publish'd</u> it because it requires in these times of <u>tempestuous</u> piety, a most careful revisal & because there are also so many & important errors of the press, but I am anxious that a complete & new edition of two-hundred & fifty or five hundred should be publish'd. I therefore submit it to you, whether it might or not answer to print it as 'Sermons on [illegible]' by the author of the Missionary –with the new matter & additions to each sermon, it would make one neat vol: – the expense of printing would be inconsiderable & I would readily go <u>halves</u>, that I think we could not possibly <u>lose</u>, which is all I care about, & I am persuaded that the novelty of tracing the actual sources of Methodistic feelings, which has been done I hope by more precision than by Bishop Lavington[149] might make it popular – If you agree, write; if not, you may take no notice![150]

George Lavington, who was Bishop of Exeter from 1747 until his death in 1762, was a strenuous opponent of Methodism and Bowles clearly thought that another attack would be popular. It seems that Murray did not agree, and so nothing more was heard of it except in a letter written by Bowles to Murray the following month:

> There is nothing to delay the immediate publication of the Missionary – I have made the Epilogue to my mind at last, & I hope you will not think it wrong to publish a few separate copies which I should be glad if you would send to Lord Lansdowne – & a copy of this edition, in my name, to Lord Holland, Honble Miss Fox, Mr Rogers & I think Augustic [?] and Eclectic Review. Have the goodness also to send in a parcel to me half a dozen copies by coach or wagon – also a copy from the author to Mr Britton Tavistock Place. I confess I was not without hope of having the poem notic'd in your valuable repository of Quarterly Fame[151] – I wish I could devise some plan of getting my discourses & theological discussions forward – I have written a review of Godwin's Lives of Milton's Nephews[152] – shall I send it for Mr Gifford's perusal?[153]

On 24 March 1816 Bowles was asked to request the prayers of his congregation for a poor woman called Ann Nichols who was seriously ill and clearly close to death. As soon as the morning service was over he hurried to her cottage and there found the woman deeply distressed by the behaviour of a Baptist minister named Warburton, who had concluded that he would not pray for her because he considered 'her doom as fixed, hopelessly and everlastingly'. As a consequence the woman was left in agony and despair. During the course of the next two weeks either Bowles or Magdalene paid daily visits to her, taking words of comfort, and, as a result she finally died, according to Bowles, 'perfectly composed, resigned and in peace'.

A detailed account of what occurred was later written by 'W.L. Bowles, the Minister', entitled *A Plain Narrative, of some circumstances attending the Sickness and Death of Ann Nichols, a poor woman late of the Parish of Bremhill, Wilts* and duly published and running to a second edition. What is particularly significant is Bowles's statement on the first page of the Narrative that:

> It should be mentioned to the honor of several Baptist Ministers, that they have refused their Pulpits to this man [i.e. Warburton]. – I trust nothing I have said here, will be construed as if I wished to throw any general imputation of unkindness or want of charity, on regular and respectable Preachers of this persuasion, of whom there are many, and I need only here mention the name of the *Rev. Mr Stennet* of Calne, a descendant of the pious and eloquent *Joseph Stennet*.[154]

This is one of a number of instances where Bowles, whose devoted attachment to the doctrine and practice of the Established Church was never doubted, nevertheless, in common with many other educated men of his time, adopted a charitable and tolerant attitude to those whose beliefs, whether as Roman Catholics or Protestant Dissenters, differed from his own.

The pamphlet met with the hearty approval of Robert Southey who wrote to Bowles:

> I was much pleased and affected by your account of the poor woman and the 'cruel Calvinist' which Peachey put in my hands. This story ought to be widely circulated as a warning and an example. I spoke of it in a paper printed for the Quarterly Review six months ago, but, still, I know not for what reason, laid aside. I look upon Calvinism as the worst corruption of Christianity; there is nothing in Popery itself so likely to produce

corruption of morals and hardness of heart, if it were followed to its legitimate consequences; – and nothing so monstrous as its doctrine, in the most revolting mythology that was ever imposed on poor human credulity.[155]

During April, or perhaps early in May, Bowles was sent a copy of John Scott's[156] *Champion,* in which appeared an article by the nineteen-year-old budding poet John Hamilton Reynolds[157] entitled 'The Pilgrimage of Living Poets to the Stream of Castaly'. Most of the readers of the *Champion* would have known that Castaly was a fountain sacred to the Muses, with its waters having the power of inspiring those who drank the water with the gift of poetry. In the article Reynolds sought to rank contemporary poets and to discriminate between the individual qualities of their poetry. In this entertaining satire he placed Byron, Moore, Rogers, Crabbe, Coleridge and Lamb and others among the first rank of poets who (in Reynolds's dream) each dipped his vessel in the waters of Castaly, and finally Wordsworth, who 'declared that the waters he had obtained should be the refreshment of his soul . . .'. Reynolds then relates:

> No other poets remained to obtain waters from the Castalian stream . . . On a sudden I heard a confusion of rogues behind me; – on turning round, I found that it arose from a mistaken set of gentlemen who were chattering and bustling and dipping at the brook, which they deemed was the true Castalian; – their splashing and vociferation and bustle, can only be imagined by those who have seen a flock of geese wash themselves in a pond with gabbling importance. There was Spencer,[158] with a goblet, lent to him by a lady of quality, – Hayley[159], simpering, and bowing, and reaching with a tea-cup at the water, – and Wilson[160] with a child's pap-spoon, – and Bowles laboriously engaged in filling fourteen nut-shells . . . There were no encouraging signs in the elements, – no delightful sounds of attendant spirits, – no springing up of flowers to cheer these worthies in their pursuits: – they seemed perfectly satisfied with their own greatness, and were flattered into industry by their own vanity and loudness.

Reynolds concludes the satire by relating how in his dream Shakespeare appeared, with Spenser[161] on one hand and Milton[162] on the other, and 'one glance of his eye scared the silly multitude from the brook . . .'.[163]

Bowles was outraged by this satire, immediately putting pen to paper and writing to the editor of the *Champion.* One later commentator declares that Bowles 'rose to the bait and sent the weekly a self-congratulatory reply that more than justified Reynolds' characterization'. Bowles wrote:

> When the name of an individual is brought into a public paper, any observation, in reply from that individual, is generally admitted in the same paper, by the liberal and generous courtesy of the conductor. – A correspondent of the <u>Champion</u> has facetiously described the numerous Poetical Characters of the present day, as dipping for water in the 'clear Castalian well,' while to me is assigned (<u>Horresco referens</u>) a place among the <u>gabbling geese</u>, at a brook mistaken for the real stream! Of this I have no right to complain, and it is a matter of indifference to me, whether I am introduced among the geese or the swans. It is a satisfaction to me, that I could appeal to those who appear highest and most adorned, in this assembled society, for a very different character than that which, as a Poet, is here given me. I could appeal to your favourite Wordsworth himself, – and none estimates his poetical talents higher: I could appeal to those who speak with delight of the feeling and affectionate sonnets 'of one of their number;' . . .
>
> I think, Sir, I could venture to appeal to your own judgment and candour, after you had given a quiet and dispassionate review of these small poems, (which are so contemptuously spoken of) because I am convinced that those writings cannot be quite so <u>contemptible</u>, of which there have been published eleven editions, of nearly one thousand to fifteen hundred each; and which have been indebted to no particle of their success, either from narratives or detraction of the fair fame of others. The writer in your paper is one of the readers of those poems which he so condemns, – one of upwards of ten thousand!
>
> This, Sir, you may call self-applause. No, – it is not; – it is plain fact. Those who know me, know how very far I am from deserving the character of 'gabbling importance', or that of ever seeking to deprecate others; – nor should I have troubled you on this occasion but on another account.
>
> Living in the country, I should have never seen or heard of your examination of our Poets; – occupied solely, as a parochial clergyman, neither my morning studies, or my evening walks, would have been disturbed by the knowledge of your correspondent's satire; but, as Sheridan says, there is generally a 'good natured friend' on those occasions, – so I would wish that 'good natured friend' to know, through the medium of the same paper which has been at the pains to convey to me, that the unmanly and despicable littleness, which could prompt his anxieties on this occasion, (lest I should be ignorant of the important contents of

your paper) in my mind, is far more offensive than the article he has been so studious to convey. I am, Sir,

Your Obedient Servant
W.L. Bowles

P.S. May I take the liberty of requesting your acceptance of my first small volume, which contains the 'nut-shells'. I almost venture to think you have not read them; if, on an occasional perusal, at your leisure, you agree with your correspondent, 'a la bonne heare!' If not, I trust I may rely on the equity of a manly judgment for your taking some opportunity of doing a piece of justice to one who may have receieved (in your unbiased opinion) unmerited abuse.[164]

In 1817 it was proposed that a District Committee in aid of the Society for Promoting Christian Knowledge should be established in Wiltshire, and the support of all the leading clergy of the Church of England would be expected. Bowles wrote to George Crabbe inviting him to dine on the day before the meeting, which was due to take place in Chippenham on 23 October. In response to this invitation Crabbe wrote:

I am in the midst of business which has been accumulating for a month past and during that time I have been gossiping with idle people of both sexes at Sidmouth. I mean nevertheless to escape from the claims of these small affairs and though I cannot dine with you on Wednesday I fully purpose to meet you at Chippenham on the following day.

Thanks for your invitation. I was mortified to receive three such notes from Mr Methuen and to know that Mr Rogers was in this part of the country and I was shut up with every-day people in Devonshire (with one exception, however). But there is no good in this retrospection. I will think of the pleasure of meeting you at Chippenham.[165]

The meeting duly took place. It was reported that before it 'a sermon was preached by the Rev W.L. Bowles on a most appropriate text . . . It would be unnecessary to expatiate on the merits of the discourse, written and delivered by so eminent a character.'[166]

Towards the end of 1817 the Irish poet Thomas Moore, then at the height of his fame, was considering renting a house in the northern part of Wiltshire, ideally within easy reach of Bowood. Bowles had become involved in helping to find a suitable house for Moore and his family and had decided that one at Heddington would be ideal for them. On 1 October he wrote to Samuel Rogers:

> I am very anxious that you should inform Lord Lansdowne that, though the house at Heddington is situate very low, yet it is within a quarter of a mile of the most beautiful views in Wiltshire, and has, I believe, every accommodation, and is in complete repair. I should think it would answer his plan very well – but verbum sapienti, he must not go to look at it with Moore, or even send a servant from Bowood, unless he wishes double price to be charged for rent, perhaps treble.
>
> If he would leave the arrangement to me, in case Moore should like the situation, I am sure I could make a much better bargain, and could either ride over with Moore, or settle with Hughes, in case of approval. I leave that, as I have said, to your and Lord Lansdowne's consideration, and have no other object than Moore's interest in the suggestion I venture to make.
>
> A word about Tytherton. I don't know whether you were in earnest about walking there with Mrs Orde, but, if so, you could come here tomorrow at about a quarter past one o'clock; you could go down with me in the carriage, and my boat, with flag, gardener, and pony, should await your arrival at Tytherton Bridge, and waft you along the canal to within half a mile of Bowood gate.
>
> I conclude all this with a song, which I hope you won't mistake for a 'vile' Baptist hymn.

Bowles then writes the words of a poem entitled *On hearing a Young Lady sing Haydn's 'Benedictus'* and continues:

> The prose you will submit to Lord Lansdowne; the verse is left to your discretion.
>
> If you could come to Bremhill, you shall have six white sticks, and stick them in where you like in the garden, and I will plant six trees, or as many as you choose, where you mark, for which I have more reasons than one, but which I shall not mention to you. You need not write; come or not, just as you feel inclined, tomorrow. I shall go about two o'clock.[167]

In the event, Moore decided not to take the house at Heddington, but settled on a cottage within walking distance of both Bowood and the parsonage at Bremhill and about half a mile from the village of Bromham. Moore, with his wife Bessy and their young children, duly moved to Sloperton Cottage and it is from Moore's journals that an intimate picture can be gained of Bowles's behaviour and of the impression he made on his contemporaries. Bowles very quickly made the new arrivals welcome as Moore wrote to his friend Samuel Rogers: 'The Lansdownes have not yet made their appearance, so I suppose neither of them has returned to Bowood. Bowles was very early in his welcome of us, and has since brought Mrs Bowles; but I was out and Bessy did not venture to encounter them.'[168]

Moore's wife Bessy, a former actress, was always very nervous of meeting her husband's eminent and often aristocratic friends. Moore had recently paid a visit to Dublin where he was enthusiastically feted, and at a dinner in his honour on 8 June, in responding to a toast to 'the poets of Great Britain', he named, among others, Byron, Rogers, Southey, Wordsworth and Crabbe, but forgot to mention Bowles.[169] This he was later embarrassed to discover, particularly, no doubt, in the light of the welcome he had received from Bowles on his arrival in Wiltshire. While Bowles was undoubtedly delighted to have the celebrated Moore as a near neighbour, Moore, in turn, was almost certainly glad to have the opportunity to become closely acquainted with a poet whose works were very familiar to him. Some years before, Moore had taken Byron to the Surrey county jail to meet Leigh Hunt,[170] the editor of the *Examiner*, incarcerated there as a result of his attacks on the character of the Prince Regent. Hunt later recalled that: 'He [Byron] came and we passed a very pleasant afternoon, talking of books, and school, and the Reverend Mr Bowles; of the pastoral innocence of whose conversation some anecdotes were related, that would have much edified the spirit of Pope, had it been in the room.'[171]

Sadly none of the anecdotes of the pastoral innocence of Bowles's conversation were recorded by Hunt who, in mentioning the spirit of Alexander Pope, had in mind the controversy between Byron and Bowles relating to the character and works of Pope that had run its course by the time these words were written.

By early the following year very friendly relations had been established between the families at Sloperton Cottage and Bremhill Parsonage, and in February Moore wrote to Samuel Rogers:

> We passed three or four days at Bowles's since I last wrote to you. What an odd fellow he is! and how narrowly, by being a *genius* he has escaped being set down for a *fool*! Even as it is, there seems to be some doubts among his fellow magistrates; but he is an excellent creature notwithstanding and if it is not of Helicon that his spirit has drunk, it is at least of very sweet waters, and to my taste very delightful.[172]

Bowles made sure that Moore was introduced to all the people of influence in his part of Wiltshire and in July, in writing to James Corry,[173] Moore reported: 'I dine today at Poet Bowles (whom I so shamefully omitted in my rigmarole of Bards) to meet Lord Lansdowne, Methuen[174] etc etc.'[175]

Moore paints a delightful picture of Bowles and his parsonage in the entry for 1 September 1818 – slightly mocking but affectionate:

> My Sheridan task in the morning – interrupted by Bowles, who, however, never comes amiss, the mixture of talent and simplicity in him delightful – His (Bowles's) parsonage-house at Bremhill is beautifully situated, but he has a good deal frittered away its beauty with grottos, hermitages & Shenstonian inscriptions – When company is coming, he cries 'Here, John, run with the crucifix & missal to the Hermitage & set the fountain going.' – His sheep-bells are tuned in thirds & fifths – but he is an excellent fellow notwithstanding, and if the waters of his inspiration be not those of Helicon, they are at least very-sweet waters, and to my taste pleasanter than some that are more strongly impregnated.[176]

Three days later Bowles and his wife Magdalene joined a large party for dinner at Bowood at which Moore was present, as well as a French judge. Moore reported in his journal: 'Bowles, who cannot speak French, holding a conversation with the Judge and bellowing out to him, as if he was deaf – highly amusing – asking him "did he know <u>Nancy</u>?" pronouncing it in the English way.'[177]

It seems that Bowles was always pleased when his friends heard him preach in his church at Bremhill, and so Moore recorded on Sunday 20 September:

> Went (Bessy, Mary D., Woolriche[178] & I) to breakfast with Bowles & attend his church – Showed us a Tract he had written to ridicule Calvinists called 'the Triumphant Tailor', with a caricature drawing he had got done for it of the Tailor in his ecstasies of Election – his sermon not so good as the last I heard him preach – all the faults of extempore eloquence, without any of the beauties he before gave us . . .'[179]

On the Friday of the following week Moore 'Set off between two & three to walk to Bowles's to dinner – Bessy & the little ones saw me part of the way'. There were seven other guests including William Linley, the composer, who after dinner sang words written by Moore to music set by him. Most of the others also sang, although the great attraction of the evening must surely have been Moore himself, whose singing always had an extraordinary effect on his listeners. One writer, commenting in

1889 on Moore's talent, declared that 'either people were more musically sensitive and sympathetic in those days than in the present, or the singing must have had unparalleled power, for both ladies and gentlemen were frequently obliged to leave the room in floods of tears over the melodies'.[180] Bowles had clearly intended all the guests to be musically talented, as among them was Miss Miles who, according to Moore, was:

> a pretty little 'tricksy spirit' of a girl whom I last singled out at the Melksham Concert, as the only thing worth looking at – the daughter of an Apothecary in Calne – most amusingly frenchified by a short visit to Paris . . .' She later sang Chi dice mel d'amore 'very much in the fashion of a dinner I once had from Catalani,[181] at Birmingham – French & Italian dishes with Birmingham cookery.[182]

Both Moore and Linley were staying at the parsonage, and on the Saturday they sang and played a great deal of music together. Moore recorded in his journal:

> Linley sung some words which Bowles had written, and addressed from Prospero to Ariel,[183] which Linley had reversed, making it from Ariel to Prospero, and said it did as well – what accommodating verses! [It ought to have been written!] Bowles showed me a part of his Library, in which was collected, he told me, all the Books illustrative of the Divines of the time of Charles the First and the theology of that period – the first book I put in my hand on in this sacred corner was a volume of Tom Brown's Works,[184] – &c. [how] Bowles was amused, in the midst of all his gravity, by this detection! – what with his genius, his blunders, his absences &c. he is the most delightful of all existing Parsons or poets . . .[185]

Moore spent another night at the parsonage and, after some conversation with Bowles on the following morning about the spirit of toleration generally to be found in the Church of England, left for Bowood with one of the other house guests in his gig.

Bowles had another opportunity of displaying his preaching skills in September – this time in Salisbury Cathedral when he preached the sermon at the service held in connection with the Anniversary Meeting of the Governors of the Infirmary in Salisbury. It was reported in the Salisbury newspaper:

> It would be impossible for us to convey to our readers an adequate idea of this eloquent discourse. It must suffice to say that the distinguished talents and erudition of the learned divine shone most conspicuosly in

this energetic manner of recommending and enforcing the great duty of charity.[186]

Moore often called at the parsonage in the hope of seeing Bowles. On one Sunday in October he wrote:

> Found Bowles at home – asked him would he meet Rogers[187] and Crowe[188] at dinner with me on Wednesday or Thursday next – cannot on account of the Sessions at Marlborough – wants to have a Statue of Melanchton[189] executed from some fine wood cut to put up in his projected Library – anxious to consult me about some Prose he is writing.[190]

Bowles's library was undoubtedly as chaotic as his writings. Many years later the son of the poet George Crabbe in describing his father's library as 'a scene of unparalleled confusion – windows rattling, paint in great request, books in every direction' adds that he could not find terms to describe it 'though the counterpart might be seen, perhaps, not one hundred miles from the study of the justly famed and beautiful rectory of Bremhill'.[191]

Accounts of Bowles's eccentricities abound and the following entry made in Moore's journal two days before Christmas show that he was perfectly happy to tell stories against himself:

> Bowles had called in the morning and was most amusing about his purchase of a great coat once in Monmouth St. which while in the shop he took for blue, but which on his appearance in the sunshine he found to be a glaring, glossy green – his being met in this Coat by a great Church Dignitary &c &c – Oh Bowles you've been to Monmouth St.[192]

On Christmas Eve Moore and a number of others, including Bowles, dined with their friends the Macdonalds.[193] Moore found the party 'noisy & dull – with the exception of Bowles, who, when the vapid chatterers would let him, was highly amusing'.[194] Moore recorded that on Christmas Day:

> Our servants had company to dinner in honour of the day, & kept it up merrily, singing choruses till past eleven – In the evening read to Bessy a MS by Miss Costello,[195] a protegee of Bowles's, taken from a story he suggested to her, and about which he is very sanguine – It cannot possibly do – which is a sad pity, as she is a respectable girl, & with her mother, much distresse26 [Saturday] Bowles called upon me to enforce my dining with him, & to ask my opinion of Miss Costello's

Opera – was sorry to be obliged to tell him how hopeless I thought it
– showed me a letter he had written to her begging acceptance of £20
Mrs Bowles had recommended limiting him to send but 10, but I gave
my note for 20, and he said he <u>would</u> send it 'without her knowing
any thing of the matter.' Went with Macdonald to dine at Bowles's – the
company Henry Joy[196] & his father,[197] Miss Calcraft, Miss Joy & little Miss
Miles – the whole day rather pleasant – sung with Miss Miles in the
evening . . .[198]

In 1818 the lawyer and politician Henry Brougham[199] instituted an
inquiry into charitable abuses, with a particular emphasis on the
universities and Eton and Winchester, Bowles's old school. Bowles felt
compelled to defend his *alma mater* and so arranged for the Bath printer,
Richard Cruttwell, to print his *Vindiciae Wykehamicae; or a Vindication
of Winchester College: in a letter to Henry Brougham, Esq; occasioned by his
Letter to Sir Samuel Romilly, on Charitable Abuses*. In this pamphlet of
fifty-four pages Bowles attempted to demonstrate that the school still
held true to the charitable intentions of its founder, and in support of
this included in it extracts from the accounts kept by his great-uncle
William Bowles when a Fellow of the college. At the end of the pamphlet
Cruttwell added: 'Speedily will be Published by the same author (a
corrected edition) of Defence of Public Schools in answer to an Article
in the Edinburgh Review'. On 9 November Thomas Moore noted in
his journal: 'Bowles called – is in a great fidget about his Answer to
Brougham – brought me a copy of it – showed me a note he had just
had, in praise of it, from his friend the Bishop of London, beginning "my
dear Bowles".'[200] Why Moore should think this form of address worth
noting is odd, as the bishop had, of course, known Bowles since their
schooldays together at Winchester. A review of the pamphlet appeared
in the *Quarterly Review* and was probably not seen by Bowles until
early in the following year, when Thomas Moore noted in his journal:
'Received a note from Bowles, in which he says –"Have you seen the
Quarterly? They are very complimentary to me *as an author*." How lucky
it is that self-love has always something comfortable to retire upon!'[201]
The review was by no means complimentary, thus explaining Moore's
not very kind remark.

In December Brougham wrote to Bowles, who responded:

I beg to express my acknowledgement of the very candid & kind manner
in which you have written respecting my late public address to you.

Sincerely hoping that nothing henceforth may prevent the
union of all hearts on a subject of such national importance & radical

benevolence, which reflects so much honour on yourself, & with the greatest respect for the purity of your motives & your high talents.[202]

However, not everyone agreed with Bowles's defence of his old school. One critic writing in 1829 was of the opinion that:

> Here he decidedly fell short, as any individual must do who tries to defend what is indefensible. The management of the public schools of England was and is notoriously defective, and in trying to uphold the discipline and instruction of Winchester school against Brougham, he was more acted upon by attachment to the place of his education than by discretion.[203]

Early in 1818 the whole of Wiltshire became convulsed by a contested election at which the freeholders of the county would return two members to Parliament. The candidates were Paul Methuen, the sitting member and a close acquaintance of Bowles, William Pole-Tylney-Long-Wellesley,[204] a nephew of the great Duke of Wellington and an 'outsider' who had married Catherine Tylney-Long, a considerable Wiltshire heiress, and John Benett, President of the Wiltshire Society for the Encouragement of Agriculture and a cousin of Bowles's wife, both being descended from Archbishop Wake. The canvassing was intense, with almost all of the freeholders being approached by either the candidates in person or their agents. It appears that one of the prospective voters, a Mr Fry, presumably either John or William Fry, both freeholders in Bremhill, had received a letter perhaps urging him to vote for Wellesley and that this was the recommendation of the Lansdownes – although as a peer of the realm, it would not have been proper for Lord Lansdowne to interfere in the election. It seems that on receipt of the letter Fry, or someone on his behalf, had promised his vote to one of the other candidates thinking that the letter might have been a forgery. As a result, and probably at Bowles's suggestion, the Lansdownes were approached. Lady Lansdowne wrote:

> The letter you alude [sic] to was certainly no forgery. As to Politicks, I never interfere I think a female has nothing to do with them. But my friendship for some of Mrs Long Wellesley's connections make me wish her husband success. I am therefore glad you are ready to give up any promise Mr Fry may inadvertently have made, and that he will of course give Mr Long Wellesley a <u>Plumper</u>[205] which I understand from you Electioneering gentlemen is the best thing.
> Best compliments to Mr Bowles

Be assured this is no forgery[206]

After an acrimonious campaign that lasted three months, the election was opened at Wilton near Salisbury on 24 June and then adjourned to a field some 3 miles from the city where the polling booths were set. As one would expect, Bowles duly voted for Methuen and cast his other vote for Benett. In the event, after seven days of polling, Benett conceded defeat and withdrew from the election.

In 1818 was also published Bowles's *The Plain Bible and the Protestant Church in England with reflections on some important subjects of existing religious controversy*. This lengthy pamphlet of 117 pages was dedicated to his friend Archdeacon Nares and commenced with the sermon that Bowles had preached at Chippenham in the autumn of the previous year, before the meeting that had been arranged in support of the Society for Promoting Christian Knowledge.

Bowles's attitude towards dissenters was ambivalent. He enjoyed a very friendly relationship with the minister of the Moravian chapel in his parish, and on several occasions spoke in flattering terms about various nonconformists in the neighbouring towns. What he appeared to fight against was the intrusion into his parish of the advocates of other Protestant sects. So it was that in 1818 he also published a *Village Dialogue: A True and Faithful Account of what passes in our Parish, between Mr New-Church, Mr Non-Church and Mr True-Church on Sunday last*. This pamphlet was printed in Chippenham and published by Hatchard in London. According to a review of it in the *Gentleman's Magazine* it was:

> the product of a clergyman, who by this and similar effusions in aid of his professional exertions, has ably defended his parish from the inroads of the enemy . . . the speakers, Mr New-Church and Mr No-Church, are introduced railing against the Church and its Ministers, and boasting of their *experiences*, when accident brings old *True-Church* to the spot, a venerable old man, who has never left the communion into which he had been baptized. They attack him, as usual, about *formal prayers*, and the *heap of old stones* in which he went to worship. Mr True-Church answers:

> 'If you call a *heap of old stones* that venerable place where your own father, and all who went before him (now mingled with the church yard dust) worshipped, I shall not reply; but I think a *heap of old stones* dedicated time out of mind to *one holy* purpose is, at any rate, as good as a heap of new bricks, whether nick-named *Ebenezer* or *Zion*; which might be thought, like some I have seen, all shew and profession on the outside.'

... The old man continues to fight them with Scriptural weapons, but with great mildness and simplicity, and powerfully defends the Liturgy and the Parish Minister ... The circulation of this cheap Tract is calculated to do good service in the cause of the injured Clergy; and we know indeed that much has actually been effected by it.[207]

In the same year Edward Lambert, rector of Freshford, who had married Bowles's eldest sister Frances, died. In accordance with his wishes he was buried at Bremhill. Bowles later related that, when digging his grave, a stone coffin was found lying across the porch of the church containing, so he thought, the bones of the founder of the church or some benefactor. The coffin was unfortunately broken but the bones were carefully replaced where they had been found.[208]

In September Maria Edgeworth and her half-sister Honora were staying with Lord and Lady Lansdowne at Bowood. During their visit Bowles was invited to dine with them and their other house guests, including Pierre Dumont who had been tutor to Lord Lansdowne. In a letter to her stepmother Maria paints a vivid account of Bowles's behaviour at dinner:

> He is a simple – not curate but rector – full of his poems and his church music and his house at Bremhill. Now there is a village of Bromham also in the neighbourhood which Lady Lansdowne had taken me to see the morning of the day he dined here and all dinner time he and I and Lord Lansdowne and Dumont were making confusion in French and English between these two names and two places, both of which have pretty churches &c. Mr Bowles was puzzled almost out of his wits and temper because Lady Lansdowne had promised to take me to Bremhill when he was at home and he suspected we had gone that morning. Still he could not believe that Lady Lansdowne would use him so and he could not possibly make her hear or venture to put a question to her from one end of the table to the other encompassed too as she was by Grenvilles. He colored and fretted and questioned me and at every one of my blundering answers changed his opinion backwards and forwards. The moment he was released from the dining room and could get to Lady Lansdowne he went to complain that for the life of him he could not make out whether Miss E had been to Brem Hill or Bromham and that very morning he had received a letter from a Member of parliament a member of a Committee reprimanding him as vicar of Bromham for some thing of which he was innocent and ignorant he being vicar or rector of Bremhill you know.

Dumont was, of course, French and it is likely that Lord Lansdowne and Maria were fluent in the language. Bowles's knowledge of French is known to have been rudimentary in the extreme, and it is certain that this, as well as his increasing deafness, caused the confusion that Maria so graphically described. Further, the thought that he had been prevented from showing his parsonage and garden to the celebrated authoress no doubt added to his discomfort.

Maria continues:

> Next day being Sunday Lady Lansdowne set all to rights by taking Honora and me and Mr Grenville to church at Brem Hill [sic] – a real country church that put me sorely in mind of the church at Ross to which dear mother we went together and with another in happy days . . .
>
> Mr Bowles is not like the clergyman that read prayers and preached that day at Ross. Mr Bowles tho simple has no dignity and is too full of himself. He preached extempore and kept one in painful sympathy lest he should never get through it. After church we went to his very pretty old parsonage newly <u>done up</u> – with good taste – walked over his little shrubbery – stuck full of inscriptions and grottoes and bowers and came at last to the weary hermitage where apropos to a hermit's inscription the question came plump upon me '<u>Have you read my poem of the Missionary</u>?' 'No.' The good natured author helped me out by saying 'No. It was published at first without my name'. He gave me a copy of it and all's well that ends well. A happier man in a house and place more suited to him I never saw. Lord Lansdowne made him the happy creature he is. His wife is a plain woman something like Mrs Alison, who has the good sense, understands the affairs of this world and is just the wife necessary for a poet. He was desperately in love with her sister – a most beautiful creature who died of a consumption. This sister comforted him and he married her and has never repented.[209]

In noticing and thinking that Lord Lansdowne had made him 'the happy creature he is', Maria realised that Bowles was for ever thrilled that the friendship of the Lansdownes enabled him to meet and converse with a wide range of people from the world of politics and literature – people with whom a country parson would not normally expect to have contact.

As Maria had noticed, Bowles had made substantial alterations and improvements to his parsonage. The most noticeable were pierced parapets and a central Gothic porch on the south elevation added in 1818. Later, in 1820, he constructed a two-storey range on the north front, with similar parapets. He caused both of these dates to be carved on his works so that future generations would be in no doubt about when the work was carried out. Bowles himself wrote that 'By parapetting the whole, with simple Gothic ornamental railing, a unity has been given to the exterior, and the long low roofs have put on ecclesiastical appearance.' The result is certainly picturesque, and in 1818 Sir Richard Colt Hoare gave to Magdalene a drawing of the south front of the house by John Buckler, who had already produced for Hoare watercolours of virtually every church in Wiltshire.[210] However, not everyone who saw Bowles's alterations to the parsonage was favourably impressed by them. John Britton, who in about 1820 painted a watercolour of the 'Vicarage Garden, Fountain, and dipping well or cascade',[211] wished 'it were in my power to compliment the parson, or the builder, for the manifestation of either taste or judgement in their weak attempt to imitate the forms, proportions, or character of any one of the varieties of genuine Christian architecture.[212]

In 1818 appeared a slim volume of poetry entitled *Sonnets and Other Poems* by 'Mariann Dark'. The authoress was in fact Mary Anne Dark,[213] the daughter of Henry Stiles,[214] of Whitley House near Calne, who had died suddenly in January of the previous year. It is clear from the preface that Stiles had discovered that his daughter had written some lines of poetry and had attempted in vain to persuade his daughter to submit them to Bowles for his consideration. However, following his death, she sent an anonymous sonnet to the Marchioness of Lansdowne and another to Bowles, and upon her identity being discovered the verses eventually found their way into print, with the preface concluding with some lines of poetry written by Bowles *On the Death of Mr Henry Stiles, many years a constant attendant on the Word of God, in the Parish Church of Bremhill, Wilts.*

It is more than likely that Lady Lansdowne and Bowles assisted Mary Dark in the enterprise, and the unusually large number of subscribers suggests that persons with very many friends and acquaintances were instrumental in securing their support. Bowles and his wife Magdalene are named in the list of some 350 subscribers as taking two copies each, as is Bowles's old friend John Benett, from the very south-western corner of the county, who is very unlikely to have known the young authoress and who very rarely subscribed to new publications.

Chapter 4
1819–1822

On 18 March 1819 Thomas Moore:

Set out between 12 & 1 to walk to Bowles's. Took the way through Bowood and had a most delicious walk of it. – Arrived at Bowles's between 3 & 4 . . . Bowles has altered his drawing room & set up an organ & books in it – The organ made by Chevirs, a common Carpenter at Calne – His statue of Melanchton[1] nearly ready – asked him whether he meant to place it in one of his grottos, in defiance of Pope's 'Nor in a hermitage set Doctor Clarke' –Talked of Calvinism (his favourite subject) after dinner – he said that almost all the atrocious crimes of the day were owing to this doctrine – mentioned several instances . . . I had found B when I came into dinner reading Campbell's[2] new work on the Poets, and very nervous at the attack which C. had made on his remarks upon Pope – told him I had seen it extracted in the Chronicle, as 'an answer to Bowles' – B is resolved to reply to it through the same channel – Dr. S & he & I sung some glees & Sacred things together in the evening – two worse voices could not well be found – Slept at Bowles's.[3]

Moore must have found it particularly painful to find himself singing in the company of such vocalists – although Bowles was a competent string and wind player, as well as a composer on rare occasions.

Bowles and Moore were in the habit of visiting Bath together from time to time, and on the following day Moore recorded in his journal:

After breakfast we set out for Bath – stopped at Corsham in our way – magnificent house – am astonished that Paul[4] holds his head so high among the natives here – but London is the place for levelling these provincial grandees – the Hall very striking – had only time to look at two fine Claudes[5] – Methuen asked us to fix a day to dine with him . . . Bowles & I (after securing our tickets to the Harmonic in the evening) dined at the White Hart – went at eight to the Harmonic – very full rooms – at least 300 persons – introduced to a whole shoal of Baronets – Sir Robert

This and Sir John That – never was so stared at in my life before . . . De Burgh, one of the Presidents, proved to be an acquaintance of mine. Told Bowles his history & that of his wife, a pretty woman, who was here with him, which set Bowles's imagination at work most unclerically.[6]

'The Harmonic' was the Harmonic Society, which presented musical concerts in Bath during the year and in March held 'a grand Gala, consisting of a Concert, Supper, and Ball' as the *Bath and Cheltenham Gazette* described it in its report. One of Moore's songs, 'The Minstrel Boy', was sung twice during the concert, and so popular was it that it was sung for a third time after supper, with Moore's health being given 'three times three for which he returned thanks in a speech of pointed gratitude and respect. – at 12 a bugle gave a signal for the dance, which was kept up with great spirit until three o'clock'.[7]

'Campbell's new work on Pope' that Moore had found Bowles reading the day before was Thomas Campbell's[8] recently published *Specimens of the British Poets*. In the first of seven volumes he included an essay lauding the merits of Alexander Pope and defending his poetical character. Bowles was determined to publish a pamphlet in reply and, on the day following their attendance at the Harmonic Society Gala, Moore wrote:

> Returned in an hour to Bowles, who wished me to read what he had done in answer to Campbell – found him in the bar of the White Hart, dictating to a waiter (who acted as amanuensis for him) his ideas of the true Sublime in Poetry – never was there such a Parson Adams, since the real one.[9]

'Parson Adams' was the country curate in Fielding's novel *Joseph Andrews*, who has been described as being notable for his goodness of heart and learning combined with courage, modesty and a thousand oddities – a very fair description of Bowles, certainly as far as 'a thousand oddities' are concerned.

On the following day Bowles called on Thomas Moore, having given him the proofs of a pamphlet that he was about to publish entitled *Thoughts on the Increase of Crimes, the Education of the Poor, and the National Schools in a Letter to Sir James Mackintosh*,[10] which he wanted Moore to look over.[11] Moore recorded in his journal: 'I had marked with a pencil the things I had particularly objected to – but the truth is, the whole is weak & confused – his head, however, is now full of his answer to Campbell, which his present intention is to publish in a letter addressed to me . . .'[12]

Thirteen years had passed since Bowles had published his edition of Pope's work that included comments on his life, about which, it has been said, 'while he omitted no detail that could harm Pope's memory, he either left out or mentioned coldly such facts as did him honour'.[13] In responding to Campbell, Bowles commenced a war of pamphlets containing many thousands of words that was to last until 1826. In April he wrote to Campbell:

> I have thought myself called upon to vindicate some observations of mine on the character of Pope in answer to your critical remarks on those observations in the 1st volume of your Specimens. I think you have hastily laid yourself open to some animadversions; but I trust you will find nothing said that might seem to imply any feelings but those of the highest regard for your acknowledged political and literary character. Your friend Moore is in the neighbourhood, as also Crabbe and Crewe. It would give me great pleasure if I should ever have the opportunity of seeing you here; and believe me that, though our aspects are somewhat warlike in print, at home I remain most sincerely and faithfully, and with many thanks for the great pleasure I have derived from your works.[14]

This letter brought forth an immediate reply from the poet Campbell:

> I received your agreeable letter this morning and I shall regard myself as at least of some use to literature if the very defects of my critical reasonings can again draw forth the pen of Mr Bowles . . . Whatever I may have to fear from the intrinsic force of your animadversions I have from the refinement of your character the most perfect confidence of being used by you in a gentlemanlike manner . . . If chance should bring you to London and if you can spare the time and the trouble you will confer an honour and a pleasure that I shall sensibly feel by spending a day under my humble roof.
>
> Believe me, dear Sr,
> With respect and admiration
> Yours truly
> T. Campbell[15]

So it was that in 1819 Richard Cruttwell printed and published in Bath Bowles's *Invariable Principles of Poetry, in a letter addressed to Thomas Campbell Esq. Occasioned by some of the critical observations in his*

Specimens of British Poetry, particularly relating to the poetical character of Pope. This work was favourably reviewed in the July issue of *Blackwood's Magazine,* and resulted in the editor writing to Bowles suggesting that while 'in the midst of far more important avocations' he would not trouble himself in writing anything for the magazine, he would be indebted to Bowles if any of his younger friends might be persuaded to do so.[16]

Thomas Moore noted in his journal: 'Received Bowles's answer to Campbell – tells me in a note with it that Lord Lansdowne considers his position indisputable & I think it is',[17] following which he wrote to Bowles: 'Your pamphlet is unanswerable, but I fear the public will not read. Corn Laws and Currency will beat you out of the field.'[18]

The newspapers at this time were full of reports of opposition to the Corn Laws, and just four months after Moore made this note in his journal a great demonstration in Manchester was violently suppressed, resulting in the death of eleven people and injury to hundreds: it became known as the Peterloo massacre.

Bowles made annual visits to London, and when in town in May 1819 he dined one day in the chambers of his friend Henry Joy in the Temple. Moore was among the company, and relates:

> Joy's Dandy dinner of mutton-chops, brought in one by one, 'like angel visits, few & far between' highly amusing – except that we were all in a state of starvation – 'Joy' – (says Bowles, in a sort of reverie) 'I want – I want' – 'What do you want, my dear Bowles?' – 'Damn it, I want something to eat'.[19]

A week later Bowles attended the annual London dinner of the Wiltshire Society when, as Moore recorded in his journal, Lord Lansdowne 'made a tasteful speech giving the health of the 3 Wiltshire poets – Crabbe, Bowles and myself, all present'.[20]

Early in July Paul Methuen, one of the Members of Parliament for the county of Wiltshire, who had successfully fought the contested election in the previous year, decided to retire: the freeholders were faced with another election for his seat. The candidates were John Benett, once again, and another landowner, this time from the north of the county, named John Dugdale Astley.[21] The campaigning was even more acrimonious than in the previous year, and the election itself was the scene of unprecedented disorder and rioting.[22] Owing to his long-standing and well-known support for the retention of the

Corn Laws, Benett was an exceedingly unpopular man with large numbers of the populace, particularly in the north of the county, and some of those who attempted to travel to Wilton near Salisbury to vote for him encountered considerable difficulties. When Bowles's friend George Crabbe, the poet and rector of Trowbridge, attempted to leave Trowbridge to cast his vote, Bowles was with him, as he later wrote to Crabbe's son:

> A riotous tumultuous and most appalling mob, at the time of the election, besieged his house, when a chaise was at the door, to prevent him going to the poll, and giving his vote in favour of my worthy friend, John Benett of Pyt House, the present member for the county. The mob threatened to destroy the chaise, and tear him to pieces, if he attempted to set out. In the face of the furious assemblage, he came out and calmly, told them they might kill him if they chose, but, while alive, nothing would prevent his giving a vote, according to his promise and principles, and set off, undisturbed and unhurt, to vote for Mr Benett.[23]

Bowles duly voted for his friend and his wife's kinsman Benett although, in the confusion at the hustings, he voted in the incorrect booth, Bremhill being in the hundred of Chippenham. His vote was duly accepted, however, but that of William Powney, his parish clerk, also in favour of Benett, was rejected, probably because he was unable to prove that he was a freeholder qualified to vote. In the event Benett was duly elected.

In August Moore recorded in his journal that he called on Bowles who was 'much delighted with an article in *Blackwood's Magazine* concerning his controversy with Campbell'. He proceeded to tell Moore:

> Of his having advised the poor psalm-writer (that comes to him for charity) to turn Dissenting Preacher – of his rigging him out with an old black coat & breeches of his own & saying 'there, now you are fit to preach before any one' – excellent this in a Minister of the Establishment.[24]

Moore's journals are so full of amusing and, in some cases, unlikely anecdotes that one wonders whether Bowles really did address a poor man who had come to his door for charity in this way.

Few of the letters written by Lord Lansdowne are dated, and so in many cases it cannot be certain when they were written. This letter, probably written in the late summer at about this time, gives a clear picture of the easy relationship that existed between Bowles and his aristocratic neighbour:

> I am ready for an expedition to Trowbridge tomorrow, but if it is as hot as I found it today coming from Longleat,[25] I am afraid we should find it rather too long a ride to be pleasant, in these dog days. Perhaps however you will come over to breakfast, and if you do I will take a ride with you at all events if we should find it too hot to proceed.
>
> I should have written before if we had not staid at Longleat longer than we intended.
>
> Will you give us the pleasure of your company to dinner on Monday the 31st.[26]

Bowles was extremely well-read and knowledgable, and mixed and conversed easily with all manner of talented men who gathered around the hospitable table of Lord and Lady Lansdowne at Bowood. It must have been surprising when the company talked of Vanini,[27] the atheist, while he was dining there a few days later, and Bowles had to confess that he had never heard of him.

Since 1803 Thomas Moore had enjoyed the sinecure office of admiralty registrar at Bermuda, but had employed a deputy to discharge his duties there. However, soon after he arrived at Sloperton Cottage his deputy defaulted, leaving Moore with a liability of £6000. Being unable to discharge such an enormous sum of money, Moore was obliged to leave the country, and in 1819 he fled to Paris. Since 1816 Byron too had lived abroad and so, in October 1819 in a letter to Elizabeth Charter, Crabbe contrasted the situation of Moore and Byron with Bowles and himself:

> Poetry does pretty well in these Times, but poets do not. I hear that Mr Anacreon[28] Moore is obliged to go abroad on Acct of the decision which calls on him for £6000 a debt contracted without a fault on his part and almost without the Possibility of Avoiding it. Lord Byron is also Self-banisshed [sic]. Bowles and I are priests struggling with the Clamour and Infidelity of the Time.[29]

Very soon after Moore arrived in Paris he embarked on a tour to Italy with Lord John Russell,[30] and it may be that when he was in Rome he acquired the pen-holder, the relic from 'mighty Rome', referred to in the letter written to him by Bowles in July of the following year:

'Squire' Locke,[31] faithfully delivered to me the relic from 'mighty Rome' with which he was charged, and it now adorns my book room under the historian of the 'Eternal City'. Sic transit. I did not know what was the composition, till I had the pleasure of having two Duncans[32] here the other day, both travelled, both learned men, who told me my new pen holder was a veritable Rosso Antico. I now write to thank you for the care you have taken of it, and for your kind note.

    Somehow or other I think I ought to have written to you before, or you ought to have written to me, which would be better, to tell how you were, and how you were situated since you left England, and that delightful corner of it called Sloperton. Somehow or other I do not write myself, for somehow or other it always appears to me that when a letter is to go so far it ought to be better than common, written with a better pen, contain better sentences, and in short look so smart and finished as to be worth sending from an English parish to Paris. I never had a good pen, and though I am, cheu fugax! on the shady side of half a century, I never could make or mend one in my life. So you and Mrs Moore, and Bessy the lesser and Tom the 'smaller',[33] must take every kind wish, written with the usual coarse materials, but made legible with all my might. I do not know what I can send better than a poetical 'votum et suspirium.' On stopping at Sloperton Gate the other day, my pony almost insisted on going in, till I told him it was of no use! So between your gate and Bowood, on a most poetical summer evening, I put the following thoughts into dactyls:-
In domum desertam
Apud Sloperton, Wilts,
Suspirium et votum.

Bowles continues with twenty lines of doggerel, beginning:

Yes, this is the Cottage! Before I pass by,
Let me stop for a minute and gaze with a sigh,
For silent and sad is the social retreat,
Where the wild harp of Erin once echoed so sweet.

Bowles goes on with his letter:

I have been to the music meeting at Oxford where I heard for the first time 'Palestine.'[34] Sublimer strains were never heard since Handel, and what is more, though I thought such music was indeed 'caviare to the general', the whole assembly seemed to feel and appreciate its beauty and excellence. You must hear Miss Stephens[35] sing 'Voices of the Dead', and songs of other years.

I wrote some lines about her when I was coming home, but cannot remember them, and if I had not written this letter to you, should have forgotten that most 'poetical morceau' at Sloperton Gate. What an Arcadian word is that said Sloperton!.

By the way, have you seen Barry Cornwall's volume?[36] I think the Sicilian <u>story</u> is exquisite! He is a most amiable and diffident young man, and I hope will not be spoiled.
Give my best regards to Bessy, and believe me ever yours,
W.L. Bowles

P.S. I am making quite a priory here; Gothic arches, turrets, pinnacles &c. salute your arrival at Bremhill Parsonage. I think you must <u>cut</u> the <u>folks</u> at <u>Sloperton!</u> I say nothing about public affairs, as you doubtless hear so much. I hope the 'Radicals' won't hang me up upon my own arch. Brougham has won my heart, by speaking so frankly, so nobly, of the country clergy, no more than, generally speaking, they deserve, but they will all go 'a la lanterne' if Cobbett,[37] and his desperado crew prevail. I forgot to say I met your interesting, sensible, and amiable fellow-traveller, Lord John Russell the other day at Holland House. Lord Lansdowne is, of course, still in town. I went to hear his speech, and never was so impressed by the powers of eloquence.

Ipse quid audes in the poetical way? Above all, is there any hope of your returning? I saw 'Rhymes on the Road'[38] advertised.

I wish they were 'Rhymes on the Road Home!'

Colburn has written to request my '<u>Face</u>' for his magazine.

I must keep this letter till I see Locke to direct it, for I don't suppose, if it were directed as I hear Lord Byron directs, it would find you 'yet'. Mrs B. says I must leave out 'yet' and add will EVER find you.[39]

In the same year the controversy over Bowles's writings on the subject of Alexander Pope was revived when the *Quarterly Review* for July 1820 contained a review of the Rev. John Spence's *Anecdotes, Observations, and Characters of Books and Men, Collected from the Conversations of Mr Pope, and other eminent Persons of his Time.*[40] During the course of the article, the reviewer states:

Warton, who first entered the list, though not unwilling to wound, exhibits occasionally some of the courtesy of ancient chivalry; but his successor, the Rev. Mr Bowles, possesses the contest *a l'outrance*, with the appearance, though assuredly not with the reality, of personal hostility. It had been more honourable in this gentleman, with his known prejudices against the class of poetry in which Pope will always remain unrivalled, to have declined the office of editor, than to attempt to spread among new generations of readers the most unfavourable and the most unjust impressions of the POET, and of the MAN . . .

And later in the review:

Provincial authors too are liable to a sort of literary hypochondriasm, where they see nothing but the creation of a morbid fancy, a phantom in a dark room. To this we owe the wild speculations of Monboddo[41] on the original state of human nature . . . It is only on this principle that we can account for the injury inflicted on Pope by the strange proceedings of his last editor, who, having probably possessed himself of all the ravings of all the dunces on their arch-enemy, dwelt on them till their sinister influence operated on his imagination, and prompted him to hesitate, and suggest, and surmise away every amiable characteristic of the poet; and, incredible as it may appear, to accuse him of the contrary dispositions!

And again:

We have already exceeded any just limits which we can assign to the defence of our great poet; but much yet remains to be said – for without following Mr Bowles, step by step, how can the sly insinuation, the obscure hint, the damning fact anxiously recorded, (but – excess of candour! – with a faint admission that it may not be true,) be rebutted? It did not become a man, whose personal virtues are acknowledged, to aggravate common infirmities into viciousness, and to tear away the veil from the sanctities of domestic life. We would grieve to incur the displeasure of Mr Bowles; but we cannot at once sacrifice Truth and Pope; and the commentator ought not to thank our delicacy for not dwelling on the indecency of some of his notes.

Mr Bowles, we suspect, does not love criticism. 'If I had written,' he says, 'half of what is attributed to me in *criticism*, I might well take to myself,

Some have at first for wits, then poets pass'd;
Turn'd critics next, and prov'd *plain fools* at last. '

It is certain that Mr Bowles is no 'plain fool'; the attempt to degrade POPE, as his EDITOR, has always appeared to us, rather a calamity. Mr Bowles has more than once complained, that his critics will not understand him as he wishes to be understood; we have seen how pathetically he asks Mr Campbell to comprehend him; and he has afforded us an anecdote of exquisite *naivete*, which passed between himself and Lord Byron. It is characteristic!

The author then proceeds to relate Bowles's own account of his meeting with Lord Byron, when he complains about Byron's suggestion that he had written that the woods of Madeira had trembled with a kiss! These are just a small number of the charges levelled against Bowles in the review. Bowles was convinced that the author of the attack on him was Octavius Graham Gilchrist,[42] who had previously defended Pope's character elsewhere. Robert Southey was not so sure. In October he wrote to Bowles:

> I was so much hurt and offended by the manner in which you are treated in the last Quarterly Review that my first impulse was to have written to you to express my indignation . . . Do not be hasty in your reply; but make the most of a good case, and you will put the Review to shame. And you should be <u>certain</u> that Gilchrist is the writer, before you make the remotest allusion to him. I never heard him mentioned as having contributed anything to the Quarterly Review. But I have no suspicion who the writer is . . . You are right to answer the Reviewer, because tho he will find more readers at present, you will be read hereafter when reviews and reviewers are forgotten. But you will not be right, if you suffer yourself to be vexed by the unhandsome and unfair attack, the futility of which must be perceived by all who understand the subject, and the manner of which must displease all who know you.[43]

On 22 October Bowles appears to have worked himself up into something of a rage. He scribbled off two letters, one to Southey and the other to Murray, in which he gave vent, at times somewhat incoherently, to his feelings about the attack on him. To Southey he wrote:

> I cannot sufficiently express my thanks for your kind & generous letter – The evidence, that the author is 'Gilchrist' I think irresistible, at all events in a <u>badinage pamphlet</u> written literally, in such terms, I think the fact may be admitted, upon the circumstance that in the London Magazine, he has <u>sign'd his name</u> & <u>promis'd</u> to attack me on the very same grounds upon which I am so crassly attacked in the Quarterly.

This is followed by two pages with many deletions and underlinings, in the course of which he writes: 'I have been engaged the last week in writing two pamphlets, in <u>different</u> styles at the same time – the one publish'd in the name of "one of the Family of the Bowles".'[44] One of these pamphlets is referred to in the letter that he wrote on the same day to Murray, who was, of course, proprietor of the *Quarterly Review*:

After the stupid, ungentlemanly [this word is substituted for 'blackguard' and is followed by the deletion of the words 'and lying'] article in the last Quarterly, destitute of even truth, so personally insulting to me, and as remote from sense as from manners, I am sure you will excuse a good-natured 'badinage' in which your name is mention'd, but without the slightest disrespect.

Without those feelings that often excite, <u>as they did in Pope</u>, vindictive asperity, I call the article stupid, for the sophistry would not deceive a child; I call it ungentlemanly [once again the word blackguard is deleted] because no gentleman ever us'd such insulting language to another; and I call it destitute of even truth [these words are substituted for the word 'lying', which is deleted] because I have endeavour'd to surmise away every amiable quality of Pope, which is false! And the writer knew it to be so! . . .

Bowles then transcribes part of the letter he had received from Southey, showing how hurt Southey was by the attack, and continues:

I shall answer the whole, with my own name, and do not fear to twist the author round my little finger, and make those interested in the success of the Review ashamed they admitted such paltry arguments and such disgraceful personal spite to a man who never offended them.

In the mean time, a small publication which has been sent to me I send to you, and as I cannnot suppose you have anything to do with the rejection or admission of most of the articles, I hope I may trust your kindness, I might say justice, to grant me one request. It is to place on your table the accompanying small publication. At all events I have no reason to complain of yourself. [45]

The 'small publication' had not, of course, been sent to Bowles but was one of the pamphlets written by him in different styles that he had mentioned in his letter to Southey. It is clear that Bowles's normally quite calm judgement had been severely affected by the attack made on him. No one was in any doubt that Bowles was the author, and it has been said that his request to Murray 'produced a good deal of amusement among his friends'.[46]

Bowles concluded his letter to Murray with a postscript, in which he wrote:

If you look at what is said in the Review concerning 'Rural Editors getting mad over Old Dunces,' you will know what I mean by blackguardism.

The same author wrote in the London Review, and attacked me with the same flippancy, ignorance, affectation, and stupidity, but the editor wrote me a manly and generous letter totally disclaiming any participation in the sentiments and accounting for the admission by illness. That such a writer (for Nature never made two such in one age) should have never been permitted [to] disgrace the Quarterly is a matter, not of exultation to me, but regret.[47]

A few days later, on 30 October, Bowles wrote to John Wilson,[48] professor of Moral Philosophy at Edinburgh University as well as editor of *Blackwood's Magazine*. Bowles begins a very lengthy letter by writing:

Tho personally unacquainted with you, I have been too long in intimate communion with the spirit of your most affecting poetry, not to address you (when I have first the honour of writing to you) as a friend. Macdonald told me he had written to you on the subject that you will naturally have suppos'd may have caus'd me some concern. – Your opinions, those of Mr Southey, Wordsworth and as well as my own, have been held up to publick derision in the Quarterly Review by a certain admirer 'of' in-door nature! which he says 'Pope preferr'd,' & he seems to think he was on this account as <u>great a poet</u> & in the highest sense of the word, as He is, who, walking at large amids't God's mighty Creation, & portraying, with a Master's hand, all the moving passions of the Soul . . .

The criticism is so <u>futile</u>, so full of pompous assertions, shifting & shuffling sophistries, studious misrepresentations, & absolutely fraudulent mistatements, to say nothing of almost insulting personalities, that one almost wonders how Gifford,[49] unless too ill to overlook it, suffer'd such an article to appear . . .

I have not a shaddow of doubt as to the author – he has attacke'd me publicly on the same subject – & exactly in the same manner before – he is as feline, as he is flippant, in style, & no less a personage than a grocer of Stamford, at the same time the trading critic of half the magazines in London . . .

But the attack now appearing in the Quarterly requires some notice – I shall answer it formally . . .

I cannot sufficiently thank you for the notice, (thinking I am indebted for it to you) that was taken in Blackwood, of my pamphlet in answer to Campbell . . .

I well know the extraordinary power with which many of the articles in Blackwood are written – If Mr Lockhart,[50] taking into consideration what I have stated, & the absolute scurrility & fraudulent mis-representations of the Monthly Review, could 'Up, & at him', he would deserve it, from the <u>general insult</u> he has thrown, on all cultivators of the highest & best kind of poetry, that which is <u>drawn from nature</u> & that which goes to the heart of all events. I hope you will excuse the liberty I have taken

With the most sincere esteem

Your oblig'd servt

W.L. Bowles

I am sorry, my kind neighbour, the Marquis of Lansdowne is still in London, which causes my sending this letter <u>so far</u>, <u>without</u> a frank. If a small article in Blackwood were written, it might be headed Poetical <u>In-door</u> & <u>out- of door</u> nature

Mr Bowles & the Quarterly Review[51]

Unfortunately Bowles failed to heed Southey's wise advice not to hastily reply to the attack made on him nor to assume that Gilchrist was its author, and immediately arranged to be published *A Reply to an unsentimental sort of critic, the reviewer of Spence's Anecdotes in the Quarterly Review for October Otherwise to a Certain Critic and Grocer, the Longinus of 'in-door' nature by One of the family of the Bowleses!!* Bowles certainly lowered the tone of the debate by heading his reply with the words 'Come, let me flap this bug!'. These words were taken from the first lines of Pope's *Epistle to Arbuthnot*:

Yet let me flap this bug with gilded wings,
This painted child of dirt, that stinks and stings,
Whose buzz the witty and the fair annoys,
Yet wit ne'er tastes, and beauty ne'er enjoys:

Further, believing that Gilchrist was the author of the attack and knowing that he had left Oxford without taking a degree in order to assist his uncle in his grocery business in Stamford, Bowles decided to sneeringly allude to Gilchrist's background in trade, notwithstanding the fact that he was later an antiquary who had been elected FSA in 1803, and wrote on the title page:

In his shop, then, let this Reviewer, this lover of the sublime and beautiful in-door nature, indulge his own poetical and romantic reveries, till the pipe in his own mouth becomes, in his glowing imagination, that of Theocritus,[52] the old ledger-book, the Georgicks of Virgil; a grove of green canisters, a grove of green trees; the dingy shop-boy, a shepherd of

Arcadia; and a lake of brown treacle, in half a hogshead by the window, more enchanting to the view than the lakes of Cumberland . . .[53]

This was immediately followed in October by a second edition of his earlier pamphlet, now entitled '*A Reply to the Charges brought by the reviewer of Spence's Anecdotes . . . against the last editor of Pope's Works and author of a letter to Mr Campbell on the Invariable Principles of Poetry* and with the words 'a Certain Critic and Grocer' removed from the title. Bowles clearly regretted his reference to the background of the supposed author of the review, and so added a note in this new edition:

> To prevent the possibility of its being conceived, that the writer had, or could have, the slightest disrespect, in alluding to any particular branch of honest and respectable employment, he begs most solemnly to declare, that such intention was most remote from his heart. If allusions of the kind occur, they are only made in good-natured raillery, as illustrative of what the Quarterly Critic has advanced about 'In-door Nature!!' If he should take them to himself, he will be reminded how little right he has to object to the application, who has not scrupled to attribute (in a most popular publication) to a literary clergyman, living chiefly in the country, and who never offended him, such a kind of DISTEMPERED HYPOCHONDRIACISM as that which made Lord Mondoddo believe in the existence of human tails!

The review in the *Quarterly Review* of July 1820 was not written by Octavius Gilchrist at all but by Isaac D'Israeli[54] (the father of Benjamin Disraeli). Further, William Gifford, the editor of the *Quarterly Review*, declared that 'in the extent and accuracy of his critical knowledge', Gilchrist was 'as much superior to the Rev. Mr Bowles as in good manners'.[55]

Although Bowles would not have known this, Murray was encouraging Lord Byron to produce his own edition of Pope's works. On 13 June, in a letter to him, Murray writes:

> All that your Lordships [sic] says about Pope – is excellent indeed & I wish you could be induced to enlarge it & I would print it with anything else in the Shape of Notes that you would make for me in an Edition of Popes Poetical Works which I am very anxious to rescue from Mr Bowles . . .[56]

By the end of the year Murray had sent copies of the different pamphlets on the controversy to Byron, who could not resist writing a glee to be sung to the tune of 'Why, how now, saucy jade?'. It read:

Why, how now, saucy Tom?
If you thus must ramble,
I will publish some
Remarks on Mister Campbell.

ANSWER

Why, how now Billy Bowles?
Sure the priest is maudlin!
(*To the public*) How can you, d–n your souls!
Listen to his twaddling?[57]

Murray continued to keep Byron, who was living in Italy at this time, supplied with information about the Pope controversy. In October 1820 he wrote:

> I much approve of your intention to preserve in notes to the Hints all that you so manfully & judiciously said about Pope – it will come a propos for there is a great discussion upon his merits on now – & Bowles who in his own edition of Pope so shamefully abused him is now furious at an article upon this subject which appeared in the last Quarterly – Gifford is very warmly on your side – by way [*sic*] he a little resembles Pope in character – I wish you may have Bowles's edition by you that you may see fairly what he there said & to prevent you from judging merely from his pamphlet to Campbell.[58]

It was not long before Byron entered the fray with his *Letter to***** [*John Murray*], *Esqre on the Rev. W.L. Bowles's Strictures on the Life and Writings of Pope* written in Ravenna in February 1821. In this it was made clear that John Cam Hobhouse was the author of the verses denigrating Bowles in the first edition of *English Bards and Scotch Reviewers*, and that in the second edition Byron had removed some of Hobhouse's words. Bowles referred to this in *Two Letters* that he was later to publish in reply, and this so incensed Hobhouse that he wrote to Byron to say that had he not been a clergyman he would have challenged Bowles[59] – presumably to a duel!

On 2 March Murray wrote to Byron: 'I now enclose the first part of a third pamphlet by Bowles more insane if possible than the former ones – he has now found out that D Israeli is the writer of the offensive article in the Quarterly – but hitherto he has abstained from naming him . . .'[60]

Early in April Bowles received a copy of the pamphlet and, although he disagreed with parts of it, he was nevertheless moved to write to Murray:

> I write once more to say that I have just got Lord Byron's pamphlet, and I could not omit requesting you to return him my best thanks for the kind terms in which he introduces my name, and also for the pleasure I have receiv'd from a work as much marked by good sense, liberal principles, and just thinking as by its peculiar tone of good-humour and urbanity, to which I have been of late so little accustom'd . . . Lord Byron is the first liberal, manly and kind-hearted opponent I have ever met, and I feel even gratitude towards him, as much as I respect him, for the manly vindication, without asperity or unkindness, of Pope's moral character . . . It is most unfortunate that the words 'Christian' community should have occurred in my last, but after I knew that Mr D'Israeli was the writer of the Quarterly, I solemnly declare I did not know his religious creed was so opposite from my own.[61]

Thomas Moore took a dim view of Byron's *Letter*, writing in his journal on 13 April:

> Found on my return home at night Ld. Byron's letter about Bowles & Pope, which Fielding had sent me to look over – the whole thing unworthy of him – a Leviathan among small fry – He has had the bad taste to allude to an anecdote which I told him about Bowles's early life, which is even worse than Bowles, in his pamphlet quoting me as entirely agreeing with the system he is combating for.[62]

Byron is recorded as having spoken of Bowles in these terms:

> I once met Bowles at Rogers's, and thought him a pleasant gentlemanly man – a good fellow for a parson. When men meet after dinner, the conversation takes a certain turn. I remember he entertained us with some good stories. The reverend gentleman pretended, however, to be much shocked at Pope's Letters to Martha Blount.[63] I set him and his 'invariable principles'[64] at rest. He did attempt an answer, which was no reply; at least nobody read it. I believed he applied to me some lines in Shakespeare. A man is very unlucky who has a name that can be punned upon; and his own name did not escape.[65]

A footnote reveals that the 'lines of Shakepeare' were 'I do remember thee, my Lord Biron etc'. In his *Lord Byron and Some of his*

Contemporaries, Leigh Hunt was to write that:

> He [Byron] was also not unwilling to be reminded of his namesake in Shakespeare, and used to mention with pleasure the quotation attributed to Mr Bowles:-
> 'Biron they call him; but a merrier man,
> Within the limits of becoming mirth
> I never knew . . .'[66]

On another occasion Bowles met Byron in London, and had the opportunity of taking him to task about one part of his *English Bards and Scotch Reviewers* to which he took particular offence. He later wrote:

> As the rest of the company were going into another room, I said I wished to speak one word to his Lordship. He came back with much apparent courtesy. I then said to him in a tone of seriousness, but that of perfectly good humour, 'My Lord, I should not have thought of making any observations on whatever you might be pleased to give to the world as your opinion of any part of my writings; but I think if I can shew that you have done me a palpable and public wrong, by charging me with having written what I never wrote, or thought of, your own principles of justice will not allow the impression to remain'. I then spoke of a particular couplet which he had introduced into his satire –
> 'Thy woods, Madeira, trembled with a kiss!'[67]

In one of his conversations recorded by Thomas Medwin,[68] after saying that 'the Lake poets were such fools as not to fish in their own waters; but this was the least offensive part of the epistle', Byron continued:

> Bowles is one of the same little order of spirits, who has been fussily fishing on for fame, and is equally waspish and jealous. What could Coleridge mean by praising his poetry as he does?
> It was a mistake of mine, about his making the woods of Madeira tremble, &c; but it seems that I might have told him that there were no <u>woods</u> to make tremble the kisses, which would have been quite as great a blunder.[69]

These conversations surely came to the notice of Bowles, who was probably pleased that Byron thought him 'a good fellow for a parson' – but not so happy to be thought of as 'fussily fishing on for fame'!

It was not in Bowles's nature to keep silent, and so he responded almost immediately by writing *Two Letters to the Right Honourable Lord*

Byron in answer to His Lordship's letter to **** on the Rev. W.L. Bowles's strictures on the Life and Writings of Pope, more particularly on the question, whether poetry be more immediately indebted to what is sublime or beautiful in the works of nature or the works of art. These were printed by Richard Cruttwell in Bath in the middle of April, whereupon Bowles wrote a long letter to Murray, the chief purpose of which was to ask him to be the publisher. He added: 'I care not a farthing about any profit. If any, it shall be yours, except what would pay the mere expense of printing.'[70] A few days later Bowles wrote again to Murray:

> I am rejoic'd very much to think my pamphlet will enter the literary world under the same auspices as Lord Byron's. This is as it should be, and I am sure the conduct of the question will be such that you will not regret it. I shall feel it doubly incumbent on me to preserve the tone of courtesy and amenity of which Lord Byron has set such an example, and shall I say that I think the question itself both novel and interesting, now it is brought to a point of such argument . . .

Bowles then sets out the title for the Advertisement for his letter to Byron, which was to include the words 'He that Plays at Bowls (with the Sun and Moon?) Must Expect Rubbers – Old Proverb', and asked to be told immediately whether he had 'the slightest objection to this motto'.[71] Several days later Bowles wrote to Murray once more:

> . . . I hope you will not be sparing in getting it advertis'd, for which, if the sale should not cover it, I would cheerfully repay you, but of this I conceive there can be no doubt. If the whole impression shall be sold, I should be glad certainly to pay for the mere printing, but all beyond, of course, will be yours, as the liberty to print on your own account as many copies afterwards as you please.
> I would wish you to send a copy to the Bishop of London, Bishop of Hereford, Sir James Mackintosh,[72] Sir Thomas Lawrence.[73] My other friends, Lord Lansdowne, Sir George Beaumont, Lord Holland, Nares &c will doubtless have copies of you, and it is hardly worth sending them: but you will do as you like . . .[74]

The Bishop of Hereford at this time was George Isaac Huntingford,[75] who was an assistant master at Winchester when Bowles was a pupil at the school.

As has been seen, Bowles wished to indulge in a little fun in the advertisement for the *Two Letters*. Byron had prefaced his *Letter to John Murray* with the motto 'I will play at Bowls with the sun and moon – Old

Song'. In the event the advertisement read:

> A 'certain family' had been spoken of, in the Quarterly Review as 'ringing changes on nature for two thousand years'.
>
> By a somewhat ludicrous coincidence it happens that the 'arms' of this 'family' are, literally, a 'sun and moon, a sun, or, and a moon, argent, secundum artem'.[76]
>
> It is, therefore, with this sun and moon, that Lord Byron, I have no doubt plays at Bowls! Not with the Sun and Moon in Nature!

As a consequence, Bowles adopted as a motto on the title page to his *Two Letters* 'He that plays Bowls, must expect rubbers.[77] That three editions of these letters should have been published, two in 1821 and another in the following year, is an indication of the public interest in the controversy.

Lord Byron had written a *Second Letter to John Murray . . .*, but having read Bowles's letters to Murray that had been sent to him on 24 April,[78] he decided, in the light of their contents, that it should not be published. In May he wrote to Murray: 'I am obliged to Mr Bowles and Mr B. is obliged to me, for having restored him to good humour,' and on 14 June he wrote to John Murray:

> I have read Bowles's answer: I could easily reply, but it would lead to a long discussion, in the course of which I should perhaps lose my temper, which I would rather not do with so civil and forbearing an antagonist. I suppose he will mistake being silent for silenced.

A few days later he wrote to Thomas Moore:

> Bowles's answers have reached me; but I can't go on disputing for ever, – particularly in a polite manner. I suppose he will take being silent for silenced. He has been so civil that I can't find it in my liver to be facetious with him, – else I had a savage joke or two at his service.[79]

On 29 May Murray wrote to Byron, with his last word to him on the controversy:

> . . . it is monstrous good Bowles cringing to you and thinking he may kick Hobhouse as he likes – Hobhouse does not like it – & thinks of cutting his (Bowless) throat – Bowles too makes an apology for the liberty he has taken [with] your 'Lordship's Motto' and mistaking your Lines f[or tho]se written by Hobhouse.[80]

Hobhouse most certainly did not like what Bowles was saying about him. A letter written by Hobhouse to Murray in May reveals his true feelings:

> I hear Parson Bowles goes about abusing me, relying on my forebearance, or on what he may think his vast capacity for satire. The dirty dog crouches and creeps to Byron, but thinks he may safely attack me. He may find himself mistaken one day or the other. In the meantime, as he is fond of parody, he may have something in that shape you will find overleaf.

> Should Parson Bowles yourself or friend compare
> To some French cut-throat, if you please, Santerre –
> Or heap, malignant, on your living head
> The smut and trash he pour'd on Pope when dead,
> Say what reply – or how with him to deal –
> Sot without shame and fool that cannot feel?
> You would not parly with a printer's hack –
> You cannot cane him, for his coat is black;
> Reproof and chastisement are idly spent
> On one who calls a kick a compliment,
> Unwhipp'd, then, leave him to lampoon and lie,
> Safe in his parson's guise and infamy.[81]

Bowles would surely have been horrified to know that the future statesman, who was later created Baron Broughton de Gyfford, should have written to Murray in this way.

An epigram bandied about at this time read:

> No more at 'bowls' let Byron play,
> Or beat old 'Bowles' about;
> For Bowles has fairly won the day
> And bowl'd his lordship out[82]

In a letter that Byron wrote from Italy to John Murray in September 1821 he revealed, probably with his tongue in his cheek, what he thought about his fellow poets, including Bowles:

> . . . I have no patience with the sort of trash you send me by way of books, except Scott's novels, and three or four other things; never saw such

work or works; Campbell lecturing, Moore idling, Southey twaddling, Wordsworth drivelling, Coleridge muddling, Joanna Baillie piddling, Bowles squibbling, squabbling, and sniveling (sic) . . .[83]

Lord Byron's decision to stay silent was not followed by the other participants in what the modern reader may well consider to be an obtuse and tedious controversy. Octavius Graham Gilchrist might perhaps be forgiven for deciding to respond to Bowles's unfortunate and mistaken attack on him: in October 1820 he published *A Letter to the Rev. W.L. Bowles in answer to a pamphlet recently published under the title of A Reply to an unsentimental sort of critic, the reviewer of Spence's Anecdotes in the Quarterly Review for October 1820 by Octavius Gilchrist Esq. F.S.A.* He had previously launched an attack on Bowles in the *London Magazine* for February 1820, in which he described Bowles's description of Pope's attachment to Martha Blount and 'the anatomical minuteness with which he examines and determines on the physical constitution of Pope, might, in charity, be deemed only seemly to a layman, and occasional critic; in an editor, and a clergyman, such conduct appears to us indecent, and insufferably disgusting'.

Bowles could not ignore these latest attacks, and so there soon appeared in the *Pamphleteer*, his *Observations on the poetical character of Pope, further elucidating the Invariable Principles of Poetry; with a sequel in reply to Octavius Gilchrist*. Gilchrist was now in full flight, and produced two further letters to Bowles, the first being *A Second Letter to the Rev. W.L. Bowles in answer to his second reply*!

As one would expect, Bowles entered into considerable correspondence with John Scott,[84] the editor of the *London Magazine*, about the attack that had been made on him. Writing to him on 27 December 1820, he declares:

> . . . Allow me to say that in the responsible situation as Editor, as a moral and conscienscious man, as a Christian in a Christian Country, it <u>did</u> behove you, independent of any personal civilities to me, to take some notice I think of the admission of an article so indecent & atrocious as that in the London Magazine!!
>
> Let me make an observation on Gilchrist's last ebullition . . . Moore will tell you how unlike the monstrous representation is! There is not a man near this place, but knows the 'poor man's cottage' is as welcome to me, as to the 'rich man's Palace' – all my [illegible] is taken up in considering & acting for the welfare of the poor and I wish Mr Gilchrist himself had seen, on Christmas Day, the spectacle, my house [illegible] of upwards of fifty poor children, fed & fully cloath'd by me;

and upwards of 100 feasted, quietly but cheerfully, in different parts of the parish.[85]

It is not easy to comprehend the extraordinary acrimony that was engendered by literary controversies at this time. When Bowles wrote this letter, Scott was deeply embroiled in a dispute with the writer John Lockhart, who had been attacked by Scott in *Blackwood's* and other magazines. Further arguments between Jonathan Christie, a friend of Lockhart's, and Scott led to a duel between Christie and Scott within two months of this letter being written, as a result of which Scott died.

Bowles had his defenders, including an anonymous writer in the *Gentleman's Magazine* of April 1821 whose opinions must have given Bowles a great deal of pleasure to read:

We cannot in the space to which we must necessarily confine ourselves, enter into any detailed criticism upon the qualifications of Mr Bowles as an Editor of the Works of our English Horace; but we will venture to assert, that notwithstanding all the elaborate invective, which has been poured forth against him, he has still the best part of the argument. That he is an amiable as well as an able man, even his enemies seem disposed to admit; and with such impressions, it is most extraordinary that they should give themselves so much trouble to injure him in the estimation of the public, by a series of charges as gross as they are unfounded and ridiculous . . . The truth is, that Mr Bowles's opponents have made him responsible for a variety of opinions which he never advanced; and much criticism of which he appears to have been equally guiltless: thus clamouring with prodigious vehemence against misrepresentations which have originated with themselves. Lord Byron is the fugleman of this literary warfare. It was he who (in his English Bards) first began to act on the offensive. Mr Campbell was the next in succession; but although he differed materially with Mr Bowles on the subject of Pope's merits, he never descended to personal invective in his criticism. He stated his objections like a gentleman: it would have been as well if the rest of the controversialists had followed his example. Against the Quarterly Review and a Writer in the London Magazine, however, Mr Bowles would appear to have more serious cause of complaint. By this latter gentleman, he has been attacked in such scurrilous terms as we hardly ever remember to have met with in the annals of criticism; and we cannot but believe that he has made a considerable sacrifice of his dignity in vouchsafing a reply to this writer . . . [86]

The writer then continues to examine and weigh 'the charges brought against this gentleman, at least such of them as are entitled to regard' at considerable length, in six full columns of the *Gentleman's Magazine.*

Having read this article, Bowles immediately wrote from Windsor to John Bowyer Nichols, part editor of the magazine, to express his thanks:

> There is so little of common truth or justice in the modern code of criticism, that I feel bound to express to you my thanks for the admission of the manly & sensible article, in your magazine for this month, in which I am vindicated from some late very inconsiderate charges, & some very atrocious slanders on account of my Life of Pope.
>
> Respecting the personal insults to which your liberal correspondent thinks it would have been more dignified not to have replied, I certainly agree with him, but there were some accusations advanc'd which requir'd to be absolutely contradicted, as acquiescing when I am no longer able to defend myself might look like <u>admitting</u>; & I am moreover convinc'd that as none deserve a somewhat coarse reproof <u>more</u>, so none are so <u>sensitive</u> as those who use the brutal weapons of attack without regard to the laws of courtesy or the dictates of justice – the controversy with Lord Byron is more like a pleasant colloquy – I shall send you my answer tomorrow, & remain dear Sir with every wish for the long health of him whose pages never have been sullied with acrimonious invectives & which for so many years have fully justified the* <u>Title</u> they first assum'd
> Your oblig'd & sincere servt
> Wm. L. Bowles
> * 'Gentleman's' Magazine –
> P.S. I wrote this on my way to London, but I would not miss a post, having just seen your magazine.[87]

True to his word, and having arrived in London, Bowles did indeed write to Nichols from 62 Piccadilly:

> I lose no time in sending you my answer to Lord Byron, the writing of which, tho' necessarily done in haste, was not unpleasing, so much more satisfactory is it to have a man of high talents & a gentleman, as an opponent . . .
>
> It is impossible not to believe that a purpose was to be answer'd & that there has been a kind of conspiracy in the business – The Blackguard who open'd the attack in the London Magazine, has been silenc'd, I hope: at all events, <u>him</u> I shall never think of answering again, & am

aware of the justness of your correspondent's remarks on this subject .
. . I believe they begin to think I am a match for all of them, but, I have
hitherto been oblig'd to fight single-handed – The first generous support
has been from you and your correspondent . . . I should esteem it a
kindness & should be much oblig'd if I might have an opportunity of
thanking him, & you, personally, before I leave Town.
I hope, at least, to pay my respects to yourself, & I am
Your much oblig'd servt
Wm. L. Bowles
You will be glad to hear that every copy of my answer that was sent to
London was sold the first day! & we have been waiting for more since
Monday.[88]

In June 1821 a long article by William Hazlitt[89] appeared in the
London Magazine entitled *Pope, Lord Byron and Mr Bowles*. He deals
mainly with the merits of Pope as a poet and generally supports Bowles
as opposed to Byron. He writes:

> In truth his Lordship has the worst of this controversy, though he throws
> out a number of pert, smart, flashy things, with the air of a man who
> sees company on subjects of taste, while his reverend antagonist, who
> is the better critic and logician of the two, goes prosing on in a tone
> of obsequious percinacity and sore pleasantry, as if he were sitting (an
> unwelcome guest) at his Lordship's table and were awed yet galled, by
> the cavalier assumption of patrician manners.[90]

Hazlitt returned to this theme when writing in his *The Spirit of the
Age* published in 1825:

> . . . In the controversy about Pope, he [Byron] claps Mr Bowles on the
> back with a coarse facetious familiarity, as if he were his chaplain whom
> he had invited to dine with him, or was about to present to a benefice.
> The reverend divine might submit to the obligation; but he has no need
> to subscribe to the jest. If it is a jest that Mr Bowles should be a parson
> and Lord Byron a peer, the world knew this before: there was no need to
> write a pamphlet to prove it.[91]

In 1821 Bowles launched into print yet again with *A Vindication of
the late Editor of Pope's Works, from some charges brought against him, by a
writer in the Quarterly Review for October 1820 . . .*, printed not by Richard
Cruttwell in Bath but by the well-known London printer Abraham
Valpy.[92] There was so much interest in the pamphlet that a 'Second

Edition, Corrected' was soon printed. Also in 1821 'Sketches of Living Poets' appeared in the *Examiner*. As one of the four poets described, Bowles was doubtless pleased to be joined by such men as Byron and Coleridge.

On 1 July 1821 the novelist Mary Russell Mitford[93] wrote to Sir William Elford[94] with an account of her meeting with Bowles at the house of Dr Valpy in London. She wrote:

> I had the honour a week or two ago to be introduced to your friend Mr Bowles, the poet. I must tell you the story. Going into Dr Valpy's the back way, I met the old butler. 'Are the ladies in the parlour, Newman?' 'Yes, ma'am – and ma'am, there's Mr Bowles, the poet,' quoth Newman.

She then proceeds into the parlour where Dr Valpy introduces her to 'Mr Bowles, the poet' and him merely, as it transpires, to 'Mary', as a result of which, to her astonishment, Bowles, who clearly had no idea who she was, turned away. A minute afterwards Miss Valpy approached and asked after Dr Mitford (Mary's father), whom Bowles had known for very many years. She continues to write:

> . . . and all was immediately right. Mr Bowles was very pleasant and sociable, talked a great deal of Lord Byron and the Pope question, in which we exactly agree, and in which, from not having read the prosy pamphlet in which he has so marred his own good cause, I was able to agree with him most conscientiously.

The letter continues with Mary Mitford's impression of Bowles's wife, Magdalene, which was not at all flattering. She writes: 'Pray do you like his wife? Is not she a coarse, cold, hard woman, and rather vulgarish? All this she seemed to me. He is very affable and agreeable.'[95] That Magdalene should be described in this way is most unexpected in view of the other few, but nevertheless favourable, descriptions of her by those who knew and had met her. The reason may surely be that Magdalene had heard quite enough of Byron and the Pope controversy, and was irritated that her husband and Mary Mitford should be engrossed in talking about little else, to her exclusion.

The controversy rumbled on, although with a little less intensity, and in 1822 another attack on Bowles's *Invariable Principles of Poetry* appeared in the *Pamphleteer*. This was written by Martin M'Dermot and was reviewed in the *New Monthly Magazine*. It resulted in Bowles's *An Address to Thomas Campbell Esq., editor of the New Monthly Magazine in consequence of an article in that publication*.[96]

In writing to Byron in 1822, Isaac D'Israeli reveals his true opinion of Bowles:

> I could tell your Lordship many pleasant 'historiettes' about Pope and Bowles! Apollo forgive him this cheek-by-jowl affair. The Review made Bowles write 1001 letters, and publish pamphlet on pamphlet. He obtained an odd kind of celebrity by the strength of his arm in writing what people only know by perpetual advertisement; and forgotten as a poet, he is remembered for a controversy with your Lordship . . . No one runs with our Bowles, so he walks over the course, and his neighing is as insolently joyous as ever. He has suppressed a letter to me, and gives promise to share in a bottle when he returns to Town, for he likes Wine, as Gilchrist asserts . . .[97]

If at this time Bowles had thought that the controversy that resulted from his work on the life and poetry of Pope had been laid to rest, he was soon to be shown to be mistaken as in William Roscoe's[98] 1824 edition of Pope's work, Bowles's comments on the poet's moral and poetical character were once again attacked. Thomas Moore recorded in his journal in September: 'Bowles called. Asked him to return to dinner with us, which he did. Is going pell-mell into controversy again; Roscoe has exposed a carelessness of his with regard to one of Pope's letters, which he is going to write a pamphlet to explain.'[99]

Whether Bowles relished the chance to once again put pen to paper in continuation of the old controversy may never be known, although he probably did. However, no one would have been surprised to see the appearance in 1825 of his *A final appeal to the literary public relative to Pope in reply to certain observations of Mr Roscoe in his edition of that poet's works, to which are added some remarks on Lord Byron's conversations as far as they relate to the same subject and the author (In letters to a literary friend)*. This rambling appeal, 190 pages long, was printed by Richard Cruttwell in Bath and caused Bowles not a little trouble in its preparation. He looked to Moore for help, who recorded in his journal, having spent the night in the parsonage after a musical evening there, 'At work for three hours after breakfast, trying to put Bowles's slipshod reasonings into some sort of order, but the task desperate.'[100] In view of what had gone before no-one would imagine that this would in reality be his final word on the subject. The 'final appeal' brought forth in 1825 *A Letter to the Rev. W.L. Bowles A.M. Prebendary of Sarum, Fellow of the Royal Society of Literature and former editor of Pope's works in ten volumes, in reply to his 'Final appeal to the literary public relative to Pope' by William Roscoe Esq.*

Needless to say, Bowles felt obliged to respond, despite Moore's advice after, one Sunday at the beginning of October, he had looked 'over the sheets of Bowles's "More last Words" to Roscoe. Having tried in vain to dissuade him from publishing it at all, did my best to get rid of some of the twaddle'![101] Despite this sound advice Bowles was not to be silenced, and so duly completed in 176 pages his *Lessons in Criticism to W. Roscoe Esq. . . in answer to his letter to the Reverend W.L. Bowles on the character and poetry of Pope.* It is perhaps a little surprising that the work was dedicated to none other than the Rev. Richard Warner, who in 1808 in *Bath Characters or Sketches from Life* had described Bowles's lines as being 'namby-pamby'. Perhaps Bowles did not know that Warner was widely believed to have been the author of *Bath Characters*, or if he did know, either did not care or was secretly amused by the satire.

Bowles was assiduous in drafting the advertisements for his works, and in making it clear to the publishers Hurst & Robinson how they should be worded and where they should be placed. He accordingly wrote to them in January 1826:

> Mr Bowles will be oblig'd to Mr Robinson to send the following announcement & advertisement to the Morning Chronicle, Courier, Times & St James's Chronicle –
> On Saturday next Jan 21st will be published
> Rev W.L. Bowles's Lessons in Criticism to a Quarterly
> Reviewer & Wm. Roscoe, Esq, F.R.S
>
> 'It is never too late to learn!'
> Published by Hurst & Robinson

Bowles followed this with the draft of a slightly differently worded advertisement to be inserted in the same newspapers on the next Monday, and then continued:

> . . . Remember that as soon as the Parcell is receiv'd to forward a copy to the Editor of the Edinburgh Review & to Mr Brougham,[102] Lincoln's Inn, MP & Sir James Mackintosh & Jeremy Bentham[103] Esq – Editor of Westminster Review, Editor of Monthly Review – Mr Harvey– Monthly Magazine, British Critic – Blackwood – Sir Walter Scott – Mr Lockhart – Professor Wilson – (Edinburgh) John Bull – & advertisement New Monthly Mag. London – News of Literature & Fashion & British Review . . .[104]

It is strange that Bowles did not ask for a copy to be sent to the *Gentleman's Magazine* (although perhaps he did this himself), but in any event the magazine soon published a review of it.[105] Someone he forgot to add to the list of those who were to be sent a copy was his old friend Archdeacon Nares, who must have seen *Lessons in Criticism* being advertised and then, perhaps, wrote to Bowles. As a consequence another letter was swiftly sent to Hurst & Robinson:

> Mr Bowles took it for granted he had sent Mr Archdeacon Nares name to Messrs Hurst & Robinson as the <u>very first</u> to whom he should have wish'd his answer to Roscoe to be sent, as a present – in all cases, if any friend of Mr Bowles's introduce himself & requests a copy of any thing he has written, it is Mr Bowles's desire, it should be given to him & is sorry he did not mention this before . . .
>
> Mr Nares, lives, No 22 Hart Street Bloomsbury & Mr Bowles will be oblig'd to Messrs Hurst, if when they send the book they will add that I had no doubt whatsoever of Mr Nares's name being on the list of those to whom I wish'd the very <u>first</u> copies to be sent.[106]

To this letter Bowles added a postscript to the effect that a copy should be sent to the bibliographer the Rev. Thomas Dibdin[107] and, with his fertile mind ever looking for further challenges, in this letter Bowles asked, 'Has any one answer'd Burton's[108] Roman Catholick Church? Would it pay expenses? It ought to be done, & I think at this moment a work done in the spirit in which Burton's book is written would be read – & popular.'

After this, what really was Bowles's last word on a subject that must by now have wearied the literary world was published, when *What is sauce for the goose, is sauce for the gander! Being an answer to an article in the Quarterly Review as far as it concerns Mr Bowles's Edition of Pope and his view of that poet's character* saw the light of day. In this pamphlet he declares that:

> My 'invariable principles' have weathered every storm, and have arrived safely in port! They ought to have three cheers: for, I believe, it has been owing to them that the question relating to Pope's supremacy in his art has taken tangible and definite shape. Pope's rank is now acknowledged; and the critic has 'degraded' him as much as I did, in assigning him exactly the same station. He stands the First in the second class. This is all I ever contended for.[109]

Many years later Bowles noticed that in an edition of his collected poems[110] published in Paris the editor said, in effect, 'In the contest with Lord Byron, the victory was manifestly on the side of Bowles; *but when he pronounced that a poem was to be judged by the subject alone!!! He gave his opponent the advantage!!'* In response to this Bowles wrote:

> As Mr Bowles was never such an obtuse dolt as to say this, the advantage is still on his side, and must be for ever his; for nothing can shake the position – that nature, not art – passion of nature, not capricious manners of life, constitute the eternal basis of what is sublime or beautiful in poetry. Whether a poet can make proper use of his materials is another question.
>
> In the memorials of his late life, Lord Byron has spoken with the greatest kindness and respect of his opponent.[III]

A later writer succinctly sums up the controversy in this way:

> Editing Pope, he [Bowles], not unnaturally, revived the old question of the value of Pope's poetry: and a mildly furious controversy followed, in which the classically-minded poets of the calibre of Byron and Campbell took part, which produced numerous pamphlets, rather fluttered Bowles's Wiltshire dovecote, but developed in him the fighting power of birds much more formidable than doves. As usual, it was rather a case of the gold and silver shield; but Bowles's general contention that, in poetry, the subject and decoration alike should be rather nature than art, and Byron's incidental insistence (very inconsistently maintained) that execution is the great secret, were the somewhat valuable by-products of a generally unprofitable dispute.[112]

While this literary war was being waged, life in and around Bremhill continued as usual. One may be sure that the great majority of the inhabitants of Wiltshire would have been entirely unware of it and, had it come to their notice, utterly bemused that so much time, energy and printing ink should have been expended in pursuing such a controversy. For those at the very bottom of the social scale, and for agricultural labourers and their families in particular, all that mattered was finding enough to eat, clothing themselves and keeping warm in the winter. Wiltshire was a county in which the wages of workers on the land were as low as anywhere in the country, and where the ever increasing number of paupers was a constant reminder to the affluent upper classes of the glaring inequalities in society as a whole. For the parson with a social conscience, and Bowles must surely be numbered among them, the question of what should be done – and, more immediately, what could he do – to alleviate their plight must always have been in the forefront of his mind.

Early in the new year in 1820 the *Devizes and Wiltshire Gazette* carried a lengthy report of what Bowles and his wife Magdalene had done at Christmas to bring some cheer to their poor neighbours. It throws some light on Bowles's thoughts on what he should or should not be doing in the face of such poverty:

On Christmas Day 55 girls of Mrs Bowles's school were plentifully fed on beef and pudding at the Rectory House, Bremhill and at 2 public houses in the parish, the parochial choir and 50 men and women had a substantial dinner of beef and beer and on the same day bread and soup was distributed to upwards of 200. We mention this donation because we think it might be serviceable at this time to notice the plan of *penny a week* club: from this alone in this one year were distributed in the parish of Bremhill 24 blankets, 40 shirts, 36 shifts, 48 pairs of stockings, 21 underpetticoats, 41 double handkerchiefs, 3 pair of shoes and four frocks. All but the blankets found in one year for a *penny* a week; the cloaks and blankets at *2 pence* a week.

Bowles addressed his neighbours:

My good friends, I have been always anxious that on this day not one of my poorer neighbours should be without the means of partaking in the cheer, which, in accordance with the customs of Old England, and the usage of the ancient church, distinguishes this Season. I most earnestly wish indeed I could see you equally comfortable every day in the year, but if I were to give up ALL I have, it would go to ease the *rich*, not to relieve the *poor*, for the Overseers would have only so much *less* to pay. In these hard times, the best I can do is endeavour to *raise* the price of labour and when I cannot do that, to take care 'the poor and needy have right'. As you surround me with cheerful looks, and I am very sure kind hearts, you will allow me to take the opportunity of addressing a few words of affectionate admonition, which some circumstances of the present awful times have suggested.

Bowles then proceeded to lecture his audience on the wickedness of those who slandered the clergy by saying that 'in general they are fonder of eating, drinking and swearing, than preaching the Gospel; of telling lies, than truth, of watching for tythes, than the good of souls, of being wolves, thieves and devils . . .' He continued by assuring his parishioners that:

I, who never went to rest, without prayer for your wordly and eternal welfare, during a connexion of 16 years, must have my share of this foul and outrageous slander . . . I can tell you, my friends, one reason why the clergy are particularly obnoxious in the present day. They stand between the poor and their oppressors. Wish so much to get rid of the clergy and magistrates, as *some overseers*, would you be better? I know what your heart answers.

Having spoken of the Church and its Ministers, you will allow me to add a word concerning those who do not attend our communion. Though my first and most affectionate concern must naturally be for those who, during a connexion of so many years, and in these days of gain-saying, have never been seduced to leave the 'household of faith' yet I wish no poor man should be left out in this distribution of small comforts . . . I do not ask *how* or *where* they call upon our common Saviour.[113]

Since 1816 when, with his friend Michael Joy of Hartham Park, he was deemed at the Quarter Sessions held in Warminster qualified to act as a magistrate for the county,[114] Bowles had duly played his part in the administration of justice. That clergymen should be appointed justices of the peace was a practice that met with the disapproval of many. Indeed, in a memoir of Bowles published in Paris in 1829 it was stated that: 'Although a clergyman, Bowles is a magistrate of the county of Wilts, after the most unseemly practice in England. No two duties can be more incompatible; but, to the credit of the poet, he has always exhibited the most assiduous attention to the duties of the office . . .'[115] However, Bowles was firmly of the opinion that clergy/magistrates, could, and did in many cases, stand between the indigent parishioner and the harsh overseer of the poor, and so could exercise a benign influence for the latter's benefit as well as attempting to mitigate so far as possible the severe penalties that he and his fellow justices were expected to impose. In his *Parochial History of Bremhill*, published in 1828, Bowles gives an example of how a resident clergyman and magistrate could come to the aid of a poor parishioner:

An old man, upwards of eighty-five, was confined to his bed with sickness. He had no one to attend to him but his wife, nearly seventy years old. The overseer was required to grant these poor people, in this calamitous situation, two shillings and sixpence a week each. No entreaties could prevail – no feelings of Christian compassion had any place. I then, as a magistrate, made a formal *order* for an allowance. Obedience was rudely and peremptorily refused. I had no power of *ordering relief* further than to the meeting of the next petty session – *four* sixpences than would have been the whole! Upon the overseer's refusal, he was summoned to the sessions, and fined forty shillings for disobedience. Would it be believed that the sum was found afterwards charged to the parish by the man who would not advance four sixpences of the parish money to a dying fellow creature! The moment the fraud was discovered an appeal was made to the quarter sessions, and this obstinate overseer condemned to pay all costs! Forty pounds my expenses, and probably twenty his own![116]

As a magistrate Bowles was not only expected from time to time to attend Quarter Sessions but also on quite frequent occasions to sign warrants committing alleged offenders against the law to gaol pending trial. On 4 February 1822, therefore, he signed a warrant that William Clark be committed as 'a rogue and vagabond, he having left his family chargeable to the parish of Calne' – he was later discharged[117] – and two days later a warrant committing sixty-six-year-old Samuel Alford to prison pending his trial at the Lent Assizes to be held in Salisbury, he having been 'found on a wood belonging to the Marquis of Lansdowne armed with a gun and having then and there killed two pheasants'. He was sentenced to spend twelve calendar months in the House of Correction.[118] Lord Lansdowne's extensive property was constantly at risk. In October of the same year Bowles was one of the two magistrates who committed Thomas Torrens, who had been an underservant in Lansdowne's family, to Fisherton gaol for trial in connection with the burglary of silver and other property from Bowood.[119]

There were many, of course, who considered that no clergyman should ever act as a magistrate. Bowles made his position quite clear in his *A Word on Cathedral-Oratorios, and Clergy-Magistrates Addressed to Lord Mountcashel*.[120] He wrote, in describing himself as 'an incorrigible sinner – in both frequenting Oratorios, and acting as a magistrate':

> I did hope my head would have been 'laid upon the lap of earth' in my parish church yard, before this most stupid accusation had been revived. I shall, therefore, state to those who think differently, my own view on a subject so important to the welfare of the country poor. It was, on account of them, not on my own, that I consented to take my place among the *squires* of the County, as a Magistrate on the Bench of the Quarter Sessions.
>
> 'Oh! But the office is incompatible,' it is exclaimed, by ten thousand, in and out of the Church.
>
> I admit that the offices are so far distinct, that, except in cases of necessity, and for the good of the community, I would not wish to see a Minister preaching on Sunday, and sending a poacher to prison,

or taking the examination of a frail parish damsel, on Monday. But I contend against the proscription, that in *no case* a Clergyman should be a Magistrate, and appointed upon the necessity of the case, and when there is no County gentleman within distance, he is as much distinguished for rectitude, integrity, and benevolence, as the best of the educated gentlemen, to whom that important post is entrusted. I will say further, that, generally speaking, this important office is not so incompatible with the most momentous clerical duties.[121]

Although Bowles occasionally had some hard things to say about dissenters from the Established Church, he was generally tolerant towards them. On 4 May, when responding to the toast to the Bishop and Clergy for the county of Wiltshire at the annual London dinner of the Wiltshire Society, he said:

Having done justice to the Church of which I am a member . . . I am sure I cannot look round me, and see a worthy brother steward now present, whose countenance beams with benevolence, without proposing the health of Mr Phillips and the Christian Dissenters of the County of Wilts, meaning by the expression, ALL THOSE of whatever religious Communion who hold their opinions without bitterness and in the spirit of Christian charity.[122]

The Wiltshire Society had been founded in 1817 for the purpose of raising money to pay for the cost of apprenticing the children of poor Wiltshire parents resident in London. In 1819 Bowles began making annual subscriptions, thus becaming a governor of the society, and attending the anniversary dinners at the Albion Tavern when visiting London in the summer. There he would have met many men prominent in the affairs of the county or those who had some particular connection with it, and so it was that it was reported that the dinner held in 1821 was attended by 'Sir Thomas Lawrence, Rev. W.L. Bowles and Mr Watson Taylor[123] and several other distinguished characters'.[124] Everyone knew that it was at the Bear Inn in Devizes, where his father was the landlord, that the young Lawrence's prodigious talent for drawing first became apparent; now that he had not only been knighted by the Prince Regent but also appointed President of the Royal Academy, the worthies of the society were doubtless more than delighted to welcome him into their midst. George Watson Taylor's considerable wealth was largely derived from Jamaican estates worked by an enormous number of slaves, so it is likely that Bowles would have been ambivalent about his acquaintance with him.

In January 1820 George III died, and as a consequence Parliament was dissolved. Another contested county election in Wiltshire was thought likely, and Benett, who had fought elections in both 1818 and 1819, began writing to men of influence throughout the county canvassing support. It is likely that he wrote to Bowles, and it seems that he sent the letter on to Lord Lansdowne who, on 10 February replied:

> I return you Mr Bennet's [sic] letter which I read with sincere pleasure & was glad to find we were not mistaken in attributing to him the liberal sentiments he professses. I conclude you will not remain in town so long as the beginning of next month, but if Mr B. comes to town at that time, I shall be very glad if you will contrive that we shall make acquaintance for in Wiltshire I am afraid with Salisbury Plain between us, some time may pass before an opportunity occurs.
>
> If you happen to be disengaged on Friday & will do me the favour to dine here at ½ past 6, I shall be happy to see you.
>
> I shall be much obliged to tell me if you hear whether the private address you allude to is to be presented to the H of Lds & if so, by whom, because I should certainly take that opportunity to say a few words upon that mode of proceeding.[125]

In the event Benett was returned to Parliament unopposed, and was soon to meet Lord Lansdowne when they both addressed a county meeting held in Devizes in March to pass a resolution that a loyal address be sent to the new King.

In 1820 the *New Monthly Magazine* printed a Memoir of the Rev. W.L. Bowles and this was reprinted in full in the *Devizes and Wiltshire Gazette*:

> The life of Mr Bowles, as far as poetry is concerned, will be that of a private clergyman, attentive to the duties of his ministry, studious to the welfare of his flock and watchful to prevent the inroads of fanaticism among them; making it at the same time his pleasure and amusement to do justice to the rural beauties of his parsonage, and to improve it with tasteful embellishments.

The writer continued by commenting at length on Bowles's writings and considered his 'larger poems as much distinguished as his sonnets'. He continues:

> But poetry has by no means monopolised the attention of Mr Bowles. Finding the religious steadiness of his parish endangered, by the

unceasing efforts of dissenting preachers and teachers, he has deeply studied the genuine tenets of our church . . . These enquiries have led him to publish sermons and other works of plain but sound divinity; and have enabled him to teach it with unusual success, by oral instruction . . . He has entered into other controversies and has most happily defended Public Schools, in reply to the buffoonery and calumnies of the Edinburgh Review. He has also defended his own *alma mater*, Winchester, against the attack of Mr Brougham . . . With all his studious occupations, Mr B. has never shrunk from active duties. Of late years he has borne his part in the magistracy of the county of Wilts . . . an annual visit to the metropolis enables him to keep pace with the world in all that is worth observing of its proceedings or its manners.[126]

Bowles's fame was clearly acknowledged when in October 1820 an engraving of a portrait of him, painted by a seemingly unrecognised artist named Mullar, was published by Henry Colburn[127] & Co. of Conduit Street in London. As expected, in this portrait Bowles is depicted dressed as a layman. Some years before his friend Robert Southey, in one of his *Letters from England*, had described how he saw a priest 'walking in his cassock from church – the only time when the priests are distinguished in their dress from the laity'.[128] Many years later, in 1837, another engraving of perhaps the same portrait was published by William Pickering[129] as the frontispiece of Bowles's *Scenes and Shadows of Days Departed* . . .

Following the death of George III, Bowles doubtless followed with interest, and probably astonishment, the conduct of the new King and his estranged Queen Caroline, who returned from abroad to assert her rights as Queen. The introduction of the Bill of Pains and Penalties, the 'trial' of the Queen in the House of Lords and the subsequent withdrawal of the bill persuaded a number of members of the aristocracy and leading gentry of Wiltshire to call a county meeting at Devizes to:

consider the propriety of declaring our unabated and unalterable attachment to the Constitution of this Country, as by law established; of expressing our deep regret at the late unjustifiable and unconstitutional proceedings instituted against the Queen, and of Petitioning both Houses of Parliament to take the most effectual steps for the removal of every obstacle to a satisfactory and final arrangement and to prevent a recurrence to measures of a similar tendency, and the revival of discussions, equally mischievous to the public morals, and dangerous to the peace of the country.[130]

Early in January 1821 Lansdowne wrote to Bowles:

> I believe Mr Douglas has written to you upon the subject of the meeting proposed at Devizes & which I am convinced you agree with me [is] unnecessary and illtimed. I only write therefore to mention that I shall certainly think it my duty to attend there, & hope to meet there those who are friends of moderation upon this important & delicate subject.[131]

Although Lansdowne thought the meeting 'unnecessary and illtimed', he was, nevertheless, one of those who signed the request to the High Sheriff to call the meeting and who addressed the crowd of some ten thousand people who gathered in the Market Place on 17 January.[132] Although not important enough to be mentioned in the press as one of those who were there, it is likely that Bowles responded to his neighbour's letter by also attending.

In June 1821 Bowles was in London again, and was one of the 100 gentlemen 'of the first rank' who attended the annual dinner of the Wiltshire Society at the Albion Tavern. It may be that it was at this time that, at one of Rogers's breakfasts at his house in St James's Street, Bowles met once again the young lawyer's clerk with whom he had played duets, Bowles on his 'cello and his fellow musician on his flute, soon after he had arrived in Bremhill. Bryan Waller Procter, although by now practising as a solicitor in London, devoted much of his time to literature and had recently enjoyed a great success with his tragedy *Mirandola*, which was staged at Covent Garden theatre with Charles Kemble[133] playing Procter's Guido. Procter later wrote:

> When I saw him [Bowles] again, after a lapse of many years, at Mr Rogers' house in St James's Place (1821 or 1822), he at once recognised me; and he seemed pleased at my having obtained a little popularity.
>
> On this occasion, I remember that after breakfast he walked with Mr Rogers and myself to Lansdowne House, in Berkeley Square (to see the pictures), he having the privilege of introducing friends there.[134]

Lansdowne House, a magnificent mansion occupying with its gardens the whole of the southern side of Berkeley Square, was the London house of Lord Lansdowne, and where Bowles was accustomed to avail himself of Lord Lansdowne's invitation that he should feel free to call at the house with his friends to inspect the collection of pictures there.

It appears that in 1821 Thomas Phillipps,[135] the antiquary and bibliophile, was considering purchasing a property in Wiltshire, and thought that Blackland Park, near Calne, might be suitable. As one of the circle of those who were assisting Sir Richard Colt Hoare in his antiquarian and topographical pursuits, Bowles would undoubtedly have become acquainted with him. Another member of this circle was Henry Wansey,[136] the retired clothier with whom Bowles had crossed literary swords while still a curate at East Knoyle and whose labours resulted in that part of Hoare's *Modern History of South Wiltshire* describing the hundred of Warminster. In February Bowles wrote to Phillipps:

> 'Maistre' Henry Wansey has been here & seen Blacklands & told me he should write to you – I requested him to say that if you had any idea of purchasing in this part of the county which you are about to 'illustrate', I should be particularly happy to see you – fixed on Wednesday the 14th.
>
> If you could come on that day & stay a day or two, or as long as you can remain, I shall be happy to ride over with you to Blacklands, tho' I would say nothing about it, fearing you might dislike it.
>
> If you had bought it, I need not say how agreeable it would be for me and Mrs Bowles to have you and Mrs Phillipps neighbours, as I can [illegible] it would be to Lord & Lady Lansdowne. I hope I shall see you on the 14th at 5 o'clock.[137]

It seems that Phillipps failed to arrive on the 14th as, soon after, Bowles wrote again letting him have further particulars of the property at Blackland: 'The house would make a handsome residence. We did not wait for you – I shall be glad if you could have come & hope Mrs Phillipps is well. I shall be at the Assizes if you can come any time.' Phillipps endorsed this letter 'Intended to go to his house therefore no answer necessary'.[138] It is certain that Phillipps did visit Bowles soon afterwards, as among his papers now in the Bodleian Library is to be found a manuscript pedigree of the Lisle family with a note written on it that 'I copied the above while on a visit to Poet Bowles at Bremhill from an ancient blazoned Pedigree on vellum in his possession 1821'.[139]

Another house in Wiltshire that was thought might be suitable for Phillipps to rent was Corsham House (now known as Corsham Court), the property of Paul Methuen. Bowles wrote to Phillipps from Bath while on his way to the Musical Meeting in Bristol, reporting that no progress had been made in the tentative negotiations that had been commenced and advising him 'most strenuously to adhere to the first suggestion of Sir Richard Hoare to take the House if they chose to let it'. However, Bowles added that he considered it was preposterous to suggest that any rent should be paid in addition to the taxes, which would amount to perhaps £50 a year. Indeed he concluded by considering that, 'if they talk of rent, I shall not think it worthwhile to say any more to you on the subject'.[140] It is as well that Phillipps's offer was not accepted, as the house was almost uninhabitable at that time owing to damp penetration and dry rot; indeed, not many years were to pass before John Nash's[141] extension was demolished.

It seems that Phillipps continued for a while to look for a property in Wiltshire, as in December Bowles wrote to him again, this time telling him that 'Scrope[142] was here last week and has written the following proposals respecting his house which I now send you. With our best wishes to Lady Phillipps'.[143] It appears that Phillipps, who had been created a baronet in July, then gave up any thought of moving to the county and in the following year set up his famous private printing press on his Middle Hill estate.

In 1820 and 1821 William Hensley, who was employed by Phillipps to transcribe monumental inscriptions in churches throughout Wiltshire, almost certainly visited Bremhill, where he noted the monuments in the church and also, doubtless at Bowles's suggestion and with Phillipps's approval, the verses that Bowles had written for the edification of the passer-by. These appeared in the six copies of the volume that were eventually printed, and are here reproduced:

Dial and Cross

There rest the Village Dead, and there too I,
When yonder Dial points the hour, must lie.
Look round, the distant prospect is displayed,
Like life's fair landscapes, marked with light and shade.
Stranger, in peace pursue thy onward road,
But ne'er forget thy long and last abode.

As you face this inscription, the dial is on the left,
And the landscape on the right.

Hermitage

To mark the few and fleeting hours,
I plac'd the Dial midst the flowers;
Which, one by one, came forth and died,
Still with'ring round its ancient side;

Mortal, let the sight impart
Its pensive moral to thy heart

Pereunt et Imputantur

Pleasure Seat

Rest, stranger, in this decorated scene,
That hangs its beds of flowers, its slopes of green;
So from the walks of life the weeds remove,
But fix thy better hopes on scenes above.

From this commands a prospect of Compton-Basset House, and other extensive Views.[144]

In November 1821 a visitor at Bowood named Ogden called on Bowles at the parsonage, and on the following day regaled his fellow guests with an account of his visit. Maria Edgeworth wrote to her aunt that Mr Ogden:

> . . . has a great deal of cool, grave gentlemanly humour with which he has just been amusing us with an account of a visit to Bowles the poet – His musical sheep bells and his susceptibility to criticism and his credulity – and his history of his loves Mr Ogden made very diverting. Bowles in the simplicity of his egotism wrote to Murray to desire that he would watch everyone who came into his shop to see whether they read the article in the Edinburgh Review that treats of his controversy with Byron and Gilchrist and begged that whenever any body was seen to take up that review Murray would pop his pamphlet by way of antidote into his hand. Conceive Murray receiving and laughing over this letter in the midst of his room filled with the bel esprits of the day. The history of his loves and of his telling them to Mr Ogden and another gentleman with Mrs Bowles sitting by I must keep for your fireside or for a walk with you to the Weir.[145]

Early in 1822 was published another of Bowles's poems, entitled *The Grave of the Last Saxon or the Legend of the Curfew*, with 500 copies being printed. In the preface to this work, which extends to 100 pages of poetry, Bowles states: 'The circumstances of the late critical controversy with Lord Byron having recalled my attention to a poem, sketched some years ago, on the subject of national history, I have been induced to revive and correct, and now venture to offer it to the public.' The poem was favourably reviewed by William Jerdan[146] in the *Literary Gazette*. Bowles lost no time in writing to him having 'just read the gratifying support your eloquent pen has given my Last Saxon'. After commenting at length on the poem, he concludes his letter:

> Could I, can I, shall I persuade you and Croly[147] & my friend Watts,[148] to come down for a week? Nares[149] is coming the beginning of July – Do pray keep us in your thoughts . . .
>
> Except when I wrote a Poem anonymously I have never had a warm word, from any Critic in my Life – but my little boat somehow or other has got on, in defiance of Cockney-Taste, or Cockney-animosity & the guarded silence of the Quarterly & Edinburgh – This I attribute to the steadiness with which I have steer'd, between Scylla & Charibdis of modern taste, false.[150]

Jerdan, who had started the *Literary Gazette* in 1817, certainly visited Bremhill at some time, and perhaps in July as suggested by Bowles, as in his autobiography published after Bowles's death he writes:

> Mr and Mrs Bowles educated nearly all the poorer class of children in the parish of Bremhill. It was a most gratifying sight to see them feted on the lawn in front of the beautiful mansion on a fine summer day. At a very short distance the Marchioness of Lansdowne was earnestly fulfilling a similar charity for the children around Bowood and Tom Moore, at Sloperton, between the two, thus had visions of a more bountiful and better world than he painted in his biting satires.[151]

Bowles sent a presentation copy of *The Grave of the Last Saxon* to *Blackwood's Edinburgh Magazine*, which had been started in 1817 as a monthly Tory rival to the Whig *Edinburgh Review*. In the July number of *Blackwood's*, Bowles would doubtless have been pleased to see long extracts from the poem printed with a largely favourable review ending with 'But, on the whole, the Grave of the Last Saxon is a far better Poem than the Missionary and corroborates the title of Mr Bowles to occupy a high rank among the living Poets of a poetical age'. He would also have been flattered to have seen himself described as one who 'formed the brightest star of a constellation of genius that rose over Trinity College Oxford' and that he had 'lived to fulfill the promise of his brightening dawn'. However, whether he would have been as amused, as the other readers of *Blackwood's* must surely have been, at the satirical account of the part he had played in the Pope controversy, is more open to doubt.

The writer, who may have been the editor Christopher North (in reality, of course, John Wilson), continues:

> We say that Mr Bowles, has lately distinguished himself as a critic. We allude to the Pope Controversy, in which we find engaged Mr Bowles, Lord Byron, Mr Thomas Campbell, Mr Southey. Mr Wordsworth, Mr Coleridge, Mr Lloyd,[152] Mr D'Israeli, Mr Gilchrist, Mr M'Dermot, Mr Hazlitt, Mr Francis Jeffrey[153] and Mr Christopher North. We know that we took some small part in the contest, but have been racking our brain in vain, to recollect on which side we fought – or indeed, what was the precise bone of contention between the belligerent powers . . . In this, we fear, somewhat irrational row, Mr Bowles appeared to us to manage his morleys with great strength and skill. He floors his man right and left, very much after the manner of our excellent and peaceable friend, the late Jem Belcher,[154] when clearing a boothful of Johnny Raws. To see a gentleman in gown and cassock acting so strenuous a part, was not a little alarming; and the Stamford grocer cried 'Foul, foul'. But the umpires decided the grocer had fallen without a blow, and that, therefore, the rector might kick him a little while down without infringing upon the immutable principles of poetry or pugalism . . . Much was said on both sides – and it was even alleged that Mr Bowles, in the exultation of victory over a man of comfits, gave a facer to our good friend Mr D'Israeli, who stripped and turned to, but the friends of both parties (among whom we were) interfered to prevent a contest; and the Rector, we answer for him, manfully held out in friendship his bunch of Fives.

On 17 June 1822 Bowles wrote to his friend Thomas Phillipps the following letter, which would now perhaps be considered somewhat high-handed:

> If this should find you at home I propose passing two days with you Thursday–Friday –28th & 29th. If I do not hear from you I shall suppose you are not at home, if you are, and this visit would not be inconvenient at this time, have the goodness to send a note to be left for me at the Plough Inn Cheltenham & with kind compliments to Lady Phillipps in which Mrs Bowles joins.[155]

By the 21st Bowles was in Clifton, from where he wrote again to Phillipps:

> Since I wrote to you proposing to go into Gloucestershire next week, I hear that the King's proclamation which will necessarily keep [me] to do duty in

my Church at Bremhill on Sunday the 30th as I will not preach a Charity Sermon upon a particular occasion without a week's previous notice.

Under the circumstances, I am compelled to relinquish coming to Cheltenham until the week after next, leaving Bremhill the 2nd July.

It is probable I shall go to Eastnor Castle, but still if you are at home, & it shall be hopefully convenient to you, I would spend Thursday the 4th instead of the day I fix'd – as there will be intervening time. Will you have the goodness to let me have a line to Bremhill & with kind respects to Lady Phillipps.[156]

Eastnor Castle in Herefordshire was the magnificent recently built seat of the 1st Earl Somers, Bowles's Oxford contemporary who had, as has been seen, in all probability assisted in arranging for him to be presented to the lucrative living of Dumbleton back in 1797. It may be that it was on this visit to Eastnor that Bowles was persuaded to resign from the living, as it was in 1822 that a new incumbent was collated to the benefice. On the 22nd Phillipps responded, writing from London:

Lady Phillipps & myself regret extremely our absence from home & I am sorry to say that illness which still continues will prevent her having the pleasure of meeting you but I wish to return for two days to arrange a few matters so would fix those two days you mention for so doing. I should be glad to know by return of post if this arrangement would be convenient to you, that I may immediately send orders for our reception. I beg my best compliments to Mrs Bowles & yourself.[157]

Having made his arrangements to return home to suit Bowles's convenience, Phillipps must surely have been a little displeased to receive a further letter from Bowles telling him that it would not after all be convenient for him to leave home at that time because he had more friends coming to Bremhill than he had expected. Having then told Phillipps that Scrope had let his house and taken an abbey in Scotland, he proceeds to write:

My 'excellent little poem'[158] is on no less a subject than William the Conqueror! & forms a six shilling volume which I hope you will get. It is published by Hurst & Robinson, Fleet Street. I have also compressed all my controversial criticisms with Lord Byron in one volume after which I commence topographical and antiquities. Pray get a periodical weekly publication call'd the Museum & Literary Gazette, last week, 8 June.[159]

In June, when the *Devizes and Wiltshire Gazette* printed a small part of *The Grave of the Last Saxon* (Bowles's 'excellent little poem'), it was described as being from the pen of 'our immortal Wiltshire bard – the Rev. W.L. Bowles'![160] At the end of the month or early in July 1822, Robert Southey wrote to Bowles mentioning a distant kinswoman of his named Caroline Bowles, and asking whether he had read her latest volume as well as her earlier *Ellen Fitzarthur*, her first books of poetry that were published in 1820 and 1822. Bowles responded:

> You mention my namesake, Caroline. If you write, do make my warmest congratulations to her. Have I read 'Ellen Fitzarthur'? There was only one copy in Bath; no one read a word of it; no one thought of buying it; no one spoke of it. I was the first in the neighbourhood to bring it into notice. I spoke to everyone with the utmost warmth of it, as deeply affecting in story, and beautiful in genuine language of poetry. I trumpeted it to Lord and Lady Lansdowne, Miss Fox, and all the <u>literati</u> of Bowood; and, without knowing the name, I flatter myself I contributed in some degree to its more general notice among some distinguished ornaments of taste and literature. I should be happy to know Caroline, and more to think her a relation. I think a poem so remote from the golden-silvery-diamond-alabaster-Pontypool-style of the present Cockney race of dandy poettasters cannot be too much noticed; and I am rejoiced the real touches of nature and passion have awakened attention.[161]

> P.S. I think I shall write a note to Caroline, with my poem.

She wrote to Bowles soon afterwards:

> . . . I thank you heartily for your good word, for the kind words I know you have spoken to many, of my first venture. Time was when such encouragement might have spurred me on, inspired me to the attempt at least, of something better, but now 'the evil days' seem come upon me, and the 'silver string so loosened' that there is no elasticity of spirit left. Enough however to wish for the pleasure of becoming personally acquainted with you, and if my health mends I <u>may</u> be in your neighbourhood about the latter end of September or the beginning of October. Till then I shall be at home, or within call from home at least, and most happy to see you should you 'wander this way'. I will venture on the ground of our <u>relationship</u> (no longer debatable land) to add that you would find a bed for yourself and shelter for your horse at my little dwelling – very homely accommodation in truth, but as comfortable as good will could make it.[162]

Following the death of her mother in 1816, Caroline Bowles had found herself in very reduced financial circumstances until her father's adopted son settled an annuity of £150 on her. Before this piece of good fortune came her way, she decided to attempt to support herself by her pen, and was encouraged in her poetic efforts by Robert Southey; and many years later became his second wife. Following their initial contact established in 1822, Bowles and Catherine met on a few occasions, and corresponded with each other occasionally.

At this time William Beckford, beset by financial difficulties, arranged to sell by public auction the spectacular contents of Fonthill Abbey in the south-western corner of Wiltshire. The sale catalogue prepared by Christie's whetted the appetite of the rich and famous throughout the land. The proposed ten-day sale caused a sensation, and people flocked in their thousands to pay to see not only the contents but also the Abbey itself. Although Bowles advised against it, John Rutter,[163] the Shaftesbury printer and publisher, seized the opportunity to write and publish *A Description of Fonthill Abbey and Demesne . . . Intended as a Guide to the Visitor, and to convey Information to the more distant Enquirer.* Bowles joined the throng of visitors on 21 August and was moved to write a poem called 'On a first view of Fonthill Abbey', which was published on 26 August in the *Salisbury and Winchester Journal*[164] and three days later in the *Devizes and Wiltshire Gazette.*[165] Although he may have been impressed by some parts of the abbey itself, the same could not be said for the contents. When writing to John Phillips of Melksham in October, Bowles mentioned 'having been on a "Fools' errand", like many others to the sale at Fonthill'.[166]

John Britton decided to write his own account of the abbey and of the Beckford family, and requested Bowles to subscribe to it and to ask Lord Lansdowne to do likewise. Bowles's later thoughts about Beckford's folly and its contents are revealed in a letter written in December to Britton in response to his request:

> I shall be happy to subscribe to Britton's account of Fonthill Abbey tho I do not think it worth describing & I am quite sure the undertaking must be a losing concern, as I told Rutter & I feel bound to say, from the most friendly feelings to you.
>
> My advice is that whatever may be your loss at present, not to add to it for the day is gone by – the <u>nine day</u> wonder is over & no possible mint of execution by any artist, no expense, no pains can ever make a productive work on a non-descript building with the [illegible] of

which the publick mind has been satiated, which never could bear the analysis of common sense & which, when it was most wondered at, was, at best a congeries of absurdity combining a Palace, a Cathedral & a shop of trinkets! I must earnestly and anxiously wish you might succeed, but, having the general feeling I would earnestly hope you might be contented with your first loss – as long ago as the beginning of October, when I first heard of Rutter's design, I requested my sentiments might be communicated to him & when I spoke to every person who knew you requesting my idea might be convey'd to you also.

The Ass[167] who has bought the place will be deservedly punished, but I shall be sorry indeed to see your pains thrown away on a subject of which every one is tired.

I will not fail to speak to Lord L, but I well know his thought coincides with mine & whoever subscribes will subscribe to a Gentleman who has illustrated our most valuable antiquities so well, not on account of this Castle of Thundertontrunk[?]!

I must confess that the view from the stairs thr' the Porch is highly impressive & the gallery & roof of the tower & on this account & to oblige Rutter I wrote a few lines but when you have said this, I think, you have said almost all.[168]

How wrong Bowles was in the advice he tendered to both Rutter and Britton! Rutter soon produced a second edition of his *Description . . .*, enlarged and corrected, and in 1823 his *New Descriptive Guide . . .* appeared. So great was the anticipated demand that his first guide could be purchased not only from Longman, Hurst and Co. in London but also from 'all other booksellers in England' as well as booksellers in Amsterdam, Brussels and Paris. Bowles, but not Lord Lansdowne, duly subscribed to Britton's *Graphical and Literary Illustrations of Fonthill Abbey with Heraldic and Genealogical Notices of the Beckford Family* that also appeared in 1823, with the impressive list of subscribers being headed by the King.

Bowles's poem inspired by his first view of the Abbey duly appeared in the *Gentleman's Magazine*, where it was stated to have been written for the second edition of Rutter's *Description of Fonthill Abbey*.[169] In the event it did not appear in Rutter's book, although it was printed yet again in John Nichols's[170] *Historical Notices of Fonthill Abbey . . .* published twelve years later, where Nichols rather quaintly states that 'the magical effect on the visitor is well described in the following beautiful lines by a sweet Wiltshire Poet'![171]

It is probable that Bowles had asked Britton to arrange for William Bartlett,[172] who had been articled to him, to sketch the north front of the parsonage at Bremhill[173] with a view to it being engraved and published in the history of Bremhill on which Bowles was now engaged. In his letter written to Britton in December, having so contemptuously dismissed the perceived merits of Beckford's abbey and its prodigious contents, Bowles continues:

> Do not let any thing be done to my picture, till I have finished what I am about, a history of Stanley Abbey, concerning which I have made, thro' the grants that Gaby has, a most interesting discovery. The spot where the first Abbey St Mary of Dragonfont was built at Lockwell as well as the name Abb-Fontis Dragonis – you will see probably some verses on it in the next Gentleman's.
>
> I would be oblig'd to you if you would let me know what I am indebted to you for the last Cathedral & what could you have paid Cattermole for on my account . . .
>
> [When] I have done what I am about I would have the <u>front</u> of the house <u>drawn upon stone</u> as I mentioned some time ago, but as nothing has proceeded in, I certainly should wish any demand from Mr Cattermole for more out-lines, which he has in his own port-folio.
>
> If an impression is taken from stone & the drawings are copied on stone, I should wish first to know what the expense would be, the size would be that of an Octave – the impression two hundred and fifty.
>
> Mrs Bowles joins in compliments to Mrs Britton.

In writing to John Phillips of Melksham in October in response to a letter perhaps seeking Bowles's advice about the setting up of a circulating library, Bowles gives his opinion about the various periodicals that were available at this time:

> No periodical publications whatever are circulated except the Edinburgh & Quarterly reviews because tho these are partial & exclusive enough, yet, as on great political questions they are oppos'd something like the truth between may be expected – The others are consider'd too fugitive for extended circulation & their criticisms for the most part too discordant & unprincipl'd to require admission – The members are undoubtedly confin'd to those who reside within a certain distance & I apprehend Melksham would be consider'd as not within the circuit.[174]

In researching the history of Bremhill, Bowles sought the assistance of a number of his friends and acquaintances whose expert knowledge exceeded his own. These included his own brother Charles, his friend Dr James Ingram,[175] President of Trinity College, Oxford, the

Rev. Dr Bulkley Bandinel[176] and Dr Philip Bliss[177] of the Bodleian Library and his friend John Shute Duncan, Keeper of the Ashmolean Library.[178] One of his friends that he consulted was Daniel Lysons,[179] the rector of Rodmarton in Gloucestershire to whom he wrote in November:

> As you are within so small a distance from this, & as I know anything relating to monastic antiquities, which no one has so ably illustrated, is interesting to you, I am not without hopes that a circumstance of which I am about to speak, may induce you, at your leisure, to favour me with your company for a few days.
>
> Having been lately at Stourhead, Sir Richard Hoare enquired what progress I had made in the history of the parish where I reside, which I had promis'd, as a contribution to his County history, & he inform'd me that less was known of the antiquities of Stanley Abbey, founded by Empress Matilda, & in my parish, than of any other antiquity of the kind. As I liv'd on the spot, & had moreover the invaluable treasure of <u>all</u> the original grants to this Abbey . . . as I had the possession of all these grants none of which were ever publish'd, except <u>two</u> by Dugdale,[180] on my return, I resolv'd to examine them all with attention & found them far more illustrative than I could possibly expect (the source being unknown & in no other hands) on the state of the country at the time, & the circumstances connected with the Abbey.

Bowles then explains to Lysons his theory about where the abbey might have stood, near a spring, and continues:

> I have interested my neighbours Lord & Lady Lansdowne with this account who are going with me to see the spring next Monday – it is at the back of his plantations but tho I have found the spring I can find no appearance of [illegible] or indications, such as I can rely upon, but as you are so much more vers'd in these matters, I am persuaded that you will not mind fifteen or twenty miles but will favour me with a visit, for a day or two – If you can fix a day, the sooner the better & the more welcome – could you come on Monday the ninth? Hoping to hear from you.[181]

Chapter 5
1823–1826

On 12 April 1823 Bowles visited Stratford-upon-Avon, and on that day wrote 'The Pilgrim at the tomb of Shakespeare', a poem of sixteen lines. He later sent a copy of it to an un-named recipient, perhaps the publisher of a magazine called *Friendship's Offering* of which Thomas Hervey[1] became editor in 1826, with a note reading:

> The inclosed has not been publish'd – pray, let me know whether Mr Hervey is editor, or any way concerned with 'Christian Remembrancer'. Mr Watts[2] has taken sonnets of mine, on the bust of Milton so this will be appropriate, tho I have purposely avoided the <u>form of a sonnet</u>. Tell Mr Hervey it is somewhat <u>singular</u> – that of five contributions of mine to the annual 'Souvenirs – Forget me not – & Friendships Offering' – every one is upon <u>work</u> of <u>Art</u> – two on the Busts of Milton – in youth & age[3] – on Chantrey's Children[4] – & on the Bust of Shakespeare! –
>
> The basis of all – is eternal & immutable Nature – in stone, in picture, or in poetry. This Mr Hervey <u>will understand</u>.[5]

In June Bowles was in London, on his annual visit to the metropolis. On the 2nd he met Thomas Moore and asked him to go with him to dine with William Linley in Furnival's Inn, where there was to be music. On the next day he breakfasted with Samuel Rogers. Moore was among the party, as well as Archibald Constable,[6] the Edinburgh publisher, and later in the day Bowles, Moore and Constable went to Sir George Beaumont's to look at his pictures,[7] several of which he later presented to the National Gallery, the foundation of which owed much to his endeavours.

Back in Bremhill in July, on Tuesday 8th Bowles called on Moore, who made him stay for dinner – after which there was much talk about the Establishment of the English Church and the attacks then being made on it. Moore noted in his journal that Bowles was a 'thorough Churchman' and 'his efforts at liberality on politics and religion, quite diverting from their abortiveness'. Before leaving for home Bowles asked him to meet the Ricardos (probably the economist David Ricardo,[8] who owned the estate of Gatcombe Park in Gloucestershire and was Member of Parliament for Portarlington, and his wife) on Friday. Realising he had made a mistake, Bowles called at Sloperton Cottage the next morning while the Moores were having breakfast to say that the Ricardos were coming to him on Saturday and not Friday. Moore recorded in his journal that Bowles was 'very amusing in his agonies and exclamations, when I found I was already tied to the Phippes.'⁹ Bowles was reassured when Moore told him that if Bowles could not put off the Ricardos, then he would come to him on Saturday. In the event, Moore went to the Phippeses at one o'clock on Saturday and left them at four to dine with the Bowleses and the Ricardos in the evening. Moore found Mrs Ricardo 'very pretty and amiable' and 'more than pretty, and may be called lovely'. Bowles, who was similarly susceptible to female charms, was doubtless also struck by her beauty. After dinner Moore sung, and was joined by Mrs Ricardo in a duet or two.

Moore spent the night at the parsonage, and the next day recorded in his journal:

> Begged him to come and christen our young one, which he promised to do on Monday. Said he would choose for his text today [it was Sunday, and Moore was to attend the service in Bremhill church] my words, 'Fallen is thy throne, O Israel,' which I sung last night, and which is one of his greatest favourites. Told him I believed these words were not in Scripture, and that he had better not venture to make them his text. He, however, introduced them thus (for he preaches extempore): – After quoting 'By the waters of Babylon,' he said, 'Such was the pathetic song of the Jews when they mourned over their lost country; but a still more pathetic song might be founded on that period, when they saw their temple itself destroyed, &c., and when they might say, "Fallen is thy throne, O Israel."' He introduced this line more than once . . . By the by, Mr Bowles copied out those pretty lines of his for me from Miss Bailey's 'Miscellany,' 'When last I saw thee, thou wert young and fair,' which he wrote to the lady whom he was so violently in love with when he composed his first sonnets, and went abroad in despair of not being able to marry her from the narrowness of his circumstances. I was with him in Bath when he saw her for the first time after an interval of thirty years, and when the lines in Miss Bailey's book were written.¹⁰

This sonnet written by the love-sick Bowles was printed anonymously in Joanna Baillie's¹¹ *A Collection of Poems, Chiefly Manuscript, and from Living Authors* that had just been published.¹²

On the next day Bowles duly appeared at Sloperton Cottage to christen Moore's young son. Bowles baptised him John Russell after his godfather by proxy, Moore's friend Lord John Russell, later Prime Minister and the first editor of his journals.

Bowles and Moore frequently dined in each other's houses, and Bowles in particular arranged dinner parties with eight guests, including Moore, who was always the star musical performer. So it was that on 5 November:

> Had promised Bowles to go and dine with him today, but the weather so bad, that it was impossible to venture in my gig; so gave up all thought of it, and dined with Bess [Moore's wife] at two. A little after four, however, a chaise arrived ordered by Bowles so was obliged to go. Company at dinner, Mr and Mrs Lysons and their two daughters (from Gloucestershire), Mr Clarke (the Winchester man, who wrote a pamphlet against Brougham on the Education question) and his wife, and Mr Hume,[13] the Vicar of Calne. Day very pleasant; music in the evening . . . Mrs L and her daughters sung 'Verdi prati'[14] to the English words. Slept there as did the Lysons.[15]

Next morning the Lysons family left after breakfast and Moore:

> Tried over some of Purcell's songs for Bowles; one that I sung at first sight rather surprised him; and with 'Mad Bess'[16] he was enchanted. Said my performance of these things (he being all for the old school) had elevated his opinion of my musical powers exceedingly. Proposed to him to undertake with me a set of biographical notes of these old composers; said he would.[17]

Nothing appears to have come of Moore's proposal.

Two days later Bowles was at Corsham as the guest of Paul Methuen and there he met William Rose,[18] the poet and not particularly conscientious reading clerk of the House of Lords and clerk of the private committees. Bowles normally found it easy to converse with all manner of people but he found Rose difficult. On the following day he wrote to Caroline Bowles and, after reporting that Rose had spoken highly of her, mentioned that so far as Rose was concerned 'his wit, when he condescended to talk, is too elaborate for me'.[19]

At the end of the month Bowles and Magdalene went to Bath together, Moore to see his daughter Anastasia who was at school there. Moore and the Bowleses dined together at the White Hart, where 'B would give me a bottle of claret' as he recorded in his journal, before going to the opera. They stayed in Bath overnight and left the next day at one o'clock. On the journey home they had 'a good deal of conversation about the religion of the Church of England'.[20]

In August the *Devizes and Wiltshire Gazette* printed a poem entitled 'Restoration of Malmesbury Abbey' 'respectfully inscribed to Lady Catherine Bisset by the Rev. Mr Bowles of Bremhill'. Following the Dissolution the nave of Malmesbury's abbey church had been given to the town to be used as its parish church, and by the beginning of the nineteenth century was greatly in need of restoration. This had now been undertaken under the supervision of Goodridge,[21] the Bath architect, and the verses 'were written under the contemplation of this singularly beautiful and unique pile being open again for public worship, by a Sacred Musical Performance'.[22]

In 1823 Bowles arranged to have published by Hurst and Robinson under the pseudonym of 'A Member of the University of Oxford' *A Voice from St Peter's and St Paul's; being a Few Plain Words addressed to the Members of Both Houses of Parliament, on some late accusations against The Established Church; particularly those contained in Number LXXV of the Edinburgh Review; with General Observations*. Why the 'Few Plain Words' should have come from St Peter's and St Paul's remains something of a mystery. The chapel of ease at Highway in the parish of Bremhill was dedicated to St Peter and the quotation on the title page of this pamphlet of sixty-seven pages comes from the words of St Paul, so perhaps this is the explanation.

At the same time Hurst and Robinson also published a poem that Bowles had written entitled *Ellen Gray: or The Dead Maiden's Curse*, once again under a pseudonym, this time of 'The late Dr. Archibald Macleod', although in one of his letters to the publishers he calls himself 'the late Dr Archibald Ma'Kettrick M.D.'!

Before publication, on 4 June while in London, Bowles wrote to Hurst and Robinson. This letter reveals how Bowles was always anxious to be fair in his financial dealings with his publishers, and also the machinations involved in attempting to deceive the public into thinking that the pamphlets were by different authors and had no connection whatsoever one with the other:

> Mr Bowles presents his compliments to Messrs Hurst & Robinson & thinks it right to inform them, before he leaves Town, that he spoke to the Printer, Mr Moyes [?], wishing to ascertain what additional expense, in the printing, he had caus'd by some important omissions, & some troublesome alterations of the letter-press.
>
> The cause was that Mr Bowles has spoken on a subject to which the person chiefly concern'd & whom he was anxious to serve, objected,

& therefore, at any trouble and expense, thought it necessary for the wishes of the person concerned should be consulted. Added to this, Mr Bowles having had the pleasure of seeing Mr Constable from his own feelings, was anxious that not one word should appear, respecting the Edinburgh Review, to which its distinguished publishers might object.

Mr Moyes told him he thought the alterations would not exceed three pounds to Messrs Hurst & Robinson, they might not be charged so much, but they might be more, & as the sale may be uncertain, & after all, these alterations take off from the profits, Mr Bowles thinks it just even in the onset, to take all additional expenses on himself.

He therefore sends a draft for Ten pounds out of which, he would request Messrs Hurst & Robinson to pay three pounds, thirteen shillings & sixpence to Hunt & Longmans, on account of his subscription to Ingram's Saxon Chronicle[23] – The remainder may be applied to the additional charges of printing, & a few advertisements, directly.

Mr Constable has acted in the kindest manner, about 'The Poem' [Ellen Gray] which will come out under a Scottish name & with Mr Constable's name as chief publisher – Mr Bowles has particular reasons for this with which Mr C is acquainted & nothing could be more fortunate than meeting him.

Pray, let the Poem, & the Pamphlet be announce'd as forthcoming, in all accessible quarters of the public press. It should hope a week or ten days at most should finish the printing of each.

As one of them, the Poem, comes apparently from Edinburgh, the other from London, there can be less objection to their being announced at the same time but I think a paragraph might be inserted in different papers that a Poem, called Ellen Gray, or the Maiden's Curse, will be published very shortly from the vast literary laboratory, Mr Constable, of Edinburgh, or some thing to this effect, if you do not object.

I hope & believe this Poem will do his name no discredit – my object is two-fold, first to deceive, if I can, some who I know would abuse, if presented with my own name; 2dly to show the difference between bold & vulgar simplicity, on the one hand, & nauseous, affected prettinesses [?] on the other; & in the announcement do not forget to say it will be dedicated to Joanna Baillie. A paragraph something like this would answer

'We have to announce that very shortly will be publish'd by Mr Constable, Edinburgh, a Poem call'd Ellen Gray or the Maiden's Curse by the late Dr Archibald Ma'cleod dedicated to Joanna Baillie'
... Mr Constable suggested Mackindoe, as a name but I think Ma'cleod would be better but I should wish him to be consulted, for nothing was so kind, as his whole manner, & you will of course give him 6 copies of

the Poem, and a copy of the 'Voice', I should also wish to give him from me, a copy of my first volume – Sonnets – & other poems if you can procure them in London. I believe this volume, however, has been long out of print, but Longman's perhaps might have a copy.[24]

The great secrecy that Bowles wished to maintain as to the authorship of these two works is emphasised by the following letter addressed to them at this time being marked 'Private':

> Mr Bowles particularly requests that Messrs Hurst & Robinson will not forget to announce . . . [here Bowles sets out the full title of *A Voice from St Peter's & St Paul's* and the name of the author] & pray also let there be <u>announced</u> on the 10th . . . [here Bowles sets out the full title of *Ellen Gray* and the name of the author].
>
> Take especial care that these appear separate publications – All Expenses, if exceeding the profits, being cheerfully paid, & all profit on five hundred copies, given up to the Publishers, it is hop'd these will be put forward . . .[25]

On 29 June Bowles was again writing to the publishers, and in this letter shows how sensitive he was to any errors creeping into his work – which he believed would instantly attract the attention of his critics:

> Mr Bowles must beg <u>the bill for the printing</u> the Prose pamphlet, as soon as it is received – Mr Bowles really must, in this point, be directed by his feelings.
>
> 'Ellen' looks very well in her <u>new dress</u>, great care must be taken to correct one fault, by a Pen, if it is too late for an Errata & <u>particular care</u> in the copy sent to the Monthly Review & Monthly Magazine.
>
> Page 26 it is printed, line 16 –
>
> Gasping he wakes and with a convulsive start
>
> It is a syllable too much – the '&' should be cross'd with a pen & the punctuation thus
>
> 'Gasping he wakes – with a convulsive start –'
>
> stroke after 'start'
>
> Mr Bowles is more particular about this as <u>such a line</u> will be <u>pointed out</u> by the Monthly Review, as a Specimen of the versification, if they quere [*sic*] as the author, as they did from one alliterative line, in the Saxon which was owing to their inadvertence no one disdaining such breaches so much as the person to whom it was objected.
>
> If a copy is sent to the Monthly let another copy be sent pointing out the correction & for the copies not sent out, a small bit of paper

might be fixed containing this one correction & <u>two more</u> the only ones Mr Bowles perceives – Page 27 – line 10 for 'where once, above the solitary main' read 'Where once, tis said, in clouds above the main'
Page 15 – note for 'British Tragedy' read 'Maid's Tragedy'.[26]

Having decided to dedicate the poem to Joanna Baillie it was, of course, necessary to inform her of this, so on 4 July Bowles duly wrote to her:

> I had some particular reasons for publishing a small poem anonymously & under Constable's auspices, as if from Edinburgh & I took the liberty of inscribing it to you. I could not for a moment think of doing this without informing you & I need not say the dedication is owing to sincere respect for you & admiration of your genius – I have only to ask one especial favour – I may possibly publish the poem with my name & if you will have the goodness to look it over with a critical eye, I should be much oblig'd to you, if you would suggest what you think would be an improvement, what passages might be corrected or what left out.
>
> No one but Rogers & the booksellers know the secret – I have doubts whether 'dead maiden's curse' does not sound [illegible] – would not 'maniac maiden's curse' do better? Or Ellen Gray – alone –
>
> If you think so, have the goodness to write by <u>the same</u> post one line to Hurst & Robinson's Cheapside –
>
> I have desir'd them to <u>wait your</u> orders – for, being here <u>alone</u> & my mind completely in a <u>mist</u> about a Prose-Pamphlet I really cannot decide – Trusting you will excuse this trouble & that my secret will for the present be <u>preserved</u>.[27]

Before publication Bowles had asked Thomas Moore to have *Ellen Gray* 'announced for him'![28] And in the preface he made some very strong comments on the literary taste of the day. In a letter written to Caroline Bowles in November, Bowles explained why he had taken what for him was a most unusual course of action:

> As to the Doctor, I did not mean to deceive you, for I thought as Caroline did not write the Poem, she would think from what I said another Bowles might. The sole reason for my putting another name was the petty malice of those votaries of 'Apollar', in a certain kingdom of Cokaine, whom I was willing to deceive as I had done once before, but surely there is not much 'treachery' in doing that by which no human being is injured and by which I might escape gross insult, for my preface

would be considered as an attack on the admirers of false simplicity, false sentiment, and false sublimity . . .

My old friend, the Bishop of London, and his family, passed a couple of days here, a few days ago, but there is no one in [the] world whom I should be more happy to see than Mr Southey, of whom I have a far higher opinion than of any other writer of the age.[29]

It was in the previous month, in October, that Bowles's old friend William Howley, the Bishop of London since 1813, had stayed at the parsonage on his way to his palace in Fulham. The *Devizes and Wiltshire Gazette* reported:

The Right Reverend Prelate attended divine service at the parish church twice on Sunday and expressed himself much gratified by the manner of the celebration, the singing, etc. His Lordship was also highly pleased by the appearance of the children of Mrs Bowles's school who assembled, as usual, on the lawn of the parsonage and there repeated their lessons and hymns. A selection of sacred music from Mozart, Haydn etc was performed in the evening by the Rev. Mr West and family, of the Moravian establishment at Tytherton in the parish of Bremhill.[30]

It is clear that Bowles much enjoyed the monthly visits paid by the Wests to the parsonage for the purpose of playing music together, and it is perhaps to the credit of Bowles that he felt no need to hide from this eminent churchman his friendship with a dissenting minister of religion living and exercising his calling within his parish. The members of the West family would no doubt recall in later years how they made music for the man who later, when Archbishop of Canterbury, would convey to the young Victoria at five o'clock in the morning in Kensington Palace the news that she was now Queen.

Just before Christmas Moore recorded that he 'went at two to assist at the opening of the new domestic chapel that Lord Lansdowne has built. Bessy most anxious to go, but prevented by the want of a new bonnet; Bowles's sermon much too long and desultory'.[31] However, the *Gentleman's Magazine* reported that it was on 21 January that 'A beautiful chapel, completed by the Marquis of Lansdowne at Bowood Wilts, for family worship was opened this day by the Rev. W.L. Bowles'.[32]

One of Bowles's more unusual eccentricities was his practice of composing epitaphs to be placed over the graves of his deceased parishioners. In January the *Devizes and Wiltshire Gazette* printed the epitaph by 'Rev. W.L. Bowles Pastor of the Parish' on Benjamin

Tremlyn, who died at the age of ninety-two and was buried on the previous 1 December:

> A poor old soldier shall not lie unknown
> Without a verse, and this recording stone
> 'Twas his, in youth, o'er distant lands to stray
> Danger and Death companions of his way.
> Here in his native village, drooping age
> Clos'd the lone evening of his pilgrimage
> Speak of the past, – of names of high renown –
> Or his brave comrades long to dust gone down
> His look with instant animation glow'd
> Tho ninety winters on his head had snow'd
> His Country, whilst he liv'd, a boon supplied
> And Faith her shield held o'er him when he died
> Hope, Christian, that his spirit lives with God
> And pluck the wild weeds from the lowly sod,
> Where dust to dust, beside the chancel's shade
> Till the last trump, a brave Man's bones are laid.[33]

This epitaph reached a much wider audience when soon afterwards it was printed in the *Gentleman's Magazine*;[34] the stone on which it was engraved now hangs on the external wall of the church at Bremhill, where it can be easily and clearly read by worshippers and others on their way to the south porch. With Bowles's name appearing at the end of the epitaph, his identity as author will be long remembered.

Another epitaph, this time for William Jenner, who died at the age of eighty-seven, and his wife, was written by Bowles in the character of a most exemplary son:

> My father – my poor mother! Both are gone,
> And o'er your cold remains I place this stone,
> In memory of your virtues – may it tell,
> How *long one* parent lived, and *both* how *well*,
> And oh! My mother, a memorial be
> Of all I owe in this sad world to thee!
> How poor, alas! This tribute to thy love,
> Whose best and brightest record is above.

In his *Parochial History of Bremhill* published in 1828, Bowles added a footnote to this epitaph:

When this last epitaph on the parents of an exemplary parishioner, William Jenner, was shewn to the stone-mason (and the writer has had *worse* public critics in his time), he observed that the lines *might* do with a *little alteration!* I think the four first lines ran thus, as altered –

My father and my mother too, are dead,
And here I *put* this grave-stone at their head.
My father liv'd to eighty-seven – my mother,
Not quite *so long*, and *one* died after *t'other!*[35]

Bowles was able to turn his hand to all manner of poetic styles. The following lines, sung by the Wild Woman of the Woods in the third canto of *The Grave of the Last Saxons*, have appeared in several anthologies of favourite poetry:

Oh! when 'tis Summer weather,
And the yellow bee, with fairy sound,
The waters clear is humming round,
And the cuckoo sings unseen,
And the leaves are waving green – Oh! then 'tis sweet,
In some retreat,
To hear the murmuring dove;
With those whom on earth alone we love,
And to wind through the green-wood to-gether.

But when 'tis Winter weather
And crosses grieve,
And friends deceive,
And rain and sleet
The lattice beat –
Oh! Then 'tis sweet
To sit and sing
Of the friends with whom, in the days of Spring,
We roamed through the greenwood together.[36]

It seems certain that by this time Bowles had met, perhaps at Bremhill, Alaric Watts and his wife. Watts's contributions to the *Literary Gazette* had resulted in his becoming acquainted with many men well known in the world of literature. In 1822 he became editor of the *Leeds Intelligencer*, and in the following year his volume of poems entitled *Poetical Sketches* was published. In December 1823 he wrote to Bowles, who responded on Christmas Day by writing:

It has given me great pleasure to hear from you, and still more to hear that you are so well established at Leeds. I thought that as an editor there was great facility and power in your pen.

I assure you that whenever I have read your poems which I am delighted to find have been so successsful, I have felt as though I had scarcely done them justice. No one can be more sensible than I am of the melody, pathos, and purity of your poetry. I hardly know anything in the English language so affecting as the lines on first hearing the voice of an infant. Your Ten Years Ago is truly exquisite. In your next edition, pray do not forget, in the beautiful lines entitled The Profession, to reconsider the imagery respecting 'words' streaming. We may say a stream of eloquence flows, for then the metaphor is entire; but the one which you use in The Profession is too abrupt. You will excuse these observations; I do not think I should object to another expression in the whole volume. I beg my best regards, and those of Mrs Bowles, to Mrs Watts.[37]

On 24 January 1824 Bowles was dining at Lacock Abbey, and on the following day his host, William Fox Talbot,[38] wrote to his stepfather Charles Fielding:

Yesterday Mr & Mrs Moore dined here and Bowles, who entertained us extremely with his naivety – He produced a letter he had just received addressed 'Revd W.L. Bowles Author of Sonnets' from the committee of chimney sweeping-abolitionists who are for the preventing the employment of climbing boys; they asked him to contribute towards a work to be written by some of the first poets of the age, in dispraise of chimney sweeping – He then asked Moore to contribute & produced his own contribution which Moore read to us, tho' inclined to laugh at first, but it proved to be a little sonnet pretty enough . . .[39]

As will be seen, the 'Author of Sonnets' in his usual willing fashion did indeed respond to this invitation.

It is likely that Bowles would have heard that in the February number of the London Magazine there appeared another satire, written once again by John Hamilton Reynolds, in which he was named. The article included a fictional report of charges brought by the 'Literary Police' against a number of literary offenders and of the hearings before the magistrates. The first offender to be brought before the magistrates was Wordsworth and the second was Coleridge, 'the same person, though much altered, who passed himself off as the Ancient Mariner, at a marriage in the metropolis some time back' and 'who was brought up for idling about the suburbs of town'. The third offender was Bowles:

> The Rev. Mr Bowles was charged with stealing fourteen lines from an old gentleman's garden, of the name of Petrarch,[40] at Putney. But he stating that he was not aware of his own dishonesty, and it appearing that the things were of little or no value – he was reproved and discharged. It was supposed that he had stolen these fourteen lines to hang himself with. This is the same person who was taken up on suspicion of being concerned in the attempted murder of Alexander Pope, at Twickenham, some time ago. But it appearing that he had no idea of what he was doing, and was generally reckoned a harmless man – he was not detained. He said he could appear to his own character.[41]

The 'fourteen lines' referred, of course, to Bowles's early sonnets, with Petrarch considered to be the creator of the model. The reference to Bowles being ready to 'appear to his own character' mocks the vanity Bowles was thought to display in praising his own works. It is likely that, if Bowles was aware of this attack on his character and works, he decided not to respond to it.

In April Bowles's old adversary Lord Byron died in Greece; his body was brought back to England for burial after lying in state for two days. Having heard that Byron's body was laid to rest beside that of his mother in the church at Hucknall Torkard, Bowles was moved to write a poem in tribute to him entitled 'Childe Harold's Last Pilgrimage'. The Rev. George Gilfillan, whose collection of Bowles's poetical works was published in 1855, considered this to be the most interesting of Bowles's minor poems:

> As proceeding from one whom the angry and unhappy Childe [i.e. Byron] had often insulted in public and laughed at in private, it was as graceful in spirit as it is elegant in composition. 'Revenge,' it has been said, 'is a feast for the gods;' and the saying is true if meant of that species of revenge which gains its ends by forgiveness. An act so noble and generous as the writing of this, is calculated to set the memory of Bowles still higher than all his poetry.[42]

In 1830 Thomas Moore's acclaimed *Letters and Journals of Lord Byron* was published. The fourth volume concludes with almost the whole of Bowles's *Childe Harold's Last Pilgrimage*, preceded by Moore's words:

From among the tributes that have been offered, in prose and verse and in almost every language of Europe, to his memory, I shall select two which appear to me worthy of peculiar notice, one of them . . . and the other as being the production of a pen, once engaged controversially against Byron, but not the less ready as these affecting verses prove, to offer the homage of a manly sorrow and admiration at his grave.[43]

On 25 April Moore wrote in his journal: 'Drove to Bowles's to dinner . . . found Bowles suffering, more from nervousness and apprehension, than from real illness; is horrified by some extracts he had seen from "Captain Rock".'[44] This is another contemporary mention of an illness from which Bowles appears to have suffered for the rest of his life. Some six years earlier, when writing to her stepmother in 1818, Maria Edgeworth had noted:

Now there is a trait of this man's character which from all that you have heard you would never guess. He is one of the greatest cowards existing – afraid in a carriage – afraid in a room by himself – afraid in a large room – afraid in a large bed – afraid like a child of 4 years old. One night at Bowood when he was to return home in his carriage in the dark he fell into agonies exclaiming that he should certainly die of it if he got into a carriage. Lady Lansdowne asked him to stay all night. So he did – but in the morning he came down all pale to breakfast. He had been so frightened when he wakened and found himself in so large a room – so large a bed. He would never sleep at Bowood again.[45]

Numerous similar anecdotes have been recorded of Bowles's increasingly eccentric behaviour, and it is certain that he had developed some sort of phobia. 'Captain Rock' mentioned by Moore refers to his first serious prose work, *Memoirs of Captain Rock*, which had just been published. It is likely that Bowles was horrified by what he had read, because the book is an indictment of the church in Ireland and of tithes in particular. A week later Magdalene called on Moore, with General Peachey,[46] and asked him to go back with her to dinner, which he duly did. There, as he notes in his journal:

. . . found Bowles in the same nervous state as before, but laughed him out of it; and he was as hearty and lively at dinner as ever. Would insist that he was a Whig; a Whig of Burke's school. I said, 'Yes, such a Whig as Burke[47] was before he turned.' Took my book to leave with him, but he refused to read it. His paper, 'St James's Chronicle,' abuses it, he tells me most violently; he will read the abuse readily enough but won't read the book . . .[48]

However, by the following month Bowles seems to have almost regained his usual health, with Crabbe telling Elizabeth Charter in a letter that he had seen Bowles in London and that he was 'much better; indeed nearly recovered and his spirits were in their usual state'.[49]

As fond of Bowles as Moore surely was, the occasional entry in his journal reveals that the constant visits between the parsonage and Sloperton Cottage could on occasion cause some irritation. On 7 August he was 'Interrupted by visitors all morning; Bowles, with Archdeacon Nares, Nugent, &c &c. What am I to do?'.[50]

In this year was published *The Ark: a dramatic oratorio. Written expressly for musical effect*. In the preface Bowles explains the background of this unusual work:

> The following poem, if poem it may be called, was written six or seven years ago and was given to Mr Bishop,[51] as an oratorio in consequence of his having signified his wish to have some words for music on this subject. As no use was made of it, it was thrown by: but some circumstances have induced me to pay greater attention to it, to revise, and print a few copies.
>
> Although MUSICAL effect was the chief object I had in view, I have endeavoured to complete it, so that it may be read as poetry, and I further hope (tho from the *confined* nature of the subject this is almost impossible) I may have added something like dramatic interest to it, by the contrasts of characters.
>
> One of the songs in the Ark (Go, beautiful and gentle Dove) was accidentally seen by Mr Moore and was sung by him. It will be published by Mr Power in the ensuing season.[52]

In the event 'Go beautiful and gentle dove: a song, from an Oratorio called the Ark, written and composed by W.L. Bowles' was indeed published.[53] The first public airing of *The Ark* appears not to have been particularly auspicious. In June 1824 Sir George Smart[54] presented a series of concerts in Bath. Some of the annotations made by Smart on his own copies of the programmes are most amusing. In reference to the performance, which occupied forty-two minutes, of 'a selection from an unpublished sacred poem *The Ark*, written by the Rev. W. Lisle Bowles, and set to music expressly for this festival by W.C. Manners', he

C. W.

indignantly says: 'A most disgraceful performance this *Ark*, owing to the incorrect state of the parts and apparent want of knowledge to correct the wind instruments.' And against the air 'Never, oh never', he writes: 'The parts were so incorrect here that first Mr Lindley [violincello] left off playing, next Mr Loder [violin]; I went on alone, receiving not the least assistance from Mr Manners who stood at my right hand.'[55]

As a county magistrate, Bowles was sometimes called upon to exercise his duties and impose his authority in quite unusual circumstances. In August 1824 he was attending the close of the Musical Festival in Salisbury Cathedral when, as the *Devizes and Wiltshire Gazette* reported:

> A Salisbury tradesman, a Mr Shakespeare, was violently assaulted by a man (who called himself a constable) who said that he was given in his charge as a pickpocket, who with another constable dragged him through the 500 or so in the cathedral (his coat and waist coat being nearly torn from his back) to a vestry where he was locked up. Soon afterwards, a friend of Shakespeare perceived Mr Estcourt[56] and Rev. Mr Bowles, two county magistrates, related the circumstances, demanded an immediate admission to the vestry and set Mr S. at liberty.[57]

Immediately after the close of the festival Bowles travelled some 15 miles to Wardour, the seat of the Catholic Lord Arundell, where on Sunday 22 August he met Thomas Moore, who recorded:

> Bowles there, having come over from Salisbury; attended mass with us . . . Bowles, himself, said to me as we knelt together, 'Only think of my being on my knees beside "Captain Rock" at mass'. The singing to a fine organ, very good. Lady Arundell herself joining in it. Bowles remarked the effect of the light falling on her face as she sung.[58]

In the middle of September Bowles called on Moore, who noted in his journal: 'Fixed for us to come to him next Monday, to his Moravian Concert.'[59] This he duly did, and when he arrived at the Parsonage:

> he found Bowles and his party fiddling away most industriously; besides the Moravians, who were six in number, there was Mr Humphreys of Chippenham, and Mr Fenwick, a parson. Had a card of the concert printed, in which I was set down both as composer and singer. The whole day highly amusing. Set to music again after dinner. Slept there.[60]

It seems that during 1824 Bowles approached Alaric Watts, who had a close relationship with his publishers Hurst and Robinson, about the possible publication of a selection of his early sonnets and poems. There was a difficulty, however, because the copyright of some had been assigned to the original publishers, and so Bowles sought Watts's advice as to how he should proceed. On 18 September he wrote:

> As to the proposed volume of selections there was an assignment to the publishers of the copyright of the first volumes. There would be no difficulty with Cruttwell, but there might, he thinks, be some with Mawman and Cadell.[61] The bargain was a gross imposition; for my poems, though I did not know it at the time, were the most saleable and popular productions of the day, in defiance of critics who did not spare them. The booksellers were proprietors, and published them almost in successive years six, eight, nine, ten, and eleven editions with little knowledge of the world, without a single literary advisor, and ignorant above all things, of such transactions, and the market value of such commodities, I received from them altogether only sixty pounds.
>
> Moore thinks that if they offer an opposition to the selection, the whole circumstances should be brought before the public for the good of poor authors; and as I am not a poor author, it should be 'marte meo'. Before I take any step, let me know your opinion.
> Believe me, ever most sincerely yours
> W.L. Bowles
>
> P.S. Whatever I have said about the sale of my poems the cause of their success was that they had something of nature, and nothing common with Hayley[62] and Seward,[63] the objects of my early scorn.[64]

It is certain that Bowles knew that he would have 'no difficulty with Cruttwell', as much later, in 1837, he described the circumstances surrounding the publication of his first sonnets by the printer 'with whose family I have lived in kindest amity from that hour'.[65]

It is likely that during the summer or early autumn of 1824 Samuel Rogers was staying at Bowood, and that Bowles, Moore and Crabbe were among the other guests. On 6 October Rogers received a letter from Uvedale Price,[66] the writer on the 'picturesque', who wrote:

> I wish I could have met you and the grand chorus of Bards at Bowood; it would have been a lucky moment, for though I so much like both Lord and Lady Lansdowne, and am so curious to see the place again after a

very long interval, that I should have wished for nothing more, yet such a party I must own would have enhanced the pleasure . . . So much for old times and the company I <u>did</u> meet at Bowood, now those I unluckily did <u>not</u>. Bowles, as you know, I am well acquainted with, but not as a flute player, and on that, as well as on every other account, I should have been very glad to have met him, and have heard him perform his water-music and do the honours of his water-party. A Greek poet is very severe on flute-players: he allows that the gods have given them a mind, but that out it flies with the first puff of their breath . . . [67]

Towards the end of October Moore described in his journal an all-male musical evening held by Bowles at the parsonage. He relates how he returned to Bowood, dressed and:

set off with Lord L [Lord Lansdowne] to dinner at Bowles'. Company, Bingham,[68] Linley, Lord L, Phipps,[69] and myself. Bowles mentioned that at some celebration at Reading school, when the patrons or governors of it (beer and brandy merchants) were to be welcomed with a Latin address, the boy appointed to the task thus spoke to them, 'Salvete, hospites celebeerimi,' and then turning to the others, 'Salvete, hospites celebrandi'. A good deal of singing in the evening; Linley, Bingham, and I sung several of Calcott's glees, which went off particularly well; Bowles in raptures. Slept there (instead of returning with Lord L) in order to look over the sheets of Bowles's new pamphlet to Roscoe, in the morning.[70]

Lord Lansdowne almost immediately returned the compliment by writing to Bowles:

Dear Bowles

Mr & Mrs Younge [?] have promised to dine here tomorrow – will you and Mrs B. do us that favour also – we shall be most happy to see you
     Yours truly
     Lansdowne

I conclude your guests have left you or we should be glad to see either Mr Bingham or Mr Linley[71]

Despite their difference in rank in an exceedingly class-conscious society, Lord and Lady Lansdowne clearly saw nothing unusual in inviting Bowles and Magdalene to dine at Bowood when their fellow guests were drawn from the very highest level of the social hierarchy. So it was that when Thomas Moore walked to Bowood to dine there at the end of November, his fellow guests were the Earl and Countess of Pembroke,[72] Colonel Young and Sir Stamford Raffles[73] as well as the Bowleses. Doubtless Bowles enjoyed hearing Moore singing in the evening with Lady Pembroke, the daughter of the Russian Count Simon Woronzow, although she did not seem to care much about Moore's singing, except in his duets with her![74]

On 1 November another musical evening was held at the parsonage, this time the regular meeting with the West family from Tytherton. On the next day Bowles wrote to Edward Phillips:

> I should be most truly happy to wait on you, but I have at present company in the house, and am not certain how long they will stay, added to which, I have scarce an hour to spare, owing to publick attacks which I feel myself bound to answer.
> Having done with Lord Byron, I now have Old Roscoe again on me, but I shall silence them <u>both</u> very shortly.
> All the Wests dined here yesterday & we had excellent music – I hope you will come over, the next concert, which is the <u>first</u> Monday in every month[75]

In 1820 the Royal Society of Literature had been founded, but it did not commence regular activity until 1823. Bowles was one of the early members of the society, whose records indicate that he was a member by 1824 at the latest.[76] The first president was Thomas Burgess,[77] Bishop of St David's but soon to be translated to Salisbury.

Bowles continued to be in receipt of income from the living of Bremhill as well as that derived from his position as a prebendary of Salisbury Cathedral and from his literary output and personal investments. Bowles was very conscious of the social evils that were prevalent in the first half of the nineteenth century, and was never slow to use some of his ample income to help alleviate the hardships endured by large sections of the people. And so when James Montgomery,[78] the Scottish poet, embarked on a crusade to see the practice of chimney sweeps sending boys up chimneys abolished by law, Bowles was one of the poets who contributed to his *The Chimney-Sweeper's Friend and Climbing Boys' Album*.[79]

An act of benevolence expected of a wealthy countryman was to treat at Christmas time the poor of his neighbourhood to a substantial meal, usually with a plentiful supply of beer. It is no surprise to find, therefore, that on Christmas Day Bowles gave a dinner of Old English fare to 400 of his parishioners.[80]

In January 1825 Bowles attended the grand opening of the Literary and Scientific Institute at Bath. Lord Lansdowne took the chair. Among the 100 or so other guests were Thomas Moore and George Crabbe. Lord Lansdowne alluded to the three poets in his first speech, and Moore reported in his journal that in referring to Bowles he said:

> His poetry was the first fountain at which I drunk the pure freshness of the English language, and learned (however little I might have profited from my learning) of what variety the music of English verse is capable. From admiration of the poet, I had been at length promoted into friendship with the man, and I felt it particularly incumbent upon me, from some late allusions, to say, that I had found the life and the poetry of my friend to be but echoes to each other; the same sweetness and good feeling pervades and modulates both. Those who call my friend a wasp, would not, if they knew him better, make such a mistake in natural history. They would find that he is a <u>bee</u>, of the species called the *apes neatina*, and that, however he may have a sting ready on the defensive, when attacked, his native element is that garden of social life which he adorns, and the proper business and delight of his life are sunshine and flowers.[81]

The healths of the three poets were given. At Moore's insistence Crabbe rose to respond, but after saying a few words forgot what he was about to say. Many years later, in 1834 and after Crabbe's death, Bowles wrote to Crabbe's son:

> I sat next to him at table, and he remarked to me it was not surprising he should have hesitated in what he was about to say, for he was seventy. On my congratulating him, I remember, that there was no appearance of his being yet in that state of decadence which has been so truly and so poetically described –
> . . . when old age began,
> And time's strong pressure to subdue the man,
> I asked him if he knew who wrote this powerful line. He instantly answered, 'Dryden'. 'No,' I replied, 'Crabbe!' He spoke, I have no doubt, with that truth and simplicity which were so characteristic of him through life.[82]

In January Bowles wrote to his old friend John Britton, who was constantly in financial difficulties owing to the ambitious and expensive production of such undertakings as *Cathedral Antiquities of England, or an historical, architectural, and graphic illustration of the English Cathedral Churches*. It appears from this letter that Britton had sent a draft or proof of his forthcoming volume of *Beauties of Wiltshire* to Bowles for him to check. Bowles wrote:

> I am sorry to hear of your serious losses. I have repeatedly requested you to let me know how much I am indebted to you now without mentioning the price of Wells Cathedral, inform me that I owe two guineas for a copy of Fonthill. I see that the price of Wells is two & ten pounds so, with the I – I – for your apprentice, I owe you

$$
\begin{array}{cc}
2 & - \; 2 \\
1 & - \; 10 \\
\underline{1} & \underline{\quad 1 \quad} \\
4 & 13 \\
\end{array}
$$

> For which I will send you a note on the other side.
>
> I have corrected your mistake about the Moravians – as to Bowood, I would now wish to say that the present noble owner has added an Italian flower-garden with two elegant marble fountains in front of the conservatory & also a new Chapel for Domestic worship built by Cockerell[83] with an excellent organ & services regularly held when the family are at Bowood, every Sunday.
>
> There is nothing also added to Bowood material. As to Gaby's book, I cannot possibly yet part with it, till I have finished what I am now engag'd in – the history of this Parish and Stanley Abbey connected with it.
>
> The discovery I made from it of the situation of Drogo's fountain was unknown to Dugdale or any human being, is exclusively my own discovery. If you happen to mention the circumstances, I am sure you will acknowledge this. I was preparing a paper from these documents to lay before the Antiquarian Society but my studies were interrupted by that stupid Old Roscoe who has made it necessary for me to turn out more about that eternal Pope!

Bowles was not the only one to refer to 'that eternal Pope'. Thomas Hood[84] in his *Ode to W. Kitchener M.D.* declares:

> Let slender minds with single themes engage
> Like Mr Bowles with his eternal Pope!

Bowles continues his letter to John Britton:

This is now finished & will be out in London on Tuesday, & I shall sit down to the Stanley documentation with greater and undisturbed attention. Gaby[85] lent them to me & till I have finish'd what I am now engag'd & till that is done, I cannot let the work out of my hands unless by a peremptory order. I have had too long experience of his kind heart & liberal & friendly disposition to think that possible. I hope to finish what I am writing before I come to London in Spring. I shall make due acknowledgement to Mr Cole,[86] publicly, but my sole discovery of which I am almost as proud, as if I was a little Bruce, in Wiltshire gives me some claim to priority in illustrating from this book the antiquities of my own parish particularly when no one, but myself, ever derived any information from the perusal, notwithstanding the book has been in several hands, & I believe, your own.[87]

Bowles continued his letter by referring to the engraving of the sketch of the north front of the parsonage that had been commissioned some three years before. Always happy to co-operate with Britton, he wrote:

I should have wish'd very much to have made you a present of the plate for your new work on Wiltshire, an engraving from the picture of the parsonage, you have sent. Could not one be finish'd in time? If so, I should be glad to have it set about immediately, at all events, I would have a plate for my own account of Bremhill and Stanley & perhaps you could put me in the best way of publishing it, I would employ Nicholls, Sir Richard does.

The engraving was indeed published in volume III of Britton's *Beauties of Wiltshire* and expressed to be presented by Bowles, who was doubtless delighted to see his modest parsonage in the company of the very grand Wiltshire mansions, such as Fonthill Abbey, Erlestoke Park and Lacock Abbey, described and illustrated in Britton's work.

In June Bowles wrote again to Britton:

I like very much the plate of 'our Parsonage' for the engraving of which you may receive thirteen pounds, thirteen shillings whenever you show this order to Mr Oliver at Messrs Drummond, Charing Cross. You will, of course, send down the impressions one of which I would request you to send to Sir George Beaumont, another to Miss Rogers 22 St James' Place and one to Mr Oliver who will pay you 'an Oliver for a Rowland !!' . . .

Get my 'Final Appeal' at Hurst & Robinson – from the author. I trust this will finish the whole of the controversy – it will on <u>my part</u> but I think it absolutely necessary to have my own character not to go down to the grave, with my opinions so nefariously mis-represented & my motives out-rag'd.[88]

There now was published Bowles's *Lessons in Criticism to William Roscoe, Esq In Answer to the Rev. W.L. Bowles on the Character and Poetry of Pope* . . . This pamphlet was destined to be Bowles's last word in the Pope controversy and was addressed to the 'stupid Old Roscoe' referred to in his letter written to John Britton in January of the previous year. A review of Bowles's work in the *Devizes and Wiltshire Gazette*[89] gave rise to a letter published a week later in the same newspaper, in which 'A Spectator' wrote:

> . . . You have said, with reference to Mr Bowles's severity, that the reader shall judge, and have given a specimen of such severity accordingly; but you have not distinctly specified the provocations given by his antagonists; so that the reader is left to judge on ex-parte evidence. A very brief statement will be sufficient to fill up the chasm.
>
> Lord Byron charged Mr Bowles with *envy, hatred* and *malice.* Mr Gilchrist accused him of *hypocrisy:* Mr Roscoe applied to him the designation of a *fiend.* Can it be wondered at, after all this, that Mr Bowles applies the spear of Ithuriel?[90] But in truth, the sarcasm of Mr Bowles has more of *contempt* than of *anger.* It is the Lion dandling the Kid.[91]

Lessons in Criticism was dedicated to the Rev. Richard Warner, who many years before had included a veiled allusion to Bowles in his satirical dialogue between well-known Bath characters of the day. It is therefore appropriate that in the epilogue to his *Lessons* Bowles should demonstrate that he was as adept as anyone in the art of humorous and satirical writing. In the course of the epilogue he declares:

> . . . that the next pamphlet Roscoe writes, which I shall never read, he might add to my title of 'writer of sentimental *sonnets*', writer of a *bit* of satire.
>
> The reader has seen some *specimens* of this kind. I shall here give him, into the *bargain*, for his money laid out in the purchase of these LESSONS ON CRITICISM, a few lines from the beginning of my great heroic Poem, to be called 'Critics, Bards, Booksellers, and Blockheads, of this enlightened aera – the *Critico-Poetico-Bibliopolo-Blockheado – Spirits of the Age!*' a Poem, by W.L.B.

BARD AND FRIEND

B. My poem finish'd. many a night and day,
Retouch'd. and polished, why should I delay
To publish it.
F. To publish it? But how? –
B. Take it to Murray.
F. Murray, Sir, will bow,
And tell you, with a simper, and a shrug,
That poetry, just now, is quite a *drug*!
B For poetry, like MINE, he would afford –
F. Yes, if you were a doctor, or a lord!
Why, man, a BISHOP'S note he scarce would squint on,
And mutter'd, 'Who the devil is J. WINTON?'

And so on, together with a footnote in which Bowles recounts a story, probably apocryphal, that: 'A note came to Mr Murray, *on dit*, signed 'J. Winton'. Who is this J. Winton, of Chelsea? said the lofty Bibliopole. It was the Bishop of Winchester, to engage the publisher of the Quarterly to be the publisher of the Life of Pitt.'[92]

In the same year, in 1826, was published *The Little Villager's Verse Book: consisting of short verses, for children to learn by heart; in which the most familiar images of country life are applied to excite the first feelings of humanity and piety*. In the preface to this book of simple verses for children, Bowles expresses his feelings after so many years of constant irritation at the criticism levelled at him, following what he must surely have thought was a not particularly controversial edition of Alexander Pope's works. He writes:

> After the somewhat severe critical contest, I have felt such a kind of refreshment from these Compositions, as an old soldier might be supposed to experience, who returns after a campaign, and wanders over the fields in Summer with the children of his native village. And if these Village Verses should ever be seen by one of my antagonists, the author[93] of the beautiful 'Butterfly's Ball', I can assure him that all unkindness is buried in my heart; although unprovoked harsh language call'd for sharper retribution than is congenial to my disposition.[94]

So popular was the little book that at least three editions were published.

In 1822 Charles Butler,[95] the Roman Catholic legal writer, had published an augmented edition of his *Historical Memoirs of the English, Irish, and Scottish Catholics since the Reformation* . . . followed in 1825 by '*The Book of the Roman Catholic Church*' in a series of letters addressed to Robert Southey Esq., on his '*Book of the Church*'. On 19 March Southey wrote to Bowles:

> Peachey tells me that you had begun to print some observations upon Mr Butler's book, but that you have suppressed them upon hearing that I was engaged in answering it. I am sorry for this, because the more answers that are called forth the better. False and shallow as the book is . . . it imposes upon shallow readers, and is gladly appealed to as an authority by the Liberals, who are at this time leagued against the Church. Every answer that may appear would have a certain circle, within which no other can act with equal effect. And I am so persuaded of this, that I desired Murray not to announce my intended work, lest it should have the effect of preventing others from coming forward in the same good cause. I hope, therefore, that you will resume the pen.[96]

In the event, Bowles did not resume his pen but Southey did, with his *Vindiciae Ecclesiae Anglicanae* being published in the following year.

One Sunday in April Thomas Moore:

> Walked to Bremhill, to take my chance of finding Bowles. Dined with him. His illness increased by his apprehensions; seemed to forget it all in the gaiety of Conversation. Mentioned his anxiety, before he died, to write the Life of Bishop Ken[97] . . . Bowles has made a pretty glee of some very charming words from Cowley's[98] Davideis.[99]

For travelling, Moore kept a gig suitable for short journeys (although he was a regular walker), whereas Bowles and Magdalene had a chaise or carriage that afforded more accommodation for passengers; they readily made this available to Moore and his family from time to time. So in July when Bessy Moore and her two sons, Tom and Russell, were to visit Cheltenham, Bowles took them in his carriage.[100] Earlier in the year Bowles used his influence to secure young Tom a place at his old school, Winchester.[101]

It may be that it was after this visit to Cheltenham that Lord Lansdowne wrote to Bowles to confess to a mistake he had made in doing what was intended to be a favour. At this time members of both

Houses of Parliament were entitled to send their own letters through the postal system free of charge, and were also able to 'frank' or sign other letters to enable them also to pass *gratis* through the post. He wrote:

> I am really concerned at a mistake I have just discovered that I must have committed. Mrs Bowles sent me (on Friday I believe) a letter asking me to frank it for you & unluckily one folded up exactly in the same shape having been sent by the post that moment with a petition that I would frank it to Ireland, the pieces of paper containing the addresses by some accident got mixed & I have this moment received back the Irish letter from Mr Cruttwell, which I am afraid yours is by this time on its way to Killarney, a tour you certainly did not intend it to take.
>
> Pray excuse this confusion, & enable me to repair my error by sending me another letter for Cruttwell to frank, & have the kindness to tell him I am sorry for the trouble I have given him.
>
> You are returned quite well I hope from Cheltenham. I am sorry that the heat of your <u>gallant</u> expedition there has hitherto prevented my seeing you but I trust we shall tomorrow.[102]

In 1822 the first volume of Colt Hoare's monumental *Modern History of South Wiltshire* had been published, with the second volume appearing in 1825. Colt Hoare had been in the habit of arranging annual meetings at Stourhead for those involved or interested in the history and topography of the county. Bowles was one of those who received invitations to these gatherings, where:

> Always hospitable, always liberal, always generous and kind, he [Colt Hoare] had long been accustomed to receive in his house persons of literary taste and habits; but now the hospitalities assumed something of a more systematic character, and those who had the honour and privilege to join in those assemblies were accustomed to expect a summons for the September week, from Monday to Saturday, as the invitations always ran. They were not confined to those who were actual labourers with him in the work; indeed some of those formed no part of the circle; but they were persons known to be devoted to such kind of studies, and who were supposed to have it in their power to make suggestions, to remove difficulties, to impart casual information, or in any other way to lend some small assistance in the design, which was still ever the central point about which the whole turned.[103]

The writer of this account of Topographical Gatherings at Stourhead concluded his paper 'with the testimony of one [Bowles] who knew him [Colt Hoare] intimately, and who thus sketches the scene, as well as the pursuits and the character of its master'. This 'testimony' consisted of part of Bowles's *Days Departed*, published in 1828, in which he pays tribute to Colt Hoare by writing:

> To thee this tribute of respect and love,
> Beloved, benevolent, and gen'rous Hoare,
> Grateful I pay; – but that, when thou art dead,
> (Late may it be!) the poor man's tear will fall,
> And his voice falter, when he speaks of thee[104]

Bowles's brother Charles, the Recorder of Shaftesbury, was responsible for that part of the resulting *Modern History of South Wiltshire* describing the hundred of Chalk, consisting of the village of Semley and its neighbourhood and the land including Tollard Royal and Berwick St John in the west and Broad Chalke in the east. This part of Colt Hoare's monumental history was published in 1833 and included an elaborate pedigree of the Bowles family, although there is no evidence that members of the family were ever substantial landowners in this hundred – the ownership of land being the usual reason for the insertion of genealogies in the work. It is more than likely that it was at the suggestion of his brother William that their family pedigree, as well as that of one branch of the Lisle family, be included as, in writing to John Nichols its publisher in 1828, he tells him that 'Baker[105] has written [illegible] the pedigrees of Lisle & Bowles, which I will send to you soon after my return'.[106]

As has been seen, Bowles had attempted to assist his young *protegée* Louisa Costello in her literary endeavours before she came to London to earn her living by painting miniatures, and at some stage she certainly visited Bowles at Bremhill as one of her poems is entitled *Lines written in November, at Bremhill, Wilts, the Residence of the Rev. W.L. Bowles*. In 1825 she published *Songs of a Stranger*, dedicated as an acknowledgement of gratitude and esteem to Bowles, who on 5 June wrote to his friend William Southeby:

> There is a small volume of Poems by Miss Costello, chaste, beautiful, & pathetic – she has been endeavouring to get a small independence by miniature painting, according to my advice & has succeeded – you would be pleased with the Poetry, & would do an act of kindness to a most deserving, ingenious young woman if you would purchase her volume, just published.

She is at present with her mother at St George's Hospital – Her mother was daughter of a clergyman, now female superintendent of St George's & she herself is the daughter of an officer in the army.

Walter Scott, the friend of her father, recommended her publishing her poems. If you can spare ten shillings for some sweet compositions, it will not be thrown away, to say nothing of the object.[107]

Louisa Costello went on to become one of the most popular writers of her day, and she and her brother achieved fame as copiers of illuminated manuscripts; they both earned a place in the *Dictionary of National Biography*.

At this time the *Devizes and Wiltshire Gazette* frequently printed poetry written by Bowles, who seemed be able to compose lines on every conceivable subject. In August 1825 it was reported that he concluded a brilliant speech at a Bible Meeting with lines on Suttee, the burning of widows in India, and that 'they were written, we understand, at the suggestion of John Huddleston Esq one of the East India Directors and the earliest friend, when resident in Tanjore, of Swartz[108] the Missionary'. The lines of poetry followed this report.[109] In the same number of the newspaper it was reported that Bowles was present at the Bear Club[110] dinner in Devizes, chaired by the Marquis of Lansdowne and described him as 'a gentleman whose poetical effusions have shed a glory on the county which gave him birth and whose works will be known and read as long as taste for pure – legitimate poetry shall exist'.[111] The writer appears to have been unaware that Bowles was not born in Wiltshire and did not live in the county until appointed curate at East Knoyle in 1788.

As well as contributing poems to the *Devizes and Wiltshire Gazette*, Bowles's verses were published from time to time in the *Literary Souvenir; or, Cabinet of Poetry and Romance* edited and later owned by his friend Alaric Watts. In the first volume published in 1824 appeared a poem 'To Miss Stephens, On first hearing her sing "Auld Robin Gray"'. Bowles was certainly susceptible to female charms and so it is no surprise that, having listened to the singing of Catherine Stephens, he should be moved to celebrate the event in verse. It may be recalled that Bowles had heard her sing in the oratorio *Palestine* in 1820, but had failed to remember the words of the verses he had composed on that occasion. Miss Stephens was 'held to have the sweetest soprano voice of her time – 'full, rich, round, lovely' – a natural manner, a simple style, disfigured by no affectation . . . As a ballad singer she was unequalled and her rendering of 'Auld Robin Gray' . . . has not been surpassed'.[112] It has been said that Bowles's poem was 'a notable departure from his usual style' and 'imitates the manner and form of the ballad, to which his first-stanza quotations and references to "Jeanie" directly allude'[113]:

Oh!, when I hear thee sing of 'Jamie far away.'
'Of Father, and of Mither,' and of 'Auld Robin Gray,'
I listen till I think it is Jeanie's self I hear,
'And I look in thy face' with a blessing and a tear.
'I look in thy face,' for my heart is not cold,
Though Winter's frost is stealing on, and I am growing old;
Those tones, I shall remember as long as I live,
And the blessing and the tear, shall be the thanks I give . . .

As well as appearing in the *Literary Souvenir*, Bowles's verses appeared on a regular basis in a number of other fashionable literary annuals published at this time. Between 1825 and 1828 his poetry could be read in the *Amulet* and *Friendship's Offering* as well as in *Forget Me Not*, *Pledge of Friendship* and *Bijou*.

Bowles must surely have thought that the last word had been said about his strictures on the life and poetry of Alexander Pope. This was not to be. He was attacked yet again in the *Quarterly Review* in October 1825, and in a letter written soon afterwards he gave vent to his feelings:

> . . . No man has been so <u>brutally</u> attack'd, & except in the solitary instance of Gilchrist, I never, in my life, us'd any expressions of severity in return! Byron's alone was outrageous, but I never thought of replying to his misrepresentations about the Madeira lovers!
>
> Gilchrist's language was scurrilous but his <u>own friend</u> the editor of the London Magazine, whom I never saw but once for five minutes, wrote me a most handsome apology in his private capacity! This is proof how little I deserve the daring charge of Roscoe that my mode of controversy is intemperate!
>
> Moore advis'd me to insert in the public papers one piece of nefarious duplicity in Roscoe, as a reason for not answering him further! but I have determined to expose, for this once, both his duplicity & absurdity – you say justly that I must repeat the same arguments over & over –
>
> This is true but when a man in the bitterest spirit, affects to [illegible] argumentatively, I like to turn his own instances against him & have a little fun at football! His arguments on poetical criticism 'cobwebs' so often destroy'd all options & too contemptible. I have been delay'd, but shall be ready in a week or ten days.[114]

Thomas Moore, writing to Bowles soon afterwards commented on the latest attack, assuring him that 'it does you honour – as it shows you are not <u>partizan</u> enough to suit the tastes of those <u>ultra</u> gentleman'.[115] Robert Southey also thought Bowles had been harshly treated, and in writing to Caroline Bowles on 4 January 1826 writes: 'I am sorry for Bowles, and the more so because the criticism has been written in perfect sincerity, and with the fullest conviction that its severity was deserved.'[116]

In October 1825 appeared Moore's *Memoirs of the Life of the Right Honourable Richard Brinsley Sheridan*, who had died in 1816 and was, of course, well known to Bowles. Having finished reading the biography, Bowles put pen to paper to congratulate Moore on his work and then to give a little 'honest criticism' such as 'The <u>Oxford scene</u> must be <u>revised</u>, and I am vexed you did not show me the sheets!' This was mainly concerned with what Bowles saw as an inaccurate description of the events that would lead up to Sheridan receiving what we would now call an honorary degree from the University of Oxford. Bowles continued: 'Pray take care this little academical history be brought out in <u>the next edition</u> a little more accurately, and let <u>me</u> see the <u>sheets</u>, and there is one most striking circumstance should be added.'

It appears from Bowles's letter that Sheridan was so certain that his degree 'would not pass' that, when the time came for him to appear before the Vice-Chancellor, he was in bed at New College, not intending to get up. However, the shouts of 'Sheridan, Sheridan, Sheridan' in the Sheldonian were so tumultuous that the Vice-Chancellor could not get a hearing until Sheridan appeared at the door of the theatre, Bowles having run to New College and hauled Sheridan out of bed after telling him how 'hotly he was called for'.[117]

The other 'honest criticism' related to Moore's style of writing, and in this he was joined by nearly all the other critics of the work. Moore responded to Bowles by writing:

> Your remarks upon the faults of my style are quite just but I cannot help letting the <u>potatoe</u>[118] show itself now and then, & the fact is, I should not produce things that people admire, if I did not run the risk also of falling into what they condemn. The same dash produces both the hits & the misses.[119]

Within the boundaries of the parish of Bremhill had been two chapels of ease, one at Foxham and the other at Highway. The chapel at Foxham had been endowed many years before by a member of the

Hungerford family with £4 per annum and by 1783 was no longer in use.[120] However, it seems that Bowles had decided to resume the holding of services there, as in 1825 he signed a document reading:

> W.L. Bowles, vicar of the parish of Bremhill, in the year 1825, in order to induce the inhabitants of Foxham, in the same parish, to subscribe for the service of the chapel there, at his own cost, as benefactor only, repaired the roof of the chapel. – Ita testor, 1825
>
> Charles Bowles, Notary Public[121]

One can detect the hand of Bowles's lawyer brother in the wording of this memorandum. It was he, no doubt, who insisted that the words 'as benefactor only' be inserted in the memorandum to guard against any future suggestions that the incumbent of Bremhill was responsible for keeping the chapel in good repair.

In 1825 Bowles was elected a member of the recently founded Athenaeum Club, his occupations being listed as 'Divine, Poet, Antiquary and Chaplain to the Prince Regent'. The membership was limited to 1000, and among the Wiltshiremen that he would have been able to meet there as fellow members were his old friends Lord Arundell and John Benett, still one of the Members of Parliament for Wiltshire.

Following Bowles's death there was found among his papers a sealed envelope with the following written on it in Bowles's handwriting and signed by him: 'To be opened after my death'. Inside was a legal document dated 17 November 1825 referring to events that had occurred some years before. It raises a question that will probably never be satisfactorily answered.

In 1813, or some time before, one Charles Harrison of Motcombe, near Shaftesbury in Dorset, referred to in the document as 'gentleman', married Sarah Bugden of Shaftesbury, a single woman who was the mother of a female child called Caroline, who had been born blind and was then about nine years old. The document stated that 'from motives of charity and humanity' Bowles had been paying for the support of Caroline. On 14 October 1813 Bowles entered into a Bond[122] with Harrison and his wife in the sum of £400 and agreed that so long as Caroline 'might continue an inmate with him and them and should be maintained and clothed by him and them' he would pay them £17 a year. Caroline now having attained the age of twenty-one, the document in the sealed envelope was signed and provided that, in consideration of £200 paid by Bowles to Harrison, Bowles would be released from his obligation to support Caroline on condition that Harrison would henceforth feed, clothe and maintain her for so long as she might remain unmarried.

If Bowles had been supporting the child purely 'from motives of charity and humanity', why had he felt it necessary to pay Harrison such a large sum of money, perhaps some £8000 in early twenty-first-century values, and why was he so anxious that the facts should not be revealed until after his death?

It is certain that rumours had been circulating relating to what might be termed improper behaviour as in 1826, in his *Lessons in Criticism to William Roscoe*, in describing what had been written by the various parties to the Pope controversy, Bowles relates: 'Lord Byron alluded to some tale, – I know not what – of my early years – it was in *bad taste*. I am ignorant, to this day, of the circumstance to which he alluded; but I suppose I was not more free from youthful indiscretions than many better and wiser men.'[123] Perhaps it was a 'youthful indiscretion' that resulted in Bowles persuading himself that 'from motives of charity and humanity' he should support the unfortunate Caroline, although it is more likely that Byron had heard, and was alluding to, the rumour that in his university days Bowles's conduct had not been entirely chaste, and as a consequence was in no position to be sanctimoniously critical of Pope's moral character.

When not themselves entertaining a string of visitors at the parsonage, Bowles and Magdalene were constantly dining at the houses of neighbouring gentry, with Thomas Moore very often one of their fellow guests. Moore found some of these parties exceedingly unexciting but was always pleased to see Bowles present. In January 1826 he recorded in his journal that one such occasion was 'cold & dull work, if Bowles and Lord Lansdowne (not forgetting Mrs Clutterbuck's eyes) had not enlivened it a little'![124]

Bowles's health was already beginning to fail. A few days later, at a dinner party at Bowood after Moore had sung one of his own songs, Moore noted in his journal that 'poor Bowles (who begins to look broken and wandering) said it was "equal to Shakespeare for the words & to Purcell for the music"'.[125]

Bowles has been described as an active though lenient magistrate, and must often have been distressed at the harsh penalties that were meted out to many of those who came before him. In May 1826 he petitioned the King through the Home Secretary of State on behalf of two of his parishioners, who had been sentenced to be transported for seven years at the last Assize for stealing poultry. As a result these sentences were commuted to one year's imprisonment, determinable on their good behaviour.[126]

Bowles's efforts to seek a mitigation of such severe penalties were referred to in the obituary that appeared in the *Gentleman's Magazine* following his death:

> Whilst resident at Bremhill, Mr Bowles was unremitting in his professional duties, zealous in the education of the poor, and manifested, in every respect, an exemplary, though happily by no means rare, instance of the union of Christian graces with the polish of taste and the amenities of literature. He took a warm interest in the welfare of the rural population, not only of his own parish, but in the surrounding neighbourhood; and on more than one occasion he exerted his influence as a county magistrate in cases which appeared to his benevolent heart to demand the exercise of the prerogative of mercy.[127]

In May Bowles paid his annual visit to London, where he met many of his friends and acquaintances in the world of letters and the arts. One day he and Moore went to the British Gallery together and called on Sir George Beaumont, who showed them some of his pictures that were soon to form the nucleus of the new National Gallery. A few days later Bowles and Moore went to the Strand to visit Deville, the celebrated phrenologist and collector of casts of heads. With them went their friends John Houlton[128] of Farley Castle and Magdalene's cousin John Benett. Moore recorded in his journal: 'Bowles, at first, a good deal unsettled by the sight of casts after death, & with much difficulty, persuaded to submit his head to inspection – some good guesses of Deville's about him soon put him in good humour . . .'[129] It is likely that one of the casts of heads seen by Bowles was of Sheridan. William Linley owned a copy of Thomas Moore's *Memoirs of Richard Brimsley Sheridan* and at the end of the book he inserted a print of a poem entitled 'On seeing a Cast of Sheridan's Countenance, taken after Death by W.L.B. 18 May 1826'.[130]

In May Bowles's sister Amy, whose son Edward had been 'barbarously murdered at Calloa, near Lima, in South America, by a banditti of robbers'[131] just three years before, was again stuck by tragedy when her husband, Peregrine Bingham,[132] the rector of Berwick St John, was killed following a fall from a run-away gig in which they had both been travelling.

Back at Bremhill in June, with Parliament having been recently dissolved, Bowles found himself involved in the election by the burgesses of nearby Calne of two Members of Parliament. The sitting members, the Hon. James Abercromby[133] and Sir James Macdonald, Bart,[134] doubtless had the support of Lord Lansdowne and would have expected to be returned without a contest. However, a majority of the burgesses, nine in number, were opposed to Abercromby and Macdonald and were attempting to find a candidate to stand against them. On Tuesday 6 June, as Moore recorded:

> Bowles called upon me in great alarm about the rebellion against Lord Lansdowne that has broke out among the Burgesses at Calne – had been all morning endeavouring to convert or neutralise a chandler (I think) who formed the one majority on the side of the malcontents – advised him to write to Lord Lansdowne, who is lying ill with the gout in town – The members arrived today.[135]

On the following Saturday the two candidates and Bowles and Magdalene dined with the Moores at Sloperton Cottage and 'drank tea in the open air', as Moore recorded in his journal. The next day, on the eve of the election, they all dined at the parsonage. The candidates urged Moore to attend the election to 'help them through', and so Bowles and Moore dutifully travelled to Calne where, as Moore recorded, he:

> Called with Bowles upon my pretty stage-coach friend who proved to be the daughter of a new chymist come to Calne – found her behind the counter, reading Voltaire's tragedies – drank some of her soda water. – took Macdonald there afterwards – all admired her exceedingly – Bowles in raptures, & will kill Himself drinking soda water for her sake . . .[136]

In the event the candidates were elected unopposed. The *Devizes and Wiltshire Gazette* explained the reason:

> It appears that notwithstanding the majority (9) of the Electors of the place were opposed to Mr Abercromby and Sir James Macdonald they contented themselves with being absent from the place of election, because – for sooth they could not unite as to the gentleman they should bring in so that the old Members were elected by the minority and now 'laugh in their sleeves'.[137]

Later in July Bowles with Magdalene and Moore paid a visit to Lord Arundell at Wardour Castle. Moore recorded: 'Bowles and Mrs

B. called for me in their carriage at ten o'clock – Bowles all in a fuss about our arrangements with Lord Arundell & Bain'.[138] It seems that Magdalene left them at Hindon to go on to East Knoyle to stay with her sister Charlotte there. Bowles and Moore left by chaise, arriving at Wardour a little after five, and in the evening 'the organist played in the Hall & Lord and Lady A sung several Gregorian chaunts – Had singing afterwards to the Piano-forte'.[139]

The next morning there was some discussion before breakfast about Latin epitaphs, with Bowles questioning the propriety of the term 'sacerdos' as applicable rather to a dignitary than a priest. One wonders whether Bowles approved of the course the conversation was taking. Moore records:

> This brought on some talk about Epitaphs, – 'Here I lies – D – n my eyes.' – 'Here I lie snug as a bug in a rug' and then near it 'Here I lie, snugger than you, you b---.' The following, quoted by Lord A. rather good

> Here I lie in the Chancel Door
> Here I lie because I am poor
> There you lie, because you are rich
> But you do not lie warmer, you son of a b----[140]

After noon Bowles, with Lord Arundell, Moore and a Mr Jones set off to walk to Pythouse, the house of Bowles's old friend and Magdalene's cousin John Benett. When they arrived Benett's wife was not well enough to see the visitors and, as no mention is made of Benett himself in Moore's journal, he was presumably away from home.[141] After breakfast the next day Magdalene arrived from East Knoyle, probably in the Bowles's carriage, which then conveyed Bowles, Magdalene and Moore to Donhead where they visited the cottage that Bowles had occupied as curate of East Knoyle so many years before. In 1828 it was occupied by Bowles's widowed sister Sarah Burlton, who was paying him an annual rental of £30 for the house and 5 acres of land.[142] It may be recalled that Bowles had planted the garden and grounds himself. Moore noted in his journal that:

> Twas to this place that he addressed his lines 'Oh no, I would not leave thee, my sweet home'. Under a tree in the grounds is an urn with the pretty Latin inscription which he has given in the 2nd Vol. of his works, written on Mrs Bowles's sister, to whom he was to have been married.[143]

The party then travelled on to Shaftesbury. Bowles's brother, Charles, was living in their old family home, Barton Hill House, which had been sold by Bowles many years before; his brother had managed to obtain a lease of it for his life. The purpose of the call was to apologise that they would not be able to dine with him as had previously been arranged. Having done this, the party visited a number of Bowles's old friends in the neighbourhood and at last arrived at East Knoyle, where they had 'a good quiet dinner', as Moore described it, with Magdalene's sister Charlotte Still. Next morning the party returned to Shaftesbury to breakfast with Charles Bowles – to make up for not dining with him the night before. Bowles discovered that his old nurse, Nanny Freke, was still alive, and Moore recorded that he 'left a *shilling* for her!' Having visited Rutter, the Shaftesbury bookseller who thrust a copy of his book about Fonthill Abbey in Moore's hands just as they were leaving, the party travelled on into Dorset to stay a few days at Heffleton in East Stoke with Dr Andrew Bain,[144] presumably another of Bowles's old friends. One of the other guests was Charles, probably the son of Richard Brinsley Sheridan.

The next day the visitors drove to see Lulworth Castle, and on the following day, as it was Sunday, they drove to a church 3 miles away. Moore recorded that it was:

> A small wretched barn, full of dingy stinking people – had no conception that the proud Protestant Establishment was ever so meanly lodged – Bowles said he never saw anything like it – Walked back from Church – no company at dinner, but some excellent champagne, hock and claret – Bowles quoted an Epigram on Dr Leed, who had a very large nose & squinted.

> The reason why Doctor Leed squints, I suppose,
> Is because his two eyes are afraid of his nose[145]

On the Monday the whole party visited Great Tyneham on the Isle of Purbeck, the mansion of the Bond family. After lunch there they set off to walk on the cliffs, although Bowles was 'obliged to turn back from his head growing giddy',[146] no doubt another manifestation of his nervouseness when in unusual situations. The roads were so bad that Bowles's carriage was damaged and needed some repair before Bowles, Sheridan and Moore were able to leave Heffleton for Salisbury, where they did not arrive until between five and six in the evening. On their way the friends talked much about George Bubb Dodington[147] '. . . and the literary men with whom he lived – Windham[148] of Salisbury has a number of MSS of Dodington, which Bowles has looked over – some most indecent poems among them [of which Bowles repeated one to me] – believes that Windham destroyed them.[149] The words in square brackets, together with parts of a number of other extracts from Moore's journal in which Bowles and others are mentioned, were omitted, for obvious reasons, from Lord John Russell's edition of Moore's journal published soon after his death, but are now able to be revealed.

Between 1825 and 1828 a number of Bowles's poems appeared in Alaric Watts's *The Literary Souvenir; or Cabinet of Poetry and Romance*, in which the works of most of the leading writers of the period appeared. In August 1826 Moore noted in his journal that 'Bowles told me that the verses C. Sheridan had sent him to chuse from for the Literary Souvenir are none of them such as any Collection would admit – expressed surprise that a man otherwise so sensible should not be aware how bad these verses were.'[150]

C. Sheridan was Charles, the son of the statesman and dramatist Richard Brinsley Sheridan by his second wife, the daughter of Newton Ogle, the Dean of Winchester to whom Bowles had dedicated the third edition of his sonnets so many years before.

Bowles, together with Southey, Coleridge and Campbell, contributed to the 1827 volume of the *Literary Souvenir* published in November 1826. Wordsworth alone of the distinguished writers of the day declined to contribute, in accordance with his resolve that his work should not appear in annual publications. Those whose poetry was included found their work exposed to an exceedingly large readership, with over 10,000 small paper copies being printed.[151]

From time to time, and in accordance with the usual practice, Bowles's sermons were printed and published. In 1823 a sermon that he had preached at Bremhill for the benefit of the National Schools was duly printed and now, in 1826, appeared the considerably more substantial publication of 154 pages of *Paulus Parochialis; or, a plain and practical view of the objects, arguments, and connection, of St Paul's Epistle, to the Romans: in a series of sermons adapted to Country Congregations.*

In the middle of September Bowles travelled to Gloucester with Lord Lansdowne and Moore to attend the music festival there, taking lodgings opposite the King's Head and occupying a bedroom next to Moore's. The star attraction was the appearance of Maria Caradori-Allan,[152] the opera singer who in 1825 had sung at the first performance in England of Beethoven's ninth symphony. Moore was introduced to Lord Ducie[153] who next day 'wished us to go to the Lay Gallery, but we remained faithful to the Spiritual & Bowles'. After listening to the music some ninety people dined together with all the aristocracy at the top table and with Moore doubting whether he would get a place, 'from the neglect of Bowles in not giving in my name'.[154]

Bowles was so impressed by Maria Caradori's performance that he wrote a poem in praise of her entitled 'On Caradori'. This he arranged to have printed by Baily, the Calne printer, with two others, a considerably reworked version of his verses 'To Miss Stephens' and a political squib called 'A Vision not by the Author of Christabelle'.[155]

In October Bowles sent a copy of the three poems to Charles Sheridan, writing his letter on the printed sheet:

> Send your other verses or at least <u>one</u> or two to Akermann <u>by my desire</u> for 'Forget me Not', where will appear <u>my verses</u> on your poor father. – I send some 'Coals to Newcastle' herewith – The Political Squib arose from something Moore said to Lord Lansdowne about the Vision by the Author of Christabelle & I said laughingly I would write a vision and – le voila.
>
> It was originally called 'Lost Lost' being my sentiments about that cursing & accursed system, lately pursued – Lord L took it in such good part, my ideas of Political Economy tho [illegible], I believe different from his own – that in compliment I added the last lines.
>
> 'A Vision not by the Author of Christabelle' describes a dream in which the writer sees a beautiful ship epitomising Old England ruling the waves being blown off course by a wizard called 'Political Economy' who tells the pilot to steer towards a deadly reef as a result of which all is 'Lost – Lost – Lost!' However, in the last stanza all is not after all lost when
>
> . . . Soft airs from heaven descend; – the roaring blast
> Dies, as she wins her stately way again,
> Her mighty shadow on the tranquil main,
> The glorious Queen of the wide watery realm –
> Hope on the prow, and ------ at the helm.

In Bowles's handwriting alongside the last line is written 'Lansdowne'. Bowles's letter to Sheridan continues: 'He [Lord Lansdowne] and Moore came to Gloucester, we had a most splendid and auspicious meeting – my niece – tres aimable – tres belle –tres Riche – was with me. Mrs Bowles wished not to go – as you were in England why did you not come? . . .' As a postscript Bowles adds:

I must not forget my lines on Alderman Wood[156] at Gloster – just stating that we received more money for the charity than has been received these fifteen years

When money our music produces
And sure such a meeting is good
Where are Beauforts & Sherbornes & Ducies
And Lansdownes – & Alderman Wood![157]

In October Bowles probably received a letter from Lupton Relfe, a bookseller in Cornhill and the publisher of *Friendship's Offering*, in which he may have suggested that Bowles would be contributing to the magazine. In reply he wrote:

Mr Bowles presents his compliments to Mr Relfe and informs him that not having heard a syllable from Mr Hervey on the subject of his letter, Mr Bowles is totally unprovided with any [illegible] publication – at the same time he begs to inform the publisher of 'Friendship's Offering' that the circumstances of hearing from him so late, only prevents his being a contributor to so elegant a work.
 Bremhill October 12 1826
 Postscript

Mrs Bowles has just found some lines of mine in her manuscript book, which are at your service.[158]

Upon his arrival at Bremhill, Bowles would have been appointed one of the trustees of the charity of Maud Heath who, by a deed of gift made in 1474, gave property in Chippenham to trustees upon trust to use the income to make and keep in repair a causeway some 4½ miles in length from Wick Hill in Bowles's parish through East Tytherton and Langley Burrell into Chippenham. In 1811 the trustees decided to arrange for John Smith of Calne 'to be employed to make estimates for building an arch or arches for raising the road at Kellaways from the Church to the Bridge to carry the waste water so as to render the road passable in times of floods and also for raising the road on the other side of the Bridge as far as may be necessary'.[159] The work was duly carried out, and part of it remains as the most noticeable and well-known section of Maud Heath's Causeway. Here in 1698 a monument was erected with three dials and an inscription commemorating Maud Heath's gift. In 1826 the trustees 'ordered that the present inscription be restored so that the paraphrase of the three Latin inscriptions on the centre of the monument which Mr Bowles one of the Trustees has written in English verse be added in such a place on the monument as shall be directed'.[160] In the very first volume of the magazine of the *Wiltshire Archaeological and Natural History Magazine*, published in 1854, Canon J.E. Jackson describes the inscriptions on the dials thus:

> There are three Dials. On the side facing the Morning, or the rising sun, 'Volat
> Tempus,' is thus paraphrased:-

> 'Oh early passenger look up, be wise:
> And think how, night and day, Time Onward Flies'.

> On the side opposite to Noon or mid-day sun, is the scriptural advice 'Whilst we have time, do good.'

> 'Qvum Tempus Habemus, Operemur Bonum.'
> 'Life steals away – this hour, oh man, is lent thee
> Patient to work the work of him that sent thee.'

> The words, on the side towards evening, or the setting sun, though appropriate when rightly applied, seem to fit less happily the case of the ordinary passer to and fro.

> 'Redibo. Tu nunquam'
> 'Haste traveller! The sun is sinking low,
> He shall return again – but Never Thou . . .'[161]

Bowles frequently made alterations to his poetry, and it seems that he did so in the case of his translations or paraphrases of these lines. According to his *Scenes and Shadows of Days Departed . . .* of 1837 the wording he proposed to the trustees for morning was:

> Oh, early passenger, a moment stay,
> And think how rapidly Time Flies Away

And for noon was:

> 'Twas morn – 'tis noon – mortal, this hour is lent thee,
> To do the Christian work of Him who sent thee.

And for evening was:

Haste homeward! For the sun is sinking now;
He shall return, but never thou.

Memorial stones were also erected at the beginning and the end of the causeway, bearing inscriptions doubtless also composed by Bowles and not, according to Jackson, 'amongst the highest efforts of the muse'! The wording on the stone at the Bremhill end of the causeway reads:

From this Wick Hill begins the praise
Of Maud Heath's gift to these highways.

And at the Chippenham end:

Hither extendeth Maud Heath's gift.
From where I stand in Chippenham clift.[162]

Portrait of Bowles by Mullar and engraved by W. Humphreys.

Bremhill Parsonage – plate presented by Bowles to John Britton for his Beauties of Wiltshire.

Pencil and water colour of Bremhill Parsonage by John Buckler presented to Bowles's wife Magdalene by Sir Richard Colt Hoare. (Reproduced by kind permission of the Wiltshire Archaeological & Natural History Society)

AUTHOR OF 'FOURTEEN SONNETS, 1789.'

Sketch of Bowles 'in the act of composing a Sonnet on the subject of a Hat's obligation to an Umbrella' by David Maclise in Fraser's Magazine.

Portrait of the elderly Bowles in the Library of Salisbury Cathedral. (Photographed by Dr John Crook and reproduced with the kind permission of the Dean and Chapter of Salisbury Cathedral)

Bowles's canonry – Aula le Stage in Salisbury Close. (Photograph by Dr John Crook and reproduced with his kind permission)

Uphill Parsonage (one of Bowles's childhood homes) as appearing in his Scenes and Shadows of Days Departed.

F O U R T E E N

S O N N E T S,

E L E G I A C

A N D

D E S C R I P T I V E.

W R I T T E N   D U R I N G   A   T O U R.

CANTANTES, LICET USQUE, MINUS VIA LÆDET EAMUS.

VIRG.

BATH, PRINTED BY R. CRUTTWELL,
AND SOLD BY
C. DILLY, LONDON.
M DCC LXXXIX.

The title page of Fourteen Sonnets . . .

Chapter 6
1827–1831

In January 1827 Bowles planned to visit Bath to attend the musical concerts and the Anacreontic dinner.[1] This year Bowles's friend John Houlton of Farleigh Castle in Somerset, just across the border with Wiltshire, was the president at the dinner, and so on 15 January Bowles wrote to him:

> I have just left Moore & Lord Lansdowne – It is fixed that at all events Moore & myself shall be at Farley Castle on Thursday the 25th. I trust there will be a place for Lord Lansdowne at the Anacreontic dinner Friday, & Moore, or rather I am sure your own feelings will suggest the rest.
>
> As Moore and Lord Lansdowne will give eclat to your anacreontic Presidentship & as I am anxious for such a selection as will give greatest satisfaction, I shall [take] the liberty of subjoining a little Sketch for I believe I may [say] that there are few who have greater knowledge of old compositions of this kind than myself from the first introduction to the present day . . .
>
> Now I will just set down a few things which I think Lord Lansdowne will like & which, according to my arrangement would have a good effect . . .[2]

Bowles then proceeds to list some twenty glees that he thought would be suitable to be performed. When he arrived in Bath on the 23rd he must have been rather embarrassed to find that it was not for him to suggest what music should be chosen, and so he hastened to write again to Houlton:

> I came to the concert & I write a line to say I call'd on Monkland to make a sort of apology for presuming to send a scheme of performances when there is a select committee for the purpose.
>
> In fact, I knew nothing of this [illegible] when I wrote to you, I imagined every composition to be perform'd was selected by the president of the night.

I can make everything quite satisfactory and have only to add I shall be with you Thursday before dark.

I should have come with Lord Lansdowne & Moore in Lord Lansdowne's carriage but one of the horses a day or two ago kick'd one of the persons belonging to the stables & I am literally afraid however pleasant such company might be to travel otherwise than with my own horses. I agree with you most cordially, as all who know him do, in your sentiments of the distinguished nobleman who happily for me [is] my nearest neighbour who will be your guest Thursday.[3]

In this letter is revealed an example of the sort of irrational fear that would from time to time overcome Bowles, and in this instant prevented him for travelling with his closest friends in case one of Lord Lansdowne's horses should misbehave and upset the carriage!

In 1827 Bowles arranged to have published *Illustrations of those stupendous monuments of Celtic antiquity Avebury and Silbury, and their mysterious origin traced by a series of deductive evidence; including observations of the great rampart Wansdike, and the adjoining highest elevation of the Wiltshire Downs, commonly called Tan-Hill. Extracted from the Parochial History of Bremhill*.[4] In the dedication to Sir Richard Colt Hoare, Bowles stated that the work formed part of a parochial history undertaken at his suggestion. It is likely that it was envisaged that the result of Bowles's researches into the history of Bremhill and its neighbourhood would form part of Colt Hoare's *Modern History of South Wiltshire*, but by this time it was clear that the larger history would be limited to the southern part of the county and that Bowles therefore would be free to publish his parochial history under his own name and on his own account.

In the event, Bowles's *Illustrations of those stupendous monuments of Celtic antiquity* was printed in advance of his parochial history, and a limited number of copies circulated in the immediate neighbourhood of the monuments so that he could 'avail himself of the comments of those few to whom such enquiries may be objects of interest', as he put it in the advertisement printed at the beginning of the work.[5] Comments were forthcoming rather earlier than Bowles had perhaps expected, as in the July number of the *Gentleman's Magazine* there appeared an essay by the Rev. Edward Duke[6] on 'The origins of Wansdyke, in answer to the opinions lately advanced by the Rev. W.L. Bowles'. Duke was a fellow Wiltshire clergyman, living at Lake House in the south of the county, where his family had been seated since 1578. For several years Duke had been contributing to the *Gentleman's Magazine* mainly on Wiltshire antiquities, and had collaborated with Colt Hoare in exploring the tumuli on his estates. As a fellow clergyman and county magistrate he would certainly have been acquainted with Bowles.

Following the publication of Duke's article, Bowles did not publish any answering pamphlet, almost certainly because he held to his views that would be repeated in his forthcoming *Parochial History of Bremhill*. Instead he wrote to the *Devizes and Wiltshire Gazette*:

> In consquence of my name being mentioned in your paper, relative to some opinions of mine, publicly given, on the ancient mound, the Wansdike, I have only to say, in answer to Mr Duke's strong series of arguments; econtra, that I must decline entering the lists with him. As I could not treat some of his opinions without a *smile*, to which *all* antiquaries are subject, and I would be unwilling to say a syllable that looked like unkindness or disrespect, to a gentleman whose character I respect so sincerely, though on *antiquarian* subjects, I differ from him so widely.
>
> Requesting the insertion of this, the only observation I shall make in the public papers on Mr Duke's hypothesis.[7]

This letter brought forth a courteous letter from Duke, in which he expressed his great personal respect and regard for Bowles and declared that, although he dissented from the major part of Bowles's hypotheses, he trusted that in delivering his arguments he did not violate the bounds of legitimate controversy.[8] This letter must have pleased Bowles, unlike another published in the same newspaper shortly afterwards under the pseudonym of Viator:

> There is a manliness of feeling in the letter signed E D which would disarm me, in a moment of any attempt to ridicule, or even so much as to 'smile', if it were possible to avoid it.
>
> Mr Bowles published his arguments, in my opinion, very substantial, respecting some of the monuments of our county . . .
>
> But what does Mr Bowles say? He tells us, in substance, he 'smiles'. Mr Duke cries out for *arguments* and if *reasons* as Shakespear says 'were as *plenty* as blackberries', Mr Bowles gives none.
>
> Mr Bowles has done *worse*, for he will neither, it seems, enter the *arena* of the Gentleman's Magazine, though his *wars* with Byron show him a *veteran* in discussion, nor does he give reasons for his 'smile'.[9]

Bowles and Duke did, in fact, then enter the arena of the *Gentleman's Magazine*, which over the next year published a number of long and erudite letters from both of them disputing the origins of Avebury.

Bowles was convinced that the stones at Avebury were a temple erected in honour of Mercury, while Duke's view was that 'Mercury Teutalis possesses not the slightest claim to the Temple of Abury'.[10]These letters were followed by others by the two clergymen presenting their views about the origin of Wansdyke, concluding, or so it was thought, with a letter from Bowles ending:

> I can assure my friend there is no one whom I would be more happy to see, and to welcome with the hospitalities of a canonical house, than the gentleman, clergyman, magistrate, and scholar whom no one respects more than myself, though I must have much stronger arguments to persuade me that Wansdike, with its immense bank and narrow bottom, was a road, that Tan-hill was derived, or *could* be derived from the Roman Goddess of Groves, Diana, or that the SUN and MOON were intended to be represented at Abury, *both* being there in the form of a *circle*, and so represented as to *travel together?* And having said this, Caestus resigno.[11]

However, Duke was not so easily silenced. Another letter from him was published in which he concluded:

> I cannot recede from this controversy which has agreeably engaged my leisure hours, without thanking my friend, Mr Bowles, for his cordial and kind invitation to the festive table of his canonical residence, with which he concludes his letter, and he may assure himself, I shall, with much pleasure accept it.[12]

The 'canonical residence' mentioned by Duke was the house in the Close of Salisbury Cathedral that, as will be seen, was soon to be occupied by Bowles for three months of each year following his election as a residentiary canon.

The editor of the *Gentleman's Magazine* must surely have received with some misgivings yet another letter from Duke, and he gracefully brought the correspondence to an end by announcing:

> We have received another letter from Mr Duke, relative to his Controversy with Mr Bowles on the Celtic Antiquities of Wiltshire, but as Mr Duke began the controversy which has been continued through several letters, we think our readers will agree with us that the question should now be left to the friendly discussion in Mr Bowles's dining room, as proposed by Mr Bowles.[13]

1827 – 1831

In 1827 the fourth edition of *The Village Verse Book*, the small collection of simple verses for children to learn by heart, appeared. Lady Lansdowne and her husband liked it, and in a letter to Magdalene she wrote:

> We are quite delighted with the Little Hymn Book. The simplicity and beauty of the compositions quite charm us, and I am sure they will be very popular amongst our children. It is quite admirable of Mr Bowles to lower his Muse in so kind a manner, to adapt it to such early readers.
>
> I beg you will send to Bowood for as many fish as you would wish to have. I am extremely happy to be able to contribute a <u>mite</u> to the bounty of Bremhill.
>
> Lord L. unites me in best compliments to you and Mr Bowles and many thanks for all the assistance you are giving us.[14]

The children referred to in this latter were the pupils in the school at Bremhill established by Lady Lansdowne and Magdalene, who dealt with many of the practical matters that arose from time to time. Bowles's kinswoman Caroline Bowles also admired the book, and in December wrote to Bowles: 'At last, my dear Sir, I send you the little sketches I promised to attempt as illustrations to your beautiful Hymn Book. It deserves a better illustrator, but you must take the will for the deed.'[15]

In the summer Bowles had at last paid a brief visit to Caroline. In the same letter she mentioned this visit and also wrote:

> Do you know you left a pledge – not a defiance, I hope – when you <u>appeared</u> to me last summer for a brief moment. You left a pair of gloves, and tho' I will not stick them in my bonnet, I will keep them till you come to redeem the token.

So far as is known, Bowles never did redeem the token.

In September Thomas Moore was dining at Bowood with a number of other guests including Bowles and Magdalene and reported in his journal:

> Bowles all rapture about an Article in his dearly-beloved Blackwood on my Epicurean,[16] of which he had already written me an account, and which he says is the perfection of eloquence, cordiality, fun and God knows what – Suspect the cause of this admiration to be, the said Blackwood having quoted him (Bowles) as one of the living examples in support of their position – that Poets always write the best Prose.

Bowles very amusing & odd at dinner – his account of his shilling's worth of sailing at Southampton, and then two shillings's worth and then three, as his courage rose. One of the boatman who rowed him had been with Clapperton[17] in Africa, and told Bowles of their having one day caught a porpoise, and on opening it, finding a black man, perfect and undissolved, in its belly – the black man having been thrown overboard from some slave-ship. After for some time gravely defending the story against our laughter, he, at last, explained that it was a shark that he meant, not a porpoise.[18]

In October Moore could not resist recording an account he had heard:

Bowles's lecture to his Curate on the use of hard words in preaching very amusing – Summoning up all his servants before the Curate, to ask them, one by one whether they understood the meaning of the word 'final'. First the Cook – then, Thomas, – 'Do you, Thomas, know what "final" means?' – 'No Sir' – Then turning to the Curate 'You see now &c &c.'[19]

On the way to Bath with Moore in November:

Bowles spoke (for the first time I ever heard him acknowledge it) of his famous song 'The origin of the P' – wrote it when he was about 20 – Said how odd it appeared to him many years afterwards to meet with Law one of his boon-companions of that time, as Vice-Chancellor of Oxford – become most grave & staid a personage, never making the slightest allusion to their early doings, but seeming to have forgotten even the possibility of them – Odd enough (as I remarked to him) that the two best songs of this description extant are by him and Sir W. Jones[20] . . . Dined with Bowles at the White Hart – Paid my share of the dinner & a pint of Madeira, but allowed the rich Poet to treat me to a bottle of claret.[21]

Any further reference to the 'famous song' written by Bowles when a young man has eluded detection.

By the spring of 1827 Bowles had completed his history of Bremhill and had arranged that it would be printed by John Bowyer Nichols.[22] However, a good deal of correspondence passed between Bowles and Nichols before the finished work was ready to be published.

On 24 April he wrote:

I hope to be in Town about the 8th of May & shall call on you, possibly on the 10th when, I hope, we shall be able to put my M.S. Parochial history to press –

I wish to have it got up in a handsome manner, but should not think of publishing more than 250 copies . . .

As the Saxon part relating to the neighbouring antiquities of Avebury, Silbury & Wansdike, may be a matter of more general antiquarian interest, & as the investigation has led me into a much larger field than I, at first, propos'd to treat over, & as I flatter myself I shall throw considerable novelty of illustration on these monuments, I have previously publish'd a few copies of this enquiry separate from the body of the work, the whole of which, including what is now disparate, will be printed at your press – & I hope, with the many original documents relating to Stanley Abbey, to make an interesting Parochial History.

I shall send you in a day or two, the part relating to Avebury & perhaps you would do me the favour of admitting a page or two with your magazine,[23] which, for so many years has been so successfully devoted to this track of literature.

I cannot forget that the first lines ever printed of mine, I here first read & I shall be happy to avail myself of your topographical press, in bringing before the public the work which may perhaps be my last.[24]

In the event Bowles did not to travel to London early in May to discuss the printing with Nichols, but at the end of the month wrote to him again:

Mrs Bowles has given up all idea of coming to London & I chiefly wish to see you, respecting my intended publication.

We search'd all Piccadilly in vain – I us'd to have, for many years, excellent lodgings for six guineas a week, but the Landlady is religiously <u>craz'd</u>, & I decline going on that account – I would not have you engage the rooms for me, for Mrs Bowles they are out of the question, but, I think from what you say, that if I come up for a week, they, or some others, could be got, such as would answer without much difficulty, for a simple room & service – when I can fix a day, I will write again.

PS See if my picture is in the Exhibition if you go that way.[25]

In July Bowles wrote to Nichols:

The three sheets which these form part had better be all sent together in a parcel, that, I may see the whole.

I know the <u>penalty</u> for <u>corrections</u>, but I must have every thing to my mind –

If I do not <u>write fast</u> I cannot write at all – & never keeping or making a copy, or seeing what I have written till <u>imperfectly</u> printed it is no wonder that I am a long time before I am perfectly satisfied.

I thank you for your kind notices

We see <u>daylight</u> at last.[26]

Bowles was continually changing his mind and requiring alterations and corrections to his manuscripts, and must have sorely tried the patience of Nichols. At the end of September he wrote:

I shall wish any sheet which, in consequence of so many <u>after-thoughts</u>, requires particular <u>trouble</u> to be reprinted de novo from the copy as it now stands arrang'd – as I suppose it would be as <u>cheap</u> & much <u>easier</u>.

On return you will be so good as to let me know the expense of the <u>printing</u> – with the account for paper separate –

I shall be glad to have this parcel return'd, <u>in shape</u>, as soon as you can. I intended to get a <u>frank</u> from the Secretary of State,[27] but he is gone to London & I suppose the next parcel will be the last.

I have not yet made up my mind about publishing, but some peculiar circumstances in the present day have induced me to dedicate to my friend the Catholic Bear,[28] of Wardour, as you will see . . .

I wish to consult you about a publisher, if I had 150 for sale & I pray, stick up a copy that I may see the whole in connection, when you send the next.

P.S. When you come this way, let me see you.[29]

It was not only the text that was causing problems but also the illustrations that were to form part of the parochial history. Bowles had persuaded his old friend and fellow parson and antiquary John Skinner to draw a plan of the ground floor of Bowles's parsonage, and also a map of Bremhill and its vicinity. These were duly printed having been engraved, doubtless to Bowles's satisfaction. The same could not be said for another of the proposed illustrations. Bowles wrote to Nichols one Sunday early in the year, adding the words 'make haste' after the date:

It is utterly impossible that any use could be made of the engraving – It should have been a mere small vignette for head of the page, but, is [illegible] too large – nothing of the character is preserved in the countenance – & it is neither sketch nor engraving! I am inexorable about this, nor can any modification do. It is so unlike, & ill done, I shall resist payment, for I am sure it is not done in a workmanlike manner.

I hope the same person will not attempt the church, which is to be the frontispiece . . . I shall alter the passage about Pope . . . I shall be in town beginning of May, but would wish the volume out by the 3rd of April . . .[30]

The engraving of the church that formed the frontispiece of the book was the work of Samuel Bellin[31] and no doubt met with Bowles's approval. On 25 October he finished writing the dedication to Lord Arundell – the Catholic Bear referred to in his earlier letter to Nichols – and had at last decided who should be his publisher. After, it is suspected, a considerable amount of hesitation, he wrote to John Murray, by now certainly the most respected publisher in London:

As life is stealing away, I hope, at last, my long 'civil wars' of the pen are over; & sincerely begging pardon, if, in the Irish order of defence a kind of side-blow may have fallen when it ought not, & trusting, at all events, to a good humour'd & manly [?] oblivion, after apology, should you, at any time, have felt a shade of offence with me – perhaps you will oblige me in one request.

I have printed at Nicholl's[32] Parliament Street, a Parochial History – comprising nearly 300 pages with engravings –

The history of a parish I have made the basis of historical information on parochial subjects – a work not un-important from its connections with miscellaneous & historical knowledge.

It will be handsomely brought out with engravings, & there will be, in the publication there will be neither expense or risk of any kind to yourself.

My booksellers, Hurst & Robinson, you know have failed, & I am left to the 'wide world' of publishers, without knowing one personally except yourself –

Will you allow me to let the 100 copies at fifteen shillings each offer with your name as publisher which I well know how to appreciate?

Requesting an answer by return of post.[33]

It is certain that Murray responded by agreeing to be named as publisher, and so, anxious now to see the book in print, on 28 December Bowles wrote to John Nichols:

I suppose the appearance of 'our Parish' is delay'd till the beginning of the year, but I must request you to send me two copies, by tomorrow's mail, that comes thro' <u>Calne</u>, as I particularly wish to have a copy before New Years day.

      The other may be sent out at your leisure, but <u>two</u> copies I must have finally & should indeed be much oblig'd to you if you could let me have your account at the same time . . .[34]

It is certain that Bowles wished to give Lady Lansdowne a copy of his new book at the earliest possible moment, and on 7 January he was able to inscribe one of the copies that he had asked Nichols to let him have before New Year's Day 'Marchioness of Lansdowne from the author, a tribute of respect and esteem'.[35]

In January 1828 a preliminary meeting was held at the Bear Inn in Devizes to consider the establishment of a friendly society upon the principles of mutual insurance by which 'a provision for old age, sickness or infirmity may be secured by means of a small monthly contribution'. The Marquis of Lansdowne chaired the meeting that was attended by most of the 'gentlemen of rank and fortune' of the county, among whom was Bowles[36] who was certainly in sympathy with the aims of the proposed society. The outcome was the foundation of the Wiltshire Friendly Society, which continues to flourish today.

In 1827 an elderly woman named Catherine Cook was convicted of stealing from her employer some cups and saucers valued at 4s 6d. She was sentenced to six months in prison and fined the enormous sum of £40. On being unable to pay the fine, the magistrates proceeded to commute it to six months' solitary confinement over and above the original term of imprisonment. Bowles was outraged, and successfully petitioned the King to have the sentence mitigated.[37] He wrote to his friend George Crabbe about the imprisonment, and was doubtless gratified to receive a reply:

> . . . I ought to express my sense of that other part of your letter in which you do me the honour of communicating your sentiments and purposes respecting the imprisonment of Mrs Cook, and I judge it right to declare my opinion on the subject, which is that you have done nobly and courageously, as a gentleman, a man, and a Christian, and I might add as a magistrate and a priest, taking it for a fact that the sentence last inflicted upon the poor woman could not be mitigated by the same authority and power by which it was pronounced . . .[38]

Many others applauded Bowles's initiative, and someone arranged to have a poem 'To the Rev. W. Lisle Bowles' published in the *Devizes and Wiltshire Gazette*. It commenced 'Friend of the sufferer! The widow's friend' and ended 'Blest was the mission forwarded to thee! Open the lonely cell, and set her free!'.[39]

Most of Bowles's fellow magistrates, however, took an extremely dim view of his conduct, and on 17 January there were reports of a rumour: 'At the Wilts County Sessions the Magistrates intend to enter certain resolutions in consequence of an aspersion which they conceived had been cast upon some of their body, in the petition of Rev. Mr Bowles to His Majesty praying mitigation of the sentence passed on Catherine Cook.'[40]

Bowles had heard what was afoot and had earlier written to George Crabbe to seek his support: 'I hear my petition will be taken up at Devizes by some magistrates, as if, in doing my public duty, I had sought to reflect on them, and I hope as a friend to equity and humanity you will attend on Tuesday the 15th . . .'[41]

A resolution censuring Bowles was duly debated. Paul Methuen supported the motion, which was carried by twenty-one votes to eleven despite being vigorously opposed by Lord Folkestone[42] (the Earl of Radnor's heir), George Crabbe and John Benett,[43] the last two, of course, being particular friends of Bowles. Despite this, Bowles's conduct continued to receive popular support, and shortly afterwards it was announced that a meeting of the inhabitants of Calne was to be called 'to give the Rev. Gent. their thanks for his exertions in the cause of humanity'.[44] The meeting was called and was 'very fully and respectably attended' and at the end of the month 'a deputation of ten respectable inhabitants' called upon Bowles to present the resolution of the meeting. Bowles duly received the motion and said 'I might indeed be proud of the generous, disinterested and unsolicited support received from Lord Folkestone, Mr Benett, your excellent neighbour Mr Heneage[45] and others'.[46]

Bowles was particularly grateful for the support he had received from Crabbe. Following the passing of the resolution of censure he wrote to Crabbe's son, who was the curate of Pucklechurch in Gloucestershire: 'I shall be delighted cum Zephyris et hirundine prima to come to Pucklechurch to meet my excellent friend your Father – who has acted like a <u>nobleman</u> towards me in my late wars with some of the merciless squires.'[47]

One of Bowles's fellow magistrates was Charles Lewis Phipps, to whom he wrote at about this time in jocular terms that he occasionally adopted when writing to his close friends:

I stole your Paper yesterday – Don't prosecute me! I should be in a solitary cell – no Bible allow'd by the chaplain for fear I should turn from Job to Bell & Dragon! And even if you humanely should let me out, he would say, compassionate creature, I was worse off than before – as I had such nice apartments to myself night & day without naughty company! . . .[48]

It may be recalled that in 1822 Bowles wrote to Daniel Lysons, the celebrated Gloucestershire topographer, who probably visited Bremhill at Bowles's invitation. In any event the two clerical historians doubtless remained in touch with each other, as in February Bowles wrote to Lysons's wife:

Mrs Bowles and myself are truly concerned to hear of our kind friend Lysons's distressing complaint . . .

Mrs Bowles has been very ill but is now quite well and I am myself confined to the house at present by an obstinate cough.

We are for the first time annoy'd by these Pestiferous Ranters now dispers'd & organised, through my village – they resolutely preach before the Church-yard gates & during Service time! I am cautious of what to do, as a magistrate, but surely this insolence might be legally prevented. I suppose Lysons has heard of my Petition to the King which releas'd a poor woman from solitary confinement which some of my brother justices were very absurdly angry. My Parochial History of Bremhill will be published by Murray in a day or two. With best wishes and regards.[49]

However, Bowles had considerable regard for very many dissenters and on one occasion, after criticising the practices of some of them, wrote: 'I cheerfully except from those implications, all Methodists of the Wesleyan communion, all Moravians, all Quakers, and many Baptists who look up to respectable leaders in their community, – as the Methodists do to the leaders in their 'Conference'.[50]

Lord Lansdowne continued to find Bowles a useful source of information about people whose character would otherwise have been unknown to him. In March he wrote to Bowles in response to a letter that he had doubtless received from him:

I shall be most happy to comply with Mr Dean's wishes. I am frequently obliged to decline such applications from persons with whom I am not acquainted, to save myself from scrapes but your authority is quite a different <u>guarantee</u> & I have heard from other quarters that Mr D is a very [ ]able & amiable character.[51]

In April 1824 Lord Byron had died, so Bowles was probably surprised and not a little flattered four years later to receive a letter from Thomas Moore telling him that it had been suggested that he might join a committee to make arrangements for a monument to be erected in his memory. Moore wrote:

I have just received a letter from Hobhouse[52] in which he suggests to me that it is possible you might like to be in our Committee for a Monument to Lord Byron, and I really think you <u>ought</u>. The tribute to him is professedly on the score of his poetical talents <u>alone</u>, which would, entirely, I think, preclude any objections you might have to sanctioning the fame <u>politically</u> or <u>religiously</u>. There are, indeed, several high Tories on our list, while in the other way we abound in sterling names, Lord Lansdowne, Duke of Devonshire,[53] Lord Jersey[54] &c – In the poetical line was have Sir W. Scott, Campbell, Rogers, <u>Goethe</u>[55] &c. Let me know as soon as you decide. The numbers are confined to those who either were his correspondents, his personal acquaintances, or personal friends.

I shall not be able to go to the Concert with you on Tuesday. The weather is disagreeable & the Anacreontic diners will take it ill of me coming away. Tell me how your cough is.[56]

In the event Bowles was not a member of the preliminary committee formed with a view to a memorial to Byron being erected in Westminster Abbey.[57]

Soon after this Bowles was doubtless pleased to see published at last *The Parochial History of Bremhill in the County of Wilts; containing a Particular Account, from Authentic and Unpublished Documents, of the Cistercian Abbey of Stanley in that Parish with Observations and Reflections on the Origin and Establishment of Parochial Clergy, and other Circumstances of General Parochial Interest, including Illustrations of the Origin and Designation of the Stupendous Monuments of Antiquity in the Neighbourhood, Avebury, Silbury, and Wansdike.*[58] This work, 285 pages in length, was dedicated, as has been previously noted, to the Roman Catholic peer Lord Arundell, who had, of course, entertained Bowles at Wardour Castle. The dedication began:

As an high and honoured character in the county of Wilts, interested and versed in its local antiquities, and in gratitude for liberal and personal kindness, I inscribe to you this volume.

But I have yet a stronger motive which dictates this public expression of my regard and esteem: – Under the same Banners of the Cross at the battle of Graun, in Hungary, one of your Lordship's heroic ancestors and an ancestor of mine fought side by side. Your Lordship's ancestor received, on the field, his creation of Knight of the Sacred Roman Empire from Rodolph the 2nd; his standard-bearer in the same battle, Sir Rowland Bowles, had the addition of the Crescent to his arms. When Sir Thomas, this first Lord Arundell, an English volunteer, took with his own hand the standard of the infidel, the noble Baron of Wardour and his brave Wiltshire comrade professed one and the same religious creed. Their descendants living in the same County, and mostly in the same neighbourhood, have diverged as far asunder as to their conscientious and religious opinions, as in stations in life . . .

Bowles added a footnote to this dedication reading:

It was said some time since in a public paper that Lord Arundell was at the castle of *bigotry* and *superstition*, Wardour. I happened on that very day to be in his company; when he laughingly said, 'Here am I publicly accused of being a bigot, when I have two *heretic parsons* to *dine with me!*'59

The exceedingly long title of the book is an early indication of the wide range of subjects that had exercised Bowles's mind and that he had decided to put together in one volume. In the introduction he could not resist making reference to the controversy over Alexander Pope's life and works by writing:

Although, indeed, an occasional writer of some years standing before the public, I have been interrupted in the pursuit of many literary objects congenial to my feelings, by having had, for the last fifteen years of life, scarce *breathing-time* from self-defence in consequence of my conscientious opinions, candidly I hope, but not unmanfully, avowed in the life and edition of a great English poet . . . If I have spoken diffidently of a great portion of life, forced from other literary pursuits by this long controversy, I can only say, with some pride, that I felt the necessity of self-defence the more necessary, because, if one-hundredth part of the charges brought against me were true, that I were little better than a compound of envy, hatred, and malice, I could never hope that one kind spirit, after I 'go hence and am no more seen', would '*bid fair peace be to my sable shroud*'.

In the introduction Bowles writes that he is enabled to throw more light on the foundation of the former Stanley Abbey in his parish, and, having done so, could not 'pass over Avebury, Silbury and Wansdike'. His opinion on the origins of Avebury and Silbury Hill are fanciful in the extreme, and echo the writings of Stukeley[60] and other eighteenth-century antiquaries. So far as Wansdyke is concerned, he declares that 'Mr Duke has attempted to prove that this great rampart was merely a *fosse road*, an opinion I shall not attempt to refute'. When describing the hamlet of Studley, he mentions the very large number of Roman coins that were frequently found in one particular field called Red-hill. In order to persuade the finders of these coins to bring them to him, he offered 3*d* for as many as should be brought to the parsonage,[61] and writes that not fewer than 200 were brought to him within a year of making the offer.

In the first chapter Bowles attempts to compare the state of agriculture with its state in the past, and provides a valuable commentary on the wages and problems of agricultural labourers in 1828. In the second chapter his thoughts on the origins and meaning of Avebury and Silbury Hill are set out, with digressions on Celtic deities and a Roman sculpture found in Bath. The establishment of parochial clergy and the history of parish churches claim his attention in following chapters – not to mention church towers, parish registers and detailed observations on 'Parochial Psalmody'. In this he writes:

> In country churches, singing to the '*praise and Glory of God*', in general, is little better than singing to the annoyance of all who have any ear or heart for harmony. Two clarinets, out of tune, and a bassoon, which hurtles one note most sonorously, while three abortive blasts succeed; a man, for treble, with long hair, and eyes out of his head; a tenor higher than the treble, which completely mars the harmony; and a quavering bass, quavering as for life; and all those voices only agreeing in one point, as to which shall be heard longest and loudest – such voices, and such instruments, not unfrequently make up the musical part in country churches, of the church service.

This is followed by an extraordinary digression in which Bowles attempts to prove that the Old Hundredth psalm tune was originally English rather than French or German. A chapter on churchyards and ancient inscriptions follows, and no reader familiar with Bowles's poetic output would be surprised to find included examples of his own epitaphs composed for his deceased parishioners. In composing some of these

Bowles betrayed a sense of humour not often found in his writings. One wonders what were the feelings of the parents of the boy who drowned in the canal when they found that their son's epitaph would be:

> Here lies a hapless youth so vain –
> He slipp'd – he fell – into – the WATERY MAIN![62]

Or of the relations of John Dark, who found that their vicar had inscribed a stone in the path to the church:

> Reader, this heap of earth – this grave-stone mark!
> Here lie the last remains of Poor John Dark!
> Five years beyond man's age he liv'd, and trod
> This path, each Sabbath, to the House of God.
> At his last hour, with his last breath, he cried,
> 'THY KINGDOM COME, THY WILL BE DONE' – and died.[63]

In the penultimate chapter Bowles gives a detailed description of his parsonage house (including a plan of the ground floor with each room identified by name[64]) and garden (very similar to the account in the *Gentleman's Magazine* in 1814), and in the introduction anticipates what many readers of today may think by writing:

> I fear it will be thought by some that I have been too minute in the description of a place so humble as the Vicarage-house and garden of this parish. But one of my objects, besides miscellaneous information on parochial matters, was, in the present age of clerical obloquy, to exhibit the clergyman and his abode in their proper moral position in English society; and with respect to the description of my own house and garden, naturally connected with the subject, it will be considered that in a very few years, when the present possessor shall sleep
>
> > Where ends the chancel in a vaulted space
> > With the departed vicars of the place;
>
> every vestige of the house as it now stands, and the garden as it appears, may be swept away. I was therefore not unwilling that some future incumbent might know what was the state of the Parsonage-house and garden in 1827. Perhaps very soon
>
> > The spade may cover all my 'care' has plann'd
> > And laughing 'carrots' reassume the land. Pope.

It not unfrequently happens that a new incumbent considers all decorations in a garden, detached from asparagus and cauliflower-beds, superfluous; on the contrary, it often happens that another,

'Thinks alteration charming work is,'

and appears busy with his spade the moment he takes possession; doubtless determining,

'His predecessor lov'd devotion,
But of *garden* – had no notion!'

On this account, if I have been somewhat solicitous myself not to do so – I hope I shall find a pardon in every liberal breast.'[65]

As Bowles leads his reader around the garden, he pauses at a root-house and invites him to sit down in the old carved chair that Bowles is proud to say has received 'amongst other visitors, Sir Samuel Romilly, Sir George Beaumont, Sir Humphrey Davy[66] – poets as well as philosophers, Madame de Stael, Dugald Stewart,[67] and – CHRISTOPHER NORTH, ESQ.!'[68] The literary minded reader would have known that 'Christopher North' was the pseudonym of John Wilson,[69] the regular contributor to *Blackwood's Magazine.*

In short, the work is, as has been said, 'a literary curiosity. It contains a variety of facts and reflections connected with its ostensible subject, inextricably mixed up with innumerable things that have no connection with it whatsoever.'[70]

However, at least one reviewer of the day thought otherwise, when he wrote in *Blackwood's Magazine* 'It is a book the most interesting of the kind we ever read . . . We are sure that we have said and quoted enough to induce all our readers, who take delight in antiquarian studies, to purchase the volume.' Bowles was, of course, delighted to read such words. He wrote to John Nichols on 6 August, while staying at the bishop's palace in Wells 'antiquity-hunting with the excellent Bishop', as he put it in a letter that was obligingly franked by the bishop:

I hope you have seen the magnificent article on my Parochial history in Blackwood's Magazine for this month. If you have not, pray get it to read – I might indeed be well proud of such eloquent praise from such a Quarter, tho' I know nothing of the writer except that I suppose it may be Professor Wilson, & this, I imagine, from the style of the writing, for I have no personal knowledge of him, whatsoever. [71]

Bowles's friend George Crabbe, the poet and rector of Trowbridge, had very mixed feelings about the work. He wrote:

The reason for my not mentioning the History of Bremhill was this. I had not read at that time more than a very few pages. I knew nothing of Wansdike, nothing of Tanhill, and could not have told you in what county, scarcely in what kingdom, were Avebury and Silbury . . . and only three days past since I could fairly say I had arrived at the knowledge of 'parochial psalmody and church-yard inscriptions,' concluding with that exquisite morsel of improvement on the epitaph of the old couple. Indeed that is the true and long approved stone-cutter style and I wonder that you would produce anything so utterly unlike it . . . He who writes concerning monuments of all or any kind, if I may judge by the little I read of them, should have no more of feeling than the things themselves. Cold, stern judges of dead and decayed materials for investigation. Perhaps I err and Sir R.C. Hoare might correct my opinion. But seriously, though I like your book the better because it engages me by subjects which I partly understand, yet I dare not affirm that a rigid antiquary would approve any portion of the work, except that which I either do not comprehand or cannot relish . . .[72]

Almost immediately after publication of the *Parochial History* Bowles's description of his garden was reproduced in *The Mirror of Literature, Amusement, and Instruction*,[73] and so reached a much wider readership than merely the purchasers of the book.

Not only did *Blackwood's Magazine* think highly of the *Parochial History* but also, in its August number, it had some very complimentary things to say about Bowles personally:

He is, we say, a well-beneficed clergyman. We make but a distant allusion to the value of his living – which is very considerable – but not more – nay, less than he deserves; for although a Whig, he is one of the most elegant, pathetic and original living poets of England. His benefice is from nature – genius. Therein he is nobly endowed. His living is in good truth immortal. We really know not whether to admire his poetry or his prose. In the famous controversy about Pope, with Byron, Campbell, Roscoe, Gifford, Gilchrist, and North, he exhibited great critical acuteness and powers of illustration. He luxuriated in examples drawn from a wide range of the best reading; and certainly, though not without a few hard knocks from his sturdy antagonists, he came off victorious and with flying colours.[74]

Early in January 1828 Bowles wrote to Murray:

I do not know whether you have received 150 copies of my topographical history from Mr Nicholls, but, I will request that no copy may be sold before the latter end of the month on account of a cancel to be inserted, if copies have not been sent.

I have settled all expenses except the advertisements, which I must leave to your superior judgement & knowledge, but will readily indemnify you for any expenses, should not the sale answer them, which I have no doubt it will, besides remuneration – 250 copies have been printed, & there are three engravings, & two plates, & the volume is handsomely got up, of nearly three hunded pages; the price, per copy, would be, I should think, fifteen or sixteen shillings, but this, also, I must leave to you.

As the printing is upwards of 100, which I have already paid, I should imagine you would think it not unreasonable if we shar'd in the profits, myself taking care you shall run no riske which, indeed, upon a local history I should think unreasonable, but, I hope, given some considerable general information. & made the volume not un-interesting to general readers,or [illegible] unworthy of the Templum Musarum[75] from which it issues! One request I trust you will hold sacred, which is this, no copy be sold under the trade price, nor will you think it unfair that I should have the copies that might remain.[76]

On 5 February Bowles wrote again to Murray:

I delay'd for some time, my Parochial History, because I think it best to add some explanatory illustrations, which will bring it to about 300 pages. You will receive 300 copies from Mr Nicholls on Saturday the 9th & I shall think it might be charg'd at twenty shillings, but of this, I am no judge.

But I am anxious that you who know how most effectively to do it, will advertise it as for publication on Tuesday the 12th.

I have not much doubt, but if this is done, directly, the 200 copies will be sold, & I should hope, by the time I come to London, we might begin another edition – but, of this I am no judge. It is local but with a good deal of miscellaneous matter, mythological, ecclesiastical – classical & Celtic, & monastic –

I can only say that Lord Lansdowne, and those who have seen it, speak [illegible] higher of it, than I could have expected, but this might not make it more saleable.

Bowles continues by instructing Murray to send copies to, among others, his old schoolfriend the Bishop of London and to William Sotheby, with suitable inscriptions in Latin, Lady Dacre '"For auld land syne" & kind remembrances' and to William Jerdan 'with the author's regards'.[77] A week later another letter from Bowles arrived in Albemarle Street:

> I write to you, really under some sort of uneasiness – I have the utmost reliance on your honour & word, more especially after your kind & gentlemanly letter in which you engag'd to be the publisher of my Parochial History. –
>
> But, Mr Nicholls, who had nearly printed it, when I wrote, informs me, he has written to you on the subject of the copies, & received no answer, & today on enquiring at my booksellers, I find no advertisement has appear'd of my work – & he thinks it possible you were under some mistake as if Mr Nicholls had any thing to do with the publication. If there should be any hesitation on your part, after your engagement, I can only attribute it to this circumstance – & therefore beg to say, that not one single copy will be sold by Mr Nicholls –
>
> I ordered him to send 150 to you, but there will be on sale 200 – having only finished 250 –& given away nearly the 50 – Trusting this explanation will be satisfactory, if my bookseller is right in his ideas, which I can hardly suppose.[78]

It is likely that this letter resolved the difficulties that appear to have arisen, although the work did not prove to be as popular as Bowles hoped as no demand for a second edition materialised – notwithstanding Bowles's optimism revealed in his next letter to Nichols, to whom he wrote in the following month:

> I must have five more copies sent here, by the coach – I see it respectfully notic'd in the Literary gazette, & if Murray sells his lot, which I hope, that it is somewhat further brought into publick notice, he will do, I should propose another edition.
>
> I am anxious to do this, on account of various additions, & corrections, & on account of not having acknowledged my obligation to the Stanley Chartulary, which was lent to me by Mr Gaby, now of Bath. The acknowledgement was inadvertently & in the hurry of the preface, omitted!
>
> Have the goodness to keep this letter, in case, any remarks should be made on the subject.[79]

The *Parochial History* was closely followed in the same year by *Hermes Britannicus. A Dissertation on the Celtic Deity Teutates, the Mercurius of Caesar, in further proof and corroboration of the origin and designation of the Great Temple at Abury, Wiltshire.* In his *Parochial History* Bowles had pointed out what appeared to him to have been the origin and designation of Avebury but, as he stated in the introduction to *Hermes Britannicus*, 'I became interested as I proceeded, particularly when all the proofs of what I first advanced seemed to accumulate, and, therefore, I pursued the track with increased ardour, till what I intended as additional notes and confirmation became a volume'. As Mark Gillings and Joshua Pollard have written:

> It seems that in the early nineteenth century you couldn't keep a good druid down. They were to make a rapid comeback in the Rev. William Lisle Bowles's argument that Avebury was a druidic temple to the Celtic deity Teutates, a god who had been introduced to them by the Phoenicians. Bowles's scheme built upon the earlier suggestion of Maurice that the Obelisk acted as the gnom of a sundial, suggesting that the stone settings of the circle formed a heavenly calendar, the whole designed to mark the passage of time. Beyond the immediate confines of the circles the 'serpent' defined by the avenues was seen as a potent symbol of rebirth and immortality, charting the course of the stars across the heavens. The final component was Silbury Hill, the platform upon which an effigy of the deity had once been placed.[80]

Following Bowles's death in 1850, a long obituary appeared in the *Gentleman's Magazine* in which the writer considered that 'these lucubrations, as may be supposed, were more ingenious than well-founded; for his poetical temperament naturally led him to adopt with eagerness many plausible, but improbable hypotheses, not only in his archaeological researches, but also in his literary biographies'.[81] And not many years were to pass before it was generally accepted that *Hermes Britannicus* was in reality a work of fiction, with Thomas William Wake Smith, the historian of Cranborne Chase, annotating his copy of it with the words 'I believe all this to be "bosh".'[82]

While in London in May 1828, Bowles was able to perform an errand for his friend George Crabbe, who had written to Bowles in the previous month:

> You have taught me to ask favours by kindly complying when I sought them and you now find how soon I repeat my requests. You are going

to town and perhaps within a few days and if so will you indulge me by receiving for me the medal voted to me by the council of the R.S. of Literature? It is in the possession of the Honbl. Mr G.A. Ellis,[83] MP, Spring Gardens, and I will venture to inform him that you will do me the honour of conveying it to me. For this purpose and at your own time I will trouble you to do this business for me, and as paper is not sufficiently defensive against accidents, I will thank you to give me credit for so much money as will purchase a small box of any material hard enough to bear pressure, and lastly (as your return will not be within two or three weeks?) I must beg of you to order the parcel directed to

    Your much obliged servant

    Geo. Crabbe.[84]

Bowles duly complied with Crabbe's request. Crabbe wrote to thank his friend, asking 'by what means I might be of use to you, though in honest truth I begin to feel that I cannot be very useful to anyone'![85]

During the same visit to London Bowles chanced to meet Sir Walter Scott. Naturally he felt compelled to record his impression of the encounter in verse by writing a sonnet entitled 'To Sir Walter Scott. On accidentally meeting and parting with Sir Walter Scott, whom I had not seen for many years, in the streets of London, May 1828.'[86]

In November Bowles was again writing to Murray:

If I am not a <u>splendid</u> Customer, I am a <u>safe</u> one, & understanding from Mr Nicholls, that he has no copy of my Parochial History, & seeing it advertis'd in the papers, those, which you have on hand, I trust, will also, before long, be dispos'd of.

    But, in the paper, which I take, St James Chronicle – the <u>advertisement</u> is – by the Rev ? W.L. Bawles – which looks so much like 'Bawl' that Mrs Bowles tells me I ought to write to you in case you advertise again, & I think further, at the same, it might be as well to say 'Canon Residentiary of Sarum' instead of Prebendary, which might induce a few of the more dignified of our order to lay out twenty shillings-worth, on a book about County – parson, matters, & antiquities . . .

    Sir Richard Hoare requested me to write the history of Bremhill & having promised him, I think it better to give Marte meo, as well as I could – a little <u>flesh & blood</u>, to an Antiquarian Skeleton, tho the Rioringtonians (?), I suppose, will be at me! particularly for a Dedication to a Catholic Peer, but I am as true <u>a Protestant</u> as the best of them.

    I shall not trouble you but, on account of another circumstance. The Bishop of Bath & Wells, having built a beautiful Cottage, near

Wells, which commands the sweep of the Severn, scenes familiar to me from Infancy, – express'd a wish that I would make this scene the subject of what he call'd a 'Justum Poem'. I have just finish'd my task – not reluctantly, but con amore – for the scene itself is most poetical, & connected with early associations that would have made me poetical, tho I had not written a line.

Now, I shall take the liberty of putting some copies under your protection, and also some copies of a sermon, lately preach'd for promoting Christian knowledge, which was requested to be publish'd. This [illegible] are already printed but I [illegible] a more splendid edition of the poem, in Spring . . . the Bishop is anxious for its prosperity in the world.

Pray, do not give yourself the trouble of writing, but I think it best to give you, hoping you will have no objection [to] this information.[87]

The poem suggested by the bishop was duly published in 1828 and entitled *Days Departed; or, Banwell Hill, a lay of the Severn Sea*. The printer was Richard Cruttwell of Bath, probably the son and successor of the original printer and publisher of Bowles's first sonnets, to whom he wrote in February of the following year before the printing of a second edition:

You may as well begin the poems directly but it must be of the size of Montgomery's vol: Omnipresence[88] & about the same number of lines in a page.

I have so many expenses here that I am unwilling to incur any expense at present, having occasion for all I have in hand in furnishing a large canonical House, but I have no doubt a new Edition will more that pay the expenses, as there will be so little to alter. Tho I am quite sure of my ground, in the notes, I should wish them completely revis'd – The preface and dedication may remain, but I think it important that my answers to the observations in the Cheltenham Gazette should appear at the end of the Preface.[89]

At the end of 1828 Bowles wrote to Nichols in some confusion about the cost of printing his latest works:

However dark Hermes was, the accounts for printing him are more so & I hope you will have the goodness to dis-entangle a little – I am of all men living the most stupid, in these things –
First – the bill for Bremhill was paid – every thing as I understood, binding and all, & now there is 6 pounds for binding Bremhill. The

whole account was paid in full – by two drafts on Drummonds & if I recollect, binding was charg'd for the whole number, they being, in a bound state, all of them, as I understood when in London.

Secondly there is a charge of printing Banwell Hill – was that the corrections for Gentleman's Magazine? – oh! no – It is all right – I remember the copies printed to give away, but shall I count accounts for binding Bremhill – perhaps this means binding Hermes – If so all is again right, but pray, let me know.

My account for Hermes, deducting sale for Bremhill, is then 76. 12. 5 – If this is so, than all is clear – & I know what I have to pay, but, as Murray's sale will cover this, I imagine you will let me remain debtor, trusting it will not be inconvenient, till the Spring when I come to London & will settle with you, whether minus or not with Murray – then we can settle about another edition of Bremhill.

PS [at the head of the letter] as you have paid money out of pocket I think I had better send you fifty pounds at once (over leaf)[90]

In one part of *Days Departed; or Banwell Hill* Bowles writes of the 'Benevolence of English Landlords' and describes the 'Ten thousand charities' that 'adorn the land' as an answer to the charge that 'England's Aristocracy . . . wrapt in sordid, selfish apathy . . . feel not for the poor'. In a footnote to these words he adds:

The English Landlord has been held up to obloquy, as endeavouring to keep up the price of corn, for his own sordid interest; but rent never *leads*, it only *follows*, as the utmost a landlord can get for his capital is *three* per cent, whereas the lord of whirling wheels[91] gains thirty. – *See Letters, by the Author, in the Bath Chronicle, signed Agricola.* [92]

In May 1829 Bowles wrote to Murray:

I am unwilling to take up a moment of your time, but one word about Banwell Hill – The 2nd Edition,[93] two hundred & fifty, will be ready in a few days – I shall transmit two hundred & forty copies to Albemarle Street . . . I could not get my old lodgings, so, if I come to Town, it will be without my family & for a few days, but, will you have the kindness to insert that 'The new Edition of Mr Bowles's Poem "Departed Days, or Banwell Hill" will be publish'd the 14th of June, dedicated to the Lord Bishop of Bath & Wells.' [Four lines are here deleted by Bowles who continues] I well know how occupied you are with more important concerns, nevertheless, pray do not forget this request. You will have the goodness to make out the small account of my other Publication, but, as I may see you, I will not bother you to write.[94]

Yet another letter to Murray followed on 20 May:

Amid your more splendid announcements, I must call your attention to a poor Poet.

My second edition of 'Days Departed', much enlarg'd, with the addition of a tale by way of episode, in a smaller volume to suit my other poems, is now printed. But have you got, or have you forgotten, my picture? Is it engraved?

The volume, done up, will be sent to you (240 copies) on account of the plates which you can get inserted, or would it be best to send the impression in sheets? If the plate is not finish'd, or perhaps forgotten, the poem must be publish'd without it.

I have received a letter from Galignani[95] of Paris, to say he is going to print the whole of my poems, but I would wish only those selected which I think would be most popular.

If you are busy, let your son or any one write a line instanter. Will you present a copy to Mr Lockhart?[96] He is perhaps sick of the sight of poems of this appearance, but I have some lines on Sir Walter Scott, and I would hope if he begins he would read my poem to the end.[97]

An extravagantly favourable review of *Days Departed* appeared in the January 1829 number of the *Mirror of Literature, Amusement and Instruction*. The reviewer considered that 'This is a delightful volume – full of nature and truth, and in every respect worthy of one of the most elegant, pathetic, and original poets of England.'[98]

Bowles was clearly flattered that Galignani was interested in publishing his poetry and in writing to Caroline Bowles told her 'You must know that the great Paris publisher Galignani has written to say he intends publishing W.L.B.'s works. This is what I never expected.' He wrote to Richard Kennet, probably Galignani's agent:

Mr Wm. L. Bowles's compliments to Mr Kennet & having been prevented coming to Town this year, sends to him for Messrs Galignani the 2nd Edition of his Poem 'Days Departed'. He sends a copy the moment it comes from the press & before its publication in Town.

The arrangements of his other Poems, Mr Bowles would recommend to be as follows –

[Here Bowles sets out in detail which of his works he would wish to be included and which excluded and concludes by writing:]

Mr Bowles will send his Poem on South American Scenery & Characters, a smaller Epic from the History of Chili –& he suggests a new name

Lauturo

Or

The Avenger of his

Country

A Poem taken from

The History of Chili

With scenes & characters

Of South America

Mr Bowles begs to return to Messrs Galignani his best thanks & submits this sketch to their judgement and decision.[99]

In the event *The Poetical Works of Milman, Bowles, Wilson and Barry Cornwall complete in one volume* containing 194 pages of Bowles's poetry was published in Paris by A. & W. Galignani in 1829. Portraits of the four poets appeared on the frontispiece and Bowles's works were prefaced by a largely flattering memoir of him. This memoir contains, however, a criticism of Bowles's poetry, and one wonders how it was received by him:

> Bowles has written much, but he ranks only as a second-rate writer of English poetry. He keeps too near the line of mediocrity, and yet all is in good style and pure in sentiment. His works are a production of a virtuous and reflective mind too little acted upon by passion, too little susceptible of high emotions, to yield 'thoughts that breathe and words that burn'. He is tender, but never impassioned; easy, but still somewhat touched with the cold correctness of the scholar; attentive to the arrangement and purity of style rather than to the elevation and novelty of his thoughts. He cannot play with the thunderbolt or ride upon the storm: he cannot hurry on with 'spurs of speed;' but his path is in the tranquil sunshine, and his pace regular and measured, even and sedate. He writes nothing to startle and surprise, but he frequently engages the kindlier feelings of the heart, and enlists the social affections of the reader on his side.[100]

Bowles was now working on a projected life of Bishop Ken, the deprived Bishop of Bath and Wells, and in an effort to find further material to assist his research he informed the editor of the *Gentleman's Magazine* of his plans. As a consequence a note appeared in the magazine that 'If any of our correspondents have any documents or letters, he will be much obliged to them to communicate either to the Editor of the Gentleman's Magazine or to himself'.[101]

In 1827 the Bath musician John Ashley had published *Reminiscences and Observations respecting the Origin of the National Anthem called 'God Save The King!'* . . . This came to Bowles's notice, as in the following year Ashley published *A Letter respectfully addressed to the Rev. W.L. Bowles, Vicar of Bremhill, Wilts (Author of 'The Spirit of Discovery')*. This letter was supplementary to Ashley's earlier pamphlet and began with the words: 'As you did me the honour of noticing my trifle respecting the origin of *God save the King*, I take the liberty of making a few additional observations on the subject.' Bowles agreed with Ashley's opinion that the words were written by Harry Carey, and in the *Life of Thomas Ken* on which Bowles was now working, after mentioning a recent publication in which Ben Johnson[102] was suggested as the author of the words, he was to write: 'I will not waste a word on such opinions, so vaguely supported; as *Mr Ashley*, an ingenious musician, of Bath, with genius allied to poor Carey's, has exposed the absurdity of such a supposition.'

On 2 August 1828 Lord and Lady Lansdowne dined at the parsonage with only two other guests, Dr Parry from Bath and Moore, who thought the day 'rather dull, for Bowles's'.[103]

Two days later Bowles's friend Lewis West, minister of the Moravian chapel at Tytherton within the parish of Bremhill, died at the age of seventy-three. For seventeen years he and Bowles had been intimate friends. Writing of the Moravians in his *The Beauties of Wiltshire*, John Britton declares that 'religion, peace and industry, characterise these amiable people; the greatest cordiality has always existed between them, and the present Minister of their parish.'[104] It is no surprise therefore to find Bowles attending his friend's funeral – although this would have not met with the approval of many clergy of the Established Church at that time. Bowles gives a detailed and affectionate account of the proceedings in his *Parochial History of Bremhill*, noting that 'the coffin is then borne into the chapel'; that 'the clergy of the established church invited, go the next in order, then the Moravian ministers, and afterwards the congregation'. Bowles could not resist adding that the afternoon service in the chapel 'is concluded by the congregation, rich and poor, taking bread together, and, what is difficult to mention with appropriate seriousness, drinking *tea!'*.[105]

Bowles had always been tolerant of orthodox dissent and regarded with respect the very often learned leaders of their established congregations. He made his position clear in the preface to his *Days Departed* . . ., published in 1829, when he wrote:

Living in the most friendly intercourse with Dissenters, of various denominations, honoured by me because they dissent from *conscience*; – making no difference, in the the church I deem Apostolical, by whatever name he may call himself, or be called by others; – a member from its commencement of that Society which distributes the *Holy Bible*, without *note* or *comment*; I trust I may be allowed, without offence to any, to express my opinions freely on '*any comment*' or *comments* on that Divine Code![106]

On Tuesday 5 August Bowles arrived at the Bishop's Palace in Wells to spend the 'weekend' (meaning Tuesday to Friday or Saturday) as a guest of the Bishop, whose other visitors included the Rev. John Skinner[107] from Camerton, the Rev. Stephen Cassan[108] from Mere and Sir Richard Colt Hoare. On the following day the Bishop, Bowles, Skinner, Cassan and two others travelled in the Bishop's coach to Banwell cave, close to which the Bishop had built a cottage for his use as a retreat. Skinner recorded in his journal:

We stopped at Cheddar to visit the Church, and Bowles employed my pencil to sketch two of the monastic crosses, as he thinks (on what grounds I know not) that they will contribute to establish a singular system he has set up respecting the Pillar of Thout, Teut, or Hermes.
We drove to the cottage the Bishop has erected on the hill contiguous to the cave, but it rained without intermission. Bowles was to be in requisition to write a poem on the occasion, myself composing some lines on the subject and contenting myself with [sketching] a view or two of the cottage and the interior of the cave.[109]

On the following day the stormy weather caused the party to remain indoors at the Palace. Skinner, who was convinced that he was 'on the track of an important etymological discovery, by which it could be proved that there was a secret significance "in every letter that entered into the composition of Celtic names",'[110] recorded in his journal:

I suffered a severe attack during our symposium from all the party (excepting the Bishop and Sir Richard Hoare), who, from not understanding, endeavoured to ridicule my system of etymology by asking me the derivation of several strange abstract words in order to perplex and puzzle me.
I told them a story, which had the effect of puttng a stop at least to the malicious criticism of Mr Cassan.[111]

Bowles doubtless employed his considerable intellect in poking fun at Skinner's unlikely theories, but probably not in a malicious way. His ability to write poetry, of sorts, 'at the drop of a hat', and his eccentricity, is graphically demonstrated by the following entry in Skinner's journal:

> I finished my drawing of Banwell Cottage before breakfast and gave it to the Bishop.
> Bowles says he has written 500 lines already on the subject, and purposes leaving them with Cruttwell,[112] so that they will soon be before the public. He is the most absent man I ever knew when engaged in his versification; no company prevents his writing, when he ought to be engaged in conversation; this morning we had done breakfast ere he came to the table, dripping with rain, having been walking backwards and forwards in the garden during the heavy storm. I was obliged actually to rub him down with a silk handkerchief, fearing he might take cold. Yesterday evening, while Sir Richard Hoare, the Bishop and two others of the party were playing at cards, he threw himself on the sofa, close to them, and snored loudly. Such eccentricities may be the companion of genius, but they certainly are not pleasing in society, especially where real distinctions ought to be made. When Bowles is in residence as Canon of Salisbury he will, I think, cut a queer figure, and read a ridiculous chapter of accidents to the people. He left after breakfast for Bath in his close carriage, as did Sir Richard for Devonshire, and Mr Cassan for his residence at Mere . . .[113]

On 8 June William Coxe,[114] the historian and writer, rector of Bemerton near Salisbury, Archdeacon of Wiltshire and one of the six residentiary canons of Salisbury Cathedral, had died, whereupon the Dean and Canons of Sarum elected Bowles to be a residentiary canon in his place.[115] It was reported that 'the election was wholly unsolicited on the part of Mr Bowles, but the Dean and Canons of Sarum, out of esteem for his character and respect for his talents, spontaneously conferred the dignity on him'.[116] It is not unlikely that the suggestion that Bowles should be elected came from his old friend William Macdonald, who had been elected a residentiary canon in 1823.

In the following month the *Annual Register* included in its Ecclesiastical Preferments not only Bowles's appointment but also the translation of his old schoolfriend William Howley from the bishopric of London to the see of Canterbury.

It was the duty of the dean and residentiary canons to keep the fabric of the cathedral in good repair, and it was reported several years later that the net revenue received by the canons from their estates amounted to £2799 per annum. The fines paid on the renewal of leases were divided equally between the dean and the six canons (subject to 2½ per cent being reserved towards the cost of keeping the cathedral in repair), and the remainder of the revenues belonged as to two-eighths to the dean and one-eighth to each of the residentiary canons.[117] However, as Bowles was later to point out when defending the function and activities of deans and canons of cathedrals, at Salisbury they also maintained a school to educate, clothe and apprentice eight boys, the cathedral choristers, and also supported various families attached to the service of the cathedral.[118] As a result, therefore, the amount of remaining revenue that would have found its way into Bowles's pocket was in all probability quite modest.

However, with this appointment came the right to occupy the house in the Cathedral Close known as Aula-le-Stage (meaning Tower House) as well as an obligation, according to the statutes, ordinances and customs of the cathedral, to be resident for three months of each year and during that time to take a turn in playing his part in the services and preaching in the cathedral. It now became Bowles's practice, therefore, to spend the first three months of each year in the Close of Salisbury Cathedral, and the rest of the year in Bremhill, when not in London, Bath or Wells, his favourite places to visit. As a consequence, while residing in Salisbury his duties as incumbent of Bremhill would have been undertaken by his curate, and not many years were to pass before this practice was being strongly criticised on the grounds that a person in Bowles's position would be unable to discharge in a proper manner his responsibilites to both the dean and chapter as residentary canon and to his flock as parish priest.

Bowles must have relished living in the ancient canonical house with its uninterrupted view of the north side of the cathedral and spire, although the story is told that so nervous was he that the spire of the cathedral might fall and cause injury to him in his house that he measured the distance between the house and the cathedral. No doubt his mind was put at rest when he calculated that, in the event of this occurring, the house would be spared by several feet!

Before Bowles took up residence the house was surveyed with a view to a schedule of dilapidations being prepared and agreed. Bowles employed John Peniston,[119] the Salisbury architect, to act for him, and on 19 November he wrote to Bowles at Bremhill to tell him that Mr Garbett of Winchester, who acted as umpire, had assessed the sum to be paid, presumably by William Coxe's estate, as £239 12s 0d. The residence of a Mrs Hinxman[120] also passed to Bowles with the canonry, and the dilapidations in respect of her property amounted to £75 15s 0d – but this sum would not be paid until the end of the remaining six years of her lease.[121]

However pleased he might have been with his new residence in the beautiful cathedral Close, Bowles could not resist adding a miniature porch and 'Gothic' arcading to the roof. At the garden entrance he added octagonal ashlar gate-piers with Perpendicular detail. He also restored mullions to the windows and added window labels. Internally he made a number of alterations, and in the tower cellar he created 'an oratory with a late medieval stained glass figure of a kneeling man in a blue habit. However, he curtailed the 13th-century chapel for use as a scullery.'[122]

Two years later Bowles erected a memorial to Coxe in the garden. This consisted of a pinnacle pedestal seen through a Gothic arch with an inscription reading 'M/GULMI COXE/LITTERIS PER EUROPAM/ ILLUSTRIS/W.L.B. /SUCCESSOR/HIS AEDIBUS CANONICIS/ MDCCCXXX'.[123] In reporting the wording of the memorial the *Devizes and Wiltshire Gazette* also added: 'Upon which the following Impromptu has been written' – surely by Bowles, the first four lines of which providing a taste of the standard of poetry now issuing from his pen:

> To William Coxe, the poet Bowles
> Devotes this willow'd spot of earth
> Inscribes this Tablet – kindred souls
> Thus pay respect to taste and worth . . .[124]

In his *Picturesque Memorials of Salisbury* published in 1834, the Rev. Peter Hall, having mentioned the memorial to Coxe, then writes:

> In the same garden appears a Dial, thus inscribed:- + Quam jucundi praeteriere dies! W.L.B. Jan. 8, 1829. Obiit. Society will have lost an accomplished poet, and a benevolent man, when the space left for the concluding date is filled up.
>
> + What pleasant days have passed away![125]

One of the duties expected of the residentiary canons of the cathedral at this time was that each of them, when in residence, should entertain from time to time the widows of clergyman living in the College of Matrons situated in the Close and near the gate separating the Close from the High Street. On one occasion, when the widows were Bowles's guests, he composed a poem entitled 'On seeing plants in the windows of Seth Ward's College, endowed for widows of clergymen, at Salisbury',[126] and in March 1830 his verses entitled 'Seth Ward's Matrons' appeared in the *Salisbury and Winchester Journal*.[127]

It seems that in October 1828 Bowles was hoping to meet in Bremhill, the celebrated engraver Joseph Skelton[128] of Oxford who, among numerous other commissions, had executed a set of fifty-two etchings of the antiquities of Bristol.[129] On the 9th Bowles wrote to him in a very formal way, which he would not adopt when writing to a friend:

> Mr Bowles is very sorry he had not the pleasure of seeing Mr Skelton on his road to Bristol, but he hopes for that pleasure when he comes this way, again.
>
> Among the beautiful illustrations of scenes, more rever'd by none, than the writer of this note, the illustrations which Mr Skelton has sent are the most beautiful, & he thanks Mr Skelton for the engravings accompanying the exquisite Picts Oxoniensis.
>
> Mr Bowles sees the price of this is fifteen shillings, which he takes the opportunity of sending by Mr Whitworth & begs to be considered as a subscriber, & also to the History of Bristol.
>
> I send you a [illegible] Picture of Bristol, which perhaps you might introduce, from a <u>Poem</u>, about to be published!
> W.L. B.[130]

On 22 October Bowles preached a sermon at Corsham on 'St Paul, the First Christian Missionary at Athens for the benefit of The Society for the Promotion of Christian Knowledge'. This was subsequently published by John Murray at the request of the magistrates and clergy present and reviewed in the *Gentleman's Magazine*.[131] The advertisement, surely written by Bowles, includes the eccentric note added as a result of the failure of his earlier publishers, Hurst and Robinson:

> It may be proper to make the preliminary observation, that in this Sermon, less has been said of the Institution on whose account it was preached, because the claims and character of that truly excellent Society had been fully and specifically pointed out in a Sermon preached on the same occasion, and mostly before the same audience. That Sermon was also published at their request, and is entitled, 'The Bible and Protestant Church in England.'*
>
> *The only remaining copies of this Sermon are under *lock and key* at the late Warehouse of Messrs Hurst and Robinson, or perhaps sold on account of *their* creditors.

One young poet who perhaps hoped to receive some encouragement from Bowles was Edward Moxon,[132] who in 1826 had published his first volume of verses dedicated to Samuel Rogers in which he describes himself as 'a very young man unlettered and self-taught'. Shortly before Christmas he sent Bowles a poem he had written that brought forth the courteous but not particularly enthusiastic response: 'I beg to thank you for your Poem on Christmas, which I have read with much pleasure.'[133]

In the Christmas Day number of the *Devizes and Wiltshire Gazette* there appeared Bowles's poem entitled 'Banwell Hill', in which the joys of innocent pleasures are extolled. It included the following lines:

> But save, Oh! Save me from the tract-mad Miss
> Who trotts to every Bible club, and that,
> Whom she SAT UNDER . . .
> The sullen Puritan, who preaches this,
> Moves, more than ev'n the Bible trotting Miss –
> My pity, my aversion, and my scorn

followed by this editorial note:

> At a time when Fanatics and Sectarians of almost every description are using the most zealous and unremittting efforts to decry and suppress every popular amusement, we feel a pleasure in presenting our readers with the sentiments upon this subject of one, whose high intellectual endowments, whose pure unspoiled and exemplary christian life, and whose known benevolence of character guarantees them from the most distant imputation of levity or uncharitableness.[134]

This poem was taken to be a criticism of the Bible Society, and so Bowles hastened to rectify this impression by asking the newspaper to print this explanation: 'I mean in what I said in respect to the Bible Society . . . the Bible *without note or comment* has been always the object of my solicitude. I hailed the establishment of such a society, without regarding sects, and equally esteeming every good man of every sect.' He continues by explaining that no reflection was meant upon the Society. He acknowledged that 'Bible trotting' was a most objectionable expression that would be corrected in another edition of his poem, and by it he simply meant 'That restless ostentation, which hurries a newly-enlightened proselyte of penny-trade from one Bethel meeting to another, through London, to the neglect of more retired and sacred duties at home.'[135]

Bowles had written to his old friend William Howley, while still Bishop of London, in which he probably mentioned his concerns. In a letter to Bowles, Howley wrote:

. . . I agree with many of your reflections on the Bible Society. The irritation which I found in the Diocese on that subject when I first was placed on the Bench has made me extremely cautious. Animosity I think has already subsided in a considerable degree and I hope nothing will arise to kindle a new flame. I have not time to enter on the discussion at large. With our best and kindest regards to Mrs Bowles
I remain my dear Bowles
Most truly yours
W. London[136]

In February 1829 Bowles wrote from his canonical house to Tom Moore:

My dear Moore
We are now settled, or shall soon be so, in our newly furnished house, and shall have got up a bed for stray friends from your part of Wiltshire. Lord Lansdowne, I suppose, is gone to the great arena, and we most sincerely and anxiously hope is improved in health. I trust also that your great task[137] is out of your hands, and what can you do better than spending a week here, to partake our canonical hospitalities, and hear our cathedral harmonies, so delightful to me in the evening of my days, yet without any 'decadence' of mind, fancy or physical strength.

Two ladies, one a young and interesting widow, sing most exquisitely Inde Gratia &c., and all such heavenly things, besides my having the command of an excellent choir in the cathedral, to sing what anthems I like. As I always write whatever I do write from instant impressions, you will have a sketch taken one morning. The old blind man dined here on Sunday, and it is an interesting sight to see him, every day, take his place.

Here is, therefore, to tempt you towards us, a fine cathedral, a hospitable canonical house, a sincere friend, two interesting lady singers, excellent music in and out of church, an old poetical parson, and a blind man whom it would do your heart good to see. Hoyle[138] is coming on the 17th. I have, at present, no spare bed, but the week after (23rd or 24th) I shall hope to have got one up and that you will come and stay over Sunday following, or as long as you find it convenient or agreeable. We will not 'teach you to drink deep ere you depart' of canonical port but of delicious harmonies and such a week will be an 'otium' to literary labours, though they are not likely to stop mine entirely.

I hope Anastasia and Mrs Moore are well. Mrs B. sends her kind regards. We shall have at this residence only a small bed, but when

better furnished, shall be happy whenever convenient to see Mrs Moore, Tom, the younger, passed though on his way to school, but the graceless varlet[139] did not call. If you come, I could take you down to Southampton for one day and bring you back, but I must not be longer out of the sound of those bells. Those 'evening' and morning bells. Write.
Yours most truly
W.L. Bowles

P.S. My works are in the greatest demand! Not a copy to be got of 'Bramhill' or 'Banwell', so to work I go again.[140]

The old blind man who dined, as he frequently did, with the servants when Bowles was in residence[141] was John Bright, who, according to the recollections of one of the choristers at the time, was 'of a singular cheerful and happy disposition, taking much interest in the music at the Cathedral and in the singing of individual Choristers, so that he was quite a favourite with us, and one of us would often take his arm, to guide him in his walk, and to have a chat with him upon his usual topic, the Cathedral music'.[142] Bright was the subject of a poem written by Bowles entitled 'The Blind Man of Salisbury Cathedral'[143] in which he describes the poor man who every day, with faltering footsteps, finds his way into the cathedral to kneel and hear the service being sung. The last of the four stanzas reads:

Oh happy if the rich, the vain, the proud,
The plumed actors in the motley crowd,
Since Pride is dust, and Life itself a span,
Would learn a lesson from a poor Blind Man.

In March 1829 Bowles's old friend Robert Nares died. Nares had established the *British Critic* in 1793 and was later keeper of manuscripts at the British Museum, being described as 'a sound and widely read scholar, and as a witty and cheerful companion to his intimates'.[144] Among his other preferments he was a canon residentiary of Lichfield, prebend of St Paul's Cathedral and archdeacon of Stafford. Following his death a monument to him was erected in Lichfield Cathedral, and some verses by Bowles were inscribed upon it.

On 1 April Bowles attended for the first time a meeting of the Chapter of Salisbury Cathedral. Present at the meeting were all the five other residentiary canons, although not the Dean, Hugh Pearson.[145] It seems that Bowles had decided that it was only necessary for him to attend the Chapter meeting while he was in residence, and so it was not until January and April of 1830 that he attended two further meetings. For nine months of the year, therefore, his large canonical house in the Close would have stood empty and unused – a situation that doubtless was to contribute towards the movement to see a reformation of the office of cathedral residentiary canons.

While living in the canonical house Bowles and Magdalene would have found themselves swept up in a social whirl of entertaining and being entertained. Six years before Bowles's appointment, in a letter to John Constable, John Fisher, the bishop,[146] wrote: 'So belly devoted are the good people here that they look upon it as a sort of <u>duty</u> imposed on the Canons-in-residence, to dine out or give a dinner every day as punctually as he goes to church.'[147]

Bowles's knowledge of and appreciation of music was extensive, so one of the pleasures that awaited him on his appointment as canon was the duty when in residence to choose, or be involved in choosing, the service and anthem to be sung by the choir, which consisted of eight boy choristers and six singing men or lay vicars. The organist was Arthur Thomas Corfe,[148] who had been appointed in 1804 and was to hold the post for an astonishing fifty-eight years. On Sundays when he was in residence Bowles would have met him in the vestry before the service to decide what music was to be sung. One observer in 1830 reported:

> Here at the hour of prayer the Bishop may be seen on his throne, the Dean at the altar, the Canon in his stall; a full and efficient choir assembled before the commencement of the exhortation, and remaining in their places till after the blessing had been pronounced. The service is performed with great solemnity in its most attractive form.[149]

On weekdays the practice was quite different. In contrast to the exceedingly efficient and orderly procedures in place in cathedrals in the twenty-first century, in the early nineteenth century the practice could at times be haphazard in the extreme. A man who left the choir in 1832 has provided a vivid account of the way in which Bowles would have carried out his duty at a weekday service when canon in residence:

> The Psalms ended, the head boy left his place to inquire of the Dean or in his absence of the Canon in residence present, what Service he wished to be sung. Having got an answer, he turned towards the boys who were waiting for the information, and gave out in a whisper the name of the author and the key of the Service chosen; he then passed on under the red curtain and through the Choir doors and gates round

to and up the Staircase to the Organ loft, to acquaint the Organis which, when done, he retraced his steps to his seat. Sometimes when the first lesson was a short one, or the Canon took a long time to make up his mind an awkward pause would ensue, accompanied by a good deal of tumbling about of music books, turning over of leaves, anxious whisperings between the Choristers and Singing-men etc; but in general all went off smoothly. Sometimes too, but not often, the Organist would play the wrong Anthem or Service, through having mistaken what the head boy had told him.[150]

Despite this, the standard of singing in the choir under the direction of Corfe was considered excellent, so Bowles doubtless took great pleasure in hearing music that he had composed being sung by such a group of singers in the splendid setting of the cathedral. Shortly after Bowles's death Corfe published *A Collection of Anthems with a list of the Services used in the Cathedral Church of Salisbury*, in which settings by Bowles of psalm 70[151] and of the collect for the Twenty-First Sunday after Trinity[152] are to be found in company with many of the greatest composers of church music.

In April Bowles received the news that Philip Bowles Burlton, the twenty-five-year-old son of his sister Sarah, had died in India. According to the memorial erected to his memory in East Knoyle church, he 'was treacherously massacred near Nunchow Assam by the natives of that place, while residing there for the benefit of his health, his remains were afterwards identified and interred on the spot where he fell'. It is likely that by this time Sarah was widowed and was living at Donhead St Mary in the house owned by Bowles that had been occupied by him when a curate at East Knoyle. The house was later known as Burltons.

On 1 May Thomas Moore dined at the parsonage and found that Bowles had with him his niece:

> A pretty girl, who had just been rescued from the claws of the Jesuits in France, when on the point of being converted by them – has the look of one ready either to 'sinner it or saint it'; and accordingly, Bowles tells me, has fallen in love with the young Captain (her cousin) to whom the father entrusted the task of bringing her safe away from the Jesuits.[153]

On 11 July Bowles wrote an unusually jocular letter to an unknown correspondent about an accident he had recently suffered:

Thank you for your very kind letter.

Not a bit hurt! But a little flinching in a <u>hop</u>, <u>step</u>, & <u>jump</u>! I had just returned, quite well, from passing a day or two, with the Bishop of Bath and Wells. – The bells ringing – sun shining out – all the congregation assembled in the church-yard – Madam, practising her voluntary on the organ – when, all of a sudden, such a cry was heard as stop'd the organ! – In stooping down to tie my shoe, I got a <u>crick</u>, like lightning, in the vertebrae – could not move an inch more than a <u>lively</u> turtle meditating on his back! For once, in twenty-five years, to dismiss the congregation & long before this far Salisbury Bowles died of an apoplexy in the church!! I got down next day, hobbled about like a crab – not a crab making it to the scupper hold, tell Ogle! & shall be in the pulpit, please God, tomorrow as well as ever – However I shall always retain a memory of your prompt and attentive kindness and believe me, most truly and sincerely W.L. Bowles

I shall indeed be happy if you could give me a lift on the 2nd as I propose a tour from Salisbury to the Archbishop . . .[154]

Bowles soon recovered from his accident, as on 16 July it was reported that he was one of the numerous bench of magistrates who attended the General Quarter Session at Warminster.[155]

It was at this time that the Rev. David Wilson preached a sermon at Christ Church Newgate Street in London following the death of a Mr Crowther, during the course of which he said that 'his *tender spirit* never recovered the oppression he suffered at Winchester from the Tyranny of the Elder Boys'. This was brought to the attention of Bowles, who had been a senior at the school when the unfortunate Mr Crowther was a junior. He was outraged that it should be suggested he should have mistreated any of the younger boys, and in a letter to the *Gentleman's Magazine* made it clear that this could not possibly have occurred, and that he took it as a personal insult to himself and to a number of fellow pupils, many of whom had become prominent members of society and were named in his letter.[156] Whatever Bowles's opinion may have been, the system of fagging and general treatment of younger boys by their seniors prevalent in all public schools at the time (and, indeed, until comparatively recently) undoubtedly had a lasting effect on some small boys. Nevertheless, the preacher confessed in a later letter to the *Gentleman's Magazine* that he had perhaps spoken hastily and meant no offence to Bowles in saying what he did.[157]

Early in 1830 Caroline Bowles wrote to Bowles, seeking his assistance in finding a suitable house in Wiltshire for her friend Lady Davenport. Not realising that Bowles was always in residence in Salisbury for the first three months of the year, she wrote to him at Bremhill, and so Bowles was not able to reply until the end of March:

There is a most beautiful villa, immediately adjoining the Town of Calne, belonging to Mr Sergeant Merewether,[158] which I think he would let, but I fear it would be dear – He resides there in Summer, but about two years since, lets it, with a most excellent & well-laid-out Garden – to Sir Guy Campbell.

Sergeant Merewether lives in Chancery Lane, & if Lady Davenport should think a decorated small villa worth looking at, she had better write to the Sergeant, first to know whether he would let it & secondly, at what price – She might use my name.

I know no other place in the neighbourhood, & I need not say, on the part of myself and Mrs Bowles, if what I have said shall induce her to apply to Sergeant Merewether – & upon inspection is found desirable, then we should [be] most happy to receive with cordiality, as the nearest neighbours, any friend of yours.

Accept my best thanks for what you so kindly say about my Poem; I can assure you your own [illegible] compositions are as often our companions in the Parsonage – & we only hope, if Lady Davenport comes to look at Calne Hermitage – so call'd – you will accompany her . . . P.S. We return on Friday to Bremhill, & after Easter or the beginning of May, jog to London.[159]

Bowles duly 'jogged' to London in April to 'see pictures and hear music' as he put it when writing in June to an old friend in Sawbridgenorth, the Rev. Mr Hutchinson, with whom he may have been at school in Winchester.

No author likes to see his work or the results of his research plagiarised, and Bowles was no exception. In April he wrote to Sir Thomas Phillipps:

Thank you for your kind communication – I think it so valuable that I have sent extracts from your letter to Slyvanus Urban, alias the Gentleman's Magazine – the only valuable repository for this kind of knowledge.

I trust you will excuse this, but I thought it right to let you know – As Miles shows you my work, I hope he did not claim my sole discovery that Avebury was the monument to the greatest Celtic deity Teut or Mercurium.

I say this for to my <u>dismay</u> Coles affix'd a paragraph in the Berkshire Chronicle asserting 'that I did not write my own history of Bremhill but that it was written by Mr Miles an ingenious & [illegible] man'!

Implied in the same paper 'That neither Mr Miles or anyone living suggested a [illegible] or communicated one sentence or one word' & there this intelligence ended.

. . . I will never allow a human to 'saw away into my Bone'! I do not suppose the Miles himself could have been the author of this information but I have been induced to mention it.[160]

Bowles added a postscript at the heading to this letter: 'I am just returned from three months' canonical residence in Sarum! Urbs Sarum! Salisbury.'

Whenever Bowles read any book, pamphlet or report in a newspaper attacking in any way the organisation or practice of the Church of England, he could be relied upon to waste no time in responding in print. When, therefore, Lord Mountcashel made some uncomplimentary remarks in Parliament, Bowles soon published *A Word on Cathedral Oratorios, and Clergy-Magistrates, addressed to Lord Mountcashel*. In his letter to Hutchinson written in June he said that when in London 'I gave Lord Mountcashel a Bremhill kick for describing Cathedrals as "Sinful" – he is a scoundrell. My pamphlet will cost you <u>two shillings</u>, if worth buying, as I hope you will find – A Word on Cathedral Oratorios & Clergy Magistrates – Murray– Albemarle Street.'[161]

As if to reinforce his credentials as the author of a pamphlet on music and clergy-magistrates, Bowles described himself on the title-page as 'Late Steward of the Gloucester Music Festival and one of his Majesty's Justices of the Peace for the County of Wilts'. He also laid down a challenge to Lord Mountcashel by writing:

As to the Christian character of the writer, if this free remonstrance should induce you to set on foot some little inquisitorial enquiries, and a Parliamentary Committee should be sent down to Bremhill, you may gratify to the utmost your pious curiosity, by ascertaining how a magistrate for the County discharges his duty to his parishioners as a clergyman. I, without much anxiety, leave you to the evidence of what 'you may hear!' or what you may find out, only informing you, that I have been a working clergyman in my parish for four-and-twenty years.[162]

Bowles concluded his pamphlet with the inevitable poem entitled 'Affiliation and Removal – A Picture by Mr Grey [*sic*] of Salisbury'. The poetry tells of a hearing before the magistrates resulting from a father's failure to support his family, and the picture is described in a footnote as 'Portraits of Magistrates. Looking in Burn's Justice [a magistrates' handbook] for case of removal, Pawlet Scrope Esq, of Castle Coombe. Standing up, Lord Arundell, of Wardour, and the writer of this description.' It is likely that this picture is the one entitled 'The Justices Room' by T.W. Gray of Salisbury, sent to the British Institution in 1831.[163]

The *Gentleman's Magazine* regretted not being able to give Bowles's address to Lord Mountcashel the notice it deserved, but thought that 'it adds another wreath to the chaplet of our amiable poet, as the able advocate of the church; of genuine piety; and of good old English common sense'![164] This pamphlet was one of the large number he had written by this time. In his autobiography John Britton writes: 'Like the generality of poets, my good friend was very sensitive, and easily led into literary controversy and contention. I now have before me a thick volume of pamphlets, mostly of this kind, which he wrote and printed between the years 1800 and 1830, amounting to nearly 2000 pages.'[165]

Bowles had been hoping that Hutchinson would have been able to visit Bremhill during June in order to meet Charlton Byam Wollaston, an old friend of Bowles's from his schooldays, but it was not to be. On 2 July he wrote to him to say that 'Sessions, assizes and family engagements fill up the whole of this month and I shall not be at liberty till the 7th of August then we are disengag'd . . .'[166] As a magistrate, Bowles would have been expected to spend a good deal of time on his legal duties, but soon after this he resigned from the bench – doubtless with a feeling of great relief. This was reflected in Caroline Bowles's letter written in the summer of the following year:

> Some time since one of the County papers announced that 'The Revd. W.L. Bowles' had withdrawn himself from the magisterial bench – and, would you believe it? – I read the announcement with a feeling of satisfaction that was anything but patriotic – for at whatever loss to the County, I could not but rejoice on your individual account that you had discharged yourself of the responsibility, 'already become one of a most anxious nature,' and in the progressive state of publick affairs too likely to be associated with the necessity of hazardous as well as harassing exertion . . .[167]

Caroline Bowles undoubtedly had in mind the widespead unrest in Wiltshire in the previous autumn and winter. In November Moore had noted that Bowles was 'full of alarm at the riots now spreading through the country'[168] resulting in the destruction of agricultural machinery and culminating in a mob of some five hundred men challenging a troop of forty-four yeomanry cavalry near Pythouse in the south-western corner of the county. This property belonged to Bowles's old friend and Magdalene's cousin John Benett, one of the Members of Parliament for the county. As a result of the confrontation one of the rioters was killed and many, including Benett, were injured.[169] As a humane clergyman, Bowles would surely have sympathised with the plight of the agricultural labourers who struggled to survive on pitifully small wages, but as a magistrate he would have been expected to impose the severest penalties of the law on the convicted men. It must be that this conflict between his personal feelings and his public duty, as well as his increasingly nervous temperament, persuaded Bowles to withdraw from the bench. The writer of a paper given to the Bath Field Club some years later remembers 'Mr William Lisle Bowles coming into our house on Belvedere with the air of a man who had the mob at his heels, and anticipating with tears the destruction of his beautiful parsonage at Bremhill by incendiaries'.[170]

On 25 June 1830 George IV died, following which a county meeting was held in Devizes to congratulate the new king on his accession to the throne. As was usual on these occasions, interminable speeches were delivered and, following addresses by Lord Lansdowne, the county Members of Parliament, John Benett and Sir John Dugdale Astley, and the Earl of Suffolk,[171] Bowles was called upon to deliver a few well-chosen words.[172]

In 1830–1 Bowles's life of Bishop Ken, which he had told Thomas Moore some five years before that he was determined to write before he died, was published in two volumes under the title of *The Life of Thomas Ken, D.D. deprived Bishop of Bath and Wells, viewed in connection with public events, and the spirit of the times, political and religious, in which he lived including some account of the fortunes of Morley, Bishop of Winchester, his first patron, and the friend of Isaak Walton, brother-in-law of Bishop Ken*. As a non-juror, Ken had been deprived of his see in 1691 and then lived mainly at Longleat as a guest of Lord Weymouth. The first volume was dedicated to Bowles's old schoolfriend William Howley, Archbishop of Canterbury, and the second volume to another friend from his Winchester days, Herbert Hawes,[173] Prebendary of Salisbury Cathedral.

Before the first volume was published Bowles wrote to Murray on several occasions. In a letter written in January he was 'in hope the

Quarterly would not be too soon for an <u>announcement</u> of my work – but I suppose there can be no chance of this' and also took the opportunity of asking 'how our account stands respecting the sale of Bremhill'.[174] In the following month he wrote to say that Murray would receive 200 copies from Nichols, told him that he was anxious that it should not be omitted from his next quarterly list and asked for Murray's account for advertising, as the printing was costing him 'a good sum'.[175]

In May 1830, while in London, Bowles wrote from the Athenaeum to John Lockhart:

> I feel I ought to have beg'd your pardon for asking your acceptance of a publication, which perhaps, <u>nobody</u>, but a <u>Wiltshire man</u>, would think of reading.
>
> Perhaps, in the steam-vessel, on a <u>sun-shiny morning</u>, you might find some small amusement from <u>Ken</u>, & <u>Banwell-hill</u>; at all events, I beg your acceptance of those particulars, & only [illegible] you will not give yourself the trouble of acknowledgement, & with best & warmest regards to those most dear to you.[176]

Before publication of the second volume Bowles doubtless worried the printer John Nichols with details of many amendments to be made to the proofs. As an example, in the middle of March 1831 he wrote:

> I write you because I forgot to mention the intended Epitaph. In the blank page, opposite the page where it is spoken of, it should be engrav'd, a fac simile of Ken's own writing with these words
> 'Ken's Epitaph, written with his own hand & intended to be placed on his tomb'.
> If not finish'd, the extract from his will had better be omitted & the fac simile of Epitaph appear alone but it does not much matter if both are engrav'd.
> There is another point I think I would request your attention, is of some consequence . . .[177]

And so on.

Although Bowles's work revived the reverence felt for Ken, it did not meet with universal approval. Bowles sent a copy of the first volume to Caroline Bowles, who wrote a kind letter to Bowles acknowledging its receipt. She later wrote to Robert Southey: 'The Life of Bishop Ken might as well be the life of the man on the moon; but surely some of the irrelevant parts (how few are relevant) are beautiful in themselves as to poetic feeling; one might make a pretty little book of such episodes.'[178]

In July Southey had written to Caroline with his thoughts on *The Life of Thomas Ken*:

> I wish very much to have reviewed his Life of Bishop Ken, who was a kinsman of my mother's family. It is only the first volume that I have seen; but that is so bad that I was really deterred from my wish by the certainty of mortifying him, even if I totally abstained from noticing any of the faults in it, and only arranged his materials as he ought to have arranged them, and thrown his rubbish overboard. But I love dearly what is to be loved in his poetry, and you will believe me when I say that I shall have quite as much pleasure in taking the first opportunity of praising him as he can possible have in being praised.[179]

In writing to Caroline in 1831 Bowles told her:

> In writing the life of the Bishop, contrary to the received custom, I have endeavour'd to vary grave subjects by the interspersion, here and there, of matter less grave; how the Dons [?] like it I do not know, nor at all care: my object was to give variety and lightness to a rather heavy subject, for am sure it would not be read without, nor perhaps with it.
>
> I have never had any connection with the Princes of the Press, nor know a single writer among them to wish me 'good speed,' and pen an article on Bowles's Life of Ken![180]

The *Gentleman's Magazine* carried a very long review of the work, and in particular commended to its readers the 'beautiful lithographic drawing by Mr Lane ARA[181] from a design by Mr Calcott RA of the parting interview between Morley and Isaac Walton and his wife Kenna at Walton's cottage'. It seems that the celebrated landscape painter Augustus Wall Callcott had for some reason been upset by some words in, perhaps, a proof of the work, as in November 1829 Bowles had written to him 'hastily, not to say, rapidly' to say:

> . . . the moment I received the sheet from the Printers, before I received your letter, from respect to your feelings, I altered the passage . . . And now, your mind is at ease, let me say, how much I thank you again – I had no conception the engraving could have been done so soon . . . The picture will be the frontispiece – Episcopal Biography is of all things, the dullest, but your Picture, and I hope the incident [?] itself, will give my Life some natural animation – the first volume will come out the beginning of February – all written and printed since I saw you.

Lord Lansdowne is gone to Cambridge, so I have no frank, but I would not delay a moment in setting your mind at rest. – and as to your [illegible] Morley, if this be your sin, I shall, very speedily absolve you from all sins – past and present or to come – for your picture is worth a thousand.

Mrs Bowles joins in best remembrances and regards to Mrs Calcott and believe me

Your oblig'd friend

W L Bowles

If you like Cathedral music, come & see us in Salisbury – our canonical residence in Jan: Feb: March.[182]

In the event Callcott's picture did not appear as the frontispiece of the first volume but later in the work, so this may have caused further offence to Callcott. However, Bowles did acknowledge in the preface that 'the thanks of the public are due, as well as my own, for the sketch from his exquisite pencil of the scene described in the work'.[183]

Shortly before the second volume of his life of Bishop Ken was published Bowles suffered from a panic attack, during which he feared that he might have laid himself open to prosecution as a result of something he had written in the preface. As usual, he looked to Thomas Moore for help and advice, as Moore recorded in his journal on 2 July:

Walked after dinner with Bowles to his printer, he being anxious that I should look at some Preface he had prefixed to his Life of Ken attacking, of course, somebody – Found it to be a fierce invective against Bulteil, a man who is preaching against the Church at Oxford, and who accuses the Clergy of being opera-goers, card players, fornicators and worse. This bitter part of the charge Bowles dives into most courageously or rather outrageously and in repelling it from the regular Church of England parsons throws it back upon such 'canters' as Bulteil in a manner that makes one almost certain he means Bulteil himself. This I pointed out to him, adding that I thought it possible Bulteil might prosecute him, which alarmed Bowles's nerves and he gave orders that the book (which was to be published tomorrow) should be suspended till he had consulted Sergeant Merryweather – It was amusing to see that I had made not the least impression upon him, as long as I merely pointed out how shocking it would be if anyone was led to suppose for a moment that he meant Bulteil by the insinuation (the person he really meant being some Dissenting parson in Dorsetshire who was charged some years since with this offence) but the moment I hinted the possibility of prosecution my sensitive friend became clear-sighted on the subject at once & perceived the whole extent of the grievance.[184]

What Bowles had written in the preface to the second volume was indeed a prolonged and fierce attack on the Rev. Henry Bulteel,[185] the curate of St Ebbe's in Oxford, who shortly afterwards had his licence revoked by the Bishop of Oxford. Bowles was probably justified in fearing that Bulteel might take action against him, but in the event nothing occurred. In the midst of the attack he could not resist making a reference to how he spent some of his leisure time when at Oxford:

> I must tell you, that when I was at Oxford, I often resorted to <u>ungodly</u> recreations and have not yet repented; so little, I must confess, that before I venture to face the whole tremendous array of Satan's crimes, here conjured up, I absolutely took up my old Oxford fiddle,and, like, Joel Collier, was obliged to play over seventeen times Arne's[186] delightful air in Artaxerxes[187] (<u>a profane opera</u>)! . . .

Bowles was pleased with his *Life of Thomas Ken*, and in June 1832 wrote to Isaac D'Israeli: '. . . you will be glad to hear, notwithstanding the criticisms of the John Knox's school, that it has succeeded infinitely beyond my Expectations, the <u>whole</u> impression of 500 copies being sold . . . .'[188]

In 1830 a poem entitled *Italy* by Bowles's old friend Samuel Rogers was published. A copy of the first edition has survived,[189] inscribed 'To the Rev. W.L. Bowles from his very sincere friend the Author'. It is more than likely that Bowles repaid the compliment by presenting to Rogers a copy of his *Life of Thomas Ken* of which he was so proud. In *Recollections of the Table-talk of Samuel Rogers*, Rogers writes:

> Bowles, like most other poets, was greatly depressed by the harsh criticisms of the reviewers. I advised him not to mind them; and, eventually, following my advice, he became a much happier man. I suggested to him the subject of The Missionary; and he was to dedicate it to me. He, however, dedicated it to a noble lord, who never, either by word or letter, acknowledged the dedication.
>
> Bowles's nervous timidity is the most ridiculous thing imaginable. Being passionately fond of music, he came to London expressly to attend the last commemoration of Handel. After going into the Abbey, he observed that the door was closed; immediately he ran to the door-keeper, exclaiming, 'What! am I to be shut up here?' and out he went before he heard a single note. I once brought a stall-ticket for him that

he might accompany me to the opera; but just as we were stepping into the carriage, he said, 'Dear me, your horses seem uncommonly frisky!' and he stayed at home.[190]

Murray's eldest son[191] began to assist his father in the running of his publishing business, and was hoping to be elected to, perhaps, the Athenaeum Club, of which Bowles was a member. It seems that Murray wrote to seek Bowles's support, as in March 1830 Bowles wrote to Murray:

> Before I received your letter, I had done as you request – immediately on receipt of it, I wrote to Sir Thomas Phillips [sic], who, requested of me some votes, adds he will be delighted to vote in return for any one I should name. I have added your son's name, and requested him, & also my friend Benett, who will send this by his frank, to give as many votes as he can & I hope I shall see your son among us next year.
>
> Had I thought of it when in Town, I could have more effectively serv'd him.
>
> If Mr Lockhart should be inclin'd for an article on public schools, now so stupidly abus'd I think, I could write something for the Quarterly which he would & I hope the public might approve. The malice against these establishments, in some quarters, is natural – The ignorance is inconscionable. Let me know if you think any more of what you said in Town.[192]

It may be that Lockhart did invite Bowles to let him have an outline of what he proposed to write on the question of public schools but that nothing further was done, as two years later Bowles again raised the matter with him, writing:

> I merely wish one word to say how very sorry I was on my return to learn from Mrs Bowles that I had been in company with Mrs Lockhart[193] without knowing it.
>
> May I request you to say to her that having had the pleasure of meeting her with her father at Mr Rogers's & Sir George Beaumont's I should instantly have remember'd her had not my eyes, us'd to green fields, more than dazzling cities, failed me, rather than my interesting recollection. Say so much for the Old Cavalier & believe me
>
> Most sincerely
> W L Bowles
>
> I wish I could see a good article on the <u>subject</u> of which I gave you a sketch – the ignorance is most extraordinary.

The ignorance referred to by Bowles undoubtedly related to the fact that many people did not realise that boys from quite humble backgrounds could achieve eminence after a free education as a scholar in one of the public schools, and so he goes on to quote two examples:

> The father of the Archbishop of Armagh was an apothecary – his sister married to a small shop-keeper of Faringdon – No one,except old Winchester boys know that the Bishop of Hereford's[194] father was <u>Dancing master</u>, to the boys . . . my Patmos is for Mrs Lockhart but pray, do not give yourself the trouble to write.[195]

At the end of 1830 Bowles stayed in Bath for a week and spent some time with Joseph Hunter,[196] the antiquary and minister of a Presbyterian congregation there for the last twenty years. They had first met when both were members of the 'Stourhead Circle', which assembled at Stourhead at the invitation of Colt Hoare. On 18 December Hunter noted:

> I met Mr Bowles in Bath the early part of the week and have seen him almost every day. He sat an hour with me in my study yesterday. He is come to Bath quite as into a city of refuge, a fenced city. He is full of alarm. I never saw anyone evince so much timidity. He thinks of nothing but an approaching convulsion, in which the clergy will be the first to suffer, & dreams of the guillotine. – I have endeavoured to draw him out of these matters to antiquarian & poetical conversation, but political economy & the prospects of the country – these are now the all-absorbing topics, both with him & with too many others also . . . Bowles told me, speaking of the condition of the labourers in his parish that there is not one amongst them who has not a pig and a watch.[197]

On 30 June 1831 Bowles wrote to Caroline Bowles:

> . . . I am coming to Salisbury on the 14th to preach to eleven hundred children in the Cathedral, the children of assembled village-schools, all orthodox, in these days of heterodoxy! We, that is, I and the Canoness, who is turn'd author[198] for the good of the publick, and our parish in particular, after resting a day proceed to my <u>Lady Sister</u>,[199] (Lady Williams) at Portsmouth, and what if my <u>long tails</u> try their luck at Buckland,[200] instead of the poney-caravan?
>
> We think we could take you, in our road at Salisbury in the summer, or, perhaps (who knows?) might persuade you to drive over and

hold a plate at the Cathedral-door, pour la charite [*sic*], at eleven o'clock, on the fourteenth? . . .²⁰¹

On 10 July Caroline replied by saying that she and her cousin Rev. George Bowles would accept Bowles's 'half proposition' about coming to Salisbury to hear him preach and would be staying at the White Hart inn in readiness for the service on the 14ᵗʰ. Bowles wrote to her on the 13ᵗʰ at the inn:

> I received your kind note only yesterday – too late for me to write to you. We shall rejoice indeed if this finds you, our only regret is that we have no household to offer such hospitalities as I could wish, the rooms being unfurnish'd, as I am not in residence, and the beds, except one, un-air'd.
>
> Mrs Bowles dines with Dr. Fowler.²⁰² Mrs Fowler is a name of ours²⁰³ –of my family, and yours, and you shall be taken care of, as one of us, deserves so well. I can answer for this, so, if you stay tomorrow, as I hope you will, you will accompany Mrs Bowles, and George can take my place, as it is probable I may be at the Bishop's.
>
> I shall call this evening, If you come and I should not see [you], enquire at church for Canon Bowles's! closet, where you will find Mrs Bowles and Fowler.²⁰⁴

The service in the cathedral was not as well attended as Bowles had anticipated when writing to Caroline. The *Salisbury and Winchester Journal* reported:

> We regret to observe that from the unfavourable state of the weather, a large number of children, particularly those resident in the country, were prevented from attending and that the Church was not as full as we have frequently had the pleasure of noticing. In the course of the service, a very affecting and appropriate Hymn, composed and set to music for the occasion by the Rev. W.L. Bowles, Canon Residentiary, was performed by the choir.²⁰⁵

Caroline did not join Magdalene in holding a plate at the door of the cathedral. The collection, as the *Journal* was sorry to add, amounted to only £18 7s 1d.

Bowles could not resist the temptation to have the words of the hymn that he wrote for the service printed at the end of his *Few Words . . . to Lord Chancellor Brougham*.

As he grew older Bowles had begun to behave in various odd and eccentric ways, all of which caused him to be compared to Henry

Fielding's[206] Parson Adams. In writing to Robert Southey the following year, Caroline related to him what occurred after the service and painted a vivid picture of Bowles's mental state at that time:

> I think I told you that I accompanied my cousin George Bowles to Salisbury last summer, on purpose to gratify the musical canon and poet by being present at his Cathedral during the performance of some hymns, of which the music and words were composed by himself for the benefit of a school charity; and we heard him preach also, in the same strange desultory style (with poetic bursts interspersed) which characterises his Life of Ken. I never saw a man so delighted and overpowered as he was at what he called my great kindness in coming; the tears actually stood in his eyes when he thanked me, as if such trifling tokens of regard and respect were rare to him now, who was once so used to them. After the service he took possession of me, to show me, as he said, every nook and corner of his beloved Cathedral, the library, &c; to tell me the stories of those who slept beneath the most remarkable tombs, and well and enthusiastically he began the task he had undertaken; but it happened that as we were returning to the Cathedral, after taking some refreshment at his residence just opposite, we spied and heard two gentlemen calling for some person to liberate them from within the grated doors of the building, which they had been locked into by accident when we came out. They seemed very impatient of confinement, and I observed to my companion, who had stopt short to look down the avenue towards the prisoners, 'I should be well content to be shut up for many hours in such a cage, and should have no objection to pass a moonlit night there quite alone'. 'God Forbid, God Forbid!' he muttered to himself in great agitation, dropping my arm; and then turning and looking strangely in my face he added, with a fearful emphasis, 'Do you know where I should be next day if I was shut up alone in that place one hour? In Finche's mad-house.'![207] Then he caught up my arm, and rather dragged than led me on. The gentlemen were liberated, and came out laughing as we entered, but Mr Bowles shuddered as he passed them, and I am sure put great force upon himself, in consideration of his promise to me, in entering at all. He hurried me over the library, the rest of the party following; then down to the body of the Cathedral, from tomb to tomb, from shrine to shrine, scarcely able to utter two connected sentences, and turning his head to look back towards the entrance every moment. At last he caught my hand, and whispered 'Good God! If we should be shut in,' and his distress was so painful to me that I feigned having seen enough. I drew him away, nothing loath, but too much agitated to be himself again while we stayed. After witnessing that scene, nothing he could say or do would affect me angrily.

Poor human nature! I suppose it is from sympathy that I feel so much for poor Bowles; and how he would resent such sympathy! . . .[208]

Nevertheless, when in the right frame of mind and among friends, and particularly at home, Bowles could appear perfectly normal and the life and soul of the party. At the end of August Moore and his wife Bessy dined at the parsonage with a group of friends. On that occasion Moore:

Never saw Bowles in a more amusing plight – played for us, on the fiddle, after dinner, a country-dance, which 40 years ago, he heard on entering a ball-room to which he had rode I don't know how many miles, to meet a girl he was very fond of, & found her dancing to this tune, when he entered the room. The sentiment with which he played this old-fashioned jig beyond anything diverting. I proposed we should dance to it, and taking Mrs Bowles, led off followed by the Powers, Bessy, Mulvany &c. &c. – Our fidler soon tired, on which Hoyle volunteered a scrape, & played so dolefully slow as to make us laugh in far quicker time that we danced – However, we brisked up his old bow & Mrs Moore taking Bowles for a partner, we got through one of the most laughing dances I have seen for a long time. In the course of the evening, I sung Alley Croker[209] accompanied by Bowles on the violin, much to the amusement of the whole party . . .[210]

The violin played by Bowles was almost certainly the violin described by him in 1837 as having had only three owners since the time of Cromwell.[211] It had belonged to Lord Crew,[212] Bishop of Durham, who died in 1721 at the age of eighty-eight and had left it to his chaplain, Bowles's grandfather, Dr Richard Grey, who in turn had bequeathed it to Bowles.

It was at this time that Bowles found it necessary to launch an attack on those who wanted to see the end of the powers possessed by deans and chapters of cathedrals, as well as a curtailment of what were perceived to be their excessively large incomes. He therefore wrote and had printed and published by W.B. Brodie and Co. in Salisbury *A Few Words most respectively addressed to the Lord Chancellor Brougham on the Misrepresentations, Exaggerations, and Falsehoods respecting the Property and Character of the Cathedral Clergy of the Church of England*. As a postscript he attempted to show what parochial work was undertaken by many of the cathedral clergy by giving an account of his own activities when at Bremhill. He wrote:

. . . I shall transcribe *one* week's work, by the Author of these pages, in the country, when he has left his canonical residence; and this is, in general, the conduct, I believe sincerely, of most of these men:-

Monday – Visited and prayed by Mrs Moore, lingering in a dropsy. Farmer's wife.

Tuesday – Visited and prayed with, and relieved, a very poor woman.

Wednesday – Summon Overseer for refusing relief to a poor old man.

Thursday – Christening a child ill – Mrs B. gone two miles off to read by the bedside of old Greenway – heard the case of the old man and overseer – relief given to poor man.

Friday – Visited Mrs Moore in the dropsy – her end approaching – prayed and offered every kindness towards her large family.

Saturday – Employed at home – read the Bible, and selected such portions as might be most impressive for Sunday's discourse.

Sunday – Two services at Church – three christenings – poor man at dinner – forty poor girls instructed by Mrs B. in reading &c., on Sundays on the lawn.

Monday – Sixpence from a poor old man's weekly pay taken off, who had seen better days, and was now 77. Take care of his being *righted*, and to have *three* shillings a week.

Tuesday – Labourer's wife, with three children, ill, and in bed – no one to look after her – took care to have one employed, and additional shilling allowed, &c.

God knows these things are not published ostentatiously, but to show the injustice of Cobbett's[213] slanders against 'the Parsons' and Clergy-Magistrates![214]

In September 1831 *Blackwood's Edinburgh Magazine* threw down a challenge to Bowles. In an article entitled 'An Hour's Talk About Poetry', the question was asked:

Ours is a poetical age; but has it produced one Great Poem? Not one. If you think it has, you will perhaps favour us with the name of the author and his work . . . Breathes not the man with a more poetical temperament than Bowles. No wonder that his eyes 'love all they look on', for they possess the sacred gift of beautifying creation, by shedding over it the charm of melancholy . . . His human sensibilities are so fine as to be in themselves poetical; and his poetical aspirations so delicate as to be always human. Hence his Sonnets have been dear to poets . . . But has Bowles written a Great Poem? If he has, then, as he loves us, let him forthwith publish it in Maga.[215]

Bowles was for ever irritated by criticisms of his work, and in an undated letter to his friend George Paulett Scrope of Castle Combe he gives vent to his feelings:

> I cannot express how much I feel for your kindness & Mr Lockhart's[216] generous intentions, the more gratifying, as, for so many years, the curses of Cockney have been yelping at my heels – & all their magpies pecking at 'my frosty pole' John Anderson! the last blockhead is more lying & [?] than all – but if Mr Lockhart lifts his little finger . . . the Old Rock may sing 'God Save the King' for the rest of his life – & I shall never forget the obligation . . . & so give my best & warmest thanks to Lockhart, and accept the same yourself for many years of kindness & regard & more particularly for this last instance.[217]

In October Bowles was at Lacock, where he heard some music that inspired him to write some lines 'To Lady Valletort, on hearing her sing "Gloria in Excelsis", with three other young Ladies, at Lacock Abbey, October 1831'. The abbey was, of course, the seat of Bowles's friend William Fox Talbot, and Lady Valletort[218] was Fox Talbot's half-sister. Doubtless she and two other young guests took the opportunity to entertain the company, probably after dinner. Bowles, by now in his seventieth year, was so captivated by the music and the beauty of the singers, and Lady Valletort in particular, that he was unable to resist composing these lines to:

> Fair inmate of these ivied walls, beneath
> Whose silent cloisters Ella[219] sleeps in death,
> Let loftier bards, in rich and glowing lays,
> Thy gentleness, thy grace, thy virtue praise![220] . . .

Chapter 7
1832–1835

As usual, Bowles and Magdalene spent the first three months of the
year in the canonical house at Salisbury, where Bowles was able to
enjoy choosing the music sung during the cathedral services. He had
hoped to receive a visit from Thomas Moore but this was not to be. He
wrote to Bowles in March 1832:

> I deferred writing for a day or two from my plans being so uncertain,
> but it is now fixed that I go to London on Monday, which puts an end to
> all visions of Music, Psalmody, Salisbury girls &c, &c. I do not like being
> routed from home just now (except, indeed, for you and such articles as
> the above-mentioned) but business makes it necessary for me to visit
> 'the City of the Plague', where I shall stay, for all reasons, as short a time
> as possible.[1]

In February 1832 Bowles's fellow poet and cleric George Crabbe
had died, and a number of his friends and parishioners decided that a
monument to his memory should be erected in the chancel of the church
at Trowbridge. Crabbe's son wrote to Bowles telling him that it was
debated by the subscribers at Trowbridge whether it should be written in
Latin or English and that, if the former were adopted, then Bowles was to
be requested to compose it.[2] In the event, after consultation with Samuel
Rogers and Lord Holland, the monument was written in English, and
still stands as a testament to Crabbe's merits. Crabbe's son, another
George, subsequently wrote and Murray published in eight volumes
the *Life and Poems of the Rev George Crabbe*. Probably in February 1834
Bowles wrote to Murray:

> I had already order'd three copies of poor Crabbe's most interesting,
> most affecting, and beautifully written Life, and am induc'd by the
> present and kinder notice from the publisher, sent to Calne, to inform
> you of two rather singular circumstances; but I must first say that the
> last copy, being sent to Calne, instead of Salisbury, where I am present
> resident, was not received till a few days ago, and Mrs Bowles, who is

now reading it, only this morning discover'd the kind note from the publisher.

I hasten therefore to thank you, dear sir, for this remembrance, and now must tell you what passed with regard to the first copy I purchased.

I had read the volume all thro, and being deeply interested, I wrote a letter to Crabbe of Pucklechurch, because I thought it would give him pleasure, being a young author. I recommended the volume warmly to the Bishop, Dean, and all here, and sent the letter to the Bishop to frank. It was not till afterwards I accidentally look'd at the front leaf, which I had not perceiv'd, and found my name and the very beautiful dedication.

As I had written without saying one word about the dedication, I instantly posted off another letter, as the author would naturally suppose I was displeas'd or ungrateful, when I could hardly read it without tears; and now, tho late, beg to thank you for your kind remembrance, as I cordially thank'd him . . .

Crabbe most gratefully spoke of the few services I was able to do to his lamented Father, of which I was scarce conscious, and propos'd dedicating the first volume to me, but I earnestly press'd him, tho deeply feeling the kindness of the intentions, to dedicate it to Lord Holland, or some other name which might be of eventual [?] advantage to him, and therefore thought no more of it, but his high disinterestedness prevail'd, notwithstanding which I hope the suggestion in the Quarterly will soon be realis'd.[3]

I beg to be remember'd to Mr Lockhart, whom I met last at poor Sotheby's table, since which I have not been in London. These things come near us at all times but more at a certain age. I shall hope to see him and yourself in the spring, and would beg the favour of you, if you will allow it, to advertise in your Quarterly my corrected edition of St John in Patmos, with my name.

Bowles could not resist a postscript:

Advertise also to be published Antiquities of Lacock Nunnery.

You never had an article on Cathedral Music. Ask Mr Lockhart if I shall send one, for him to do as he likes with it. I think it a most interesting subject in these times, and I am able historically and practically to speak of it, and should like the task.

Every body here speaks in the highest terms of the Life, particularly the Dean.[4]

The dedication that very nearly reduced Bowles to tears read: 'To the Rev. W.L. Bowles, Canon of Salisbury, &c.,&c.,&c., these memoirs of his Departed Friend and Brother-Poet Are Inscribed, in Testimony of that Grateful and Affectionate respect, Which Has Descended from Mr Crabbe to his Children's Children'.

The village of Bremhill contained only a very small number of houses that were occupied by educated people with whom Bowles and his wife would have been expected,in an exceedingly class-conscious age, to be on 'visiting terms'. One such appears to have been Richard Smith, described as an 'esq' in the Poll Book published after the 1818 contested county election. Following Smith's death in 1832 Bowles wrote a poem published in the *Devizes and Wiltshire Gazette* as being 'To the memory of Mr R.S. Smith, of Bremhill, by the Minister of the Parish'. It begins:

> I think upon the village-scene,
> I think of him with tears,
> Who there has like a brother been
> For well nigh thirty years[5]

And so on.

It may be recalled that in 1820 during the course of the Pope controversy the author Isaac D'Israeli contributed to the *Quarterly Review* a review of Joseph Spence's *Anecdotes, Observations, and Characters of Books and Men . . .*, which contained such severe criticisms of Bowles's *The Works of Alexander Pope . . .* that Bowles was as a consequence consumed with rage, although he did not discover until later the true identity of the author. However, between 1828 and 1830 were published D'Israeli's *Commentaries on the Life and Reign of Charles I*, a work that met with Bowles's wholehearted approval. This may explain why he was happy to overlook the disagreements of the past and lobby for D'Israeli's achievements to be recognised by an honorary degree from Oxford.
On 3 May Bowles wrote to D'Israeli:

> A thought has occurr'd to me, as the Oxford Commemoration is approaching, to ask, whether you should have any objection to those honours, which, for your defense of poor Charles, you ought to have in Sheldon's Theatre at Oxford?
> I have been a humble soldier, on your side, in my Life of Ken . . . I should be glad to hear from you, as I will write instantly to my friends, the President of Trinity Coll & President of Magdalen . . .[6]

D'Israeli must have signified his consent, as on 20 May Bowles wrote to him:

> I shall write, at all events, by this day's post, to my friend Dr Ingram, the President of Trinity, hoping, that, if it should not this year be <u>too</u> late, you would not have any <u>serious</u> objections, to such honours, as, I think, the University of Oxford as would be willing to pay – most willing to pay – to the historian, the ablest, of those who defended the memory of Charles, & in so doing, the Character of the Church, in this University, which boasts the name & munificence, of Clarendon.
>
> One of your objections, I believe, I can answer directly – I know of <u>no expense</u>, whatsoever, except <u>hiring</u> a <u>gown</u>, for which the sum of <u>one</u> pound is paid, not 100! But of this I cannot speak for certain. I am going to London tomorrw & shall desire Ingram to give me every information
> . . .
> P.S. If you are in London, pray call at No 178 Piccadilly, or leave a note at the Athanaeum. What <u>will</u> become of us?[7]

Bowles continued with his lobbying. On the 26th he wrote from London to the antiquary and biographer the Rev. Dr Philip Bliss,[8] who held the post of the registrarship of the university as well as keeper of the archives.[9] A few days later he wrote again to D'Israeli telling him that he had written to Dr William Buckland,[10] who was canon of Christ Church, and, on the way to London, he had spoken to Dr Martin Routh,[11] who had been President of Magdalen College since 1791. Martin fully agreed that an honorary degree should be conferred. However, a difficulty had arisen in that Ingram had now told him that there would hardly be time for the necessary applications to be made before the Commemoration, and that, contrary to what Bowles had understood, the fees would amount to £70 – a very large sum of money indeed.[12]

Despite this, on the 31st James Ingram, the President of Trinity College, wrote to Bowles:

> You will be glad to hear that your friend and brother biographer D'Israeli has been proposed, seconded by me and proposed <u>nem. com</u> as far as our board is concerned but will not be on the printed list till a few days previous to the Commemoration. I rejoice at this the more, because we may look forward to <u>your Canonical</u> appearance in the area along side your friend. Perhaps <u>you</u> ought to take your degrees of B.D. & D.D. in the regular manner having your name on the books – otherwise I should propose you at the same time. We are to have an innundation of

Philosophers here on the 18th June the members of the new Scientific Association having agreed to meet here under the auspices of their worthy President Dr. Buckland . . .

I congratulate you on the success of Ken which looks as if some intent was still felt in the fate of Episcopacy. Lord Kerry[13] is to be the new member for Calne, I understand, Benett, Astley, Long and Methuen are named for the County. I hope the waters of the deluge will soon be abated & that the Ark of the Constitution will rest in safety after all. I suppose our Archbishop is as placid as he can be. Give my respects to him if you see him again before you leave town. You of course will come to us, bring your friend D'Israeli with you.[14]

It is certain that Bowles would have dearly loved to have had the degree of a doctor of divinity conferred upon him, but it was never to be. Ingram had been born at Codford St Mary near Salisbury, and this doubtless explains his interest in the future representation in Parliament of Wiltshire following the expected passing of the Reform Bill.

Bowles wrote to D'Israeli yet again on 1 June, adding a characteristic postscript: 'I am going to Bremhill from here, with my servant, in a safe pony carriage. I could dine and sleep at Bradenham[15] on Wednesday . . . let me hear – I write in great hurry, How far is Bradenham from Reading. Let us all meet at Oxford.[16]

It appears that Ingram's suggestion that a large fee would have to be paid was a mistake on his part, and on 4 July Bowles's lobbying met with success when an honorary degree of Doctor of Civil Law was duly conferred on D'Israeli. It is likely that Bowles was in Oxford to witness this and remained there until 10 July, when he left in a great hurry leaving a note for Ingram: 'I am sorry I think it best to set off early, as I wish to avoid the heat, I think "indoor heat" in this weather preferable'! Ingram added a note at the top, addressed perhaps to Bowles's unknown host in Oxford:

Poet Bowles scribbled as follows in my study just before he set off, alarmed at the prospect of out of doors nature in hot weather. I suppose I ought to have delivered it to you as his apology for so abruptly quitting us; but our literary curiosities diverted my attention from his epistle. It has just fallen in my way; I send it as it is, to avoid giving you double postage as single postage may be considered quite equivalent to its merits. It nevertheless gives me an opportunity of saying how much I am, Dear Sir, Yours ever, J Ingram.[17]

Among Bowles's wide circle of friends was George Law,[18] since 1824 Bishop of Bath and Wells. Bowles paid a number of visits to him, sometimes staying in the Bishop's Palace in Wells and at other times in Banwell Cottage, Law's favourite retreat that he had built in Banwell, on a small estate belonging to him. In September 1834 Thomas Moore recorded in his journal:

> After dinner Bowles amused us very much (being in one of his most happy moods for showing himself up) by an account of his miseries during a late visit to the Bishop of Bath & Wells's cottage at Banwell – his being put in a room to sleep where he was intercepted from all means of sortie or access to certain nightly conveniences (on which he dwelt most ludicrously) by his ladies' maids who occupied the room next to his – his offering the maids half-a-guinea to sleep in his bed &c. &c. – the naivete and the sense of the ridiculous with which he told this convulsed both himself and us with laughter. 'Not for his bishopric (said he) would I sleep another night in the Cottage of the Bishop of Bath & Wells – I thought his Palace bad enough when I slept there, but the Lord save me from his Cottage.'[19]

Bowles's account of what occurred does not entirely agree with what was told to the Rev. Julian Young by the bishop's son and recorded in Young's journal quite soon after the event:

> As usual, the first thing he did, when he went to his room to dress for dinner, was to inspect his quarters, and see if he could detect any assailable point from which danger might be expected. He crept about suspiciously, looked to the fastenings of the windows, tested the working of the door-locks, peeped into the closets, and then into a small adjoining dressing room, in which there was a tent-bed unmade. From that fact, and the absence of washstand, towel-horse, &c., &c., he concluded it was to be unoccupied. Out of this dressing-room (if I remember rightly what I was told by one of the Bishop's sons) there was a door of outlet on to a back stair. The idea of sleeping alone in a room so exposed to nocturnal assault on two sides so appalled the poor Bowles, that, when a maidservant brought him up his hot water, he took her by the hand, and told her that, if she would consent to occupy the vacant bed in the adjoining room, he would give her a sovereign. Conceiving that he meant to insult her, she bounced out of the room, and told the Bishop that he must get someone else to wait on the nasty old clergyman.

This account continues by relating how the Bishop set the maid's mind at rest by explaining that all the timid cleryman wanted was to have someone within ready call, and asking her and the under-housemaid to sleep in the room, placing their bed against the door between their room and Bowles's. What the bishop failed to do was to tell Bowles of this arrangement, so when he awoke in the night and decided to lock the outer door of the adjoining room he found a resisting object against the door, and, of course, whispering! The journal continues:

> This at once confirmed his conviction that there were thieves in the house. He ran back to the other door, bawling out 'Murder! Thieves!' with such stentorian energy, that the Bishop and all his family were roused out of their beds, though not frightened (for the Laws are remarkably fearless); and it was long before their guest could be reconciled to his position, and induced to go back again to bed.[20]

While visiting the bishop at Banwell in 1832 Bowles learned that his father's old gardener, William Collins, was still alive. It will be recalled that Bowles's father had been rector of Uphill and Brean, small villages not far from Banwell and the scene of Bowles's early childhood. Anxious to visit a man who would have known him from his earliest years, he was taken to the old man's cottage at Uphill and there, after not immediately recognising his visitor, he was moved to tears to find 'Master Billy' talking to him. Bowles visited his old friend again in 1834, having, following his earlier visit, made arrangements for an allowance to be made to him to enable him to end his days in some comfort. He paid another visit at the end of September 1835, accompanied by Magdalene and Bishop Law. On that occasion Bowles recalled that on seeing the old man the bishop said, with a gentle smile:

> 'My good old man, in the present days, I fear, a "Bishop's blessing" may not be thought so valuable as it has been in ages past, but' – placing his hand on the old man's head, he added, in a manner and voice most affecting – 'such as it is, it is given most warmly.' He gave him, not only a 'Bishop's blessing', but what some, in the present day, would consider more valuable, he ordered coals, &c., to last till the long nights of winter were over, if this aged man should live to be out in the air once more, and hear the cuckoo or the blackbird sing again.[21]

The bishop did not forget the old man, as in 1837 he wrote to Bowles to tell him that he had been to see him again and was happy to be able to supply him and his daughter, who looked after him, with some more of their needs.[22]

In 1832 *St John in Patmos: A Poem. By One of the Old Living Poets of Great Britain* was published by Murray. This was soon recognised as being written by Bowles, and a second edition was published in 1835 entitled *St John in Patmos; or, the Last Apostle; a Sacred Poem, from the Revelations*. In the preface Bowles berated 'the laureat Apollo of the living golden lyre' – a thinly disguised reference to Robert Southey, the poet-laureate – for commending in a literary journal 'a bashful livery-man' and 'a poetical semptress' while neglecting 'the elder living bards of Britain' and deserving young authors such as John Pennie.[23] The 'poetical semptress' so contemptuously mentioned by Bowles was Mary Colling, whose poetry Southey had commended.

When sending Caroline Bowles a copy of the anonymous edition in 1832 Bowles wrote:

> ... I need not point out to whom I allude, in my preface, which, I hope, will be taken in good part, tho I could not avoid some notice of greater attention in distinguish'd literary journals, paid to disgusting and stupid bards of the <u>pantry</u> and <u>wash</u>-house, than to cultivated intellect and real genius. But the heart is sick with far more serious considerations.
> God preserve us from the storm that seems impending[24]

On 9 June Caroline wrote to Southey:

> I believe every Bowles has more or less of what the Scots call 'a bee in the bonnet.' I am sometimes sensible of the humming of mine, and I am sure our poor friend of Bremhill is haunted by a very tormenting familiar. Have you seen his late publication, St John at Patmos? If you have, I am sure you have felt compassion for, rather than anger towards, him for the effusion of pique and disappointment directed towards yourself in the preface ... It is evident that from year to year he cherished hopes of being noticed by your pen, a few words of commendation from which would, I believe, have consoled him for the heartless neglect and cutting scorn of a world which cares less than nothing for one who has nearly outlived the generation as well as the age that hailed his youthful Muse with lavish favour ... I tried to soothe him in my answer ... which brought me another letter by return of post, so characteristic of his infirmity of temper, and simplicity and real goodness of heart, that I must let you see it ... .[25]

Southey was soon writing to Caroline Bowles:

You are perfectly right, dear Caroline, in supposing that I should feel anything rather than anger at poor Bowles's effusion of spleen . . . I forgive him everything except his giving a proud and contemptuous nickname to one whose family history and whose character ought to have touched him, whatever he may think of her rhymes. I am sure that if he ever sees her portrait he will be pitiably ashamed of his.

The first time I ever saw Bowles was in 1802, and I took a dislike to him which did not wear off till I learnt from Sir George Beaumont what was his real character, many years afterwards; but the cause was just such an effusion of spleen against the Welsh bard Edward Williams,[26] to whom he denied anything like genius because he wrote commonplace English verses, unmindful that the Welshman was writing in a foreign tongue.

More than once I have taken an opportunity of complimenting him, as he well deserves, when he came in my way, though I believe Gifford[27] sometimes intercepted such compliments. And now, for your sake, if he does not come in my way, I will, on the first occasion, go out of mine to bring him in neck and shoulders.[28]

Bowles did not perhaps deserve the kindly letter that he received from Southey, writing from Keswick, soon after this:

This morning I received your St John in Patmos . . . I have just read the poem through, and with much pleasure. Yours I should have known it to have been by the sweet and unsophisticated style; upon which I endeavoured, now almost forty years ago, to form my own . . .

You will not, I am sure, suppose that I could for even a moment feel hurt by your remarks in the preface . . .

Southey went on to explain why he no longer reviewed the work of living poets but nevertheless wished to render Mary Colling some service by telling her story, and concluded his letter:

Would that there were a hope of seeing you here, that I might show you this lake and these mountains, and these books, and talk with you upon subjects which might make us forget that we are living in the days of William IV., Earl Grey,[29] the Times newspaper, and the cholera morbus. God save the first, and deliver us from the rest!

Believe me, my dear Sir,
Yours, with sincere respect and regard,
Robert Southey[30]

In the summer of 1832 Bowles must have heard of civil unrest in Canterbury and so wrote to his old friend William Howley, who had been archbishop since 1828, to enquire after his well being. The archbishop replied:

> I have just found time to thank you for your most kind letter having this evening reached home after completing the visitation of my Diocese. You and Mrs Bowles will be very glad to hear that I have not suffered in any way from the rabble of Canterbury. I was neither alarmed, nor did I receive any personal injury: a few stones were thrown which struck the carriage, and one of them broke a shop window. A man attempted to pull one of the postillions off his horse but got a cut with his whip across the face, which made him run off, and he has hid himself ever since for fear of being recognised by the watch: had the boy been dismounted the horses would have run away & the consequences might have been serious. On the whole I have great reason to be thankful to Providence, and during the week which I passed afterwards in Canterbury I received so many marks of respect and attention from the people of the Town and the gentlemen of the neighbourhood as to have no reason to regret the annoyance I was exposed to on my entrance to the city. As far as I can learn, the Radical interest there has been much hurt by this transaction; which is universally reprobated by all respectable persons, and by none more than by the Reformers [?] who are not Radicals. I agree with you however in thinking that the aspect of the times is very alarming. I am prepared for the worst, but I still have the confidence in Divine providence which makes me hope we will weather the storm . . .[31]

It is likely that at this time arrangements had been made for Bowles's old friend, the composer and Sheridan's brother-in-law William Linley, to pay a visit to the parsonage. However, it can be inferred from the following letter that Magdalene had heard reports of Linley's alcohol-induced misbehaviour and wrote to him about 'excesses which are distressing to every one, and lamentable to see', presumably making it clear that she would not expect to see him behaving in this way at Bremhill. This letter brought forth a long reply from Linley, in which he wrote:

> . . . That I may occasionally have drank wine to a certain point of elevation, even at Bremhill, I will not deny; but if I have been so besotted as to have justly deserved the character your words would imply, a character 'quite altered' as you say from my proper one, it would be better that I kept

away from the risk of giving further offence, and withdrew from society altogether.

I am naturally of a social turn, and like my glass of wine; I will not deny it; – but there are some dosey, formal people – and Wiltshire is one, who if a laugh happens to be too incorrectly loud, or an argument too ardently pursued in conversation, immediately attributes the temporary excitement to drunkenness . . . You surely cannot seriously fear that I shall run riot at Bremhill, and disturb the serenity of the friends you are expecting? – If so, anxious as I am to preserve the small remains of regard you and Mr Bowles may still retain for me, I had better, perhaps, postpone my visit.

But I won't think so. You have had stories told of me that are not true, or else that have been greatly exaggerated . . .

God bless you, my dear Mrs B. ! And believe me that I shall be able to defend myself better than you are aware of from the attacks that 'some good natured friends' may have made upon me.[32]

On receipt of this letter it is more than likely that Magdalene responded by urging Linley, who had known her husband for more than thirty years, not to cancel or postpone the proposed visit.

By now Bowles would have been well advanced in the research that was to lead to the publication of his history of Lacock Abbey, the seat of his friend William Henry Fox Talbot, celebrated as a pioneer of photography. In September 1832 he wrote to Fox Talbot at Cowes in the Isle of Wight:

. . . I intended writing a short note on the lines to your Sister, respecting the peculiar fate of Ela,[33] but I found the subject increasingly led me so far. & was in itself so very interesting & affecting & Romantic, that, I said to myself, 'I have nothing to do – & will tell her story' . . .

. . . How long the fit of writing will last, I cannot tell – I have some four or five chapter, con amore.

I wish you would let me see you when you come down – for William being on the King's side, at Runnimede, I should imagine the copy of 'magna charta', in the Tower at Lacock, is [?] the one Wm & the Barons signed, on the spot, for each of the attestors, had each, I have no doubt, a copy.

Pray – examine all the papers – I am sure you will find some original, if not valuable documents & believe me

Yrs (?) most truly

W L Bowles

Oh! That I were on the Edge of Southampton waters, this beautiful day[34]

In September Bowles and members of Lord Lansdowne's family were in Wells, perhaps as guests of the Bishop, and on 6 September the *Devizes and Wiltshire Gazette* reported: 'On Sunday last, the Marquis of Lansdowne, the Marchioness, and Lady Louisa Fitzmaurice with the Rev. Canon Bowles attended service at Wells, and never at "the high altar of public praise" was the Choir service of the Church of England more impressively performed.'[35]

It is noteworthy that although Lord Lansdowne was closely involved with the management of his estates and of the park and gardens surrounding Bowood, his close friendship with Bowles enabled him to hear of various matters that would otherwise not have come to his notice. For example, on one occasion he wrote to Bowles:

> I am glad you spoke to me about Eastwell also certainly how without my knowing it <u>stepped out</u> of the garden business – the cause is that his blades are not so short as other people's – but I have given directions for him always to be employed except in peculiar cases & then on speaking to me – for I believe him to be a very honest man.
>
> In the meantime he has no great reason to complain as last year's bill for my work amounts to £170.[36]

Bowles and Magdalene were frequently asked to dine at Bowood, in particular when friends or acquaintances had also been invited. On one occasion Lord Lansdowne wrote:

> Many thanks for your satisfactory letter – perhaps it may be as convenient for you to dine here Sunday as Monday, we shall be equally happy to see you both days, but I mention it because I think you will be glad to see Jekyll if he is obliged to leave on Monday morning. [37]

'Jekyll'was undoubtedly Joseph Jekyll,[38] who had been Member of Parliament for Calne until 1816 and then a master in chancery.

On 13 September the *Devizes and Wiltshire Gazette* printed a squib or satirical poem by Thomas Moore (taken from the *Metropolitan Magazine* for September), entitled *Song of the Departing Spirits of Tithe*. This very bad piece of verse included such lines as:

Ah never shall rosie Rector more
Like shepherds of Israel idly eat
And make of his flock 'a prey and meat'
No more that shall be his pastoral sport
Of suing his flock in the Bishop's Court[39]

Such an attack, albeit good-humoured, on the clergy and their receipt of tithes was sure to enrage Bowles. Ten days later Moore lunched at the parsonage, and reported:

Bowles, by the by, has been writing a most twaddling answer to my Tithes Squib, which appeared in the Devizes paper – looked a little nervous on the strength of it today. Bessy said, when I showed it to her, – 'it is lucky for him he is your friend' – and I could to be sure have made rare reprisals on him[40]

Bowles's 'twaddling answer' consisted of a letter to the editor, not signed with his name but with an 'X', reading:

Some apology ought to be made for attributing the lines you have published 'On the Death of Tithes' to the distinguished author of the beautiful lines on 'Crabbe's Inkstand'. To this author, however, though it could scarcely have been believed, the 'Death of Tithes' has been publicaly [sic], and universally attributed; you will therefore only act up to your own motto by publishing the following.[41]

Then followed a long satirical piece in answer to Moore's attack with numerous explanatory footnotes so characteristic of Bowles's style that no one could have been in any doubt that it was his work.

In October Bowles's friend Joseph Hunter spent a few days at the parsonage at Bremhill. Hunter noted:

. . . He took me to see Lacock Abbey. He is preparing a kind of history of it. My visit was very pleasant: though I found him saddened by the times, anticipating all kinds of evils, & fiercely engaged in defending the Church as it is.

His library is a very miscellaneous collection. The basis of it, the books of some good old Divines, but poetical & historical works intermingled . . .

His family consists of himself & Mrs Bowles, who is a [?] helpmate: managing him & his affairs very well: a very kind friendly woman. She is aware of his peculiarities which are many & [?]. He is 70, rather too old to begin Lacock. He visits frequently Lord Lansdowne.[42]

On one occasion in October, when Bowles and Magdalene were dining at Bowood with, among others, Lord John Russell and Moore, Bowles amused the company by saying, as Moore recorded: 'that he had once an offer to be made a member of the Whig Club. On our looking a little surprized – "Yes!" he added, "and of the *Linnaean* too". I said that in *both* instances it must have been a mistake as he was neither Whig nor Naturalist.'[43]

During 1832 Bowles attended only one meeting of the Chapter of Salisbury Cathedral, and that was when he was in residence in April. At the meeting of the Chapter held in October Bowles was elected as Master of the Choristers, thus confirming his interest in and some measure of control over the cathedral music. At the same meeting, not attended by Bowles, it was ordered 'that a visitation of the Library be made by the Chapter on 24 October and that Mr Greenly[44] be informed thereof'. Bowles and his fellow canons were responsible for maintaining the fabric of the cathedral. It has been said that when Sir Thomas Phillipps visited not many years before he found 'The windows of the Cathedral Library were at that time broken, and the jackdaws, with free ingress and egress, nightly found both "perch" and "dormitory" on the piles of choice volumes, including an Anglo-Saxon MS, which were heaped up in a state of "chaos" on the tables within.'[45] Perhaps some slight improvements had been made by 1832 but some years later, when Bowles was still a residentiary canon, it was reported that 'Many volumes still remain buried in dust, and when the cobwebs of the last century have been brushed away, some works may probably be found not undeserving of notice'.[46] It seems, therefore, that despite his interest in antiquarian matters Bowles was either unwilling or, perhaps, unable to persuade his fellow canons to take proper care of the magnificent contents of the library, including one of the original copies of Magna Carta, tenth-century psalters and over a thousand books left by Bishop Gheast, who died in 1577.

At the foot of Derry Hill, quite close to Bowood Park, was a covered well and, half-way up the hill, a drinking spout with the following inscription, composed by Bowles:

> Drink traveller drink and more than worldly wealth enjoy
> God's greatest earthly blessing health[47]

In January 1833 there appeared in the *Devizes and Wiltshire Gazette* a poem that must surely have brought a smile to Bowles's lips:

A Lay on Derry Hill

Drink! Drink! Quoth Bowles
To thirsty souls –
'And a fig for worldly wealth.
This fountain clear
Is pregnant here
With the first of blessings – Health'*
A simple swain
Who conn'd the strain
Seduc'd by inspiration
In copious draught
The liquor quaff'd
To his bowels' sore vexation
For at once he found
To the very ground
The cursed cholera level'd him:
And with groan he swore
That never before
Had drink so vile bedevil'd him
But alas! He died
By Derry's side
A warning most pathetic
To all who view
As strictly true
The puffs of pens poetic
Then let thirsty souls
Beware of Bowles
Whenever he praises water
Against whom when found
On the fairest ground
A verdict of – Manslaughter.

*Vide Bowles' lines by the roadside.[48]

From his ample income Bowles endeavoured to relieve distress among the poor, and on one occasion in particular, when a fellow writer and poet, John Banim,[49] fell on hard times Bowles was happy to join with others in responding to an appeal for his support that appeared in *The Times* and other papers. The *Devizes and Wiltshire Gazette* at this time was frequently fulsome in its praise of him and was 'happy to learn that the Rev Canon Bowles of Salisbury Cathedral with that liberality for which he is remarkable has forwarded a draft towards the relief of the distresses of the poor Banim, the author of "Tales of the O'Hara Family" and numerous other works of acknowledged ability'.[50]

Some measure of parliamentary reform having been achieved in 1832, the moves to see the Established Church reformed, the deans and chapters of cathedrals in particular, gathered pace. In June 1832 the new Church Revenues Commission was charged with carrying out a complete investigation into the finances of the Church, with the huge disparities between the income received by the bishops and some deans and chapters as compared with the majority of clergymen being sure to be under scrutiny.

One particularly vociferous critic of the Church at this time was Lord King, Baron of Ockham,[51] who supported Catholic emancipation and the commutation of tithes and was well known as a fervent opponent of the episcopal bench. In a speech in the House of Lords he had asked the question 'Of what use are the Deans and Chapters?'. Bowles lost no time in writing in 1833 *A Last and Summary Answer to the Question 'Of what use have been, and are, the English Cathedral Establishments?' with a Vindication of Anthems & Cathedral Services . . .* However, before the work could be fully advertised and published Lord King died. The *Devizes and Wiltshire Gazette* reported that:

> The Rev. Canon Bowles, with a truly amiable and characteristic feeling, has, for the present, suspended his work on English Cathedral Establishments, in consequence of the death of Lord King 'lest' (as the Rev gent. himself says) 'one unkind word should be heard over his lordship's grave' . . . As the printing of the answer was completed, Lord King was taken ill upon which Mr Bowles immediately prohibited all advertisements relating to the work in the London papers and suspended publication on his Lordship's death. The work it appears will undergo some explanations and corrections and be published within a few weeks.[52]

It seems that Bowles decided that his *Last and Summary Answer* should be addressed not to the deceased baron but to Lord Henley,[53] a well-known advocate for the reform of the Church of England and who, in his *A Plan of Church Reform* published in 1832, had called for, among other things, cathedrals to be turned into parish churches, with their incomes being equalised and canonries being suppressed. As a consequence, shortly after Lord King's death Bowles arranged to have published *A Last and Summary Answer to the Question 'Of what use have been, and are, the English Cathedral Establishments?' with a Vindication of Anthems & Cathedral Services in a letter to Lord Henley by Rev. W L Bowles . . . To which is added An Answer to an article in the Edinburgh Review on the Relative Number of Learned and Eminent Characters Furnished by the Scottish and English Churches.* When Bowles was happy for the pamphlet to be published he wrote on 11 May to Carrington, the printer at the Chronicle Office in Bath:

> This <u>new plague</u> absolutely frightens me, from Bath, & I shall <u>not come</u>, except for a morning, till it is over.
>
> From one thing or another, I have delay'd my pamphlet, but I would wish you to do it up & send copies to British Magazine, directly, Gentleman's & a hundred & twenty-five copies to Rivington's & seventy to Turrill's. I shall not advertise it in Bath, till I see you, which I hope to do next week (Thursday morning) therefore you will send copies to London & let it lie in Bath, till further orders, as to advertisement.[54]

The pamphlet was a vigorous and generally well-argued piece of writing in favour of the existing governance of English cathedrals and in particular of the worthy work, as Bowles saw it, done by the prebendaries who, with very few exceptions, received a very modest income from their office. However, at the end of his comparison of the eminent characters in the English and Scottish churches, he added a note headed 'Dulwich and Durham', commencing with: 'If the principles of the Plan of Lord Henley be just, they would apply to the "College of God's Gift" in Surrey, as well as to Durham, or any other cathedral'; that is, to Dulwich College as as well as to any cathedral. Bowles's argument was that if 'the people' have a right to confiscate the ancient endowments of cathedrals and do away with the prebendaries and substitute a dean with two assistants, then by the same right Lord Henley might say that in the case of Dulwich College, whose founder willed that there would be a master and warden with four clergymen of the church of England, he would take away 'either the accomplished master or the amiable and excellent warden' and substitute them for a commissioner, who would allow one master to be paid a salary and two clergymen their stipends, with the remainder of the founder's property being given to the neighbouring vicars of Surrey![55]

The master of Dulwich College at this time was John Allen,[56] the political and historical writer who assisted Lord Holland in the composition of his parliamentary speeches and in Lord Byron's view 'the best informed and one of the ablest men' that he knew.[57] Bowles sent a copy of his pamphlet to Allen, and was dismayed to receive a reply in which Allen took exception to it, on the grounds that it would be seen as a suggestion that Dulwich College was as worthy of reformation as the cathedrals of the Church of England.

Bowles's reply was doubtless immediate:

My dear Sir

I am truly most sincerely concern'd that you should have thought for one moment, that my mode of introducing the interesting establishment of Dulwich College, was, or could be intended with the slightest disrespect, particularly when I have received so many kindnesses there, & have the highest esteem for the Master, & the sincerest regard for the Warden.

No! dear Sir – it was the farthest from my thought – and as to sheltering Durham under the wing of Dulwich, I did not want or think of it, in that light. I merely, in a manner which I hoped could not be offensive, combated the arguments which applied to the principles of the Establishment of either.

As they struck me, both resting on the same grounds, according to Lord Henley's vision.

It is quite sufficient that you, whom as a scholar, & most amiable character, as I have ever esteem'd see what I have said in a different view – & to show my sincerity I have written instantly to Rivington <u>not to sell a single</u> copy more for it is enough for me to shew I have written <u>differently</u> from <u>what I ought</u>, if one sensible & excellent man sees in a light different from <u>what I intended</u> whatever I have written 'Dulwich a fit subject of <u>reform</u>'!! Never, never! I mean quite the contrary.

Another copy of the pamphlet should not be sold for <u>ten thousand chapters</u> of Durham, and their Bishop into the bargain if, I have un-intentionally said what might justly be consider'd as unfair, which was indeed never my intention. – I beg you will not trouble yourself any farther by writing a single line, because I feel I must have done wrong, but, surely I could not have thought of sending the pamphlet to you, <u>of all men</u>, if I suppos'd you could see any thing disrespectful in the sentiments or unfair in the arguments, but I thought merely upon public grounds, that if Lord Henley's principles, applied to one establishment of benevolence, learning & piety – they must apply to all, & certainly I did not think the cases were paralel [sic].

It is quite sufficient for me that you see the argument in another light, & deeply regretting I introduced the comparison at all.

P.S. I order'd no advertisement to be inserted in the London papers because I heard of Lord King's illness, so I imagine scarce a copy of my pamphlet is sold.[58]

This letter must surely have been painful for Bowles to write, and at the end of it he scribbled another, rather incoherent, note: 'Pray, say a kind word, if my friend Allen, the Master – if he sees what I have said in the same light . . . I beg my respects to Lord Holland, thro whom I have taken the liberty of sending this hasty note.' As the letter itself was addressed to Allen, the Master, perhaps Bowles had intended to refer to the warden.

It was not only the cathedral clergy who attracted the support of Bowles at this time but also the Protestant clergy in Ireland. An appeal was launched to provide funds for their relief. In Wiltshire the Bishop of Salisbury contributed £100, Lord Lansdowne £50 and Bowles £10.[59] At a time when an agricultural labourer would be fortunate if he was paid £23 a year to support himself and his family, Bowles's response can be seen to be more generous than it might at first appear.

Bowles never hesitated to seek assistance from his friends when pursuing, without initial success, historical research, and so it was that in July he wrote to Sir Richard Colt Hoare in somewhat demanding terms:

My dear Sir Richard
I hope this will find [you] among your books – & well!
I write anxiously – Gratefully
I only want facts – leave me to <u>adorn</u> them as I please. I only want so to colour them as may make them look alive! You must find out for me the date if you can of the endowment on the Priory of Farley, in Wilts – by Humphrey de Bohun & his wife Margaret.[60]
I have such a chain of evidence as will surprise you and convince both you and Hunter[61] that the book of Lacock is veracious to a Title.
But I must know the date of the endowment of Humphrey to Farley – I also [illegible] do you get the formation that Edward of Salisbury was in the Battle the 20 of Henry the 1st.
God keep you & believe me
&c The Poor Canon![62]

In May Bowles had received a visit from his old friend Joseph Hunter, who noted: 'Mr W.L. Bowles entertained me with a long history of Mr Dallaway, as we rode together between Bremhill and Drycote, May

31, 1833.'[63] Bowles delighted in regaling his friends with gossip and anecdotes, a great fund of which he possessed, and Hunter proceeded to record the life history of James Dallaway, another antiquary and writer.

In the summer the ancient chapel of ease at Foxham within Bowles's parish was reopened for worship after its restoration largely at Lord Lansdowne's expense. Later it was reported:

> An additional place of worship having long been wanted for the inhabitants of Bremhill who lived at a distance from the parish church. It was wished that the ancient chapel should be restored. The Rev. Canon Bowles liberally contributed towards carrying the object into effect. The rector of Bremhill with that Christian benevolence which distinguishes his whole life, also readily consented to provide for the duty of the chapel ... The chapel was opened in the summer last year on which a sermon was preached by Rev the Rector and such was the interest taken in the event that it is calculated there were nearly a thousand persons present, though only about three hundred could gain admission.[64]

Bowles continued to be excellent company when among friends, as he was early in September when dining at Bowood. Thomas Moore found:

> Bowles in a most amusing mood, during the evening, showed himself up with a degree of <u>abandon</u> which convulsed us all with laughter – His account of his course of education at Strasburg, where he was for a short time, when young, – his having learnt French fortification and the *pierres gravee* (*Peer gravvy*, as he pronounced it) and the specimens he gave us of his proficiency in two of these branches of learning – French & the Peer gravvy, was, beyond measure ridiculous – Lady Lansdowne declared that her sides were sore with laughing Fixed to go with him on Saturday to Stonehenge, a long projected expedition.[65]

On Saturday Bowles and Magdalen set off in their carriage from Bremhill and collected Moore and Bessy from Sloperton Cottage at about nine o'clock. At Lydway, some 4 miles beyond Devizes, the party transferred to Bowles's pony carriage, which had been sent on there the night before. They then proceeded to Stonehenge, Moore seeing it for the first time. They found some 'sensible Quakers' there with whom they had a conversation. Moore noted in his journal:

Dined at the Bustard well and cheaply, and taking the carriage again at Lodway, were conveyed back comfortably by our Reverend <u>Vetturio</u>, reaching home before eight o'clock. Nothing could be managed better or more agreeably than the whole journey – Bowles and I talking Druidical learning the whole way, much to Bessy's edification and amusement.[66]

As he got older and more absent-minded, Bowles's behaviour on social occasions was undoubtedly a source of amusement to his friends and of astonishment to those who were not so well acquainted with him. A writer on the life of Bowles in 1894 recounts one such example:

The following anecdote was told me by a friend Dr. Prior, who had it from Mr John Benett, who was present when the incident occurred. At a dinner party at Bowood, the Marchioness of Lansdowne introduced Canon Bowles to an elderly lady, and they sat down chatting away pleasantly about things of the day. Bowles was perfectly oblivious that this was the very lady to whom he had been engaged to be married when he had very little income besides his curacy. The marriage had been broken off in consequence of their mutual want of means. The lady of course was perfectly well aware that she was talking to her quondam lover; but her married name had in no way enlightened him as to her personality. After a time, she said, having touched upon old days

'But, Mr Bowles, don't you remember me?'
'No, ma'am, I don't.'
Then she added, smiling – 'You used to know me and pretend to be very fond of me. I was Miss ---'
'Oh, what a wreck!' was the spontaneous exclamation of the poet.
Happily the lady enjoyed the joke immensely, for she was a remarkably handsome woman for her age, and his burst of surprise was really only a compliment to the extreme beauty of her youth. One must come to the conclusion that the reverend canon had been an often engaged man in his time, and if his constancy was at fault, his good taste was indisputable.[67]

It seems that Bowles could never forget the way in which Byron, in his *English Bards and Scotch Reviewers* published as long ago as 1809, had made fun of Bowles's lines in his *Spirit of Discovery* about the woods of Madeira trembling to the lovers' kiss. And so it was that when in 1833 he arranged to have a part of the *Spirit of Discovery* entitled *The Grave of Anna in the Island of Madeira* printed and published in the form of a pamphlet, he could not resist reminding his readers of what had passed almost twenty-five years before by including the following explanation:

> This affecting story is well known. I have taken some poetical liberties with it, but adhered substantially to the narrative.
>
> Without reference to a palpable absurdity, attributed to me by Lord Byron, in his well-known Satire, I have thought it right to revise and correct this Episode, and to leave the story as I would wish it to appear, when I shall have no power to re-call a sentiment or word.

The revision and correction is so extensive that this version of the story bears little, if any, resemblance to the verses published in 1804. What is certain is that all reference to the lovers' kiss in the woods of Madeira is entirely absent!

Bowles was apparently pleased when, in the September 1833 number of *Blackwood's Edinburgh Magazine* in an article on painters and poets, his views were mentioned:

> There is a passage in Lord Byron's letter to Mr Bowles, which, as he was not practically a painter, shews, that if he had been, he would have transferred all his poetry to his canvas. His views on nature were not very different from those I have given. It is true he neither minutely enters into the theory of form or colour, but he would have directed, had he sat in the chair of Professor of Painting, studies from nature, or, at least, the use of them, with a view to engraft the poetry of the mind on nature.[68]

At the end of August and the beginning of September Bowles paid one of his visits to Bishop Law in Wells and on his way home, while in Bath and perhaps where he saw the latest number of the magazine, he wrote to John Wilson, the 'Christopher North' of *Blackwood's Magazine*:

> . . . Having the advantage of a frank, I hasten to return my most grateful thanks for the kindness with which you have spoken in introducing my name.
>
> I am now on my way Home, & hope to send you my last oratorio 'pro Ecclesia'. If you could find an opportunity to say a word or two, I need not say how oblig'd I shall ever feel, myself, as indeed I have so often felt . . .[69]

In February 1833 Edward Moxon published the young lawyer Abraham Hayward's[70] translation into English of Goethe's *Faust*. Having been born at Wilton near Salisbury in 1801, Hayward would have been well acquainted with his fellow Wiltshireman's reputation, and so, soon after his translation – that he had arranged to have privately printed – was published, he visited Salisbury with a copy to present to Bowles. However, Bowles was away when he called, and so in October he wrote from Bremhill to Hayward:

> I am sorry the translator of Faust should have thought it necessary, when I was at Salisbury, to have any one but his book to introduce him. However, I shall most truly value the book, from the author, tho the author is personally to my regret unknown, & I hope the next time he comes, to see at the Canonry-House, if I am in residence, the author of a work so interesting.[71]

Having subscribed to Nicholas Lee Torre's[72] *Translations of the Oxford Latin Prize Poems* in 1831, another translation that Bowles was no doubt pleased to see published at this time (1833) was *The Siege of Gibraltar Translated from the Latin poem recited in the Theatre at Oxford AD 1799*. This was Nicholas Lee Torre's translation of Bowles's poem, which had won the Chancellor's Latin verse prize when he was an undergraduate so many years before and he had himself recited at the Commemoration Day in 1799.

Bowles was well known as a fluent *extempore* preacher, and in April 1834 it was reported that at a service in aid of the fund for building and enlarging churches held at Bremhill his sermon was 'a powerful and affecting discourse, and delivered with touching eloquence'. Nearly seventy children of the Marchioness of Lansdowne's school and the girls belonging to Magdalene's school were compelled to listen to the rector's oration, with each of them putting a half-penny in the collection plate and remaining silent while the village choir sang a hymn written for the occasion by Bowles. In reporting the occasion the *Devizes and Wiltshire Gazette* printed the words of the hymn for all to read. [73]

In July the *Gentleman's Magazine* printed a review of 'a Sermon preached at Bremhill on Sunday 20 April 1834 by the Rev W.L. Bowles'. This most flattering piece was written by Bowles's old friend John Mitford, who in the previous year began contributing to the magazine and continued to do so every month without fail for the next seventeen years. At the end of the review Mitford wrote:

> Will Mr Bowles pardon us, if we venture to address him in the Poetic language, though we cannot bring to it the Poetic strength? At least, he

will accept our song as the expression of gratitude for the many hours of of delight which we have received, in common with others, from the harp that still hangs in the sacred groves of Bremhill.[74]

Then follow some poetic lines composed by Mitford and addressed to Bowles – the quality of the poetry matching that produced by Bowles in his later years.

In June the *Devizes and Wiltshire Gazette* printed a poem that had been separately printed and published, written by Bowles after hearing the Choral Music and Coronation Anthem in Westminster Abbey on 24 June. In introducing the poem, Bowles writes: 'It is a full fifty years since I heard last Handel, thy solemn and divine strain.'[75] In the following month Thomas Moore noted in his journal:

> A visit from Bowles, who came rather tipsy & headily after dinner by himself at the Boar – very amusing, though, notwithstanding. His account of his writing his verses on the Westminster Abbey Festival, while the Music was going on – walking off with them between the Acts to Nicholl the Printer, and having them in type before dinner – all amusingly characteristic of the man – the verses too being some of his best.[76]

Having published his life of Bishop Ken, Bowles continued to take an interest in him, and so visited Frome in Somerset where the bishop was buried after his sojourn at Longleat. He was not at all pleased to find that there was not even a stone to mark the bishop's grave, although he learned that some years before one of the churchwardens had been induced to plant a few flowers around the bishop's last resting place. Bowles therefore composed 'Some Lines for an intended Monument to Bishop Ken', which he arranged to have published in 1834 in the *Devizes and Wiltshire Gazette* – a newspaper always ready to accept his poetic offerings.[77]

Also in 1834 was published *A Brief History of Old and New Sarum*[78] by the Rev. Peter Hall,[79] who had been curate of St Edmund's Church in Salisbury until dismissed in the previous year. Like Bowles, Hall had been educated at Winchester. The history included a sonnet by Bowles: 'On Old Sarum composed and communicated expressly for the present work'.

Bowles was continuing at this time with the research for his history of Lacock Abbey. On 26 July John Britton wrote to Fox Talbot with his views on the project:

I am glad to hear that Mr Bowles is going on with his vol on Lacock, tho'
I am confident he will never sell enough to repay his expenses – however
it is a rational amusement, & much better than writing about politics &
church reform on neither of which can he write or talk with composure
. . . I am not <u>desirous</u> of embarking in any new publication either on
Lacock, or any other subject; but offered my cooperation with you in case
Bowles gave up his vol . . .[80]

On 25 July Samuel Taylor Coleridge died. Many years before, as
a young man, he had enlisted as a private soldier under a false name,
and following his death the literary journal the *Athenaeum* speculated
on how it came about that he was soon discharged from service. Bowles
knew the true facts and so wrote to *The Times*:

> . . . I trespass for a minute on your time and paper, as I am, perhaps the
> only person now living who can explain all the circumstances from Mr
> Coleridge's own mouth with whom I became acquainted after a sonnet
> addressed to me in his poems; moreover, being intimate from our school
> days, and at Oxford with that very officer in his regiment who alone
> procured his discharge, from whom I also heard the facts after Coleridge
> became known as a poet.
>
> The regiment was the 15th Elliot's Light Dragoons, the officer was
> Nathaniel Ogle, eldest son of Dr Newton Ogle, Dean of Winchester and
> brother of Mrs Sheridan; he was a scholar, and leaving Merton College,
> he entered this regiment a cornet. Some years afterwards, I believe he
> was then Captain of Coleridge's troop, going into the stables at Reading,
> he remarked written on the white wall, under one of the saddles, in large
> pencil characters, the following sentence, in Latin,
>> 'Eheu! Quam infortunii miserimum est fulsae fellcem!'

Bowles continues by explaining that the identity of the writer of
these words was soon discovered; that, having come down from Jesus
College, Cambridge, he had enlisted when he found himself in London
without any means, and when asked his name replied 'Comberback',
the name over a shop door near Westminster Bridge. Bowles writes that
Coleridge was discharged 'from respect to his friends and his station' and
was soon carried away in a chaise to the cheers of his old companions.[81]
    While living at Calne with the Morgan family Coleridge enjoyed
very friendly relations with Bowles, but it is said that Coleridge later
recorded 'I injured myself irreparably with him by devoting a fortnight
to the correction of his poems. He took the corrections, but never forgave
the corrector'.[82]

In September Southey wrote to Bowles from Keswick:

> In the course of this month I am about to leave home on a long circuit, with my son, – an over-grown lad in his sixteenth year . . . Should you be at Bremhill about the second week in October, and you can conveniently receive us, I would gladly take the opportunity, – which may never again occur – of passing two days with you.
>
> I saw your letter in the Times, concerning poor Coleridge, and can tell you more circumstances concerning his campaign . . .
>
> The General is expected here in the course of the autumn, but is not likely to make any long tarriance, for his own house will not be in a state to receive him . . . It has undergone a radical reform . . . Mrs P has also undergone a reform; she has become <u>evangelical</u>, – and the poor General when he arrives will be taken to sit under many a dolorous lecture . . .[83]

The general referred to by Southey was undoubtedly General Peachey, who had a house at Vicar's Island near Keswick in which he was accustomed to reside during part of the summer season. Bowles replied:

> Our <u>penates</u>, & Mrs Bowles & myself will be rejoic'd to welcome you and your son at the time you mention.
>
> I have just recev'd a letter from Bristol respecting the monument to Butler, in which I am told, you propose going there & I could easily take you from this place, if you and your son would accompany me, & I should like to see it with the writer of the inscription.
>
> The inscription is most appropriate but, had there been space, I could have wish'd, in these days, the singular circumstance <u>touch'd</u> on, that, so profound a mind, from reason of conscience, left the communion of dissent, for the established church.
>
> I think nothing can equal the design of the monument or do more credit to the youthful artist, & its cheapness is as extraordinary as its design & execution.

The monument to Butler referred to by Bowles was the memorial belatedly erected in Bristol Cathedral to Joseph Butler,[84] Bishop of Bristol from 1738 until 1750, the son of a retired Presbyterian draper and educated at a dissenting academy. Bowles continues:

> So Mrs P is, at last, among the incurables, in this age, when the disease of fanaticism is [illegible], as in the times of Cromwell & Barebones.

Alas for the General! Both on account of the House & Housekeeper! I have known him from our school & Oxford days, & have great esteem for him, on account of his unvaried attachments to old scenes & old acquaintances, tho his flux of talk is sometimes too much for me, but now illumination spiritual has possess'd itself of his household he will meet his match! . . .[85]

In the event the state of health of Southey's wife prevented the planned visit from taking place.[86]

On 1 January 1835 Bowles preached a sermon in Salisbury Cathedral on the martyrdom of Charles I, not from choice, as he mentioned when the sermon was published in 1838, but according to his canonical turn. He also stated that when delivering the sermon he held 'the identical Prayer-Book of the murdered Charles, marked, as it seems to me in many passages appropriate to his sorrows and fate, in prison – with traces of tears shed in solitude, nearly two hundred years ago'.

In this year the last of Bowles's major works appeared: *Annals and Antiquities of Lacock Abbey in the county of Wilts; with memorials of the foundress Ela Countess of Salisbury, and of the Earls of Salisbury of the Houses of Sarisbury and Longespe; including notices of the monasteries of Bradenstoke, Hinton, and Farley.* The book, over 400 pages in length, was the joint work of Bowles and the young John Gough Nichols,[87] eldest son of the celebrated printer and antiquary John Bowyer Nichols. Still under thirty years of age, his work with the now elderly Bowles was one of the first of an immense corpus of topographical, heraldic and genealogical works that he was to produce over the next forty years, with his great contribution to Sir Richard Colt Hoare's *Modern History of South Wiltshire* appearing only two years later. He had visited Lacock Abbey with Bowles in the course of their joint research, and, in a letter written by Bowles to Fox Talbot in the previous year he refers to 'Mr J.G. Nicholls, the intelligent young Man who called with me at Lacock'.[88]

In the preface Bowles pays a handsome tribute to Nichols by declaring that 'not only myself, but the literary world, is indebted for his scrupulous antiquarian researches, and for everything more especially relating to antient genealogy, contained in these pages'. It is clear that Bowles could not possibly have produced the work without the assistance of Nichols and the other scholars mentioned in the preface. During the course of their joint research Bowles wrote to Nichols:

I have [illegible] on you, as a far better judge than myself, & should be happy to adopt all & every suggestion of yours.

What you have sent is most important, & I am very oblig'd to you for the care you have taken and the interest you have shown.

The additions are most valuable – how to bring them in, I shall leave to you.

The print from Buck[89] is totally unlike Lacock, in its present appearance but if you think it is better to show it just as it was when Buck drew it, I shall be happy to have another engraving, but the <u>River</u> could never have been where Buck has plac'd it. – When we are done with Edward, all will be easy

P.S. I doubt whether an engraving from Buck would be worth the expense – should rather prefer to take very beautiful additions to south gallery.[90]

Bowles seems to have kept in touch with very many of his old schoolfriends, and it was to one of them, Charles Byam Wollaston, 'one of my kindest and oldest friends from school days at Winchester', that he dedicated the work. The drawing of the Abbey in the frontispiece was by Constance, the 'accomplished and amiable Mistress of the Mansion' as Bowles describes her in the preface. In typical 'Bowlesian' fashion, he could not resist devoting one of the final pages of the book to an entirely irrelevant matter, the origins of Stonehenge, and makes no apology for 'taking this opportunity of publishing my final sentiments on this mysterious structure that is Druidical, a vast Temple raised to the Sun, the second Deity of Celts mythology [that] seems now to be the universal opinion . . .'

How printers managed to decipher Bowles's manuscripts, produced in enormous numbers during his adult life and in particular as he grew older, is something of a mystery. He was well aware of the difficulties that he caused them, and in the introduction to his *The Parochial History of Bremhill* went so far as to publicly thank John Bowyer Nichols 'for his great care and attention in bringing out a work of which the manuscript was almost illegible'. Some fifty years after Bowles's death a member of one of the firms who printed his work gave an account of the difficulties experienced by them, and the challenges faced by the compositors and printer:

> . . . There is before us as we write some of the 'copy' which came from his hand. We have seen some slovenly copy, we still (occasionally) see such. But we think we can say conscientiously that we have not seen any more slovenly than this. It is a mass of scrawl (there is no other word

to properly describe it) the greater part of which is scratched out, and re-written between the original lines, only again scratched out, either by line or by dash of the pen down the contents of a half or a third of the page. The inter-leavings and over-leavings are, of course, correspondingly numerous – and we would add exasperating.

The writer then proceeds to attempt to unravel and make sense of what appeared to be part of chapter 2 of *Annals and Antiquities of Lacock Abbey*, and then continues:

Then we come to a footnote, apparently relating to the excised interleaving, and the page ends. It took the good man all a page of foolscap to secure his opening sentence. What it cost in mental agitation and distress, and how many interuptions he had as he sat in his study at Bremhill and got that far, are things we do not know. Probably the one sentence last quoted was the result of a morning's literary work.

And so it was Chapter 2 started on its way, fifteen lines follow with scarcely an alteration; the succeeding pages are a series of lessons in patience and thoroughness in literary work; a series of examples of how a gifted man laboured to produce his best and was not satisfied till he produced his best.[91]

On a Saturday at the beginning of May Thomas Moore, Bessy and their visitor went to dine at the parsonage and to stay until the Monday. Moore recorded:

The only company, Barry, the Curate of Calne, and Calcott, son to the celebrated musician and nephew of the Painter – Bowles in high spirits – In talking of my squibs, said there was nothing he envied so much as my power in that way, and suggested to me as a subject, the preaching of some canting fellow lately about the year when 'King Jesus' is to begin to reign, and the story of the two horses which Lady Hester Stanhope,[92] it is said, keeps always ready saddled in that event, and on one of which King Jesus is to ride into Jerusalem, while she herself mounts the other – Told him I thought this somewhat a ticklish subject & would rather leave it to Canon Bowles to undertake.[93]

Moore's journal continues the following day:

Bowles who has not preached for a long time was induced by Mrs Moore's entreaties to give us a sermon this morning, and we were all much interested in his discourse. The manner in which it was delivered was very touching and the feeling throughout, <u>Christian</u> in the best sense of the word.[94]

Bowles certainly enjoyed the company of the rich and famous. When he was visiting Moore in June he was shown a card that Moore had received from the Duchess of Kent[95] inviting him to meet King William IV and his Queen. He exclaimed, 'Good God, what an honour! You mean to go up, don't you?', and expressed his surprise when Moore told him that he hadn't the slightest notion of doing so![96]

On 6 May Bowles's old friend William Linley died, and later in the year Bowles's *Recollections of the Late William Linley, Esq* appeared in the *Gentleman's Magazine*, followed by a sonnet 'On the death of William Linley, Esq' written, of course, by him.[97]

The novelist Anna Maria Hall[98] first knew Bowles in London in 1835:

> . . . he was a hale, hearty old man. He seemed to me a happy blending of the country farmer with the country clergyman of old times, and recalled the portraitures of 'parson' of the days of Fielding and Smollett. He rarely quit Bremhill. Now and then he visited the metropolis, when he seemed as much out of place as a 'daisy in a conservatory' – that was his own simile during one of my conversations with this eccentric but benevolent clergyman . . .
>
> 'I never', said he, 'had but one watch, and I lost it the very day I wore it', Mrs Bowles whispered to me 'and if he got another today, he would lose it as quickly' . . .
>
> Another peculiarity of his was an inveterate tendency to give away his chattels to those who happened to casually admire them. Mrs Bowles was compelled, in consequence, to keep a watchful eye at all times upon his proceedings in that way, and is said to have controlled his simple-minded irregularities as well as his indiscriminate liberality.[99]

In August Bowles was able to repay some of the hospitality that he had enjoyed in the Bishop's Palace in Wells when his old friend George Law, the Bishop, came to Devizes, where he confirmed almost a thousand young people in St John's Church.[100] Some short time before a hayrick had caught fire on the parsonage farm at Bremhill and had been extinguished by the efforts of a large number of villagers. Bowles decided to reward them while his friend was with him, and the *Salisbury and Winchester Journal* reported:

. . . As a result of such meritorious and cheerful assistance, the Vicar, W. L. Bowles gave a dinner of substantial English fare to seventy people all of whom had assisted in extinguishing the fire. The evening was beautiful, and the sight very impressive. The Poet addressing his parishioners with the Bishop standing by his side, and the guests who had dined at the parsonage, thanking them in a loyal and eloquent speech for the good example they had set. The kind Bishop appeared much affected, when the whole assembly simultaneously rose and drank with loud cheers the health of their venerable vicar . . .[101]

According to another account of the dinner, Bowles arranged for his parishioners to be entertained in an unconsecrated part of the churchyard rather than in the garden of the parsonage.[102]

By the autumn of 1835 Bowles was wondering how sales of *The Annals and Antiquities of Lacock Abbey* were proceeding and so wrote to the young John Nichols:

I have not heard from you a long time, & have now, more reasons than one for writing to you!

How do we get on? Are any copies gone? What can be the reason, the Literary Gazette is quite mute? Has he had a copy? & <u>two advertisements</u>? I suppose he is silent not from want of friendliness, but, from being little acquainted with the subject! If you could get Hunter, with my kind remembrances, & regards – to write ever so few lines I am sure they would be admitted instantly! Pray, speak to him – I speak on your account as well as my own.

I should not known of the abuse shower'd on me from old jack-asses of Cockney, but for Blackwood's generous deference – who the author is I neither know nor wish to know, but if [illegible] hopes to get fame or profit from publishing such authors he is not like the old and honour'd Sylvanus Urban! with whom he is in partnership.

My chief object in writing is to enquire after the painted glass you advertis'd –. Lord Lansdowne gave us one beautiful painted window, & I hope the church will purchase another.

Give my kind regards to Sylvanus pater
& believe me dear Sir
Your affectionate & sincere friend.[103]

On 18 September Bowles was in Gloucester and was moved by a performance of *Messiah* in the Cathedral to write 'On Hearing the

Messiah last performed in Gloucester Cathedral September 18 1835'. This was printed in the *Gentleman's Magazine*[104] after appearing in the *Devizes and Wiltshire Gazette* – having been 'taken from A Gloucester paper'.[105]

It seems that Bowles could not get enough of Handel's music, as only three days later he was writing to Thomas Estcourt, soon to be elected Member of Parliament for Devizes:

> Be assur'd nothing in the world would give Mrs Bowles & myself more pleasure than to avail ourselves to your kind and proffer'd hospitality, but we are engag'd with company here on Wednesday, & on Thursday is the night of the Choral performance of some of Handel's most sublime strains at Bath, alas not in such a Cathedral as Gloucester but at the Rooms! As I sleep at Bath Thursday it would not be so convenient to us to be from home Friday, the day of my return, but we should both rejoice to avail ourselves of your kindness before another summer like this is hastening away if we live so long, & delighted should we be, if when you come to Macdonald's[106] in the <u>Salisbury season</u>, you would not forget with Mrs Estcourt his brother Canon and, believe me, dear Sir, ever most sincerely & gratefully.[107]

In the following month the Devizes paper printed another of Bowles's poems, 'On Children gathering Flowers in the Cathedral Churchyard of New Sarum'.[108]

In October Moore had one of his oldest friends, Dr Thomas Hume, staying with him. He was anxious to see Bowles's parsonage, so on Saturday the 12th Moore ordered a fly and drove him to Bremhill, calling in at Bowood on the way where they briefly saw Lord and Lady Lansdowne. Moore related in his journal:

> Found Bowles, with his old friend Hoyle,[109] in full feather of fun – though in a great rage also against some new publication (or rather old one revived) 'The Modern Dunciad,' in which he is called 'Dunce Bowles', and (what ought to console him) Sydney Smith[110] is called 'Leaden Smith' – To be sure, what asses do browse on Parnassus![111] – Wanted me very much to attack the fellow for him. Bowles mentioned that he was to preach at Bowood on the morrow and, in his thoughtless way, asked me to come & hear him. Hume, accordingly, very eager to go, but I felt that, without an express invitiation, or, at least, previously asking the Ls. it would not be warrantable to take a stranger to their private chapel. Hume seemed to think otherwise.[112]

On the next day Bowles nevertheless called for Moore and Hume on his way to Bowood, and found Bowles:

> as eager that Hume should hear him preach as Hume was to hear – but I soon made him perceive the impropriety of thus going *sans ceremonie* to a private chapel, and told him, if he found on arriving there that they had no objection to my taking Hume, he might send back the carriage for us. He was, however, too late.[113]

Early in October Bowles called on Moore who recorded that he was 'Still full of the attack upon him in the Modern Dunciad, and, noticing that a Second edition of my Fudges[114] was commenced, expressed an anxious wish that I should give a lash to this unknown for him'.[115] 'This unknown' is presumably the 'lying & obscure railer' mentioned in Bowles's letter written to the young Nichols on 9 November:

> I hope you received my <u>little</u> work! All my friends without exception entreat me to take no notice whatsoever of a lying & obscure railer; so you <u>will not let the</u> letter I sent on <u>the subject appear</u>, as they think any notice whatsoever, will answer his end, the more, & they even think the very kind and able critique in your pages, calculated in some measure to extend the sale of this impoverish'd piece of Cockney spite
> Believe, with best thanks to Mr Mitford & your partners.[116]

In November Moore noted in his journal:

> A visit from Bowles, bringing with him Mr West,[117] a young man who had been a pupil of the Academy of Music and has set an Oratorio of Bowles's 'The Ark' – played over for me one of the Choruses, which I thought very good – the words being admirably adapted for musical effect. – Bowles spoke of the delight it always gave him to come & see Bessy & me – we 'met him with such cheerful faces.'[118]

As has been seen, the words of *The Ark* had been written many years before, and 'Go beautiful and gentle dove: a song, from an Oratorio called the Ark, written and composed by W.L. Bowles' had been published.[119] Bowles was doubtless delighted to hear the oratorio performed in Bath on 9 December, the words having now been set to music, perhaps by William West, and more successfully composed and performed than when first played and sung in Bath in 1824. Moore and Bessy went to hear it, and Moore thought it 'went off very well'.[120]

Two days later Bowles wrote to his old friend George Poulett Scrope of Castle Combe and the Member of Parliament for Stroud:

> Mrs Scrope told me you were at the Performance of 'our Ark, on the Waters'! How sorry I was that I should not have seen you. I saw Mrs Scrope at Hartham Park[121] – & pray tell her my coqueting, as becomes <u>my youth</u> – with a <u>very young</u> Lady was occasion'd by my discovery that she was the daughter of a <u>brother</u> Poet, the tragical father of whose two sons, drown'd in the Severn, in the sight of a broken-hearted & accomplish'd father – was the subject of something I had poetically written. – This young Lady, was the sister of these, who were lost, & whom I had <u>never seen</u> before.
>
> I had honour paid me by Benett[122] in the Agricultural Chair for Lord Lansdowne – my old labourer, past ninety, each had served one master & his son, <u>fifty years</u> of <u>faithful servitude</u> & who was lately robbed of all he had sav'd up for his last days . . .
>
> And I who interested myself about this <u>old man</u>, for an <u>old man</u> is as interesting to me as a <u>young Lady</u>, a subscriber to the Society for 40 years! – not, be assured, to encourage the breed of infernal <u>fat</u> pigs & bullocks! . . .
>
> Our Ark went off – swimmingly![123]

For very many years Bowles had been, rather surprisingly, a member of the Bristol and West of England Society for the Encouragement of Agriculture, and in December he attended the annual meeting of the society. Magdalene's cousin John Benett, the president of the society, although by no means a churchman proposed the toast to the bishop and clergy of the diocese and 'paid honour' to Bowles, as he put it in his letter to Scrope, by coupling it with 'my oldest and most valued friend Mr Bowles . . . not as a farmer, but as a philanthropist who has always most earnestly, and in a manner which reflects on him highest honour, done all in his power to promote the welfare of the lower classes'.[124]

Bowles responded to the toast, in the course of which he said:

> he was himself a humble agriculturalist, he had been connected with this Society longer perhaps than any one in the room, having belonged for upwards of forty years, his object in being a member was not, however, agricultural only, but as far as he was concerned, it was the cause of humanity by which he was sure he was not separate from the hearts of any one present.[125]

The King had given to Lord Lansdowne some glass copies of Raphael cartoons[126] for the new chapel at Bowood, and in December Moore related that:

> Lord L. mentioned to me that Bowles was to preach on the Cartoon of the Draught of Fishes (he has been going through a series of sermons on the cartoons in the Chapel) and hoped I would attend. He told Bowles (as he mentioned to me afterwards) that I meant to attend his sermon, and Bowles said 'I am very glad of it – I do not think that there is any thing in my sermon that can annoy him – Do you think, my Lord, he is likely to be offended at what I say about St Peter?' – Poor dear Bowles! He is the cause of many a good-natured laugh at Bowood. After the sermon (in which he had disposed, in the usual way, of the supremacy of Peter, the Rock &c.) he came up to me, to the great amusement of the lookers-on, and was proceeding with 'I hope there was nothing in my sermon that –' when I interrupted him laughing, and said 'my dear Bowles – I am by no means so <u>touchy</u> about St Peter as you seem to suppose.'[127]

It may be recalled that in 1833 Bowles had contributed to an appeal launched to raise funds in support of the hard-pressed and in many cases poverty-stricken Irish Protestant clergy, who were attempting to work and survive in the midst of a largely Roman Catholic population. It is no surprise, therefore, to find Bowles speaking in forcible terms at a public meeting that was held in Devizes shortly before Christmas for the purpose of entering into a subscription to further mitigate their distress.[128] Bowles subscribed £15 and £67 was collected at the door.[129] In the event the considerable sum of £462 15s 11d was raised in Devizes and its neighbourhood to be sent to Ireland.[130]

Soon after the meeting in Devizes Bowles wrote a long letter to George Scrope, who had recently published two pamphlets on the Irish question:

> I cannot express with how much interest I have dwelt on your pathetic pictures of miserable Ireland – you have done the whole article well & eloquently – <u>save</u> & <u>except</u> – <u>one half sentence</u> 'with ease & quickening' a mode of verbiage which a moment's thought would have obviated.
>
> I alluded to your representation in which I said – 'of the clergy' added to the perishing poor in my speech at Devizes but the rogues of the press made me say 'beyond human and' instead of 'beyond human aid'!! However my speech is the shorter & most to the purpose.

With these criticisms on 'ease & quickness' – which sounds like a man's putting on a pair of <u>new breeches</u> – I send you a little work for Criticism – a visit to my father's old gardener, at Uphill & which I hope may entertain you and Mrs Scrope.

'Master Billy's memorabilia! From the time he put on, in this life, 'with ease & quickness' his first pair of breeches . . .

I intended to have sent a few copies for sale to London, to my friend with whom I have had so long commerce in the publishing way – the golden John Murray, of Albemarle Street, with a wish that he would publish the entire work & shew it to Mr Lockhart [illegible]. Brodies sent to Murrays & he had heard nothing about it!! No! because the greater part was sold in Bath.

But it occurs to me that you might do me, in my Old Age, this kind act – send two copies, for Murray & Lockhart. If Lockhart likes it, perhaps he would allow you, who <u>know me</u> to write a kind article (& I have had many <u>unkind</u> & undeserved ones from that Quarter!) . . .

Bowles continues this long and somewhat rambling letter by mentioning several proposed publications and, 'if Lockhart will allow, some of my old songs . . . and some of my Life also as you have known me – so long – I shall, for what remains of it – 'Eat, drink,& be Merry!' He then writes:

I could indeed ardently wish this particularly as a <u>certain bill</u> broker & Cockney poet – of Islington – who never saw or <u>knew</u> me – has asserted in a stupid Poem that I am 'obscene' who never wrote a line I would [illegible] 'profane', who spent my days in dispensing the religion of the Bible – a sordid money cover, who ever since I have had <u>ninepence</u> have expended <u>sixpence</u> in subscriptions & among the poor – & this wicked is the [illegible] – of the 'obscene', 'profane' – sordid – 'spiteful' – Pope! Whom he says I have 'calumniated' & been an advocate of the 'licentiousness of Byron'! My other virtues, my tres spiteful, is chiefly prominent! As of me, who never did an unkind act – or said an unkind word of him or of man, woman or child . . .[131]

And so on. Scrope must have despaired that his old friend still harboured such bitterness against his old opponent in the Pope controversy, William Roscoe, who had died in 1831; and when referring to Roscoe in the preface to his *Little Villager's Verse Book* published almost ten years before, Bowles had declared that 'all unkindness is buried in my heart'.

At the very end of 1835, on 28 December, Lord Kerry, Lord Lansdowne's heir, called on Bowles at the parsonage and asked him to write to Sir Thomas Phillipps on his behalf about some documents that he had heard Phillipps was holding. Bowles accordingly immediately put pen to paper and wrote:

> Lord Kerry has just call'd and requested me to write to you as he is meditating a life of his ancestor Sir William Petty[132] and has learnt that you are in possession of some manuscripts. Pray either write to him, Bowood, or to me, Salisbury, where we go in Friday . . .

Phillipps endorsed the letter in his usual efficient manner: 'answered 7 Jan. requesting Lord Kerry to write to me'.[133] In the event, Kerry's early death prevented his research into the life of his ancestor being completed.

Chapter 8
1836–1837

In 1835 a second edition of Bowles's poem *St John in Patmos* had been published, following which the *New Monthly* printed a review that surely gave Bowles a great deal of satisfaction, particularly as it was reproduced in the *Salisbury and Winchester Journal* and so would have been read by very many people who would not have seen it when it first appeared:

> Mr Bowles furnishes another instance, in addition to that of Dryden[1] that the most vigorous efforts of imagination are not at all times incompatible with advancing years, and that the lamps of poetry may burn with increased brightness . . . as its bearer proceeds amidst the gathering mists and shadows, which beset the path of man, when approaching the undiversified and wintry regions of age . . . Mr Bowles is one of the oldest of our living poets; how little hazard he runs of seeing the laurels pass from his own brow to those of his junior competitors in the tuneful art the present volume affords a convincing illustration.[2]

From time to time verses by Bowles appeared in the *Devizes and Wiltshire Gazette* and occasionally in the *Salisbury and Winchester Journal*. In February 1836 the Salisbury newspaper published 'On a Painting of Zuccharelli in possession of Mrs Batt of "New Hall" near Salisbury'.[3] Mrs Batt[4] was the widow of John Batt,[5] almost certainly an acquaintance of Bowles's who was moved to write a sonnet in celebration of the landscape by Zuccarelli[6] hanging in Mrs Batt's dining room at New Hall at Bodenham.[7]

In *Fraser's Magazine* for March 1836 appeared a portrait of Bowles dressed to go out and representing him, according to a contemporary, 'in the act of composing a Sonnet on the subject of a Hat's obligation to an Umbrella, in cases of excessive heat, not less than rain. It is one of the best likenesses of the long series of Literary Characters immortalized by Croquis . . .'[8] The image was published to illustrate a piece about Bowles, affectionate in tone, in the magazine's Gallery of Literary Characters. The story was told, apparently originating from Thomas

Moore, about a nocturnal adventure during a recent visit to London to attend the musical festival in Westminster Abbey. He was lodging with his old friend Samuel Rogers:

> Bowles amused himself now and then during his stay, as old Crabbe had done in like circumstances before him, with an evening stroll to the theatres; where, in the sweet security of *incog.*, he might either laugh his sides sore at Liston,[9] or strain his optics dim at Taglioni.[10] The first night he did not come home till somewhere between one and two. 'My dear friend', said his host, 'I was afraid something had happened – you must have lost your way!' 'I did', quoth Bowles; 'I turned east instead of west, I believe, and I don't know how far I might have gone astray, had I not fallen into conversation with two very elegant ladies, who were so kind as to conduct me safely to your door.' 'Lucky man! – and did you part company without finding who they were?' 'No', said our original, 'they gave me their tickets; and one of them was a particularly merry young lady – perhaps you know her (here he handed a card across the table). And she said, to make sure of my calling to thank her for her convoy, I must give her a keepsake by way of pledge'. 'By all means', grunted Sam; 'be sure you call on *Mrs Stafford, 15 Lisson Quadrant,* and reclaim the *little sixpence.*' Stafford! – 'tis a high name!' observed the sonnetteer; 'should not wonder if she were an honourable'. Moore did not mention if Rogers actually allowed the old boy to make out his visit to the lovely aristocrat of Paddington.

After describing something of Bowles's career and his early influence on Wordsworth and Coleridge, the article concludes:

> It has pleased Jeffrey[11] to say, that Bowles will only be remembered for his controversy with Byron. We think he was wrong in that dispute: but we reject the sentence of the Northern, as false, faithless, and worthy of no acceptance. Bowles is an original genius, if our age has produced one; and, if he had never penned a single syllable of prose, his place would have been secure as even Byron's own – to say nothing of the puisne judge's.
>
> Farewell, dear old bard! Long may you continue to enjoy your morning fiddle and your evening pipe – the affectionate respect of your parishioners, and the worshipful admiration of your brethren of the clerity. And whenever you revisit the great city, even Babylon, the mistress of abominations, be sure you remember not to forget that OLIVER has a rump and dozen at your service – and that our niece, Miss FITZYORKE, will see you safe home to No. 22.[12]

It seems that Bowles was highly amused, and perhaps quite pleased, with what had been written about him for, in 'Epistles to the Literati' that appeared in *Fraser's Magazine* quite soon after, was printed a letter above Bowles's name and so presumably written by him in response:

Bowles to Yorke

Friend Oliver . . . I must have a word with you, 'learned Theban' as you may be. You have held me up to public notice, with a visage somewhat rueful, having my own name under it, in my own hand – held up to public gaze and public notice – me, Master of Arts, of Trinity College, Oxford – me, canon residentiary of Sarum – me. A member of the Atheneaum Club, Pall Mall – . . . – me as, *not* Parson Trulliber,[13] to be sure, but as Parson Adams, who aspires no further than the kitchen, in the country, at the mansion of Squire Booby!

Now, Oliver, I appeal to yourself, and to the public through your pages, was it right to hold me up in that character – me who has been received a guest, half my life, in the houses of lords and ladies, and archbishops, and bishops, ministers of state, and last, though not least, at the *Tusculum* of Sylvanus Urbanissimus, at his suburban villa at Hammersmith? Is it right, that I should be held up as so *unacquainted* with London streets, as to mistake the east for the west? And, what is worse, to mistake for *ladies of fashion* two young ladies who civilly led me to their lodgings between one and two o'clock in the morning? Shame on you, Mr Yorke!

Now if you believe one word of all this story, you must yourself be much more simple than Parson Adams; and I verily believe some wicked wag . . . must have completely *gulled* you! For, if I dine often at the *fashionable* hour of seven, I am always in bed before eleven, and generally before ten; as my good landlady, No. 178 Piccadilly, where I have lodged for nearly twenty years, will tell you.

But you have amply made amends, 'dear' Oliver, for any *jokes* about me, old bard, by your kind wishes and criticism on my poems, and also by your kinder invitation, the next time I arrive amidst 'the busy hum of men', to 'a rump and dozen' with you. Remember, I never smoke a pipe, nor ever was in company where a pipe was smoked in my life, except once with old Parr [?] *after breakfast*. But I shall be most happy if you visit my pastoral parsonage to play on my grandfather's fiddle (see *Scenes and Shadows*, a most delectable history to be published by Murray) 'Maggie Lauder'[14] or 'Over the Water to Charley',[15] till the

old bard forgets age and grey hairs. And then, dear Oliver, when I come again to Regent-Street, we will talk of the rump and dozen and drink a health to Miss Fitz-Yorke. But remember, if the 'old blithe bard' dines with you, it is on one condition, – that as soon as the cloth is cleared, we drink the *old toast*,which brought tears into my grandfather's eyes, 'Church and King!' So 'Church and King', Oliver (*cheers*) – 'Church and King', Yorke! (*cheers*) – 'Church and King!' *One cheer more!* 'Church and King!' – Hurrah! hurrah! Hurrah! Bless me, I had forgot myself – the bell goes for church! More when I write again: and I remain, &c. forgiving all your jokes,
W.L. Bowles

N.B. Buy at Nicholls' my *Letters in Criticism* of which a *'few copies* remain', and you will never again speak of poor Byron's unsubstantial and rhetoric about nature and art, in his controversy with Bowles. *Verbum* [?][16]

By this time Bowles's eccentricities were frequently manifesting themselves and had become widely known. One that has often been repeated was his constant refusal to be measured by his tailor. The Rev. Julian Young recorded in his journal that when he lived in Wiltshire in 1836 Bowles was a neighbour to whom:

> . . . it was a matter of equal indifference to him whether he had to measure swords with Lord Byron, the merits of Pope the battlefield; or to wrestle with deans and chapters, church patronage the bone of contention between them. But to confront a situation involving the slightest personal risk was beyond his powers of nerve. For instance, he never entered my doors without first sending his footman forward on a reconnoitring expedition, to ascertain that there was no stray dog or cat prowling about for his special discomfiture.[17]

Bowles's friend of many years standing, the antiquary John Britton, describes one well-known example of Bowles's absence of mind:

> I am assured that he started from Bremhill, on horseback, to ride to Chippenham, dismounted to walk down a steep hill, leading the horse by the bridle slung across his arm, and continued to the turnpike gate, when he offered to pay the toll, and was not a little surprised when the man said, 'We doont charge nothing for your honor, as you beant on osback'. On turning round, he perceived the bridle dangling from his arm, but could not descry his horse.[18]

Between 7 January and 1 April 1835 Bowles had attended no fewer than six meetings of the Cathedral Chapter but then, as was his custom, no further meetings during the remainder of the year while he was not resident in the Cathedral Close. The business of these meetings was normally limited to approving the granting or renewing of leases of property belonging to the Chapter, and was never concerned with the maintenance of the fabric or the services or ministry of the Cathedral. However, at the meeting of the Chapter held in March 1836, Bowles, as Master Warden or Governor of the Choristers, reported that:

> the education of the choristers is now and for some time past has been much neglected by the Rev. John Greenly[19] the Master of the Grammar School. It was therefore resolved that the Master be requested to certify at the next Chapter the course of study pursued by the choristers and the number of hours daily in which they are engaged in at the same school.[20]

At the next Chapter meeting held in April the Chapter Clerk reported that 'the Rev. John Greenly attended the Chapter and the choristers having been examined in his presence and found very deficient in learning. It was resolved that Mr Greenly be admonished to bestow in future much more attention on their education.'[21]

In accordance with what appears to have been the practice at the time, there is no record in the Chapter Act Book of any inquiry by the Chapter to discover whether the admonition had any effect on Mr Greenly who, as a naval chaplain, had been wounded at the battle of Trafalgar and was by now Vicar-General of the Close, the Cathedral Librarian, Curate of St Thomas's Church in Salisbury and rector of Sharcote in Dorset, as well as master of the choristers' school!

In March 1835 the new Ecclesiastical Duties and Revenues Commission had proposed a reconstruction of episcopal boundaries and incomes, but the cathedrals were not touched. However, this reprieve was short lived, as the Commissioners' second report published in March 1836 proposed the abolition of non-residentiary canonries and the limiting of residentiary canonries to four in each cathedral. Bowles lost no time in responding, and so soon afterwards he arranged for Simpson,[22] the Devizes printer, to produce *Further Observations on the last report of the Church Commissioners, particularly as respects the Patronage of Deans and Chapters, and Cathedral Music.* In the same year he looked, for the only time it seems, to a firm in Bristol, Gutch and Martin, to print and publish for him. It is possible that the reason was that John Gutch, the proprietor and printer of *Felix Farley's Bristol Journal*, had been a schoolfellow of Samuel Coleridge Taylor at Christ's Hospital.

This booklet was dedicated to Lord John Russell and Bowles's old schoolfriend William Howley and entitled *The Patronage of the English Bishops. Two Addresses to the Houses of Lords and Commons of England, and to the British Nation, on the Proposal of the Church Commissioners, to transfer to the Bishops, the patronage of Deans and Chapters, and to make the Cathedral Churches dependent on the Bishops.*

It is certain that Bowles made sure that he was aware of the patronage that might be available to himself and his fellow canons, and it was at about this time that a living became vacant that Bowles's enquiries led him to believe that, as Custos Puerorum or Master of the Choristers, was in his gift. His claim resulted in what was described as 'a friendly dispute' with the Bishop. Having taken legal advice, he relinquished it on 'finding that it had for many years been the practice of the Bishop to present'.[23]

At the end of January 1836 Bowles preached a sermon in Salisbury Cathedral on the martyrdom of Charles I and, soon after, was published with *Some Account of the last days of William Chillingworth, author of 'The religion of Protestants a safe way to salvation' with remarks on the character of Cromwell.* So incensed was Bowles that the Commissioners were recommending that the patronage exercised by the deans and chapters of Cathedrals should be transferred to the bishops that he incorporated in this work not only a sequel to the sermon but also 'remarks on the late report of the Church Commissioners'. The *Salisbury and Winchester Journal* published an extract from the sermon and was fulsome in its praise:

> In common with every production from the pen of that truly amiable and accomplished writer, the sermon in question gives ample proof of the true inspiration of genius tempered by the sober and rational piety of the Christian Minister. It would be an insult to the good taste of the public to suppose for a moment that such a production, from such a pen, and on so interesting a subject, should not be extensively read, and as generally admired.[24]

Bowles was such an ardent admirer of Chillingworth,[25] who was made chancellor of Salisbury Cathedral in 1638, that he resolved to arrange for a tablet in his memory to be erected in the cathedral. On 14 March the Salisbury newspaper reported:

> The Rev W.L. Bowles has, at his own expense, just placed in the South East transept of that noble edifice a beautifully-chaste Gothic monument

to the memory of the celebrated Chillingworth. The design and execution confer great credit on the sculptor, Mr Osmond.[26]

    'The Bible is the Religion of Protestants'

    To the Memory of William Chillingworth, the immortal Author of the words inscribed above and formerly Chancellor of the Church . . .[27]

These are the first lines on the memorial, composed, of course, by Bowles, the final words reading, 'This tablet is erected in his own Cathedral in reverence to so great and good a man by William Lisle Bowles Canon Residentiary A D 1836'.

Not content with erecting one tablet in memory of a long-dead luminary of the cathedral, Bowles at the same time erected one in memory of Richard Hooker[28] who had been instituted to a minor prebend in the cathedral in 1591. Among the other virtues of Hooker mentioned by Bowles on the tablet was one that he probably thought was particularly worthy of notice, that Hooker 'successfully vindicated the forms and Ordinances of the Episcopal Church of this Nation and her primitive usage of the sweetest songs of Sion, Anthems and Antiphonal Harmonies, adapted to the words of the inspired Psalmist'. To this was added, so that the reader should be in no doubt as to the identity of the author of these words, 'This tribute of Respect and Veneration for so great a man is offered here by William Lisle Bowles Canon Residentiary 1836'.

Having reported on Bowles's second offering, the Salisbury newspaper informed its readers at the end of March that the example of 'the amiable "Bard of Bremhill"' was about to be followed by the Bishop and the Dean and Chapter in the erection of a monument to Bishop Jewell,[29] who had built the library at the cathedral in the sixteenth century. This took the form of stained glass windows at the end of the south-west transept, with Lord Lansdowne and Bowles each contributing the sum of £100 towards the cost.[30] At the same time the *Gentleman's Magazine* also reported on the erection of the memorials, describing Bowles as a man 'who, though best known as a poet, is scarcely less estimable as a sincere and liberal friend of our scriptural church'.

One day in April Moore noted in his journal:

A visit from Bowles who is in a most amusing rage against the Bishops on account of the transfer into their hands by the new Church Reform of the preferment & patronage hitherto vested in the Dean and Chapter – no Radical could be more furious on the subject than was this comical Canon in his own odd way; – on driving off from the door, he exclaimed to Mrs Moore, 'I say, Down with the Bishops!'[31]

Soon afterwards the *Devizes and Wiltshire Gazette* printed a long extract from Bowles's *Observations on the last Report of the Church Commission*, in the course of which he wrote:

> . . . I have written from the feelings of my heart; and I am bound to express these feelings, had the election [of himself as a canon] been in any other way than by the unbiased vote of the Dean and Chapter, having been indebted for my preferment to no Bishop – King or Minister of State – but only to my brethren of the Chapter, and than unsolicited, unsought and unexpected . . . I ought to say, and I say it *proudly*, that, though the Bishop was not *consulted* . . . he was the first to send me his cordial congratulations and approval.[32]

At the same time the Salisbury newspaper also published 'some further powerful observations [of Bowles] on the Report of the Church Commission as respects the patronage of Deans and Chapter', in the course of which he wrote:

> But sure I am, if this additional patronage and power be granted to Bishops, of which the Chapters are to be despoiled, the natural effect will be, that the Bishops will only look upon the members of their Chapters, not as liberal and learned coadjutors – but as sycophantist slaves; unless that convulsion should first take place which should hurl Bishops from their thrones, and tread down equally Church and State – Independence – Property and Laws together.[33]

In writing in this way Bowles was articulating what many members of the monied and landowning classes were fearing at this time – that there might be a repetition of the violent disorder that had occurred at the beginning of the decade; and that such lawlessness might lead to a revolution not unlike that in France, well within the memory of Bowles's contemporaries. One of Bowles's oldest friends, John Benett, had been injured when rioters attacked his property in 1830, and in the following year the Mansion House and Customs House in Bristol had been set on fire and looted, with the Bishop's Palace being destroyed on the following day.

Bowles was constantly seeking Moore's opinion on all manner of matters relating to his prodigious literary output. One day in May Moore recorded:

Visit from Bowles – Gave me a new pamphlet of his (the superfortation of his pen being endless) to ask my opinion as to the title 'Popish & Protestant Intolerance – the latter the least excusable of the two'. Cried, of course, 'Bravo' at this – nothing in the world being truer – the people who appeal to reason are the very last who should find fault with others for making free of it.[34]

Bowles was a frequent writer of letters to the *Devizes and Wiltshire Gazette*, and on some occasions he sent to the editor, George Simpson, copies of letters that he had written to others, with a request that he should publish them. He frequently travelled to Devizes to see the editor, who had founded the newpaper in 1816, and to hand the letter direct to him.

One of Bowles's oddities was his fear of mad dogs. A writer to the *Gazette* in 1926 related:

On one of these occasions Mr Simpson's dog alarmed him, and on Mrs Simpson going into the room to which he had been shown, she found him on his knees, either praying for deliverance or offering thanks for it. Bowles's manuscript, by the way, was an awful jumble with erasion over erasion – a kind of multiple palimpsest; only printers accustomed to it could decipher it.[35]

So George Simpson and his compositor would no doubt have risen to the challenge of understanding a letter that Bowles wrote towards the end of June. He had seen a report written by a 'Home Missionary' from Christian Malford, a village adjoining Bowles's own parish, that there was no Sunday school in the area. He therefore hastened to write to Lord Bexley,[36] one of the vice-presidents of the Society for Establishing Sunday Schools, to tell him that he would be surprised to learn that there was a 'resident, zealous, pious and exemplary clergyman' at Christian Malford and under his care and management a school for some 150 poor children on every day of the week as well as on Sunday. A copy of Bowles's letter was duly published in the Devizes newspaper,[37] as well as a report two weeks later that Bowles had received a letter from Lord Bexley telling him that the Home Missionary's letter would be struck out of the communication that was to be circulated to the subscribers and friends of the Society.[38]

The printers were likely to have had no difficulty in reading the manuscripts of two little pamphlets that Magdalene had written. In 1833 her *John Harding: a tale of a churchgoing Christian* appeared, and there was now published in London and dedicated to Bowles's old friend George Law, Bishop of Bath and Wells, *Summer Visits to Cottages in a Country Village with Observations on the Morals and Habits of the Inhabitants and particularly exemplifying the Pernicious Effects of Beer Houses*, which provides a graphic picture of her visits to some of the poor villagers in Bremhill. It commences with the words: 'Again winter has passed and after a sojourn of some months in a crowded city, amidst the "busy hum of men", we return to the quiet scenes of this lovely village, now dressed in all its early bloom.' The 'sojourn' was spent in the Bowles's house in the Close at Salisbury – a very quiet part of a not particularly busy place!

In June 1836 Bowles proposed to Thomas Moore that while the fine weather lasted they should take a trip to Clifton, and agreed that Moore's son Tom should go with them. As a result, a few days later Moore recorded in his journal:

> Called for Bowles in his chariot & long-tails, the object being to reach Bristol in time for a Concert which was to take place today, but Bowles had not ascertained whether it was a morning or evening one – Could learn nothing on the subject in Bath, from whence we started (Wondrous to say, for the honour of Bowles's courage) in a one horse Fly – the Long-tails not being able to proceed farther without rest. Found on arriving at Bristol that the music was not to be till evening – Put up at the Gloster, and had a most [illegible] drive before dinner to Lord Clifford's[39] – the day splendid & the view (which I never had before seen) magnificent. Our dinner very good & [MS damaged] being in high feather. The concert no great thing nor the company very [MS damaged] Came away in the middle of the Second Act and was rather taken by surprise by clapping, there being nobody performing, but which was soon explained by shouts of 'Moore –Moore' accompanying it [MS damaged] acknowledgment to those around [MS damaged] bowing – one young man stretching forth his hands, begging that I should shake [hands] with him, and said 'You would have [had this] long before, Sir, had the company known who you were'.[40]

As can be learned from this, and many other entries in Moore's journal, his celebrity was such that he was invariably recognised when entering a room, and even noticed when walking in the street.

Following the visit to Clifton, Moore wrote to Mary Shelley:[41]

> One of the *lesser* pleasant things I have been doing – but still very agreeable – was an excursion with *young* Tom (as he is now insultingly

styled) and myself took to Clifton with Bowles, who is, in himself always a treat and would, I am sure, please and amuse you exceedingly.[42]

It seems that in July Bowles was in Clifton once again, probably to attend the marriage of the daughter of Sir William Parker,[43] as at the beginning of August the *Salisbury and Winchester Journal* published a poem he had written in Clifton on 20 July entitled 'On the Marriage of Miss Parker, daughter of Sir William Parker, Bt. to Lionel Clive esq on 26 July 1836 at Clifton' and commencing:

What shall an aged poet say,
To Bessie on her wedding day?
He offers no poetic flowers
Gather'd from the Muses's bowers
To form a garland for her hair . . .[44]

It is likely that Bowles was intimately acquainted with the bride's family, as in the poem he refers to the familiar name used by the bride to address her grandmother.

Towards the end of August Bowles paid yet another visit to Clifton. Moore arrived after Bowles, and recorded some days later in his journal:

Bowles asked his bar-maid (at the Mall) whether she meant to go see the grand doings at the Suspension Bridge – 'Oh Sir' she answered 'don't talk to me about bridges and sights – I have seen Mr Moore'. She then pointed to Lalla Rookh[45] which lay, I suppose, among the cream-jugs at the Bar and which Bowles took up and read to her in his most pathetic manner the passage at which the leaves opened – 'I never loved a dear gazelle'. All this I heard from Tom [Moore's son who was in Clifton with him] to whom Bowles told it & the scene altogether would have been worth witnessing.[46]

Earlier Moore had noted:

Went to look for Bowles at the Mall Hotel, and was most smilingly received by the pretty Bar-Maid who as he tells me, is so well read in Lalla Rookh – Found that Bowles had just gone out to look for the Bishop of Bath & Wells whom the waiter gave me a long account of, always calling him the Bath of Bishop & Wells – should like much to know what sort of aqueous divinity he conceived him to be. Called upon Strong the bookseller – found Bowles at last, and agreed we should dine at the Ordinary together – a most mobbish affair – no less than between five & six hundred diners . . . Bowles and I separated far assunder.[47]

Bowles doubtless remained in Bristol for a few days, probably going to the theatre and perhaps even attending a lecture on Steam Communication with America, which Moore enjoyed.

In August the twenty-six-year-old Earl of Kerry, Lord Lansdowne's son and heir, died. Bowles would, of course, have known him well for all his life, and so had some difficulty in controlling his emotions when, in a sermon preached at Bremhill, he spoke of the young earl. It was reported by those who heard the sermon 'That anything more impressive or pathetic was never delivered from the pulpit while speaking of the late Lord Kerry; it was with difficulty that the Rev gent could restrain his feelings. The whole congregation was also visibly affected – there was scarcely a dry eye in the church.'[48]

In the same month Parliament passed the Tithe Commutation Act, with the intention of bringing to an end the disputes and confusion that so often arose in the payment of tithes to the clergy of the Established Church. There is no knowing how Bowles reacted to what he probably saw as a further attempt by Parliament to alter the age-old practices of the Church to which he was so devoted. The Act provided for an annual rent-charge to be paid in lieu of the old tithes and to be such sum as might be agreed, or, failing agreement by 1 October 1838, as would be awarded by a commissioner appointed under the Act. In the case of highway within the parish of Bremhill, agreement was duly reached in July 1838, as a result of which £170 was to be paid to Bowles each year.[49] So far as the rest of the parish of Bremhill was concerned no agreement was reached, with an award being made after Bowles's death.[50]

On 24 September Bowles attained the age of seventy-four years. His letters began to assume a rambling character that doubtless amused and at times, perhaps, infuriated the recipients. So it was that on the following day he wrote again to the long-suffering Murray:

> Having attained this day <u>seventy four years</u> I am reminded imprimis to write to you amongst other worldly matters.
>
> You requested to publish my biographical sketch. I have scratched out a few pages, like interweaving poetry & prose, as far as leaving Winchester school having become possess'd of some <u>classical learning,</u> with little 'land' & my Grandfather's fiddle – how I far'd in my infancy – I have already told, what is written on to my launch into the world. –

When I am quite at or shall have left the scene for ever – will be consign'd to your hands from the <u>writing case</u> which holds the only unique sketch – of 'Billy's memorabilia'! what first put me on it, was the sight of old Collins, at Uphill where I am going on Thursday with the Bishop of Bath & Wells, and a memorandum of my mother – which I shew'd Moore – '1779 paid for Billy's boots'!

But now for what is more immaterial.

I have written a series of sermons, & preach'd some extempore & some written, on the subject of the Cartoons of Raphael in the windows of Bowood Chapel from copies in glass of these celebrated works of art – presented by his <u>present Majesty</u> to the <u>Marquis of Lansdowne</u>.

The first of the series, I send you, & to the <u>learned</u> for criticism!

and perhaps with such names & 'Billy's' we might sell a few copies – at all events I have sent 150 or 200 copies & request you will advertise as you best know.

Bowles then sets out the wording of the proposed advertisement and continues:

The Bishops have done that which they ought not to have done! & I wish all the members of Deans & Chapters in England with Sydney Smith are up in arms!

I have [illegible] two addresses & am printing them at Bristol, together! Will you take me in 'pugnantem' (which I never expected to do) contra episcopos! But their conduct – I mean that of the commissioners – is indefensible!

I hope you will take my discourse, if you ever read such things & I hope some thing novel, if not some little eloquence, will be found in it. I saw your son at Bristol & beg to assure you of my regards & respect.[51]

Having enjoyed the company of Southey at the parsonage at Bremhill for a few days in November, Bowles wrote him this, in places somewhat incoherent, letter on 30 December:

I write this, trusting when it will find you, on <u>New Year's Day</u>! It is to beg you, if possible, to spare us a few days of your company, with your son, – now you are so near us at Salisbury – the Bishop is not here, but the Dean is . . . & my brother Residentiary Archdeacon Macdonald &c all of whom would receive you with open arms, and warmest gratulations and we have besides such a Cathedral Library, as perhaps, is not, for MSS & [illegible] Church-historians – to be found in the Kingdom!

At all events, I feel my duty to write . . . if anything canonical hospitality could offer, with the warmest & most affectionate esteem, could induce you – non long & est via – to bend your course – into the North – a few miles to the right! At all events let me hear from you (Canonry House) and wherever you go, and wherever you are, be assured, till death, my best and kindest remembrances with those of Mrs Bowles who parted from you with sadness – will be with you and yours – and with affectionate kind remembrances to your accomplish'd and amiable Mistress – believe me

> Ever – most sincerely and truly
> W L Bowles

We should have been upon our journey today but from the snow, but hope to reach Salisbury Wednesday next. I am sorry to say my health is not quite so good as when you were here . . .[52]

On 11 January Southey replied:

Here I have found your most friendly invitation to Salisbury . . . Few things would have pleased me more than to pass a few days as agreeably with you in your residence in the Close, as I did at Bremhill. But this cannot be. The time of my absence from home has already been inconveniently extended, tho many things which I wish to do have been left undone, and tho the pleasure of meeting an old friend has been too quickly followed by the pain of saying farewell to him . . . God bless you, my dear sir. My son joins with me in thankful remembrances to Mrs Bowles. When I come again into these parts, I will not fail to visit you again, God willing, whether you are at Bremhill or Salisbury.[53]

The Christmas Day number of the *Examiner* had devoted the whole of its front page to a leading article on a feud that had been raging between bishops and deans and chapters about the proposed transfer of the rights of patronage vested in the deans and chapters to the bishops – a proposal that was, as has been seen, fiercely opposed by Bowles and his fellow canons. In the course of a humorous article the *Examiner* wrote:

For our part, if we were to offer a word on the subject of the quarrel it would be an expression of surprise at the moderation of the Bishops. It seems wonderful to us that while these holy men were considering how they could do some good to themselves, they contented themselvers with grasping the patronage of the Deans and Chapters, when they might have declared those bodies altogether useless, and proposed to abolish them and add their revenues to the Bishops' incomes. If the Deans and Chapters were wise they would thank heaven it is no worse, and that they have escaped so well from the shears of the Bishops . . . Instead, then, of making such a noise about what the Bishops propose to take from them, the Deans and Chapters should feel infinite gratitude for what they have left, and should deem it a very miracle of Prelatic grace that they have not been altogether absorbed by their superiors . . .[54]

Needless to say, having read this attack Bowles put pen to paper, and on 3 January wrote to the editor of the *Examiner*:

I shall not be deterred from making an aberration on a leading article in your paper last week, by the mastery of wit and humour, which that article, on the present contest between Commissioners, Bishops and Deans and Chapter, displays. I cannot easily believe that you, or any man, would write that deliberately, which he was not <u>persuaded</u> was the truth. But it is <u>not</u> the truth, as far as I can be a witness that 'Deans and Chapters' may have connections and relations for whom to provide as well as Bishops. A Canon-Residentiary, at least, of Salisbury can only present to <u>one living</u> most probably – <u>one living</u>, taken in turns, on they becoming vacant, during his whole life! Whereas a Bishop may present in hundreds, including all lucrative ecclesiastical stations, treasurer etc.

This one canonical living, so taken in his turn, by a Residentiary, if he has a son in orders, and in every other respect qualified, he gives to his son; and he would be an unworthy father if he did not; for he, most probably, whatever his interest might be, could get no <u>preferment from a Bishop</u>. Therefore, a canon <u>cannot possibly</u> provide for his relations and connections, as a Bishop may, and that sometimes to two and three generations . . .

You may seem to think that I, and they who think with me can be actuated by no motives but base and selfish ones.

'Mr Bowles has no objection to worldly wealth' I forget the words!!

Mr Bowles was twelve years, with nothing to subsist on, in the Church – at least, but a curacy – value at that time <u>forty</u> pounds a year – and 'passing rich' included – for he, entering the Church <u>voluntarily</u> has no right to complain, if he were a curate still.

Without solicitation he was patronised – he was elected a canon – he has no son – his only anxiety has been for some friends serving curacies – unknown, uncomplaining, <u>serving curacies</u> till their hairs are grey, and <u>one</u> exemplary curate, near his own residence. Neither of them would have any <u>chance of any independence in the Church</u> from a Bishop. By succeeding, in my turn, to a Chapter living, I would give to one old friend, or to my own curate, a living. Neither have any chance from anyone else in the world.

Having been Canon of Salisbury eight or nine years, it has come to my turn, on the next vacancy to present to a living – This living I am in grateful duty bound to present to my own curate . . . This patronage was left to the Canon who fills my place by Bishop Osmond,[55] the founder of the first Cathedral. I have no other means of getting a living for a friend or a curate – and shall 'ewe-lamb' be forcibly snatched from a meritorious friend or curate to be placed at the disposal of the Episcopacy?

Therefore you are wrong, and I hope that you will acknowledge that Canon residentiaries can lavish no preferment on their connections . . .

P.S. Till this heartless and crafty bill, curate and canon I have been the most warm and disinterested defender of Episcopacy and only of those who had any hand in concocting the bill, have I spoken so harshly 'mild' as I am.

The editor of the *Examiner's* reply to this letter brought forth another from Bowles:

Revd Canon Bowles is oblig'd to the Editor of the Examiner for the manly candour with which he so promptly admitted his explanatory letter, explanatory as Mr Bowles thought it respecting the difference in the patronage belonging to Deans & Chapters and Bishops. Mr Bowles, with the simplicity of Parson Adams to whom the Editor compares him, & which character he hopes he shall ever retain, whatever may be his station ['in the Church' deleted] did, in his simplicity opine that the difference would have been understood, but, as it seems, in this instance the interpreter is the hardest to be understood of the two – Mr Bowles trusts the Editor's impartiality for making one observation on the Editor's observation that 'he scarce knows what Mr Bowles, by his reasoning, intended'.

This is exactly what Mr Bowles would say & does say, of the reasonings of the Examiner!

According to his conclusion, the reasoning on Mr Bowles reasons, appears to be something after this kind.

The fox and the lamb equally deserve hanging! The Fox for purloining Hens &c & leaving the bones to be pick'd by his numerous relations & connections & the Lamb because if he had been a fox, he would have done just the same!

A specimen of democratical reasoning, justice & mercy – from which he prays almighty God, to protect poor

1836 – 1837

'Parson Adams'!
Canonry House Salisbury Jan:ry 17th 1837.[56]

Bowles's letter of 3 January was reprinted in the *Devizes and Wiltshire Gazette*[57], which early in February also published 'Canon Bowles's last answer to the Examiner': '. . . the Editor liberally acknowledged my letter but giving me credit for the <u>simplicity</u> of Parson Adams (a character which I hope I shall always deserve, though a Canon of a Cathedral) he remarked that I scarce seemed to <u>know the tendency of my own argument</u>'. Bowles then repeats part of his earlier letter, and continues:

> The fox and the lamb equally deserve hanging! – the <u>fox</u> because he seized all the hens and lavished them on his relations! – and the <u>lamb</u>, because if the lamb had been a fox, he would have done the same!! From the 'tendency' of which truly democratical reasoning God Almighty defended poor <u>Parson Adams</u>! This answer the Examiner refused to insert, quoting my motto on Lord Byron 'he who plays at "Bowles" may expect a rubber' – My answer, I rather think, was a rubber, the Examiner did not expect. At all events, he refused to publish it; and in the expectation of seeing it in your paper, I am etc W.L. Bowles.[58]

In the following year Samuel Best's[59] *Case of the Deans and Chapters Considered in an Answer to the Rev. W. Bowles* was published, but Bowles appears not to have made any reply and to have decided to let the matter rest.

In February Bowles wrote to Moore, probably asking him to visit Salisbury. Moore replied:

> I am delighted to learn that you and Mrs Bowles had escaped this minor pestilence that has being [*sic*] going about. I have not myself been so lucky, having had a short but sharp attack of the disease, which still obliges me to be careful, at least as long as this ungenial weather continues. Such being the case, my dear Bowles, it is quite out of the question my being able to face the air of Salisbury Downs tomorrow, where I should be sure to meet the <u>Grippe-Fiend</u> before I got half way, and come in for a second scratch . . . Mrs Moore's maid and myself have been the only sufferers, I am glad to say at Sloperton.[60]

Bowles's handwriting is often very difficult, if not impossible, to decipher. In February 1837 he wrote to an unknown correspondent who had written to him enquiring, it seems, about Bowles's early life.

Bowles ended his reply (which appears to have been sent to Pickering, his publisher) by writing:

> Tho your letter was so late in finding me you have given <u>no directions</u> to yourself – or rather I should say, the name is so difficult to [?] that I doubt whether I read it exactly right but presuming you will receive this address I beg to express my thanks for your obliging communication.[61]

In the same month he received a letter from a correspondent who perhaps merely wanted Bowles's signature or a specimen of his handwriting, for Bowles replied:

> The Revd Canon Bowles informs Mr Saml D Knott that if his handwriting is worth sending so far & Mr Knott has no objection to pay eightpence for it, he herewith sends it, & with many thanks for Mr Knott's kind expressions, he remains his obedient & sincere
> Servt W.L. Bowles
> Canonry Salisbury, Feb: 20th 1837

> Our poor Bishop died yesterday morning at 2 o'clock – how earnestly we wish Exeter to succeed him.

Following the death of Bowles's fellow Wykehamist Thomas Burgess, the Bishop of Salisbury, he was moved to write in Latin a poem headed:

> *In Obitum Doctissimi*
> *et Pientissimi*
> *Praesulis Sarisburiensis Thomae Burgess,*
> *D.D., qui ob. Feb. 19, 1837*

The poem with an English translation also, of course, by Bowles duly appeared two weeks after the Bishop's death in the *Salisbury and Winchester Journal*[62] and was also separately printed by W.B. Brodie in Salisbury.[63]

Bowles's wish that Henry Phillpotts,[64] the forceful and controversial Bishop of Exeter, should be translated to Salisbury was not fulfilled.

Bowles and Southey continued their correspondence, with Bowles receiving a very long letter from his old friend in April in which he acknowledges the pleasure he had in reading Bowles's early poetry:

. . . I have also to thank you for the honour you intend me in your forthcoming edition – a very great honour I cannot but consider it, especially remembering (which I shall never forget) the improvement as well as the delight which I derived from your poems more than forty years ago, and have acknowledged in a general preface (just drawn out) to my own . . .[65]

A collected edition of Southey's poems was soon to appear, and in the preface he indeed acknowledged the delight and benefit he had received from Bowles. The 'honour you intend me' was the dedication of a proposed edition of Bowles's poetry to Southey. In June 1837 William Pickering sent Bowles a proof, and Bowles returned the page on which the dedication was printed, amended by him and annotated: 'This should be much larger to fill the page'. A rambling letter was also written on it:

I have <u>done</u> the job as it must remain when I am gone & none can tell with what anxiety – both of recollection & revision & least one expression should have [illegible] that any friend of mine might wish to have recall'd when the turf is on my head. – I am not yet determined about the immediate publication but when I wish you to do this – to make up a dozen copies & send them to me & send another sheet of this last corrected page to Mr Rogers & send a copy of the whole Poems to him & a copy to Mr Mitford for the present this is all I have determined & this you will do as soon as possible.[66]

It seems that this further edition of Bowles's poetry was never published.

In September 1837 the *Mirror of Literature, Amusement, and Instruction* published an engraving of Bremhill Parsonage, describing it as 'the abode of the oldest of our living poets, and who has adorned the literature of our country for the last half century'. A description of the parsonage follows, taken from Bowles's *Parochial History*, with 'a short collection of village epitaphs, in Bremhill churchyard, placed there by the pastor to commemorate the guiltless character and virtues of a few of the humbler part of his flock'.[67]

Southey paints a delightful picture of the gardens at Bremhill and of Bowles himself at this time:

The garden is ornamented, in his way, with a jet fountain, something like a hermitage, an obelisk, a cross, and some inscriptions. Two swans, who answer to the names of Snowdrop and Lily, have a pond to themselves, and if not duly fed they march to Mrs Bowles's window. The view from the house extends over a rich country to the distant Downs, and the White Horse may be distinctly seen. Much as I had heard of Bowles's peculiarities, I should very imperfectly have understood his character had I not passed some time under his roof. He has indulged his natural timidity to a degree little short of insanity, yet he laughs, himself, at follies which he is nevertheless continually committing. He is literally afraid of every thing. His oddity, his untidiness, his simplicity, his benevolence, his fear, and his good nature, make him one of the most entertaining and extraordinary characters I ever met with. He is in his 73rd year (1837) and for that age is certainly a <u>fine old man</u>: in full possession of all his faculties, though so afraid of being deaf, when a slight cold affects his hearing, that he puts his watch to his ear twenty times in the course of the day.[68]

It was in this year that a third edition of Bowles's *The Little Villager's Verse Book: consisting of short verses, for children to learn by heart*[69] was published. The *Devizes and Wiltshire Gazette* printed some verses from it and declared that 'Mr Bowles is too well known as an author, a philanthropist and a worthy minister of Christ, to need our commendation. His name bears with it its own panegyric.'[70] It seems that the first edition of this book had been published in 1834, as in December of that year it was reported:

The Rev. W.L. Bowles, who has powers to interest the most manly intellects, has not thought it beneath him, like the excellent Dr. Watts,[71] to accommodate his mind to the understandings of children, and has published a little book of moral and religious verses, such as a child may easily learn by rote. They are worthy to be learned by heart; we give one as a specimen.[72]

The newspaper then printed a short poem entitled 'Star-light Frost'. When a new edition of this book was advertised for sale in 1835 it was described as 'consisting of short verses to be learnt by heart in which the most familiar objects of country life are applied to excite the feelings of humanity and piety'.[73] The flavour of these simple but very popular verses can be gauged from the first of the three verses of 'Path of Life':

O Lord, in sickness and in health,
To every lot resigned,

Grant me, before all worldly wealth,
A meek and thankful mind![74]

Another of the verses written especially for children and included in *The Little Villager's Verse Book* was entitled 'The Butterfly and the Bee':

1
Methought I heard a butterfly
Say to the labouring bee:
'Thou hast no colours of the sky
On painted wings like me'

2
'Poor child of vanity! Those dyes,
And colours bright and rare,'
With mild reproof, the bee replies,
'Are all beneath my care.

3
'Content I toil from morn to eve,
And scorning idleness.
To tribes of gaudy sloth I leave
The vanity of dress.'

It is likely that it was at about this time that there was another manifestation of Bowles's fear of the unknown. This occurred when he was invited to dine and stay the night at Bowood, something that he had done many times before, and in the company of his old friends, Thomas Moore and Samuel Rogers among others. Julian Charles Young was also a guest, and he recorded in his journal:

Bowles was no sooner dressed, than, on entering the drawing-room, he walked up to Lady Lansdowne, and made some complaint or other to her, which caused her at once to leave the room. He forthwith followed her. In a few moments they both returned. As Lady Lansdowne passed me, she said, 'Bless the dear man, there is no pleasing him'. I did not know what she alluded to, until Bowles came up to me with a face of blank dismay, and asked me if I was going to sleep there. On my telling him that I was not, he exclaimed, 'I wish I were going home too. I shan't sleep a wink here. I was shown to a bedroom to dress in, in which I was intended to pass the night, where there was nothing whatsoever to prevent thieves from getting in and cutting my throat!

I have remonstrated to Lady Lansdowne, and the dear lady, by way of rendering me easier in my mind, has transferred me to a room so high, that, in case of fire, I shall be burnt to a cinder before I can be rescued!'[75]

It had been arranged that, as the house was so full of guests, Magdalene would return home for the night with Bowles remaining to enjoy the company of his friends. However, so nervous was he of spending the night in his elevated room that, as the ladies were leaving the dining-room, he whispered to Magdalene, 'I won't stay. Go home with you I must, and will.' However, as they were about to leave later in the evening there was a violent thunderstorm, as a result of which he changed his mind yet again, telling Magdalene that as she was not afraid of the elements and he was, he would remain in the house for the night and that she should start at once and leave him to his fate. Young proceeds with his account:

> This she did; and after giving infinite trouble to his noble host and hostess by his childish fears and vacillations of purpose, it was at last arranged that he should sleep in a room adjoining Rogers', with the door between the rooms left open, so that he might have the protection of his more valiant brother poet.[76]

Not only did Bowles suffer from irrational fears of this kind, but he was also exceedingly absentminded. On one occasion he presented a copy of the Bible to someone as a birthday present and, on being asked to write in it, inscribed it as being a 'gift from the Author'!

It is probable that it was in 1837 that Moore, while at Bowood, wrote this letter to Bowles:

> I am delighted to learn from our friends here that you are yourself (and you could not be any thing much better) once more again. Now that your mind is at ease about Bishops & Archbishops, I hope I shall find you in sufficient good humour with them to oblige me (who am always you know in good humour) by subscribing only a guinea to a History of the Archbishops of Dublin which a friend of mine is about publishing. He is a Protestant and a man well acquainted with the subject, so that you may, I think, depend upon the work being well worthy of your patronage. Lord Lansdowne has already given his name for it.[77]

Bowles complied with Moore's request and John D'Alton's *Memoirs of the Archbishops of Dublin* was duly published in 1838 with

Bowles named as one of the subscribers.

It will be recalled that Bowles had for many years been a trustee of Maud Heath's charity. In 1828 in his *The Parochial History of Bremhill* Bowles wrote, 'Whatever has become of other charities, that of this benevolent spinster still flourishes, and, as one of the trustees, I hope to live to see a monument more worthy of her name, erected on the hill which overlooks the extensive vale'.[78] Bowles had to wait almost ten years for his ambition to be fulfilled, as it was not until 1837 that he and Lord Lansdowne, one of the other trustees, decided to erect a more visible and imposing monument to Maud Heath than already existed by the side of her causeway. They therefore arranged to have constructed, it is said at their joint expense, a column on Wick Hill surmounted by the seated figure of Maud holding her basket and looking towards Kellaways – the tradition being that the causeway was intended to ease the journeys of those travelling to and from market.

In May 1837 Lansdowne wrote from London to Bowles:

> I am glad to hear that our pillar is likely to rise & still more that you are returned safe to your Bremhill quarters – tho it will be tempting [illegible] to ascend for a more extended [illegible]. I should with you be sorry to part with old Mansel (?), besides which I can hardly conceive how that facility could be obtained without altering the proportions of the column which would be very detrimental to its effect as at present and [illegible] I should be inclined to adhere to the first design.
>
> I am obliged to write in haste being in a [illegible] to other duties the Chairman of a very laborious committeee on education which will last all the session.
>
> Remember me kindly to Mrs Bowles.[79]

It is clear that a good deal of care was taken in Maud's appearance. In one letter written by Lady Lansdowne to Magdalene, perhaps shortly before her husband had written to Bowles in May and after their usual sojourn in Salisbury, she writes:

> I am very glad to hear of your safe return to dear Bremhill. Of your warm reception there could be no doubt. There is always so many lamentations at your absence, and such a blank is felt in all the neighbourhood when you cross the plain[80] . . . I hope Maude Heath looks well and that you approve her head-dress. It cost a great deal of research to get it correctly designed.[81]

The column was duly erected and, needless to say, Bowles composed the lines inscribed on the monument:

> Thou who dost pause in this aerial height
> Where Maud Heath's pathway winds in shade or light.
> Christian wayfarer, in a world of strife
> Be still, and ponder on the Path of Life.

In Pevsner's view 'the quality of the poetry matches that of the statue'![82]
A stone by the gateway at the side of the road is also inscribed:

> From Wick Hill begins the praise
> Of Maud Heath's gifts to these highways

In 1837 John Murray published a volume containing six of Bowles's sermons, all of which seem to have been printed separately during the previous two or three years, three of them by E. Bailey in Calne, one by George Simpson in Devizes and two by Murray himself.[83]

In the middle of October Lord Lansdowne was hosting a large party of politicians at Bowood, including the Prime Minister, Lord Melbourne,[84] Sir John Cam Hobhouse, the President of the Board of Control, Lord Glenelg,[85] the Colonial Secretary, and Lord John Russell, the Home Secretary.[86] On the 16th Lord Lansdowne took Lord Melbourne to the parsonage at Bremhill to meet Bowles. It is not unlikely that he thought Bowles's unpredictable behaviour, as well as his increasing deafness, made an invitation to dine with the Prime Minister at Bowood inadvisable, even though Bowles's old friends Thomas Moore and Samuel Rogers were among his guests. In any event Bowles was delighted and flattered that he should receive such a distinguished visitor. He could not resist calling on Moore after breakfast on the very next day to tell him the exciting news. Moore recorded in his journal:

> Bowles came after breakfast – more odd & ridiculous then ever – his delight at having been visited by the Prime Minister & Secretary of State, Lord L. having taken them both to Bremhill – The foolish fellow had left his trumpet at home, so we could hardly make him hear, or indeed do anything with him but laugh. Even when he <u>has</u> his trumpet, he always keeps it to his ear while talking himself and then takes it down when anyone else begins to talk – Today he was putting his mouth close to my ear, and bellowing away, as if I was the deaf man, not he – We all pressed

him to stay to dinner, but in vain and one of his excuses was – 'No–
no–indeed–I cannot. I <u>must</u> go back to Mrs Moore'. – Rogers was very
amusing about this afterwards – 'it was plain,he said where Bowles had
been all this time' – taking advantage of Moore's absence &c. &c. Rogers
arranged to go with his sister to Bremhill on Saturday, to stay there some
days – no room for me, which (all circumstances considered) I was not
at all sorry for.[87]

Very few of Bowles's letters contain any touches of humour, but when
writing to his friend George Poulett Scrope of Castle Combe, Member
of Parliament for Stroud, he invariably includes light-hearted passages
and allusions to what must be private jokes. Scrope started out as plain
George Thomson but on marrying Emma, the only child of William
Scrope of Castle Combe, in 1821 he assumed the surname of the
Scropes, who had been in possession of the Castle Combe estate since
the fifteenth century. In November Bowles wrote, addressing the letter
to Paulet Scope Esq. MP, St James's Place, London:

Mrs Bowles often writes to you, & the kind Lady, you have left behind in
the valley of Bagdad, so why should not the old Vicar & Poet say a word to
you as he has experienced from none, more friendliness as he has from
such as he has not work'd with for forty or fifty years!

But he would not take up the time of a senator except upon a
literary topic that concerns himself & one of the most amiable of the
Queen's counsellors, & indeed prime of Counsel, Lord Lansdowne.

That I, a great Theologian, have employ'd my learned leisure
not in verses only, but on a subject more kindred to my profession & I
pride myself, not a little in hitting on some Scriptural views, which have
excell'd all the old women who have contributed their notes to Mant's
great Bible![88]

. . . I know you and I differ about a race with Pink Gloves and
polish'd shoes call'd High Priests but you do not dislike the old Poet &
Parson, the same, rich or poor who, says what he thinks & feels without
regard to anyone.

Now my dear friend, if you can spare half an hour on Sunday
– accept from the profound author another one of his little works of
Theology, an Oration in these days of obloquy, pro clericis – Desire young
John Murray to make you a present from me, & to make this narrative go
down better, when you go into the City, desire Pickering of Chancery Lane
to give you one of the author's 'Melodies of Melancholy fancy thro life
call'd 'Poems by W.L. Bowles with a head of the Author'! Just printed . . .

Bowles was here referring to *Scenes and Shadows of Days Departed* . . ., published by William Pickering earlier in the year. He then tells Scrope about the problem, as he saw it, with Murray over the price to be charged for the volume of sermons that had just been published. He continues:

> As to the sermons, lend me your attention for five minutes.
>
> I printed 50 copies & think I had a right to charge what I lik'd for my <u>own Articles</u>, & considering them at 50 copies, which might be called somewhat <u>scarce</u>, when the <u>value</u> of the article is taken into consideration. I directed Murray the Maecenas of Albemarle Street – <u>not</u> to sell <u>one copy</u> under <u>twenty shillings</u>!! He writes by return of post to say the author & bookseller would be [paper torn] – I wrote in answer He might <u>sell them</u> for a <u>shilling</u> if he likes – instead of weekly!
>
> And having [illegible] about the business, I dislike writing again on the subject I should wish you, when you go by, to call there & inform me whether the said Sermons have been <u>advertised</u> & whether any body has heard any thing about them . . .

He adds a postscript: 'Think of my having you Scrope at Stroud and the Prime Minister in our vicarage garden, Lord Melbourne, the Great British Maker!'[89] Bowles never forgot, and probably enjoyed reminding whoever would listen, that he had once entertained the great Melbourne at the parsonage at Bremhill!

In 1835 John Murray had published for Bowles in the form of a pamphlet, dedicated to his old university friend John Wiltshire,[90] priced at one shilling and stated to be 'for the benefit of an old labourer', just two chapters of *Scenes and Shadows of Days Departed with Selections from Poems, illustrative of a long journey through life from the earliest recollections to age*. In the February 1836 number of the *Gentleman's Magazine* a most favourable review appeared: 'We have here two very interesting chapters of a work, which we hope will be continued by the author: for few narratives of personal history have been more gracefully or more affectively written . . .' Here are printed two long extracts from the pamphlet, with the review concluding:

> We think the selection of picturesque images here very happily made, described in very poetical language and with fine modulation of verse; we hope Mr Bowles will not think of leaving a work so happily commenced, an *opus imperfectum* – let him set sail, and let the *Aldine Dolphin*[91] sport around the prow.[92]

Bowles certainly had it in mind to arrange for a fuller version to be placed before the public, and approached Murray to see whether he would handle its publication. On 2 February 1836 he wrote:

I ought to have written before to say, I had taken the liberty, of putting your name as publisher, to an affecting incident, I had occasion to relate, in consequence of which incident, I was induc'd to say something of my early days, & long career of passing long!

Both Moore, & every one, who has seen this literary [illegible] have express'd great gratification, I am tempt'd to go on, & indeed have written enough to make almost a volume.

The reason why I did not write, or send copies to you, for sale, was, because the greater part of these recollections of departed days, being printed in Bath, few were left.

Now, Mr Pickering, is about to publish two volumes of my best selected poems, but if you should have no objection, to be the publisher of these memoirs, I think, they would <u>answer</u> to <u>us Both</u>, considering my long life, connected with so many literary & distinguished characters – to you [illegible] with whom I have had so many dealings I make the <u>first</u> offer.

I have little doubt of their popularity, should they, as I hope, <u>obtain</u> a <u>smile</u> from Mr Lockhart before my Sun is set! I would print them myself, or if you like, you might <u>go halves</u> – in all events, I make to you the <u>first offer</u> – I hope you will lend a hand & if so, take care to advertise the title with [illegible] in your next quarterly list of publications they say – <u>in no time</u>!

Pray speak to Moore, about this projected scheme.[93]

Murray's response was very favourable:

As soon as I had finished my letter to you I went to the Athenaeum to read, in the Gentleman's Magazine, the interesting extract from your little Tract. I have since received (about an hour ago) the 6 copies of the Tract itself which you have had the attentive kindness to send me, and, upon my word, the appearance of it is so neat, & novel, & taking, that I think we cannot do better than continue the work, in the same attractive form, & publish a Number every Saturday. I will undertake the expense of it & leave, at your disposal, half the profit. I will not send your note to Mr Nichols until I shall be favoured with your opinion upon this plan. I observe that his note is accompanied by a neat drawing for engraving in wood, I presume – now I should like very much to have the work illustrated by several prints of interest to your narrative – and, above all, we must have the best portrait of the Author, in his <u>Studio</u> – I possess a very pretty drawing by Westall,[94] of your House & Church at Bremhill – but I hope you possess others, which could offer variety. – Pray write me fully upon these matters.[95]

However, in the event Murray did not publish because Bowles always resolutely refused to see any of his work published in weekly numbers. However, Murray's decision did not prevent Bowles from writing to him yet again, this time on 7 March, wishing to encourage a young talent:

Having a frank, I send you this drawing, <u>not</u> in the remotest hope, wishing you to undertake any thing that concerns the picture, but, merely, for the <u>boy's sake</u>, <u>who drew</u> it – & as a specimen of what I could offer as embellishment in case, I should myself, at any time, think of publishing, in the manner you suggested.

The likeness, is, exactly as it must be suppos'd (and the age) of Wm Collins my father's gardener after <u>both Masters were</u> dead, & he, the old labourer, beginning to droop with age – He is represented as feeling for the first time weary with his work, & resting on a style – In the background is Uphill Parsonage house, and he is thoughtful with many remembrances . . . Pray take care of it – the penciling is very tender, tho so <u>powerful</u> & if the penciling could be fix'd I would have it, <u>instantly</u> put into the very best engraver's hands, at my own expense, for which I will pay you, in May.

Pray let it be done, for the sake of this truly original drawing & beautiful design . . .

I do not think an <u>artist</u> in London, could do better.

Now a word about the artist – he is a boy of about sixteen – he could furnish a <u>hundred</u> such drawings for ten or twelve shillings a piece & it might answer to you, occasionally to employ him, on any design you might want . . .[96]

Finding that Murray would not publish his new work in one volume, Bowles approached William Pickering, whose publishing and bookselling business at 57 Chancery Lane was by now attracting widespread attention and whose finely printed books were widely admired. Doubtless very many letters travelled from Bremhill and Salisbury to Chancery Lane before Bowles wrote to him on 6 February 1837, again on the following day and yet again on 22 February, when he wrote:

The sheet requires little correction . . . I will try to get 'Scenes & Shadows' for it is absolutely important to our little volume that they should be prefix'd – & I shall be glad if there was a well-engraved vignette – either of me or my parsonage in the country, in respect to the last Bulcock,[97] to whom I gave permission to publish for his own profit – the first and another [illegible] of 'Little Village Verses' (not yet before the public) has had a view of my country parsonage, engraved. Of this we could have as many copies as we like if on inspection of the publication you should not disapprove . . .[98]

On the very next day, following the death of Dr Herbert Hawes, for many years rector of St Edmund's Church in Salisbury and an old friend of Bowles, another of Bowles's letters arrived at Pickering's premises in Chancery Lane:

It was not till yesterday, that I was aware, poor Hawes, in every thing regarding his will, had acted so justly – & since, his executor, so nobly! He only wrote yesterday to inform me that, contrary to every thing which had been absurdly reported, all his books – Latin, Greek, Hebrew &c he had left to the Dean & Chapter – & cathedral library – Isaak Walton's[99] picture to the National Gallery – The Young Man, whom he in his benevolence, to those who had liv'd with him, & his sister, so long & faithfully, to show how much he deserv'd the [illegible] – of his own accord he has presented to you the prayer-book – to whom indeed I should have done the same had I been a purchaser – but, moreover to me, Hawes' oldest & warmest friend – the writer of Ken's Life – Ken's watch,[100] he has gratuitously given – to me. I could not resist the importance of writing to you, fearing I might, from ignorance, have done this young man whom Hawes bred up, a [illegible] injustice.

   After the Assizes, do come down & we will dine together at the canonry & drink to the memory of my old friend in silence, & with affectionate respect & now to business – I hope you receiv'd yesterday my parcell – let the last proof of poems be put by for the present –

   The title, & all the papers I sent you, let them be typ'd as soon as possible – & sent here. I can arrange them afterwards but omit nothing – I hope you will be entertain'd with Master Billy's memorabilia! Murray was so pleas'd with it . . . Pray set about the job immediately.[101]

Hawes was descended from both Bishop Ken and Isaac Walton, and the prayer book with Walton's memoranda passed to Pickering as 'illustrator and publisher of the splendid edition of Isaac Walton's Work', as Bowles put it.

In April Bowles wrote to John Mitford at Pickering's office:

He may begin the Sonnets as there printed – all of which are correct and many as they were <u>first</u> meditated – and after the sonnet on the 'Cherwell,' Oxford included that on a Lady,

'When last we parted,' &c

This finishes the first series of sonnets – written in early youth from disappointed passion. The tale is <u>too</u> affecting to me, even at these years, to enter on – if I pursue my 'and Shadows of Remembrance!'

Pickering can begin printing directly, as when I come to London the 3rd May I can look over as far as he may have got, according to my scheme in last letter.

I do not care two-pence about being indemnified for expense, but if Mr Pickering thinks it best to print 500 he may do so. My chief object was to leave on record what I had written in this way, taking the **best** of the Poetical compositions, with the arrangement beginning as I marked in my last letter. I thought it best to have an octavo size as it would suit the size of my 'Scenes and Shadows', for which I purpose having engravings should I go on.

Apropos of this projected publication, the moment Murray of Albemarle Street read this brochure of mine, he wrote to say that 'upon his word' he thought it 'so attractive (this was his expression) that he should be happy to publish it in weekly numbers,' pay all costs of printing and engravings, take upon himself 'every expense and give me half the profits'.

This was the most magnificent, and I might say the only, offer of the kind I have had in my Life, or Poetical Life!

I wrote to say that I thought the offer was 'princely', but that no pecuniary advantage could tempt me to engage in a weekly job! It might be otherwise, perhaps, if the work were to be monthly instead of weekly, but as to profit it never had any consideration with me, notwithstanding what 'Daniel says' or sings. Since this, I have heard nothing from 'John' of Albemarle Street. But if he chooses to publish, I have made him the first offer and I shall be glad, if he only is willing, to do so at my expense, and not his own . . .

I am afraid I have put you to a somewhat perplexing job, but on considering it, I hope here will be no difficulty to you or Mr Pickering . . .

P.S. If Murray declines publishing Scenes and Shadows, it would be best to include them just as they are in the Introduction to this edition or [as] a few more chapters, making three volumes – one of Introduction and two poems. I am sure I have chalk'd out as much as Pickering can do till I come . . .[102]

There can be little doubt that Bowles was still constantly writing to Pickering at this time, and was very conscious of this when in June he wrote:

> I deeply regret giving you a moment's more trouble, on my petty affairs, but I write to say my opinion is decided, that the general title should be:-
>> Scenes & Shadows of days departed, a narrative
>> accompanied with Poems of youth and some other
>> poems of melancholy & fancy in the journey of life from
>> youth to age
>>> price 5 shillings. Motto
>>>> contents
> and this must be the title of the work present'd in the second page . . .
>
> I am <u>determin'd</u> on this & the narrative is accompanying all future numbers – if I print any more – so 'gird up your loins', my good friend – this came into my head this morning on receiving my papers from Rogers & observing <u>every page</u> of the <u>Narrative</u> was <u>cut open</u> & the poems, which indeed he knows by heart – <u>uncut</u> . . .
>
> If you have a day of leisure leave the smoke of Chancery Lane on the twentieth & look at Bremhill before its last incumbrances is departed! A coach comes from Calne every day – you will meet a Gentleman, literary & intellectual who alone is worth coming to see . . . you can go back to work as soon as you like – but, if possible, come & believe me, writing to you as an old friend, not the Prince of Printers . . .
>
> Do come – Mrs Bowles says come – Hoyle of Overton, vicar – my guest would say come . . . but do not 'come' without your <u>fishing-rod</u>![103]

Pickering duly accepted this pressing invitation, and before the visit Bowles wrote to him to tell him what to expect at the parsonage:

> As you are coming so soon, I think, it would be better before I have the pleasure of shaking you by the hands – to notify a few particulars. You say Mr Mitford will read papers – I hope he will do the morning duty, & <u>preach</u> in the parish church. My curate will do the duty in the afternoon at a chapel in the parish. <u>Bring down interleav'd copy</u> of poems.
>
> Being more bow'd down by the last [illegible] of sadness & sickness at upwards of seventy-four years, I think it also right you should be previously acquainted with habits absolutely necessary for my health. – We dine at five & I go to bed – at nine! You may stay and chat with Mrs Bowles till eleven. I never departed from this rule when the Bishop of

London (Howley) or the Bishop of Salisbury were here – it has been the rule of my life for nearly twenty years – therefore I am still active. I shall have no one here to dinner but Hoyle, if he is well enough on Friday & large parties fatigue me but Saturday, after fishing, you will meet a very intelligent gentleman, Mr Loscombe [?].

I wish you would bring down with you Dr Buckland's work,[104] printed & published by you – the publications I have of yours are among my best books in Salisbury – except Mitford's edition of Parnell & Armstrong – My bookroom is an omnium gatherum of papers – pamphlets among the papers – my continuation of Scenes which, if you could get anyone to decipher you might take back – & harken, there is a little machine – not applied by hand but hitch'd on the ear, behind it – If you could lay hand on such a machine, in London, you would do well to bring it with you – tho my hearing has return'd comparatively well, it might be gone again before you come down, for which I should be sorry.

And bring down the new Title & the errata among these, one is of consequence – relating to the time, on which I speak, in my little narrative of leaving Bristol. I have no exact recollection, but it must have been late in the afternoon, as I perfectly remember it was quite dark when I heard the sound of the waves at a distance on approaching Uphill – therefore in the page mark'd it would be best to say 'When we left Bristol, the sun was declining' instead of 'between nine or ten' or 'between one and two' – neither will agree with the other circumstance & another pondering – I think our title should be . . . [Bowles then sets out yet another version of the proposed title of Scenes & Shadows]

I have said all this I thought would be more comfortable for you to have, before I welcome my friendly guests at my little Priory Porch & so God send you a safe journey & believe me

Yours truly &
W.L. Bowles

I am afraid you will find me sad, very sad company – but you will kindly make allowances. If I should be better, you will find it more agreeable. I should be happy to shew you Lacock and Malmesbury Abbeys.[105]

Mitford, who as well as being editor of the Gentleman's Magazine was also ordained in the Church of England, was at Bremhill at the same time as Pickering and stayed on for a few days after Pickering had returned to London. During that time Bowles took the opportunity of showing him some of the neighbouring sights, including Lacock Abbey. On the following day Constance, the wife of the owner of Lacock Abbey,

William Henry Fox Talbot, wrote to her husband in London with an account of the chaotic visit:

> Yesterday I had an unexpected visit from Mr Bowles a few minutes after twelve – He brought with him Mr Mitford, a friend & brother Poet to see our Abbey – first Mr Bowles pleaded ill health & refused to get out of the Carriage; upon which I sent him a message expressive of my regret that you were not at home to show the Abbey to his friend – & saying that I would come & speak to him at the door, as he would not come in – But by the time I had my Bonnet on & was proceeding to the hall, he had changed his mind & met me in the South gallery. – But instead of sitting down quietly, he immediately became anxious about his friend whom he fancied he had left sitting in the carriage – although the friend was in fact busily engaged in admiring the Cloisters &c – under the guidance of Cooper[106] – Not finding him in the Carriage we pursued him into the Cloisters – but he had fled from thence also – & Mr Bowles's agitation might have become serious – had not Mr Mitford at length joined us – hearing that we were in search of him. – We returned to the Library & Mr Bowles gave me a detailed account of the Column which is going to be built in honor of Maude Heath from a design of his (Mr Bowles's) – I am to be presented with a Memoir of his Life . . .[107]

While staying with Bowles, Mitford took the opportunity of looking at the proofs of *Scenes and Shadows* with Bowles. Having done this, he wrote to Pickering from Bremhill with a number of amendments to be made, with the carefully spaced wording of the dedication to Robert Southey, and instructions that 'You are to print the Inscription as I have now adjusted it: and when done, you are to send down a dozen more copies to Mr Bowles.' This instruction Pickering duly carried out. Mitford added a note: 'Young the actor has just called.' This was Charles Mayne Young,[108] who had retired from the stage in 1832 but in his day was the country's leading tragedian.

On 24 July Bowles 1837 wrote to Pickering:

> Since you left us – 'coming & departing, like a shadow' – I receiv'd a kind letter from Mr Mitford – he stay'd, I think, a few days & went away sooner than I wish'd but was gratified with his wanderings in Wiltshire & has promised to assist me in the last sheets which I begin to dread the appearance of – For I doubt whether I may not be quite like poor Moxon!!

The letter continues with some reminders of amendments presumably already notified to Pickering, and a postscript:

By the way, Coleridge's Poem M.S. sent to me from Stowey on a visit of Charles Lamb is most beautiful – Do you wish it? I think Mrs Bowles shew'd it to Mitford but she is from Home. I did not know that she had preserv'd it, but it is at your service or the editor of C.'s remains.[109]

Towards the end of July Constance Talbot was pleased, and perhaps slightly embarrassed, to receive a rather unusual gift from Bowles. She immediately wrote to her husband for his guidance:

Think of my having received some complimentary verses from Mr Bowles! – evidently suggested by his visit to me during your last absence – They are so pretty & so very poetical that I long to show them to you – They were transmitted to me by Mr Moore with a note from himself . . . I suppose some notice ought to be taken to Mr Bowles of his Poem, but the case is an unusual one, I know not how to act – do tell me, please . . .[110]

At the end of August Bowles was at Weston-super-Mare in Somerset, and while there wrote to Pickering that, 'Being in the neighbourhood I thought I would not omit a Sonnet written two or three years ago on Woodspring Abbey, founded by three of the murderers of Archbishop Becket' – and then proceeds to give Pickering the words of the sonnet.[111] On his way home from Somerset and while at Clifton on 27 August he was inspired to write a poem entitled 'Art and Nature. The Bridge between Clifton and Leigh Woods'. In 1836 the foundation stone of the tower on the Somerset side of the gorge had just been laid, so Bowles could only write:

> . . . But Art, high o'er the trailing smoke below
> Of sea-bound steamer, on yon summit's head
> Sat musing; and where scarce a wandering crow
> Sailed o'er the chasm, in thought a highway led;
> Conquering, as by an arrow from a bow,
> The scene's lone Genius by her elfin-thread.[112]

Little was Bowles to know that almost thirty years would pass before the highway mentioned in his poetry would be opened.

At last the much expanded edition of *Scenes and Shadows* with extra poems was duly published, having been printed by Charles Whittingham[113] who was responsible at that time for producing some of the very finest specimens of typography.[114] Facing the frontispiece is an engraving of Bowles as a young man by William Humphreys,[115] well known as the the engraver of the head of Queen Victoria on postage stamps. In the introduction Bowles tells the stories of his childhood journey from Bristol to his father's new parish at Uphill in Somerset and of his visit to his father's old gardener while staying at Banwell Cottage in 1832 as the guest of the Bishop of Bath and Wells. This is followed by a passage in which Bowles thought that:

> a few memorials of my departed days, before I 'go hence, and am no more seen', might not be unacceptable to some readers of my prose and verse.
>
> Many years after my grey head shall have been laid to rest, in Bremhill Church-yard, or in the cloisters of Salisbury Cathedral, the reader of the memorable controversy with Lord Byron, in which, I believe, all dispassionate judges will admit his lordship was foiled, and the polished lance of his sophistical rhetoric broken at his feet; or, perhaps, some who may have seen those poems of which Coleridge spoke, in the days of his earliest song, so enthusiastically, may enquire, 'Who was W.L. Bowles, *et quo patre cretus?*'"

Then follow 118 pages of poetry, beginning with his verses 'On Leaving Winchester School, written in 1788' – almost half a century before.

In November 1837 Pickering wrote to Bowles:

> The total [?] of printing your little volume including portrait and boarding up 71 copies which you either had or have been presented to your friends is £74/1/10. Now if agreeable to you to send me £50, I shall be quite satisfied . . . Should you, as you once named, leave me the copyright of your poems, I shall have much pleasure at a future day printing the entire collection. I like opera omnias better than parts, and I should think that they would pay their expenses, if not too many corrections. This, however I leave entirely to yourself, to do as you may now or hereafter think right. Should they come to me at any time, I think no one will feel more interested for the author. Many of my friends are much pleased with the little volume. If I could have foreseen how slender it would have been, I should have used thicker paper.[116]

To this letter, written on 16 November and seemingly delivered to Bremhill on the same day, Bowles responded with unusual brevity, also on the 16th: 'Had I foreseen how meagre our little volume would have look'd, I would not have been satisfied with <u>fifty pounds' worth</u> of printing, but 50 I send instantly with many thanks & believe your oblig'd friend – W.L. Bowles.'[117] At much the same time he also wrote:

> I think there was a great error in our not assuming [?] that the whole would be publish'd in six numbers or volumes with a continuation of the narrative. Could not this be done now? You are quite welcome to whatever may be the worth of the copyright & I shall be glad of being in such hands – I have the <u>vanity</u> of believing that <u>one day</u> the Grave of the Last Saxon – The Missionary – the Sonnets will survive . . . I willingly consign to Mr William Pickering, printer & publisher, of Chancery Lane the copyright of all my poems
> Bremhill Nov 15th 1837
> Of course reserving any interest to Mr Bowles.[118]

At the end of October the *Salisbury and Winchester Journal* had printed an extract from a new edition of Southey's poetical works, which doubtless afforded Bowles a good deal of pleasure. Southey wrote:

> . . . I am conscious also of having derived much benefit at one time from Cowper,[119] and more from Bowles; for which, and for the delight which his poems gave me, at an age when we are most susceptible to such delight, my good friend at Bremhill, to whom I was then, and for long afterwards personally unknown, will allow me to make this grateful and cordial acknowledgement.[120]

It seems that Bowles could never be allowed to forget the controversy arising out of what he wrote so many years before on the life of Alexander Pope and his poetry. The author of an article on Bowles, written soon after his death, mentions:

> Byron's line is familiar to all:
> 'And Pope, whom Bowles says is no poet'
> He [Bowles] thus refers to this subject in one of his letters to me dated Oct 28, 1837:
> 'I never said "Pope is no poet". I never thought so. I put the epistle to Abelard[121] before all poems, of the kind, ancient or modern. The Rape of the Lock, the most ingenious, and imaginative . . .'[122]

It may be recalled that in 1826 Bowles had written and arranged to be published a book of simple verses suitable for children to learn by heart. Anxious to bring this poetry, as well as other earlier works, before the public once again, he decided to use the services of a London publisher and bookseller that he appears not to have employed before. Between 1832 and 1836 he was corresponding with James Bulcock[123] in King's Cross, who had published one or more of his longer poems (although none is recorded as having survived). Early in 1836 he wrote to the recently bereaved Bulcock at his new place of business in Hackney:

> I am truly sorry for your great and irreparable loss, which the Almighty only can enable you to bear.
>
> I am concern'd, also, tho this is trifling, that the sale of the longer poems did not repay you the expenses & I fear in the present agitated times any <u>long</u> poem, particularly on a religious subject, would not find general readers – unless religious readers of a peculiar disposition, & they would read only without any regard to poetry what suited their own exclusive views on religion. Sternhold and Hopkins[124] are more sublime and pathetic that the psalmist & maukish, methodistical hymns than the finest serious poem that ever was written, unless in unison with their own views!
>
> I shall bring with me some <u>smaller</u> poems & hope they may repay what you have lost by the <u>longer</u>, when I come to London in May & I remain with sincere regard and condolences
> Faithfully yours
> W.L. Bowles[125]

In the event Bowles did not travel to London, but wrote again in June:

> I could not come to London as I had hop'd to have done, the illness being so general & lodgings so difficult to get.
>
> Perhaps your business might lead you this way, & if so, I should be most happy to see you & shew, that I have not been unmindful of you – but it was useless to send a little collection of things, which I hope might answer your purpose – unless fairly written which I cannot do . . .[126]

The 'little collection of things' referred to in this letter and which Bowles eventually sent to Bulcock consisted of a number of his verses suitable for children to learn by heart, as well as some epitaphs that Bowles had composed. It seems that rather than confuse Bulcock with his almost illegible handwriting, Bowles asked Magdalene to write on his behalf, as in November she wrote:

Mrs Bowles begs to return her best thanks to Mr Bullcock for his kind present of some beautiful prints the receipt of which would have been acknowledged before had she not waited for Mr Bowles's accompanying verses for the Child's book she now sends <u>all</u> that can be muster'd up and hopes it will be sufficient to form a little book.[127]

Early in 1837 Bowles must have received a proof of the proposed book containing a number of errors, and this caused him to write to Bulcock:

I expected to have heard today, being most anxious to know what <u>is</u>, or what <u>can</u> be done, in this singular business! The ryme [*sic*] alone I should have thought would have prevented that ludicrous 'Oh!' appearing, however, it got there!

But at whatever trouble or expense which I will take upon myself, the two leaves <u>must</u> & <u>shall</u> be cancell'd – as soon as possible – I did not think I could have been so disturb'd by such an <u>unfortunate</u> incident, the <u>worse</u> as it subjects an author to eternal ridicule . . .

After mentioning several other corrections to be made, Bowles continues:

Do you know Pease, the quaker who frank'd the letter, to the Canonry? If so, give my regards to him & two or three copies of both verse-books and say I shall be happy, if he ever should come near Salisbury 'Steeple House' to see him!

I have great respect for all quakers, as truly benevolent & conscientious men . . .[128]

Mr Pease referred to by Bowles was John Pease,[129] who, as a Quaker, was unwilling to take the usual oath on taking his seat in Parliament in 1833 and was the first Member of Parliament to be allowed to affirm instead.

Over the next few months many letters passed between Bowles and Bulcock, with Bowles becoming increasingly exasperated at the small errors in the printing of his verses. When Bulcock suggested that his reader was responsible for some of them not being noticed, Bowles responded with 'why is not such a "reader" turn'd into the street' and, when the word 'Oh!' was substituted for a full stop, with 'Oh! Oh! the ass!!'

In May Magdalene wrote to the hapless Bulcock:

Mrs Bowles begs to inform Mr Bullcock that his corrected copies arrived this morning and threw Mr Bowles into a perfect agony at reading 'Silent sorrows' for 'silent snows' in the [?] Robin. – Mrs Bowles hardly knows what to advise in the business, it was a great pity Mr Bullcock had not sent a proof, which Mr Bowles says he desir'd he would do. – The mistake of the unfortunate 'oh' was not to compare with the present one, as silent sorrows makes absolute nonsense. – Mrs Bowles hopes she shall be able to prevail upon Mr Bowles to lay down his pen and not print any thing more on this most [?] subject, for he feels so strongly upon the subject of these mistakes that it effects his health and spirits which at his advanced age should be carefully avoided. – If anything can now be done to calm Mr Bowles's mind Mr Bullcock will write to Mrs Bowles and inform her.[130]

The Little Villager's Verse Book was eventually published as the Second Series in 1837, with the lengthy title also reading '*to which is added, a brief Account of the Parsonage House and Garden; also Village Epitaphs*'.[131]

It seems that at the end of the year Bullock was suggesting that another edition might be published (although the following letter implies that the sales of the first had not covered the cost), and that there might even be a market for it in America. On 23 December Bowles wrote to him, with the letter being franked on Christmas Day by Wadham Wyndham,[132] one of the Members of Parliament for Salisbury:

The way is so chok'd up with all sorts of literary traffickers, bawling 'Buy me' & with every kind of literary ware . . . I never heartily approved a second series of anything. But I was willing to oblige, & last year I thought I should be driven out of my senses – But that is over, & I cannot for a moment blame you – only for your sake, I am sorry the book is not likely to answer. – In America where the field is fresh and the way less obstructed I have no doubt of your success, with both works, & I am glad to hear that you can make way, so far across the Atlantic . . .[133]

In the event, a further edition was indeed published in the following year.

Chapter 9
1838–1850

While in Salisbury in January 1838 Bowles made his last will. He had signed what appears to have been a 'home-made' will in 1828[1] but the will that he made on 23 January, which was drafted by a lawyer, was duly proved following his death. By this will Magdalene was to receive all his household goods and effects both in his house in Salisbury and in the parsonage at Bremhill, and all his books except those in which his family arms had been inserted, presumably on a book plate. She was also given half of all his money in the 3 per cent Consolidated Funds and a life interest in the remainder of his estate. After his death Bowles was found to have possessed the very large sum of £17,252 10s in 3 per cent consols. Bowles did not forget his servants to whom legacies of various amounts were given. It must have saddened Bowles that he had neither son nor close relations bearing his surname and so after Magdalene's death his pedigree of the Bowles family and all his books with the Bowles arms were to pass to the sons of his sister Margaret Erle, one of whom, William,[2] was later to be knighted and appointed lord chief justice of the common pleas. After Magdalene's death the property in which she had a life interest was given in different shares and various trusts to his three sisters and their children, and to Margaret, the only child of his brother Charles (who had predeceased him) and her children.

Having signed this will, he had second thoughts about the provision he had made for his sister Sarah Burlton and her children, and so in a codicil signed at the end of February he made a number of changes and also gave the watch that had belonged to Bishop Ken and had been left to him by his old friend Herbert Hawes to Sergeant-at-Law Henry Merewether, a lineal descendant of the bishop.

Bowles was always happy to co-operate with his fellow antiquaries and to assist them in their research if he could, but his advancing years made this more difficult and sometimes impossible. So when Henry Ellacombe,[3] the vicar of Bitton in south Gloucestershire and particularly well known as an authority on church bells, sought his help early in 1838, Bowles replied from Salisbury:

[?] as I am, or rather, as I have been, in antiquities, you have set me a job utterly beyond my strength, in this declining stage of historian's life – If you can come up here, I shall be happy to give you as long as you stay a knife and fork at the Canonry, & should be happy if I were allowed to join in your pursuits.[4]

On New Year's Day 1838 Bowles wrote to Murray's son:

Perhaps you have seen, if not I would have you look at what is said of our Cartoons Sermons, p. 269 Quarterly Church Review, Church of England, & I write this to say, that a New Edition corrected, will be printed uniformly, under my eye, at this printer's office.

Of these, I shall print 250 copies but among my more splendid meditations is an edition with engravings of the Cartoons & I have no doubt Lord Lansdowne would go halves, & if your father would assist I think we could get up a work that we might boast of & perhaps the young Queen's name, as patroness.

These are among my visions tell your father, but, at all events, I hope to have a complete edition, on your counter, before I leave Salisbury.[5]

Young John Murray duly responded to this letter and this was followed by Bowles's reply:

I am very much oblig'd to you, for your letter, & your father's kind and ingenious advice.

Depend upon it, I shall implicitly abide by his opinion, but I ought to say Mr Rickerby never has been applied to by me, & I know not, whether he is at all aware of my sentiments, that, if I could legally do as I suggested, I have too much of the feeling of honour, to do any thing that might, in the least degree, tend to injure an honourable tradesman in the course of business, if I knew I should do so! I should merely ask his permission, & if, what I propose could not be thought injurious to him, that he would not object to my publishing a very limited number of copies, so illustrated . . .[6]

It seems that Rickerby had already published a book illustrating the cartoons, and that Murray senior had perhaps suggested that the publication of Bowles's sermons with plates of the cartoons might give rise to difficulties. With this letter, therefore, Bowles sent to Murray for his approval a draft of his suggested letter to Rickerby, seeking his consent to the publication of a very limited number of the sermons containing one of the plates to his work as frontispiece.

On 5 March Bowles reported to Murray that he had received 'a most kind and frank letter' from Rickerby in which he agreed that one of the plates from his book could be used as a frontispiece to the sermons[7] and that any advertisement in the papers should state that the publication by Murray was with his permission. Bowles made it clear to Murray that he wished the advertisements for the sermons to include a quotation from the *Church of England Gazette* that they were 'the most animated, eloquent, & beautiful sermons, we ever read'![8] Further letters to Murray followed on 8, 12, 15 and 17 March, in one of which he asked that six copies of the book should be bound 'in a beautiful manner' and sent 'with the author's respects' to the Marchioness of Lansdowne, The Honourable Miss Fox,[9] Lady John Russel [*sic*],[10] Lord Melbourne, the Duke of Wellington[11] and the Archbishop of Canterbury'. In a postscript Bowles adds, 'It is not often that I do these things but when I do I <u>do them handsomely</u>! So I leave all to your father's discretion.'

At the end of the month he wrote to Murray:

> . . . I find & am glad that Lord Melbourne had received his – & I wrote expressly saying that 'I did not expect a Minister would read Sermons & was most anxious that he should not <u>give himself the trouble in these stirring</u> times even to acknowledge the present'. He instantly wrote the most kind & courteous letter with which I was so gratified I send you a copy
>
> > Lord Melbourne to Mr Bowles
> > My dear Sir
> > I beg to return my best thanks for your recollection of my visit to your beautiful residence in the country & for the very valuable present which you have made me as a memorial
>
> . . . I wrote also to the Duke of Wellington, but, it appears, from a very civil acknowledgement that he has only receiv'd my letter not the book![12]

For some unknown reason Bowles caused a corrected copy of his letter to the Duke of Wellington to be printed and sent to Murray so that, as Bowles wrote on the copy, he 'might see what it has been thought more just to omit'.[13] Although this letter was printed it appears never to have been published.

In yet another letter to Murray written at the beginning of April Bowles tells him: 'I go down into the Country, I thank the Lord, I hope with reasonable health but I am <u>piteously</u> – I fear, <u>hopelessly deaf</u>! I am persuaded to consult an <u>Ear-Physician</u> – if I do, you will see me in Albemarle Street'.[14] It may be that Bowles's deafness made him reluctant to attend the Cathedral Chapter meetings while in Salisbury, as he failed to attend any of the meetings during the first three months of 1838 while in residence. One would have thought that he might have wished to be present at the meeting held on 4 April when it was resolved that the Dean and Bowles's old friend Macdonald should travel to London to be at the meeting called by the Dean and Chapter of Canterbury to organise a defence of cathedral bodies.

When Bowles wrote to Murray on 13 April to thank him for a copy of the *Quarterly Review* in which a review of Bowles's work appeared, he mentioned that he had thought of continuing 'the scenes and shadows' but 'perhaps it is best to leave off'. He could not resist transcribing part of a letter he had received from his old schoolfriend William Howley, now Archbishop of Canterbury, who had just seen a republication of Bowles's sonnets. The archbishop wrote: 'I cannot tell you the pleasure I felt in seeing a republication of your sonnets – their intrinsic beauties must recommend them to all Lovers of Poetry but my gratification was increas'd by the recollections of Old Times.'[15]

Two days later another letter from Bowles arrived in Albemarle Street:

> I enclos'd a letter yesterday to your father, in a frank to the Archbishop to thank the writer of the kind article in the Quarterly which will gratify the archbishop, as much as myself.
>
> But to <u>you</u> I write about my sermons, & their pictures again! Supposing the <u>copies to be sent to Salisbury</u> – & all the <u>presentation</u> copies, made up & dispatch'd – & the advertisements on the London papers, <u>not yet</u> having appear'd <u>could you announce</u>, they will be <u>publish'd not before Whitsuntide</u>?
>
> Pray, let me know, & begging pardon for the trouble, if any unnecessary trouble has been given.
>
> The fact is, as I wish to be in perfect tranquillity on the decline of my days, I wish to soften the passage in the advertisements to the sermon on Charles – also the infallible porkers! . . .[16]

In writing to young Murray just three days later with anxious enquiries about the cost of the production of the sermons, Bowles prefaces his letter, written from Bremhill, by telling him, 'You are punctuality itself, but your letter went to Salisbury, & I am waiting for the cuckoo, which I am too deaf to hear, at Bremhill – but to business!'[17]

It is clear that Bowles possessed ample funds to respond generously to any appeals that were made to the public, and so when in February the wealthy – and not so wealthy – inhabitants of Salisbury were asked to give money for the relief of the numerous poor of the city, Bowles joined the mayor and the bishop at the head of the list of subscribers by giving the sum of £5.[18]

Moore makes no mention of Bowles in his journal in 1837, but in March 1838, when 'little worthy of record occurred', he noted that:

> In default of other matter I shall here transcribe from a late publication (or rather re-re-publication of Bowles's) a note respecting myself, which in his usual good-natured sensitiveness he has thought it necessary to insert. What the passage about 'the Sorcerer Poet' was to which he refers I have not the slightest notion.[19]

Moore then proceeds to quote Bowles, prefaced by the words 'Sorcerer Poet', in which he is clearly describing Moore as the 'consummate master of song, who if in the unthinking gaiety of premature Genius, he joined Syrens, has made ample amends by a life of the strictest virtuous propriety, equally exemplary as the husband, the father and the man . . .'

Now approaching his seventy-fifth year, Bowles was clearly beginning to lose both his mental and physical faculties, and was reluctant to visit London to meet his old friends. It is likely that in April he wrote to Samuel Rogers inviting him to Bremhill, as on the 19th Rogers responded:

> A thousand thanks for your very welcome letter – welcome indeed, for it told me that you were both well after a winter that has swept away many I could ill spare. You say nothing of a journey east-ward. Salisbury has supplanted London in your regard and we are never again, I fear, to see either of you, unless we climb your hill. My sister desires to be very affectionately remembered to you both. I am Eastering at Stratfield Saye and have asked an old school fellow of yours to frank this letter, because I knew it would give pleasure to him and to you.[20]

In July, Rogers did, indeed, 'climb the hill' to the parsonage, and when he and Bowles went to dine at Sloperton Cottage, Moore found 'Bowles very desponding about his health, though looking as well as he has done for years, and when poked up a little as full of fun & oddity as ever'.[21] Despite his advancing years Bowles continued to entertain members of his wide circle of friends and acquaintances at Bremhill. The very modest scale of the accommodation at the parsonage must have contrasted very sharply with that enjoyed by many of his visitors and their servants at the other houses in which they stayed, and Bowles was very conscious of this. He expressed his concerns about it to the very wealthy poet Samuel Rogers, as in a letter written by Rogers to Magdalene he writes: 'As to our man and maid they are sure to be delighted under your roof. A second table (what Bowles alluded to this morning) they never knew under our own.'[22]

After Wadham Wyndham, the Member of Parliament for Salisbury, had spent three days with Bowles and Magdalene in August, he went on to spend a few days with the Earl of Suffolk at Charlton Park, near Malmesbury,[23] and in April Rogers was writing to him from Stratfield Saye, the estate in Hampshire that had been granted to the Duke of Wellington by Parliament in 1817 – two great houses as far removed in size and grandeur from the parsonage as was Lord Lansdowne's mansion at Bowood.

Although it was very many years since Bowles had published his *Fourteen Sonnets*, which had so quickly captured the imagination of the public, his life and works were still thought worthy of notice, and so it was that in April the *Devizes and Wiltshire Gazette* reprinted from the *Quarterly Review* some 'Reminiscences of the Rev. Canon Bowles':

> We are not aware that the claims of Mr Bowles, as a poet, have ever received any detailed notice in our journal. Nor are we sorry, at this late period, and towards the decline of his life, to pay some tribute in respect to the sweetness of his verse – the effect, which has not been un-important, on the poetry of the day – and the singularly benevolent and amiable simplicity of his character, as it appears in all his writing.[24]

It is likely that it was these comments in the *Quarterly Review* that persuaded Bowles this was the time to republish some of his work, and as a consequence, on 4 May, he wrote to William Pickering:

> It is a long time since I have heard anything of you or <u>our works</u>, which according to the Quarterly 'made some impression on the age' & after this review & others as favourable, if they are not <u>all sold</u>, the copies – they may as well <u>now</u> be <u>cancell'd</u> I imagine at least I should wish it, and then another edition <u>larger</u> & handsomer with a <u>less price</u> might be propos'd directly, accompanied with a 2ⁿᵈ volume.

It was <u>my</u> fault that it was so small, <u>not</u> yours! Pray, let me know if this could not be set about – & you & Mr Mitford, to whom I owe obligations I cannot repay – Come down again – one with a pen & the other a <u>fishing</u>-rod.

Ever sincerely

W L Bowles

I expect Miss Martineau's[25] Trumpet, I expect tomorrow! & Southey says I shall hear again 'the birds sing, the bees <u>humming</u> & the waters flowing!' If this is so, Miss Martineau's trumpet is worth cartloads of the sapient Lady's philosophy & Tommy Moore shall write a Pindarick[26] in her praise!

Mrs Moore, alas! has been very ill – but is much better I rejoice to hear!

I have had a kind & affectionate letter from the Arch-bishop about the poems he says 'their intrinsic beauties will recommend them to every lover of poetry' – but that pleasure is increas'd to him by the remembrance of old friends & Old Times, but, my mind is taken up with the Cartoon Sermons –

'Write'!

What is become of my account of pedigree & Sir Rowland Bowles the brave? Answer! You printed the <u>arms under my picture</u>[27] is my sketch in existence – it will do well for another volume[28]

This letter rambles on for another page with disjointed comments and remarks, and ends with with an NB: 'How many copies, bona fide remain? Let a new Edition, at all events, be <u>advertised</u> widely . . .'

On 8 May Pickering replied:

I am glad to find you at Bremhill and in good spirits. Your little volume has gone off very well, I have 163 left and shall be ready to go to press whenever the copy is prepared for a thicker one, or two if you please.

I hope you are aware that when I first charged 7/6 for the book, it was under the supposition that <u>it was to bear all the charges</u>, but that I afterwards made it 5/-, as it was too high.

Mr Mitford I expect in town daily who will, I am sure, do every thing to please you – and as for making the book I will do my best. I should much like to see Bremhill again, but at present I have so much to keep me at home that I dare not think of it.

With kind remembrance to Mrs Bowles.[29]

This letter arrived at Bremhill on the following day, whereupon Bowles immediately put pen to paper. It is a tribute to the wonderfully efficient postal service of the day that Bowles's letter addressed absentmindedly simply to 'Messrs Pickering Chancery Lane', with no town mentioned, should be delivered in London almost certainly the next day. He wrote:

> Your letter has given me great satisfaction but, pray send me down <u>ten</u>, out of the 163 copies, or fifteen rather.
>
> I thought I was understood to take all charges, & <u>risks</u>, upon myself. So I intended to do, but was astonish'd, shall I say somewhat mortified to find for so <u>little</u> a volume so much was charg'd! but it is all well – & as for the 163 – sell or not, the <u>sale</u> has indemnified you for the twenty-five pounds, when you kindly & generously agree to take fifty pounds, instead of the whole of your bill, 75!
>
> Pray, advertise a <u>second edition</u>, directly –!
>
> To tell you the truth, when your bill was only seventy five, I expected a <u>great deal more</u>, owing to the great trouble I gave, in correcting & re-corrections, chiefly owing to my endeavouring to recollect faithfully impressions & verses made so many years ago.
>
> But now, all is fair. – I shall make <u>no corrections</u>, nor shall I see one proof, but leave the <u>second edition</u> entirely to <u>your care</u>, consulting Mr Mitford, whenever at fault. Advertise the 2<u>nd</u> edition instantly. The Ark, an <u>original</u> poem, never before publish'd, the letter to Campbell & extracts from letter to Lord Byron on Nature and Art . . . This will make a good sized volume, & I think I have <u>corrected</u> every thing, in my latter poems, which wanted correction, there will be no trouble at all, but ever remember <u>Five shillings</u> is the utmost selling price. .
>
> Let this be done immediately – you have <u>no loss</u> to fear & I hope you have found <u>none</u> about the twenty-five pounds which you <u>generously</u>, I must think, deducted from your bill.
>
> I do not think I shall now <u>go on</u> with my personal narrative as, tho there was kindness in the article of the Quarterly, for which I cannot be <u>too</u> thankful, the adverting to the Infantinaty [?] when I was no longer an infant might have been spar'd! . . .
>
> However I am very anxious about the 2nd edition, & getting the history of <u>Sir Rowland</u> ! . . .
>
> P.S. I am just return'd from Moore's who is all wonderment at the magic of Miss Martineau's trumpet for the ear.[30]

In the postscript Bowles repeats once again what Southey said about the trumpet, quite forgetting that he had already related this in his earlier letter to Pickering! It seems that neither the second edition nor the history of Bowles's ancestor, Sir Rowland, ever saw the light of day.

However, 1838 saw the publication of the sermons that Bowles had preached in the new chapel at Bowood under the title *The Cartoons of Raphael. A Series of Discourses, preached in Bowood Chapel on subjects from the Cartoons of Raphael; to which are added a Sermon preached on King Charles's Martyrdom; and some account of the last moments of Chillingworth.* Bowles sent a copy to his old friend Robert Southey, and it is clear from the preface that he now realised that his writing career was drawing to a close. He declares:

> . . . and to this volume of sermons, if God gives him life and health, it is the intention of the Author to add one other volume of 'The Village Church,' with Parochial Sermons, and the two Verse-Books for Village Children, – and he hopes then to conclude his pensive song of many years, and his long and last ministerial labours, with a Farewell for ever, thankful that, amongst his works of prose and poetry, no sentence, from youth to old age, has, he trusts, escaped his pen, that may cause him pain, on reflection, when, he is called to his Account.

In May Bowles wrote a very long and rambling letter to his old friend Isaac D'Israeli, who, it will be recalled, had been a severe critic of Bowles during the course of the Pope controversy but whose honorary doctorate from Oxford had been conferred at Bowles's suggestion and as a result of his support. In the course of this letter he wrote:

> . . . You have doubtless seen the Quarterly Review – There is a kindness about it which must have given me great satisfaction tho I have held on my way, & if I have sometimes read what I thought undeserved harshness, it never mov'd me from the path my judgement had chosen, & I have never said harsh things in return, I am sure [to?] you, my dear [friend?], as I never felt angry, beyond the perishable moment & was always the most unhappy 'till I had shaken hands, & left all unkind feelings behind me, like the clouds of yesterday.
>
> Tho Poetry was, by accident, a distinguishing feature of my youthful days & from youth 'till old age. I always was intent on studies more congenial with a clergyman's life – tho an humble Master of Arts & not a Doctor of Divinity, notwithstanding I recognise so much in contributing my aid to make you, so properly, a Doctor of Law at Oxford for your important service of King Charles.
>
> But I wish'd my studies to be not unworthy a D.D! & always thought there would be quite time for these things, when, lo! I look'd

round with 'Bless me – the Night is coming'!

So I printed as fast as I could The Cartoon Sermons & then on the death of Charles the 1st but not till after the sermon was publish'd did I perceive that the printer had left out the Dedication to yourself! It shall be carefully & gratefully replaced, if there should be another edition called for & I am sure when you consider, I was under the greatest affliction last year, on account of the loss of my brother & with dejected heart, bow'd myself to thoughts of writing any thing, you will rather wonder I have muster'd up so much matter & forgive the hasty injustice for I should have done what was most urgent, if I had [?] what I had written on purpose and designedly.

I have just receiv'd a friendly letter from one, whom I have been intimate with from school-days – The Archbishop of Canterbury & mentioning that few of those with whom we set out on life are left, I pointed out many, many still active & he himself an instance, tho two years younger. I am rejoiced man that the Sermons of which I sent him a copy, are approv'd by so good a man & so judicious a critic – but I am getting [?] when the quarterly review [sic] calls 'am the [illegible] of age', so with kind remembrances believe me, dear Sir, very Sincerely, Your oblig'd friend

W.L. Bowles

I hardly know whether I shall see London & the Athenaeum again, but, if in the summer, you should wander to Bath or Clifton, come, with any part of your family & see my Monument 'cresting the hill' – Rogers was here last summer from Bowood! Adieu!

Southey here, some time in the Summer – He is entitled to my gratitude, more than on account of literature and regard, & the highest esteem, for having recommended me a trumpet call'd after Miss Martineau! Worth all her foolish Philosophy for it makes me social, if it does not as Mr Southey expresses it – make me hear 'the birds sing – & the bees hum'! Moore is just gone to Town & I wish I could go too for Lord Lansdowne is in the chair, at the Literary Society dinner.

I do not know whether you read Sermons, but I hope mine would repay you, in more senses than one, from their original views – but they are garnished with all the beautiful Plates from the book of the Cartoons, Murray will give you a copy unless you are dispos'd to give nine shillings to a Poor Parson & Poet!![31]

Bowles seemed to be not a little obsessed by his new ear trumpet, as on 7 July *Felix Farley's Bristol Journal* published his sonnet entitled 'On a Trumpet for Deafness', with the added words 'Recommended by Mr Southey, who said "You will again hear the birds sing, the bees hum, and the waters flow."' Beneath the sonnet is a note: 'These lines were composed on the road from Clifton to Bremhill after having heard Mrs Pillinger sing "Angels ever bright and fair".' The editor added: 'Let us hope that we may have many more beautiful effusions from the Bremhill lyre.'[32] The sonnet also appeared in the July number of the *Gentleman's Magazine* and in the *Salisbury and Winchester Journal* on 23 July.[33] It may seem strange that a poet should compose lines on such a subject but Bowles's inventiveness knew no bounds. The first few lines provide a taste of poetry that at the time found favour with the public – and, indeed, his fellow poets:

> Faithful interpreter of sounds – to me
> How faithful! For I hear, indeed, the birds
> Sing, and the low of home-returning herds
> Once more, and murmers of the morning bee
> In summer lanes; . . .[34]

It seems that before the poem was published in July Bowles had sent the text to Southey, as he makes reference to it when writing from London to Bowles in April 1838 before embarking on a visit to northern France:

> Your sonnet gave me great pleasure, both for its intrinsic worth and for the gratifying reflection that my chance meeting with a lady whom heaven knows I never desired to meet, should have been the means of bringing the sweet sounds of the country again within your reach . – I wish I were out of reach of the abominable noise of the town, never again to hear it.[35]

It must be that Southey, on meeting the writer Harriet Martineau who suffered from deafness from a very early age, discovered the usefulness of an ear trumpet as an aid to hearing.

A story is told of the amusing consequences arising from Bowles's faulty hearing:

> Latterly Bowles became very deaf, but he kept up the habit of going out as long as he could. Once on the occasion of the archdeacon's visitation to Chippenham, Mr Julian Young, as the last instituted incumbent in the district, had to preach the sermon. This gentleman, the son of Young the actor, was a very popular preacher, but full of gesticulations and display in the pulpit – a manner by no means approved by all his

hearers. After church, the assembled parsons always had a luncheon at the Angel Hotel. My informant, Sir Gabriel Goldney,[36] tells me that 'It was the duty of Canon Bowles, as the oldest incumbent, to thank the new incumbent for his sermon. In the somewhat droning but still emphatic way that Bowles had in speaking, he said – "Excellent sermon, Mr Young – wonderful sermon. I never heard a word of it, but the acting was admirable."'[37]

Many years had passed since Bowles had first corresponded with John Wilson, 'Christopher North' of *Blackwood's Edinburgh Magazine* as well as Professor of Moral Philosophy at Edinburgh University. Since 1837, when his wife had died, Wilson's contributions to *Blackwood* were less frequent than formerly but, probably after some initial hesitation, Bowles decided to make contact with him by writing in August:

I have never forgotten & never shall forget, that Professor Wilson was among the warmest & kindest friends of my Poetical Life, so feeling, when my small unpretending volume of selections came out, I wrote a grateful letter & prepar'd to send that volume in remembrance of his kindness last year.

But some reports I had heard to which delicacy & respect to sacred feelings made me unwilling to advert lest I might un-intentionally have added to conscious sorrows – caus'd me to suppress that letter at the time, but since having seen some late articles, accidentally, by which I learn, that that singularly gifted individual is yet employ'd, as engag'd as of yore, I write this time to him, with some what of diffidence, but with the warmest congratulations, if this writer be the ancient 'old man El [illegible]', who made a track of himself, when in deep pathos, & the [?] humour was never rivall'd in Blackwood's Magazine or any periodical publication in the world!

I am anxious therefore to hear from him, (having had many letters before) & if I am answer'd of the fact, from his own hand that he is living, writing & adorning as usual the old pages where I have read with tears of delight & is indeed restor'd to health & happiness . . . I should communicate some things relating to 'Scenes & shadows of days departed' or perhaps he would do me the favour of some kind of critical notice, in the next Review – & hoping I have not intruded rashly, I remain his sincere and grateful friend, tho personally unknown.[38]

It is not known whether Wilson responded favourably to this letter, but it is certain that he would have acknowledged it.

On 30 August 1838 the Bishop of Gloucester and Bristol[39] was at Chippenham, where he confirmed a large number of young people[40] after which he held his triennial Visitation of the Deanery of Malmesbury which, with Cricklade, had recently been annexed to the newly formed diocese of Gloucester and Bristol. Some part of his charge to the clergy so incensed Bowles that he immediately penned what was published as *A Final Defence of the Rights of Patronage in Deans and Chapters: being a few plain words in answer to one material part of the Bishop of Bristol and Gloucester's Charge, delivered at Chippenham August 30th, 1838*. It appears that as soon as what Bowles had written was printed he was advised that part of it was probably libellous, as is made clear by a note in the second impression in which Bowles writes:

> Having been informed that some expressions in a former edition might be regarded as 'libellous', whether so or not, I was certain that no sentence, of which this might be said, became a Clergyman addressing a Bishop. I therefore cancelled the whole impression; and, I trust, in the present impression, I have not exceeded the display of strong remonstrance which my view of the case appears to demand.[41]

The *Final Defence* was printed in Bath and Murray was named as publisher. Soon after it was printed Bowles wrote to Murray:

> I hope you have receiv'd by this time the copies of my somewhat strong answer to the Bishop of Gloucester's charge. It is <u>not</u> stronger than the case deserves – but the Board is now sitting & I trust you will have sent to every individual of the Commissioners my letter to the Bishop of Gloucester & to every Bishop besides & to all Ministers . . .
> I will settle all accounts for this pamphlet & the other on the same subject in Spring & for the Cartoons! . . .[42]

It is likely that Bowles had written to the reforming parson Sydney Smith, now canon-residentiary of St Paul's, about his *Final Defence*, as in December Smith wrote to Bowles from his parsonage at Combe Florey in Somerset: 'Depend upon it I will crucify Simon and make him as detestable to good churchmen(?) as is Simon Magus.[43] I shall immediately procure, read, and profit by your pamphlet. Bishops should not write at all, seldom speak, and confine themselves to voting.'[44]

Part of the Bishop's charge related to the soon to be enacted Pluralities Act that would forbid any clergyman from holding two livings, except by the disposition of the Archbishop of Canterbury, where, among other conditions, such livings were less than 10 miles apart. The Bishop said that he did not think that the bill that would lead to the Act would be 'disliked by the clergy in general'.[45] Bowles probably did not like it, having for almost twenty years held the livings of both Bremhill and Dumbleton.

During 1837 Bowles attended just one of the meetings of the Cathedral Chapter and in the following year none at all. Perhaps he knew that in October one of the other canons would be appointed Master of the Choristers,[46] and so any influence he might have had over the conduct of the music in the cathedral was now at an end.

In January 1839 the *Devizes and Wiltshire Gazette* printed some remarks on Bowles's pamphlet that had appeared in the *Gentleman's Magazine*:

> This animated and interesting pamphlet has appeared in answer to some part of the Bishop of Gloucester's charge, delivered at Chippenham, in which the Bishop vindicates the Board . . . Mr Bowles falls tooth and nail on the proceedings of the Commission and the defence which the Bishop has set up for it, and we confess, we think much of his argument unanswerable . . .[47]

One other pamphlet was printed, probably in 1838, at the office of E. Baily in Calne, and this was almost certainly the last of Bowles's literary offerings to the public. Published anonymously, it gloried in the title of *Prudens and Claudia of St Paul. On the earliest introduction of the Christian faith to these islands, through Claudia, certainly a British lady, supposed daughter of Caractacus: intended to be added to the sermon on Paul at Athens, as an historical note in sermons on the cartoons*. It appears that there was a second edition of this pamphlet and that a third edition, bearing Bowles's name, was published in Bristol in 1839.[48]

In November 1838, in an announcement that plans were being made to erect a new church not far distant from Bremhill, reference was made to the 'moral destitution of the inhabitants of the hamlets of Studley, Derry Hill and the extra-parochial of Pewsham',[49] Bowles lost no time in writing to the paper:

> I cannot read a statement respecting the destitution and ignorance of the neighbourhood of the intended District Church without saying a few words in favour of my faithful out lying parishioners from Studley, in that district and to shew their deep attachment to the Church. The distance is two miles with a long and steep hill to climb; yet 40–50 are every Sunday attendants at my church, and, reckoning their families,

upwards of a hundred and have been so ever since my residence, now nearly 35 years. I do not think I have missed one face, except from death or illness for all that time . . .[50]

Having put pen to paper in this way, Bowles could not resist doing the same again very soon afterwards, writing to the editor of the *Devizes and Wiltshire Gazette*:

The spot on which it is proposed to erect the New District Church having been fixed, you will perhaps allow a subscriber, and an old topographer of county localities to send you a few, I hope, not uninteresting remarks . . . it will stand on a section of extensive hilly plain called Red-hill . . . where, 1700 years ago the Romans in Britain had a *speculatory camp*, and, where, when about to leave this country, their legions buried innumerable coins proposing to return . . .[51]

Bowles proceeds to relate how, many years before, he had offered a small reward to all those who found Roman coins and brought them to him, and describes in some detail a number of the coins so found.

At the end of the year Moore recorded in his journal:

Bowles sent me, this morning, a Latin epitaph (ancient, I believe) and his own translation of it, with both of which he seems mightily pleased. The original (as well as I can remember) is as follows: '*Hic jacet Lollius juxta viam, ut dicant praeterientes, Lolli vale!*'

Translation

'Here Lollius lies, beside the road,
That they who journey by
May look upon his last abode,
And "Farewell, Lollius," sigh.'

The last line as bad as need be, and so Lord Holland seemed to think, as well as myself. I suggested, as at least a more natural translation of it,

'And say, Friend Loll, good bye!'

Which Lord H. improved infinitely by making it,

'And say, Toll Loll, good bye!'[52]

In common with most classically educated men of his day, Bowles was proficient in Latin and ancient Greek, and delighted in demonstrating his ability by not only composing epitaphs in Latin but also by translating into English all manner of ancient texts. One famous example is his translation of the epitaph by Simonides[53] on the monument erected where the Spartans fell and lie buried after the battle of Thermopylae:

> Go tell the Spartans, thou that passest by,
> That here obedient to their laws, we lie.

Bowles could not resist saying more about the coins that had been found, and so he wrote again to the editor of the newspapers published in both Salisbury[54] and Devizes:

> Alas! Many of my rarest coins are gone – and I know not where – and the coins I have spoken of among the rest, drawn up and left at my house by Mr Stoughton Money[55] – a young gentleman of promising talent and extraordinary information, son of my most valued friend the Rev. Mr Money of Whitham, and far better versed in this part of antiquarian lore than myself. Here follows a list of those (amidst innumerable others) most valuable coins –valuable in throwing a great light on the original records of history and of the Christian Church.[56]

A list of some of the coins follows, with a note about the derivation of the name Derry Hill, showing once again Bowles's belief in the existence and importance of the Druids:

> . . . and I would have concluded this letter; but I am desirous of saying a word on the origin of the name Derry-hill – more so, as in my history of Bremhill, I gave a wrong definition of it. The name shews that the whole district was Druidical: Derry Hill being derived from Dern, an oak, sacred to the Druids. In my next letter I shall return to the coins . . .[57]

In reality, it is likely that the word 'Derry' is merely a variant of the word 'dairy'.[58]

Bowles did indeed write again to the newspapers with a further list of coins and also a telling list of spelling errors[59] in his earlier letter – a clear indication of the printer's almost impossible task in deciphering Bowles's handwriting.

In the following number of the *Salisbury and Winchester Journal* appeared yet another letter from him, written in the characteristically eccentric style that the seventy-six-year-old Bowles now adopted:

> In putting down my pen, for the present on the subject of the antiquarian discoveries, and relics of the olden times, at Derry-Hill, I shall here only observe, that I had no other object, in addressing the general reader, than because I thought such reflections serviceable to truth; and if I have felt in looking back on such objects
> 'Mortem mortalia tangunt' –
> 'That which relates to mortality touches the heart'
> I hope to be excused, besides confessing the solace of such silent studies, as won my youth, and soothe my age.
> I shall therefore further, only add, in the beautiful classical lines of Chief Justice Abbot, my competitor for the prize of Latin verses when we were both 'poor scholars' 'pauperes scholares of Oxenford'
> – 'Sic mihi floribus
> mulcere me, fessum senemque
> carpere quos junvenis soleiam'[60]

A certain naïvety had for many years been recognised as one of Bowles's characteristics, and this is clearly demonstrated in a letter that he wrote to young Murray early in January 1839. The purpose of this letter was not 'a project of a new edition of any works of mine' but to recommend to Murray as a possible employee 'an excellent young man to whom I made a present of my little volume of village verses. By attention, he sold not less than eight-hundred, the <u>present year</u>, what he has sold since, I know not but he embark'd in a much larger concern, & – has failed!'.[61]

On 3 April 1839 Bowles was at a Cathedral Chapter meeting, doubtless before returning to Bremhill for the rest of the year. This was the first meeting that he had attended since January 1837. Since he had been elected a residentiary canon in 1828, Bowles had attended only 26 out of a possible 112 meetings, the lowest number of any of the canons – approximately a quarter of the total and equivalent to the three months of each year during which he was in residence.[62]

In April Bowles had the pleasure of meeting once again the poet William Wordsworth, whom he had not seen since he was a very young man. Wordsworth was in Bath, and Bowles wrote to him on the 15th:

Connected by so many and affecting reminiscences, and so much of more higher reason for veneration, it would have been of great satisfaction and gratification if you could have look'd on me in my old parsonage domain. You will find the Fishers, and their wonderful child, and I tru[ly] regret not being there. But I shall come to Bath, and shake you by the hand, not having seen you, I think, since you and I, and Rogers, were in a boat together on the <u>Thames</u>, and I <u>got out</u> and <u>run away</u>, and I heard you <u>pronounc'd</u> – My the <u>boldest man</u> in England!

Whether this be true or not, I shall face all dangers of <u>two post</u> horses to come and see you <u>Thursday</u>, at <u>one</u> o'clock.

I am much alter'd in phiz., but not, I hope, much either in heart or head, at least I persuade myself so; but with respect and regard for you, privately and publickly, I am not sure; and believe me

Ever, &c.,

W.L. Bowles

Do not write, if Thursday will suit you. Southey is with my namesake, Caroline – I hope, and believe, the attachment will lead to happiness the most enviable in his life, and who but must wish so, who ever read Southey's exquisite Hymn <u>to the Penates</u>[63]!

I am truly glad to find your <u>outward machine</u> is only a little worse for <u>wear</u>! I am as <u>Wizen</u> as a witch, and as <u>Deaf</u> as a <u>Post</u>![64]

Wordsworth's cousin, Elizabeth Cookson had married William Fisher,[65] a canon of Salisbury, and it appears from this letter that they may have been staying at the parsonage with their daughter Emmeline, a child with extraordinary poetical gifts. Bowles duly travelled to Bath where he met and dined with Wordsworth and his wife, and soon after returning home he wrote once again:

I should have written to you sooner to thank you and Mrs Wordsworth for your <u>more</u> than <u>kind</u> welcome, but I wished to hear first from the oldest friend I have, and whose unrivalled pictures I mention'd to you.

I hope by this time you have seen him and them! I mention'd to their owner the interesting anecdote which you told me, and I trust the sight of pictures, landscapes and portraits so beautiful upon earth will inspire you not to let the design slumber!

To-day I have been over to Moore's and told him that I went to Bath on purpose to see you, and how glad I was to find you so well.

He is anxious to see you, and was easily persuaded to come over to a morning's concert on Friday! He, Mrs Moore and young Tom come in my carriage, and he and myself mean to call on you and Mrs

Wordsworth, about one o'clock, before the concert, and believe me, ever, my dear Mr Wordsworth - - -

If our calling on you at that time should be in the slightest manner inconvenient write a line to me at the White Hart, and how rejoiced I should feel if you would partake of our fare, at the inn, for which I order'd the very same fare as that with which you treated us so sumptuously, and we shall sit down as soon as the concert is over, and get back in the evening.

Mrs Bowles desires to send her best remembrances, hoping you have heard a good account from your son.

Ever truly and affectionately

W.L. Bowles [66]

Soon after this Rogers wrote to Magdalene:

How ungrateful you must have thought me, so kind as your letters were and so welcome too . . . I can only say that I thought of you both, morning, noon and nights, and this is the third frank I have procured for the purpose of thanking you – tho' I am half angry when I think of your long absence from this town of ours – from Piccadilly now so gay and from nightingales now in full song.

Wordsworth is still here, delighted with the glimpses he had of you both at Bath. Pray tell Moore, when you see him, to come before we break up. Farewell, my dear Mrs Bowles, till we meet at Bremhill. [67]

By now Bowles's physical and mental health was deteriorating to a marked degree. However, this did not prevent him and Magdalene continuing to receive an almost continuous flow of visitors, several of whom he insisted upon taking to view Lacock Abbey in which he appears to have acquired something of a proprietary interest since writing its history. In May he wrote to William Fox Talbot, who earlier in the year had sent to the Royal Society *Some Account of the Art of Photogenic Drawing, or the process by which natural objects may be made to delineate themselves without the aid of the artist's pencil*:

I am conscious I ought to have written before this to hail the photo-genic Ladies at Lacock. We feel giddy in general which indisposes me to small wanderings – I expect Mr Reade[68] the author of Italy, a beautiful poem on Saturday, & propose bringing him over if you are at home about one o'clock & with best regards remain yours truly

W.L. Bowles

If you hear or see nothing of me, my giddiness you may rely on it has prevented me – do not write – I will stand all <u>chances</u>.[69]

Mr Reade was the author of *Italy: a poem in six parts: with historical and classical notes* recently published. Later in the year, in September, Bowles troubled the master of Lacock Abbey with more inquisitive visitors:

I propose paying another visit to your interesting abode, chiefly because I wish to show the Abbey, whose story I have told, to Mr Sergeant & his new bride Mrs Sergeant Merewether. If you are at home <u>we shall</u> rejoice, if not I shall trust to the welcome <u>Old</u> Bowles has always found & believe me, still <u>giddy</u>, but sincerely
W.L. Bowles

We shall come <u>Thursday</u> next about <u>one o'clock</u> and are anxious to see a specimen of the Photo-genic art – by its Inventor, in his own Abby [*sic*].[70]

Mr Sergeant Merewether[71] was the son of Henry Merewether of Calne and an immensely successful barrister earning, it is said, the enormous sum of £5000 a year; in 1842 he was elected town clerk of London. The Mrs Merewether mentioned was the sergeant-at-law's second wife.

The party duly called at the Abbey, and on the following day Fox Talbot's wife, Constance, gave her husband an account of the visit:

We did not show ourselves to the party yesterday, because they were all strangers, & Mr Bowles did not come to introduce them . . . One Lady fainted in the Cloisters & the young gentleman was pulled off his horse at the entrance gate, by the impetuosity of another Steed which he was leading for a lady . . . No desire <u>was expressed to see</u> the Photogenic-Drawings, so that I was not called upon to do the honors of them . . .[72]

On 6 May yet another letter appeared in the *Salisbury and Winchester Journal* once again headed 'Roman Coins Found at Derry Hill', but having very little to do with the discovery of the coins and more with a controversy that appeared to be brewing relating to the form of the sacramental bread used at the celebration of the Lord's Supper. It seems to have followed an open letter written to Bowles by Augustus Pugin.[73] Bowles wrote:

I now beg the reader to remember, not in the harshness of uncharitable zeal, but in the spirit of truth and candour, that in the Scripture all the Gospel accounts agree, in the plain and simple narrative of *one fact* that Christ, at the last supper, after he had given thanks, took the bread and '*brake it*'; this is an universally admitted fact. Then how came, in one communion, the form of sacramental bread to be ROUND?[74]

As the correspondence appeared to be moving in a controversial direction, in the same number of the newspaper the editor felt it necessary to justify the publication of such letters:

A preceding page contains another paper by the Rev. Canon Bowles in continuation of the interesting subject of the ancient coins found on the site of the intended new church at Derry-Hill. We always open our columns with a feeling of pleasure to the communications of our amiable, learned, and highly-gifted correspondent and should on the present occasion have felt that pleasure in no degree lessened had the paper in question been of a less controversial character . . .

Bowles's letter resulted in the two following numbers of the newspaper carrying exceedingly lengthy letters from Johannes Gnatenfordiensis to which Bowles felt compelled to respond with a long letter that managed to bring the controversy to an end, for the time being at least. He concluded:

. . . But although I declare, and have declared, that no irritation from critical controversies in newspapers shall lead me astray from the path of peace and gentleness again in this mortal life I OWE IT TO TRUTH AND THE GOD OR TRUTH, and to his INFALLIBLE WORD, firstly to declare, that what I hold most sacredly, as the only truth, unmixed with error, and ONLY INFALLIBLE – (though I confess the greatest human deference to the Apostolic Fathers, and the Fathers, and to traditions when they are proved) I will never relinquish as my only hope in death, but MAINTAIN it firmly and faithfully while I have breath – if I am not say till fire and fagot is lighted under my feet (of which this letter in my old age, quietude, and infirmities is ominous) – I will never relinquish TILL THE PEN DROP FROM MY HAND – Amen.[75]

In May Moore recorded in his journal:

A visit from Bowles one of these days – showed me some new progeny of his Muse, which really breeds rabbit-fashion – This was prose, however, and theological, tracing the Catholic adoration of the host to the circular image of the sun worshipped at Heliopolis[76] – But why not take the Cross itself which formed part of the religious worship of the Egyptians?[77]

Mercifully it seems that this 'new progeny' of Bowles was never published.

Despite the deterioration in Bowles's health, he could still be good company at dinner with his friends. In August Moore noted:

> Went all to Bowles's to dinner. Bessy [Moore's wife] having given Bowles some venison for the occasion that had been sent to us – she herself not well enough to join the party. Two or three parsons (Mr Salt one of them) and a <u>she</u> parson, Mrs Archdeacon Knares, our company – the <u>she</u> by far the best of the group . . . Bowles in high fun and folly – his fears of death mixing so ludicrously with his thorough enjoyment of all the nonsense of life – 'how do you think I look?', being his constant and anxious question – Has put a cast of a head of Christ in his Church, and chuckles at the notion of being taken for an idolater. Miss Kenny[78] charmed them all by playing (beautifully as she does) some valses on Mrs Bowles's atrocious old Piano-forte – they wanted me to sing – but no – with such an instrument, and such <u>parsons</u> it would never do. Got home very agreeably, the evening being delightful . . .[79]

In the summer the foundation stone of the new church at Derry Hill was laid by Lord Lansdowne. Bowles, who was a member of the building committee, was of course present, accompanied by the Anglo-Saxon scholar James Ingram, President of Trinity College, Oxford.[80]

In October Bowles's old friend John Skinner, who had so memorably recorded the weekend spent in the Bishop's Palace in Wells in 1828, shot himself dead in the woods near his parsonage at Camerton in Somerset. In a codicil to his will made only two months earlier he left to Bowles 'a little useful poney which his old friend Mr Wiltshire gave me and for the same reason, because I know that he will have it taken care of as long as he lives'.[81]

At the very end of 1838 Bowles had convinced himself that there would be a market for new editions of his history of Bremhill and his life of Bishop Ken. So it was that in writing to the young John Murray, asking him to send 'one of my garnish'd copies of the Cartoons to John Harford[82] of Blaise Castle near Bristol', who was shortly to publish a life of Thomas

Burgess, Bishop of Salisbury until 1837, he continued:

> . . . and in the spring I will settle with your Father for this job – but I propose publishing an edition (the second) of Bremhill & the Life of Ken, & Mr Nicholls Junr will prepare them – Bremhill sells at ten shillings more that its original price, at first very dear, & your father knows how soon the Life of Kenn [*sic*] – went off – I wish he would speak, to you, or young Nicholls & I would offer to your father the copy-right first, with Mr Nicholls, who would prepare the Life of Ken in one volume & in the 2nd History of Bremhill or rather the History of Bremhill & the Life of Ken – . . . Please send the Cartoon Sermons to Mr Harford immediately.[83]

The Murrays were quite clearly not enthusiastic about Bowles's suggestion, and had neither accepted nor rejected it when Bowles wrote again in April of the following year to young Murray, asking whether his father would give him anything for the copyright of the history of Bremhill. In the same letter he wrote:

> I must beg again to trouble you? Have you sent to every Bishop on the Bench & the commissioners generally a copy of my letter to the Bishop of Gloucestershire [*sic*]?
> If not I beg you to do so, without loss of time, to the Bishop of Gloucester especially.
> Our Bishop[84] dining with me yesterday made some observations which induce me to ask this question and I am doubtful whether I gave directions.[85]

Bowles continues this rambling letter by asking Murray to 'have the goodness to send as presents to the Bishop of Oxford, London, Lincoln, Exeter, Rochester & all the Bishops, except Bath & Wells a copy of my Cartoon Sermons along with the letter to the Bishop of Gloster' and proceeds to give somewhat incoherent directions for all manner of advertisements to be inserted in the newspapers. It is perhaps doubtful whether Murray thought fit to comply with Bowles's directions. What is certain is that no further editions of the *History of Bremhill* or of the *Life of Ken* ever appeared.

Bowles's letters written at this time are on occasion almost incomprehensible and irrational and on others perfectly sensible, as is the case of the last two letters written by Bowles to Murray that appear to have survived:

It is impossible for me to say how much I am pleas'd with the punctuality & accuracy of every thing you have done, & let me also acknowledge, gratefully, that I am also pleas'd that the amount of the balance, in my favor, considering the expense I put you to, – for the rest let 25 pounds, be paid into the hands of my bankers, Messrs Drummonds Charing Cross, at whatever date your father pleases (say six weeks or three months if he likes) – and let the odd money go, for an advertisement or two, or three, in the St James' Chronicle, with a present of a copy.[86]

The second of the letters was written in July 1839:

Dear Mr Murray

In consequence of a most kind letter from Lord Mahon,[87] owing to some misunderstanding on my part of a particular passage of his unrival'd historical work, I have ventured to beg his acceptance of my edition of the works of Pope.

If you have not got a copy, you can procure, and place it to my account at the original selling price.

Then let me know when this is done & I will pay you instantly & with many thanks I remain

Sincerely &ce

W L Bowles[88]

In January 1840 the *Salisbury and Winchester Journal* informed its readers: 'It is with deep regret that we have to announce the alarming state of health of the venerable Poet of Bremhill, the Rev Canon Bowles, who, we hear, is sinking fast. The religious, no less that the literary world, can ill spare so amiable a member.'[89]

Bowles failed to attend any Chapter meetings in 1840, and although he appeared to be 'sinking fast' he certainly failed to drown but managed to survive for many years to come!

In July 1840 the Devizes newspaper carried an announcement concerning the formation of the Wiltshire Topographical Society.[90] Had Bowles been younger and in reasonable health, it is likely that he would have been a member of the original council of the society. Further, the absence of his name from the list of original members is a sure sign of his failing faculties, which were to entirely curtail his literary activities. The following year his name appeared for the last time in the list of those who subscribed to the Wiltshire Society – a society that he had supported since 1819. It is clear that from time to time his mental health showed signs of serious deterioration. As an example, at the end of June Magdalene wrote this letter to an unknown recipient, perhaps Isaac D'Israeli: 'In my dear husband's name I beg to thank you for your kind present and I am sure you will be sorry to hear that he is not well enough to write his thanks. His bodily health is tolerably good, but his spirits in a very depressed state.'[91]

In August 1840 the Ecclesiastical Commissioners Act became law, and among other measures fixed the number of canons of each cathedral to four – with the canonries above that number being suspended as they became vacant. Bowles would have known, therefore, that his own position as residentiary canon was now secure for the rest of his life.

In October the last mention of Bowles in the journal of Thomas Moore appears:

> Bowles called at Bowood yesterday and was altogether much better than I expected to see him – Rogers unluckily out of the way & Bowles would not wait – The only signs of wandering I saw in him more than usual was his saying to me 'How beautiful you look! You ought to get your picture drawn immediately' – He said much the same to Rogers – Poor Bowles![92]

Later in the year Bowles was seriously ill once again, but recovered before Christmas. The Devizes newspaper reported: 'We sincerely rejoice to find the venerable Canon Bowles is sufficiently recovered from his late severe illness to resume his duties as one of the Canons of the Salisbury Cathedral.'[93]

In 1837 the thirty-six-year-old Edward Denison[94] had been consecrated Bishop of Salisbury in succession to Bowles's old friend Thomas Burgess, and in 1841 Denison's friend Walter Kerr Hamilton[95] was appointed Dean. Hamilton was so dismayed at what he found on his arrival in Salisbury that he seriously considered returning to Oxford but he was persuaded by his Bishop to remain. Bowles, by now almost eighty years old, was undoubtedly not happy when confronted with the reforming zeal of the new Dean who was soon appointed Precentor, a position that gave him virtual control of the choir. Further, Hamilton made no secret of the fact that he considered that constant residence of the canons should be enforced and, having refused his father's old living, would certainly not have approved of Bowles holding the living of Bremhill as well as his canonry.

Although increasingly infirm, Bowles continued to live during the summer and autumn months in Bremhill, spending the first three months of the year as usual in his canonical residence in the Close. When the national census was taken on 6 June 1841 Bowles and Magdalene were at the parsonage at Bremhill. In the house were four servants, Charles Rawlings, their thirty-year-old manservant, Catherine Eastwell, forty-five years old and probably the cook, and two other female servants, twenty-year-old Amelia Powney and twenty-five-year-old Louisa Ford, almost certainly Magdalene's maid and either the house or kitchen maid. It is certain that when Bowles and Magdalene moved to Salisbury after each Christmas their servants would have moved with them.

In December 1841 Bowles must have been pleased to receive a letter from his old friend William Howley, since 1828 the Archbishop of Canterbury. He writes:

> . . . You will naturally be more interested in recollections of former days which have just been forcibly brought to my mind by a present I have received from the widow of Dr Nares (formerly of Merton who died last Summer) of a copy of our poor friend Russell's[96] poems with a portrait of him in profile (in French silhouette) and with an extract in Dr Nares' hand in the blank leaf in the beginning from an elegy written by you at Hotwells Bristol[97] in which a very pathetic passage occurs relating to Russell's death[98] and my recovery. This carries one back to days long bygone of which the occupations the cares and the anxieties of my present situation have by no means effaced the remembrance and I trust never will. Though it is some time since I wrote to you, I have never lost an opportunity of making enquiry and I trust from what I last heard you are on the whole more comfortable than you were last year. We cannot of course expect to retain the pleasures of youth in advanced years but it is a great blessing to be free from pain and a greater still to enjoy the care and kindly attentions of those who are most dear to us. In this respect both you and I are most happy in excellent wives. To whose affection we are indebted for the ease of our households and for a thousand little services which add to our comfort, and soothe our afflictions. I beg you to make my kindest regards to Mrs Bowles and Mrs Howley unites with me in affectionate remembrances to you and her. With every good wish I remain, my dear Bowles
> Yours affectionately
> W. Cantuar[99]

On 21 March 1843 the eighty-year-old Bowles's old friend Robert Southey died, following which he managed to write 'Epitaph on Robert Southey' – probably the last of his poems to be published.[100]

For very many years Bowles's activities had been recorded in the *Devizes and Wiltshire Gazette*, but now that his literary career was at an end only very rarely does his name appear in the newspaper's columns. In 1843 his name was included in the list of subscribers to a fund established to equip a chapel in the Infirmary at Salisbury and to pay the stipend of a hospital chaplain.[101]

Despite his age Bowles continued to visit Bath from time to time, and was there in December 1843. On his return to Bremhill he found a letter waiting for him from his fellow clerical antiquary, the Rev. Henry Ellacombe of Bitton in Gloucestershire, and in typical fashion immediately put pen to paper in order to acknowledge it. However he did succeed in misspelling his correspondent's surname by addressing the letter to 'Rev. Mr Elicome' – something he would never have done in his younger days:

> I beg to thank you for your kind communication, respecting the grant of some lands in Bitton, from the Abbess of Lacock . . .
>
> You would have had an earlier acknowledgement of your kindness, but your letter having been directed to Salisbury, instead of this place. I did not receive till today, on my return from the annual Athenaeum meeting at Bath.
>
> A seal of the Abbey, very perfect, I have now engraving, with other illustrations, but you will, in my name, thank the Possessor of this seal, & I shall solicit an inspexion, if I can come to Bath, before I go to Salisbury.[102]

This last sentence seems to make no sense at all, and appears to be clear evidence of Bowles's now muddled thinking.

In November 1843 an election was held in Salisbury to return a member to Parliament and Bowles was registered as entitled to vote. It may be that it was his infirmity of mind as well as body that persuaded him not to cast his vote.

The household account book kept by Magdalene and beginning in April 1843 has survived.[103] Among the entries for the month of April are 10s for 'boots for the poor', £5 6s 10d 'for dinners for the poor people at Christmas and for the singers' and £2 paid to Thomas's wife 'for taking care of our house at Sarum', and in August £5 was 'sent for the poor in the manufacturing and mining districts'. On 1 May 1844, however, Magdalene's handwriting becomes almost illegible, and on 7 May 1844 Bowles suffered a severe blow when his wife of nearly forty-seven years died. She died intestate and was buried in the Cathedral beneath the floor of the south aisle of the choir. John Britton, who knew both Bowles and his wife well over very many years, wrote:

> Mr Bowles was noted for absence of mind, abstraction from the affairs of every-day reality, whence the temper and stoicism of his good and truly philosophic wife were often tested, and, fortunately for her, were efficaciously exerted...[his eccentricities were] such as would have made wives of a nervous irritability miserable, were borne by Mrs Bowles with exemplary equanimity, and almost without murmur. Hence she proved to be an invaluable wife and companion; and it is believed that she not only prolonged his life, but guarded him against many accidents that might have been fatal.[104]

Bowles doubtless received many letters of condolence following Magdalene's death, but none can have given him more comfort or pleasure than the moving letter written on 14 May by William Wordsworth:

> The newspapers informed me of your mournful bereavement, and deeply did I sympathize with your sorrows, but I could not bring myself to write to you immediately, being persuaded that my condolence had better be deferred till you had time to feel what through your own heart and mind the goodness of God would effect for your Support and Consolation. It is a sad thing to be left alone, as it were, after having been so long blessed as you have been with a faithful companion; no one can judge of this but they who have been so happily placed, and either have been doomed to a like loss, or, if the tie still be unbroken, are compelled to daily to think how soon it certainly must, by one or the other being called away. Under this consciousness, I venture to break in upon you, and to offer my heartfelt sympathy. The separation cannot be long between you, nor would I advert to so obvious a reflection were it not that from the advanced age which my wife and I have, through God's blessing, attained together, I feel the power of it to soothe and mitigate and sustain, far beyond what is possible for your young friends to do. –
> It is more than half a century since, through your poetry, I became acquainted with your mind and feelings, and felt myself greatly your debtor for the truth and beauty with which you expressed the emotions

of a mourner. My Remembrance is thrown back upon those days with a Sadness which is deep, yet far from painful. A beloved Brother with whom I first read your Sonnets (it was in a recess from London Bridge) perished by Shipwreck long ago, and my most valued friends are gone to their graves. 'But not without hope we sorrow and we mourn'.[105] So I wrote when I lost that dear brother. So have I felt ever since, and so I am sure in my heart, you do now. God bless you through time and through eternity.[106]

When writing this letter Wordsworth was seventy-four years of age, and was obviously very conscious of how many of his contemporaries had died. In writing to Basil Montague[107] some four months later, he remarks: 'I don't wonder at your mention of the Friends whom we have lost by death. Bowles the poet still lives, and Rogers, all that survive of the poetical fraternity with whom I have had any intimacy'.[108]

It is probable that when Wordsworth mentioned in his letter the 'truth and beauty' with which Bowles 'expressed the emotions of a mourner' he was remembering Bowles's lines 'Influence of Time on Grief' – not one of his original fourteen sonnets but included in *Sonnets (3rd edition) with other Poems* published in 1794, which found a place in Sir Richard Quiller-Couch's *Oxford Book of English Verse*:

O Time! Who know'st a lenient hand to lay
Softest on Sorrow's wound, and slowly thence
(Lulling to sad repose the weary sense)
The faint pang stealest unperceived away;
On thee I rest my only hope at last,
And think, when thou hast dried the bitter tear
That flows in vain o'er all my sould held dear,
I may look back on every sorrow past,
And meet life's peaceful evening with a smile:-
As some lone bird, at day's departing hour,
Sings in the sun beam, of the transient shower
Forgetful, though its wings are wet the while:-
Yet ah! How much must that poor heart endure,
Which hopes from thee, and thee alone, a cure!

After his wife's death Bowles's health, both mental and physical, deteriorated to a marked degree and as a result he resigned the living of Bremhill in the following year. For some time the care of the parish would have been left largely in the hands of a curate and as a consquence it seems that, with Bowles being absent for a considerable period, the care of the people was neglected. Following Bowles's resignation the Rev. Francis Fisher was ordained to the curacy of the parish just as Bowles's successor entered on his duties, and in its obituary of Fisher published in 1858 the *Gentleman's Magazine* referred to 'The Rev. W.L. Bowles, whose great age and consequent non-residence had left ample scope for the energy and industry of his successor'. Until his death in 1850, therefore, Bowles remained in his house in the Close, where he was looked after by his servants – including Charles Rawlings, who on 4 June 1844 continued to keep the book of household accounts kept by Magdalene before her death, after it had been checked by Bowles's barrister nephew William Erle.

The Rev. Julian Young relates in his journal an incident that occurred one day during the long period of Bowles's declining years:

> When very old, and when his mental faculties were painfully on the wane, he was seated in his armchair at the window, in his prebendal house at Salisbury, when he perceived an unusual crowd of people of all sorts, tag, rag, and bobtail hurrying with eager steps in one direction.
>
> He enquired of his attendant the cause of this ferment, and was told that it was the first day of the great assizes. On hearing this, he hung his head and betrayed symptoms of profound depression. Presently, with an abruptness that might have startled men of less sensibility, the loud blast of a trumpet was heard, 'Good heavens!' he cried out, 'what is that?' His servant informed him that 'the Judges were come'. He had no sooner heard this, than he fell to the ground, crying out in accents of piteous alarm, 'Guilty! Guilty!' Then turning his silvery head to the person nearest him, he said, 'If my doom is sealed, and I am to go to prison, I implore you not to allow that solemn coxcombe F--- to attend me.' N.B. A clergyman against whom he had conceived an unaccountable antipathy.[109]

According to John Britton, the death of his wife left Bowles:

> . . . disconsolate, forlorn and almost helpless. He, however, lived, or rather existed, some years afterwards, at his official home in the Cathedral Close of Salisbury, but was deprived of mental consciousness: his existence was a blank, a sort of mechanical routine of motion and action, devoid of all those sympathies and enjoyments which distinguish man from the lower race of animals.[110]

In July 1845 a public dinner was held in Richmond as a tribute to Britton on his seventy-fourth birthday. Had he been younger and in better health, it is certain that Bowles would have been in the company assembled there, but it is an indication of the failure of his mental capacities that he is not even named among those who subscribed to the testimonial to Britton.

In October 1845 Charles Rawlings recorded in his account book that payment was made for 'carriage of wheel chair from Bath', and so it is probable that Bowles was wheeled out into the Close and perhaps into the Cathedral when he was no longer able to walk unaided. In May £1 19s was paid for making a suit of clothes for him, with the same amount being paid for more clothing in April the following year. There is a much repeated story that Bowles consistently refused to be measured by his tailor when ordering new clothes. It is certain that Ingram,[111] the Salisbury tailor who made and supplied the clothes at this time, would have done so without attempting to measure the old man.

In September 1845 a meeting of the Cathedral Chapter was held in Bowles's house, with just the Dean and Kerr Hamilton being present with the chapter clerk. In the autumn of the following year another meeting was held at his house with the same persons being present. It is unlikely that Bowles was able to make any useful contribution to the discussions, and it is probable that the meeting was held at his house merely to humour him. In the autumn of 1847 the same procedure was followed for the last time. It is certain that the Dean and the other canons by now would have realised that Bowles was, in John Britton's words, 'devoid of mental consciousness'.

By 1849 it is likely that Bowles did not remember that it was customary for him to pay for tea for the widows living in Seth Ward's college, just inside the Close and near the High Street gate in Salisbury, and so Rawlings paid £2 for this purpose in February 1849 and again in January 1850.

As Bowles's marriage had been childless it is certain that such of his siblings as were still living and their children would have seen to his welfare during his last years. One of his sisters, Amy, had married Peregrine Bingham, at one time rector of Berwick St John in Wiltshire, and after his death in 1826 she had married a soldier, Sir Richard Williams. He too predeceased her, and in 1855 she was living in the Close. Amy died in 1859 and was buried in the cloisters of the cathedral.

Bowles eventually died on 7 April 1850 at the age of eighty-eight in his canonical house in the Close, and was buried beside his wife in the Cathedral – not at Bremhill where, for many years, he had believed that his mortal remains would be laid to rest. He is said to have been the last person to be buried within the Cathedral.[112] He outlived all the poets whose work he had influenced or whom he had known, except for William Wordsworth who survived Bowles by just sixteen days.

In his biography published in the year of Bowles's death, John Britton describes his old friend in this way:

> Devoid of guile, as harmless as the dimpled infant, as bland and affable as courtesy and kindness in union, he gained the love and excited the sympathy of all who knew him; but he often aroused the pity and the fears of those who had witnessed or heard of the negligences and hair-breadth scrapes in which he was occasionally involved.[113]

A little later Alaric Alfred Watts, in a narrative of the life of his father, Bowles's friend Alaric Watts, wrote of Bowles:

> It might have been said of Bowles, as Lord Thurlow[114] said of Crabbe, 'he was like a Parson Adams as twelve to the dozen'. While of a tender and sensitive nature, and the parent, as I have said, of the poetical school of tasteful sensibility, he was a man of vigorous and independent judgement, great critical discrimination, and upon questions of argument feared no man living, laying about him in controversial conflict, when it presented itself, with all the readiness and aptitude to the use of his weapons of the admirable athlete and sound divine with whom I have ventured to compare him.[115]

Arthur Houlton[116] wrote:

> So death has bowl'd out old Bowles. 'I do remember him' – a queer, vain & eccentric fellow, good hearted & like Acraclitus wept while surveying 'the wicked actions of man' . . . some of the 'notes' from his fiddle were sweet, plaintive & harmonious – I shall never forget his reading to me from the play of [illegible] – he was suffering at the time from <u>tooth-ache</u>, groaning & ramming his head up the chimney.[117]

A monument was soon erected in the Cathedral as a memorial to both Bowles and his wife Magdalene. On the large Gothic tablet[118] he is aptly described as 'A Poet, Critic and Divine'. The memorial was erected 'by their kindred as a tribute of respect to departed worth, of which the writings of the Poet afford a more enduring and unimpeachable memorial'. It is perhaps doubtful whether his poetry will indeed be a more enduring memorial than that in the great cathedral in Salisbury, but these lines written by Coleridge may prove to be the more lasting of all:

My heart has thank'd thee, Bowles! for those soft strains,
That on the still air floating, tremblingly
Wak'd in me Fancy, Love and Sympathy!
For hence, not callous to a Brother's pains
Thro' youth's gay prime and thornless paths I went;
And when the *darker* day of life began,
And I did roam, a thought-bewilder'd man!
Thy kindred lays an healing solace lent.

Notes

Chapter 1

1 W. Lisle Bowles, *Scenes and Shadows of Days Departed* . . . (London 1837), pp. xvii–xviii.

2 John Collinson, *The History and Antiquities of the County of Somerset* . . .(Bath 1791), vol. III, p. 608.

3 W.L. Bowles, *The Parochial History of Bremhill, in the County of Wilts* . . . (London 1828), p. xvii.

4 The present Barton Hill House, part of the boarding complex of Shaftesbury School, is the successor to the Barton Hill House in which Bowles passed much of his childhood.

5 Mountain in central Greece revered by the ancient Greeks as the abode of Apollo and the Muses.

6 Wm. Lisle Bowles, *Days Departed or Banwell Hill* . . . (London 1829), p. 163. It is stated that this letter was writtten in 1779. This date cannot be right, however, and is probably a misprint for 1769.

7 Ibid., p. 165.

8 John Hutchins, *The History and Antiquities of the County of Dorset* (Westminster 1868), vol. III, p. 51, where a transcription of the wording on the stone above her grave can be read.

9 W.L. Bowles, op. cit., p. 260.

10 Joseph Warton (1722–1800), critic.

11 John Oglander (1737–94).

12 W.L. Bowles, op. cit., p. 226.

13 The author is indebted to Suzanne Foster, the Winchester College Archivist, for information about the admission of Bowles and his fellow scholars to the school.

14 'stomachy' meaning 'sullen'.

15 In Salisbury.

16 The street in Salisbury, now known as the Canal, had in Bowles's day an open drain or sewer running along it.

17 Wm Lisle Bowles, op. cit., pp. 191–4.

18 *Manual of Prayers for the use of Winchester Scholars* by Thomas Ken (1637–1711).

19 W.L. Bowles, *The Life of Thomas Ken D. D. Deprived Bishop of Bath and Wells* (London 1830/1), vol. 1, p. xiii.

20 Thomas Russell (1762–88), poet.

21 Thomas Warton (1728–90), historian.

22 George Gilfillan, *The Poetical Works of William Lisle Bowles with Memoir, Critical Dissertation, and Explanatory Notes* (Edinburgh 1855), vol. II, p. xiii.

23 W.L. Bowles, *Vindiciae Wykehamicae: or a Vindication of Winchester College* . . . (London 1818), pp. 31–2. The reference in the toast to Three Score and Ten relates to the number of scholars.

24 George Gilfillan, op. cit., vol. 1, p. 136.

25 Thomas Moore (1779–1852), poet.

26 William Lisle Bowles and John Gough Nichols, *Annals and Antiquities of Lacock Abbey* . . . (London 1835), p. xi.

27 George Gilfillan, op. cit., vol. 1, p. 77.

28 Henry Headley (1765–88), poet.

29 William Benwell (1765–96), classical scholar.

30 'Memoir of the Rev. W.L. Bowles' from the *New Monthly Magazine* reprinted in the *Devizes and*

Wiltshire Gazette (hereafter *DWG*) no. 253, 2 Nov. 1820.

31 Charles Abbott (1762–1832), lawyer.

32 John Hutchins, op. cit., p. 41.

33 Ibid., p. 50, a transcription of the wording on the memorial now no longer to be seen.

34 W.L. Bowles, *A Word on Cathedral Oratorios and Clergy-Magistrates Addressed to Lord Mountcashel* (London 1830), pp. 22–3.

35 Henry Kett (1761–1825), writer.

36 James Dallaway (1763–1834), topographer and writer.

37 Josiah Dornford (1764–97), writer.

38 George Richards (1767–1837), poet.

39 Leslie Stephen and Sidney Lee, eds, *Dictionary of National Biography* (London 1908) (hereafter *DNB*), vol. 17, p. 472.

40 Samuel Romilly (1757–1818), law reformer.

41 W. Lisle Bowles, op. cit., p. xliii.

42 The author is indebted to Colin Pedley whose 'Dating Bowles's Sonnets' in *Notes and Queries for Readers and Writers, Collectors and Librarians* (Oxford 1990), vol. CCXXXV, p. 403 brought the existence of the publication of Bowles's sonnet in November 1785 to his attention.

43 Wiltshire and Swindon Archives, Chippenham (hereafter WSA), D/1/14/1/20, ordination papers.

44 Charles Wake (1721–96), clergyman.

45 In 1801 East Knoyle is recorded as having 853 inhabitants, see *The Victoria History of the County of Wiltshire* (hereafter *VCH*) vol. IV, ed. Elizabeth Crittall (London 1959), p. 351.

46 *DWG*, no. 1095, 5 Jan. 1837, letter Bowles to the Editor.

47 William Beckford (1760–1844), author and connoisseur.

48 Henry St George (1581–1644), herald.

49 Sampson Lennard (d. 1633), herald.

50 For a pedigree of the Bowles family see Charles Bowles, *The Modern History of South Wiltshire* (London 1833), vol. IV, The Hundred of Chalk, pp. 36–7.

51 Shute Barrington (1734–1826), clergyman.

52 Mary Ransome, ed., *Wiltshire Returns to the Bishop's Visitation Queries 1783*, Wiltshire Record Society (Devizes 1972), pp. 131–2.

53 Christopher Wren (1591–1723), clergyman.

54 Thomas Grove (1758–1847), landowner.

55 John Kneller (1751–1811), landowner.

56 John Benett (1730–1808), clergyman.

57 Thomas Benett (1729–89), landowner.

58 James Still (1720–1803), landowner.

59 The *Gentleman's Magazine*, vol. LVIII for the year 1788, pt 2, pp. 1104–5.

60 Richard Cruttwell (c. 1747–99), printer.

61 W. Lisle Bowles, op. cit., p. xviv.

62 Charles Dilly (1739–1807), bookseller.

63 Footnote to the Introduction of the edition of the sonnets published in 1837.

64 *The Analytical Review or History of Literature, Domestic and Foreign . . .* (London 1789), Jan to April, pp. 339–40.

65 Richard Blackmore (c. 1655–1729), physician and writer.

66 Charlotte Smith (1749–1806), poetess.

67 The *Monthly Review; or Literary Journal* (London 1789), Jan to June, p. 465.

68 100 copies of the first edition were printed. Cecil Woolf in 'Some Uncollected Authors XVIII, William Lisle Bowles, 1762–1850', *Book Collector*, vol. 7, 1958, states that he had traced six copies of the first edition. One can be seen in the Public Reference Library in Bath.

69 *Bath Chronicle*, no. 1485, 14 May 1789.

70 Ibid., no. 1486, 21 May 1789.

71 Bowles was referring to *Elegaic Sonnets and other Essays* written by

Charlotte Smith and first published
in 1784, with a fifth edition
appearing in 1789.

72   Mary Locke (b. 1768), poet and
children's writer.

73   John Howard (c. 1726–90),
philanthropist.

74   Edward Easton (1720–95), publisher
and printer.

75   Edmund Burke (1729–97),
statesman.

76   This poem was translated into
French by Madame de Stael.

77   William Howley (1766–1848),
clergyman.

78   George Gilfillan, op. cit, p. 59.

79   The Gentleman's Magazine, vol LXI,
pt 2, p. 1114.

80   Ibid., vol. LXII, pt 2, p. 690.

81   Samuel Taylor Coleridge (1772–
1834), poet.

82   Thomas Fanshaw Middleton
(1769–1822), clergyman.

83   Biographia Literaria in H.J. Jackson,
ed., Samuel Taylor Coleridge The
Major Works (Oxford 2000) p. 164.

84   Ibid., p. 168.

85   Earl Leslie Griggs, Collected Letters
of Samuel Taylor Coleridge (Oxford
1956), p. 29. For a discussion as
to precisely which book of poems
Coleridge sent to Mary Evans see
Tomoya Oda 'The Book of Bowles's
Poems that Coleridge sent to Mary
Evans' in Notes and Queries for
Readers and Writers, Collectors and
Librarians, September 1994,
vol. CCXXXIX, p. 329.

86   Christopher Wordsworth (1774–
1846), later Master of Trinity
College, Cambridge.

87   J.B. Beer, Coleridge the Visionary
(London 1959), p. 76.

88   DNB, vol. 2, p. 978.

89   Douglas Brooks-Davies, ed., What
Sweeter Music: Poems on Music
(London 1999), p. 49.

90   Norman Fruman, Coleridge, The
Damaged Archangel (London 1972),
pp. 222–9, 231–5.

91   Ibid., p. 227.

92   See Tim May's 'Coleridge's Slave

Trade Ode and Bowles's' The
African' in Oxford Journals, Notes
and Queries, vol. 54, no. 4,
pp. 504–9.

93   William Wordsworth (1770–1850),
poet.

94   Robert Southey (1774–1843), poet.

95   Charles Lamb (1775–1834), essayist.

96   Howard Cooper, William Lisle
Bowles: A Wiltshire Parson and
his Place in Literary History, The
Hatcher Review (1989), vol. 3, no. 27,
p. 322.

97   Alexander Dyce, ed., Recollections
of the Table-Talk of Samuel Rogers
(London 1856), p. 261 n.

98   Garland Greever, A Wiltshire Parson
and His Friends: The Correspondence
of William Lisle Bowles together with
Four Hitherto Unidentified Reviews by
Coleridge (London 1926), pp. 21–2.

99   Robert Lovell (c. 1770–96), poet.

100 W. Lisle Bowles, op. cit, p. xlx.

101 The Poetical Works of Robert Southey
collected by himself (London 1838)
vol. 1, p. ix.

102 Garland Greever, op. cit., p. 20.

103 For an analysis of this sonnet see
Howard Cooper, op. cit., pp. 320–1.

104 Arthur Thomas Quiller-Couch
(1863–1944), man of letters.

105 Earl Leslie Griggs, op. cit., p. 94.

106 Joseph Priestley (1733–1804),
theologian and scientist.

107 Marquis de Lafayette (1757–1834),
French soldier and statesman.

108 Richard Holmes, Coleridge Early
Visions (London 1989), p. 81.

109 DNB, vol. XI, p. 425.

110 Richard Holmes, op. cit., p. 36.

111 Presumably the wife of John
Thelwall (1764–1834), the reformer
and expert on elocution.

112 Earl Leslie Griggs, op. cit., p. 287.

113 The Church Rambler; A Series of
Articles on the Churches in the
Neighbourhood of Bath (London
1878), pp. 406–7. This report of
Bowles's behaviour erroneously
suggests that it took place in the
office of William Meyer's Bath
Herald rather than in the office of

Cruttwell's *Bath Chronicle*.

114 *Salisbury and Winchester Journal* (hereafter *SWJ*), no. 2953, 12 Jan. 1795.

115 William Markham (1719–1807), clergyman.

116 Robert Burns (1759–96), poet.

117 William Cowper (1731–1800), poet.

118 E.V. Lucas, ed., *Letters of Charles and Mary Lamb 1796–1820* (can be viewed online).

119 Letters in H.J. Jackson, op. cit., p. 486.

120 E.V. Lucas, ed., *The Letters of Charles Lamb to which are added those to his sister Mary Lamb* (London 1935), vol. I, p. 51.

121 Ibid., p. 56.

122 Ibid., p. 73.

123 Donald H. Reiman, *William Lisle Bowles* (New York 1978), p. xi.

124 Richard Brinsley Sheridan (1751–1816), dramatist and parliamentarian.

125 Newton Ogle (1726–1804), clergyman.

126 Thomas Moore, *Memoirs of the Life of the Rt. Hon. Richard Brinsley Sheridan* (London 1825), p. 558.

127 Joseph Richardson (1755–1803), author.

128 John Petty Fitzmaurice, 2nd Marquis of Lansdowne (1765–1809).

129 *DWG*, no. 1013, 11 June 1835.

130 Sarah Siddons (1755–1831), actress.

131 John Philip Kemble (1757–1823), actor.

132 Garland Greever, op. cit., pp. 29–31.

133 William Linley (1771–1835), author and composer.

134 Sir Stafford Henry Northcote, 7th baronet (1762–1851).

135 Garland Greever, op. cit., pp. 154–5.

136 John Thelwall (1764–1834), reformer.

137 Earl Leslie Griggs, op. cit., p. 294.

138 John Prior Estlin (1747–1817), Unitarian minister.

139 Earl Leslie Griggs, op. cit., p. 327.

140 Molly Lefebure, *Samuel Taylor Coleridge: A Bondage of Opium* (London 1974), p. 24.

141 Richard Camplin (d. 1792), Deputy Receiver of the Royal Exchequer.

142 Garland Greever, op. cit., p. 33.

143 Ibid., pp. 32–3.

Chapter 2

1 Wiltshire and Swindon Archives (hereafter WSA) D/1/14/1/22, ordination papers.

2 *VCH*, vol. 13, ed. C.R. Elrington (London 1987), p. 141.

3 WSA, 2667/1/5/141, conveyance dated 23 Apr. 1793. In 1799 and 1803 he purchased two more cottages in Donhead St Mary with a small amount of land belonging to each, see WSA 2667/1/5/160 and 2667/1/5/179.

4 James Everard, 10th Baron Arundell of Wardour (1785–1834), landowner and historian.

5 Richard Colt Hoare, 2nd Baronet (1758–1838), landowner and historian.

6 James Everard, Baron Arundell and Sir. R.C. Hoare, *The Modern History of South Wiltshire* (London 1829), vol. IV, The Hundred of Dunworth, p. 36.

7 This letter and all the following letters passing between Bowles and Harriet and Magdalene Wake are deposited in the State University of New Jersey, New Brunswick, New Jersey, USA.

8 Dr Wake's sister Magdalen, widow of Bowles's kinsman William Bowles.

9 Shute Barrington (1734–1826), clergyman.

10 Harriet's sister.

11 Frances, the wife of Dr John Benet, rector of Donhead St Andrew. Dr Benet spelt his name in this way.

12 Cranborne Chase.

13 John Still (1761–1839), clergyman. His brother James married Harriet's sister Charlotte.

14 Peter Still (1759–1832), barrister and

brother of James Still.

15 The *Gentleman's Magazine*, vol. 63 (1793), p. 380.

16 *SWJ*, no. 2916, 28 Apr. 1794.

17 Ibid., no 2937, 22 Sept. 1794.

18 James Easton (1727–99), printer and publisher.

19 There is a copy of this pamphlet in the Hoskins Library, University of Tennessee.

20 Francis Rivington (1745–1822) and Charles Rivington (1754–1831), publishers.

21 Thomas Cadell (1773–1836) and William Davies (d. 1820), publishers.

22 John Murray (1778–1843), publisher.

23 The *Gentleman's Magazine* (1797), vol. LXVII, pt 2, p. 547.

24 Jeremiah Whitaker Newman, ed., *Lounger's Common Place Book . . .* (London 1796), 2. 133–5.

25 John Saville Ogle (1767–1838), clergyman.

26 Charles Cocks, 1st Baron Somers (1725–1806).

27 William Markham (1719–1807), clergyman.

28 The personal representatives of a deceased incumbent would normally be responsible for the cost of putting the parsonage in good repair, but in this case Bowles probably knew that Ogle would bear the cost himself.

29 Newton Ogle, Dean of Winchester.

30 Probably John Wall Callcott (1766–1821), composer.

31 The Archbishop of York's palace.

32 George O'Brien, Earl of Egremont (1751–1827).

33 Presumably in connection with Bowles's pursuit of another living.

34 Frederica, daughter of William Markham, Archbishop of York.

35 David William Murray, 3rd Earl of Mansfield (1777–1840).

36 John Colpoys (c. 1742–1821), admiral.

37 This was a false rumour.

38 John Somers (1760–1841), later 2nd Baron Somers and 1st Earl Somers.

39 *SWJ*, no. 3074, 27 May 1797.

40 The whole of the poem is reproduced in John Hutchins, op. cit., p. 41.

41 Richard Gough (1735–1809), antiquary.

42 The whole of Gough's verses are reproduced in John Hutchins, op. cit., p. 112.

43 *SWJ*, no. 4005, 25 Dec. 1797.

44 Ibid., no. 4026, 21 May 1798.

45 Ibid., no. 4047, 17 Sept. 1798.

46 Ibid., no. 4026, 21 May 1798.

47 John Britton (1771–1857), antiquary.

48 John Britton, *The Biography of John Britton, F.S.A. . . .* (London 1850), part 1, p. 291.

49 The *European Magazine*, July 1798.

50 Ibid., Nov. 1803.

51 David J. Jeremy, 'A Local Crisis between Establishment and Nonconformity: The Salisbury Village Preaching Controversy, 1798–1799', *Wiltshire Archaeological and Natural History Magazine*, 61 (1966), pp. 63–84. The author is indebted to the writer of this paper that drew his attention to Bowles's part in this controversy.

52 John Douglas (1721–1807), clergyman.

53 *SWJ*, no. 4038, 20 Aug. 1798.

54 Henry Wansey (c. 1752–1827), antiquary.

55 John Hatchard (1769–1849), publisher.

56 *SWJ*, no. 4050, 5 Nov. 1798.

57 John Malham, *A Broom for the Conventicle . . .* (Salisbury 1798), one of the Wanseyan Controversy pamphlets.

58 William Kingsbury (1744–1818), dissenting minister and author of *An Apology for Village Preachers . . .* (Southampton 1798), one of the Wanseyan Controversy pamphlets.

59 David J. Jeremy, op. cit., pp. 77–8.

60 George Canning (1770–1827), statesman.

61 The *Anti-Jacobin Review and Magazine or, Monthly Political and Literary Censor, from January to April*

(Inclusive) 1799 . . ., vol. II, p. 301. No copy of this sermon appears to have survived although, as well as being mentioned in the *Anti-Jacobin*, it is also referred to in George Baker's account of Bowles's career in his *History and Antiquities of the County of Northampton* (London 1822–41), vol. I, p. 703.

62 Charles Dilly (1739–1807), bookseller.

63 The *Anti-Jacobin . . .*, op. cit., p. 426,

64 John Gifford (1758–1818), author.

65 Richard Polwhele (1760–1838), clergyman, poet and historian.

66 Emily Lorraine de Montluzin, *The Anti-Jacobins 1798–1800: The Early Contributors to the Anti-Jacobin Review* (Basingstoke 1988), p. 177.

67 Elizabeth Hall, 'Sheridan and the Rev. William Lisle Bowles: an Uncollected Bowles Poem and the Dating of Two Sheridan Letters' in *Notes and Queries for Readers and Writers, Collectors and Librarians*, March 1976 New Series vol. 23, no. 3, p. 107.

68 In *Blackwood's Edinburgh Magazine*, July 1822, in a review of Bowles's *Grave of the Last Saxon*, the writer refers to 'that beautiful Latin poem which we heard the author recite in the Theatre on Commemoration Day, five lustres [25 years] ago'. It was in reality twenty-three or twenty-four years before.

69 *SWJ*, no. 5002, 23 Sept. 1799.

70 Samuel Rogers (1763–1855), poet.

71 Garland Greever, op. cit., p. 94.

72 Ibid., p. 96.

73 Nathan Drake (1766–1836), literary essayist.

74 Tom Sheridan (1775–1817), colonial treasurer.

75 Charles Knyvett (1773–1852), musician.

76 Garland Greever, op. cit., p. 92.

77 Probably William Preston (1742–1818), printer.

78 Sons of the famous Salisbury violin maker Benjamin Banks.

79 There is a copy of Bowles's duet in the British Library, shelfmark H. 1663 (32).

80 William Sotheby (1757–1833), author.

81 Earl Leslie Griggs, *Collected Letters of Samuel Taylor Coleridge* (Oxford), pp. 855–9.

82 Perhaps *Translation of a Latin Poem by the Rev. Newton Ogle* printed in George Gilfillan, op. cit., vol. I, p. 100, in the title of which Ogle is mistakenly described by Gilfillan as Dean of Manchester rather than Dean of Winchester.

83 Earl Leslie Griggs, op. cit., p. 812.

84 Ibid., pp. 862–7.

85 *DNB*, vol. 2, p. 56.

86 John Willes (1721–84), landowner.

87 The *Gentleman's Magazine*, vol. LXXV, pt 2, p. 732.

88 Alexander Pope (1688–1744), poet.

89 Davies to Bowles, 10 Jan. 1802: Harvard University, MS. Eng. 505.

90 Dr William Vincent's commentary on Arrian's *Voyage of Nearchus* (1797).

91 Davies to Bowles, 17 Jan. 1802: Harvard University, MS Eng. 505.

92 Bowles to Cadell & Davies, 22 June 1802: Box/Folder Bor-Brou/Bowles, Manuscripts Division, Department of Rare Books and Special Collections, Princeton University Library.

93 Account, Apr. 1802: Huntingdon Library, Art Collections, and Botanical Gardens, San Marino, California, ref. CD 3.

94 Garland Greever, op. cit., pp. 94–5.

95 Henry Bowles (1765–1804), physician.

96 *The Poetical Works of Milman, Bowles, Wilson and Barry Cornwall* (Paris 1829), p. 149.

97 *SWJ*, no. 3512, 22 Aug. 1803.

98 Ibid., no. 3513, 29 Aug. 1803.

99 John Hely-Hutchinson (1757–1832), military commander.

100 William Preston (1742–1818), printer.

101 Colin Pedley, 'Two Uncollected Poems by William Lisle Bowles' in *Notes and Queries for Readers and*

Writers, Collectors and Librarians (Oxford 1990), vol. CCXXXV, p. 404.

102 *SWJ*, no. 3547, 23 April 1804.

103 George Augustus Frederick (1762–1830) later George IV.

104 *SWJ*, no. 3552, 28 May 1804.

105 Garland Greever, op. cit., p. 93.

106 *The Victoria History of the County of Buckingham*, William Page, ed. (London 1927), vol. 4, p. 148.

107 John Moore (1730–1805), clergyman.

108 Charles Spencer, 3rd Duke of Marlborough (1706–58).

109 Garland Greever, op. cit., p. 7.

110 *SWJ*, no. 3536, 6 Feb. 1804.

Chapter 3

1 John Britton, *A Topographical and Historical Description of the County of Wilts . . .*(London 1814), p. 534.

2 *VCH*, Elizabeth Crittall, ed. (London 1959), vol5   W.L. Bowles, *Poems (Never before Published) Written Chiefly at Bremhill* (London 1809), p. 2.

3 WSA, 451/12, schedule of dilapidations dated Aug. 1804.

4 Henry Petty Fitzmaurice, 3rd Marquis of Lansdowne (1780–1863).

5 W.L. Bowles, *Poems (Never before Published) Written Chiefly at Bremhill* (London 1809), p. 2.

6 See Christopher Thacker, *Masters of the Grotto: Joseph and Josiah Lane* (Tisbury 1976).

7 Lansdowne to Bowles, 4 Sept. 1810: William L. Clements Library, University of Michigan.

8 Bryan Waller Procter (1787–1874), poet.

9 Richard Willard Armour, *Barry Cornwall: a Biography of Bryan Waller Procter with a Selected Collection of Hitherto Unpublished Letters* (Boston 1935), p. 37. Bryan Waller Procter (Barry Cornwall), *An Autobiographical fragment and biographical notes* (London 1877), pp. 131–2.

10 The famous Nelson Pillar was duly completed in 1808 and stood until 1966, when it was blown up by the IRA.

11 Lansdowne to Bowles, 10 Jan. 1806: William L. Clements Library, University of Michigan.

12 This poem is printed in George Gilfillan, *The Poetical Works of William Lisle Bowles with Memoir, Critical Dissertation, and Explanatory Notes* (Edinburgh 1855), vol. 1, p. 216.

13 George Gilfillan, ibid., p. 217.

14 Harriet Grove (1791–1867), daughter of Bowles's friend Thomas Grove of Ferne.

15 Desmond Hawkins, *The Grove Diaries: the Rise and Fall of an English Family 1809–1925* (Wimborne 1995), pp. 87–8.

16 William Cunnington (1754–1810), antiquary.

17 Philip Crocker (1780–1840), surveyor and artist.

18 Sir Richard Colt Hoare, *The Ancient History of South Wiltshire* (London 1812), p. 239.

19 The *Gentleman's Magazine*, vol. 87 (1812) pt 2, p. 122.

20 Bowles to Colt Hoare, 16 June 1823, letter on the reverse of a printed broadsheet of one of Bowles's poems offered for sale by Bonhams in 2004.

21 Wiltshire Archaeological and Natural History Society's Library, Devizes, Wiltshire Cuttings, Vol. 11, p. 169.

22 George Gilfillan, op. cit., vol. 2, p. xv.

23 David Wilkie (1785–1841), painter.

24 Joseph Mallord Turner (1775–1851), painter. The painting described as *Morning* by Bowles was, perhaps, Turner's *Sun rising through Vapour* exhibited in 1807.

25 Augustus Wall Callcott (1779–1844), landscape painter.

26 George Howland Beaumont (1753–1827), connoisseur and landscape painter.

27 Philip James de Loutherbourg (1740–1812), painter.

28 George Gilfillan, op. cit., vol. 1, p. 163.

29 Benjamin West (1738–1820), painter.

30 Frank Sayers (1763–1817), poet.

31 *DNB*, vol. 17, p. 881.

32 Presumably Thomas Gray (1716–71), poet.

33 Letter published online: http:/198. 82. 142. 160.

34 George Gordon Byron, 6th Baron Byron (1788–1824), poet.

35 Hafiz (b. 1310–25–1388), Persian poet.

36 Frederick Page, ed., *Byron Poetical Works* (London 1970), p. 117.

37 Ibid., p. 866.

38 Ibid., p. 118.

39 Ibid, p. 118.

40 John Cam Hobhouse (1786–1869), statesman.

41 Jacob Johan van Rennes, *Bowles, Byron and the Pope-Controversy* (New York 1966), p. 4.

42 Frederick Page, op. cit., p. 118.

43 A reference to Bowles's sonnet written at Ostend and published as one of the original fourteen sonnets.

44 Thomas Moore's original poetry was written in the name of the 'Late Thomas Little'.

45 Words from Bowles's *Spirit of Discovery*.

46 John Hervey, Baron Hervey of Ickworth (1696–1743), memoir writer, attacked by Pope as 'Lord Fanny'.

47 Edmund Curll (1675–1747), bookseller, attacked in Pope's *Dunciad*.

48 David Mallet (1705–65), poet and writer who attacked Pope's memory.

49 John Dennis (1657–1734), critic, replied to Pope having been satirised by him.

50 James Ralph (1705–62), poet, attacked Pope in a satire.

51 Pope's *Dunciad* (1728).

52 The *Gentleman's Magazine*, vol. 87 (1816) pt 2, p. 333.

53 Leslie A. Marchant, ed., '*So late into the night*' *Byron's Letters and Journals* vol. 5 1816–1817 (London 1976), p. 241.

54 Richard Warner (1763–1857), clergyman and author.

55 Peter Paul Pallet [Richard Warner], *Bath Characters or Sketches from Life* (London 1808), pp. 80–1.

56 Lansdowne to Bowles, 19 Nov. 1808: William L. Clements Library, University of Michigan.

57 Henry Thomas Fox-Strangeways, 3rd Earl of Ilchester (1747–1802).

58 W.L. Bowles, *The Parochial History of Bremhill in the County of Wilts . . .* (London 1828), p. 154.

59 Bowles to Phillips, 2 Nov. 1824: Huntingdon Library, Art Collections, and Botanical Gardens, San Marino, California, ref. HM 11457.

60 Emma Peachey was Elizabeth Charter's sister and the first wife of General Peachey, a friend of both Bowles and Robert Southey.

61 A.M. Broadley and Walter Jerrold, *The Romance of an Elderly Poet: A Hitherto Unknown Chapter in the Life of George Crabbe Revealed by his Ten Years' Correspondence with Elizabeth Charter 1815–1825* (London 1913), pp. 63–4.

62 The *Gentleman's Magazine*, vol. 79 (1809), pt 1, p. 551.

63 Ibid., vol. 80 (1810), pt 1, p. 648.

64 William Wyndham Grenville, Baron Grenville (1759–1834), statesman.

65 The *Gentleman's Magazine*, op. cit., pt 2, p. 263.

66 Isabella Henrietta, Countess of Cork and Orrery (d. 1843).

67 W.L. Bowles, *Poems (Never before Published) Written Chiefly at Bremhill* (London 1809), p. 91.

68 The *Gentleman's Magazine*, vol. 82 (1812) pt 2, p. 261.

69 W.L. Bowles, *The Missionary; A poem* (London 1815), pp. vii–viii.

70 William Miller (1769–1844), publisher.

71 The first volume of Colt Hoare's *The Ancient History of South Wiltshire* published by Miller in 1812.

72 Bowles to Miller, 14 June 1812: National Library of Scotland, John Murray Archive, MS 12604/1137.

73 Garland Greever, *A Wiltshire Parson and his Friends; The Correspondence of William Lisle Bowles with Four Hitherto Unidentified Reviews by Coleridge* (London 1926), pp. 139–40.

74 Walter Scott (1771–1832), novelist and poet.

75 Bowles to Murray, 26 June 1812: National Library of Scotland, John Murray Archive, MS 12604/1137.

76 Bowles to Murray, 14 Dec. 1812: ibid.

77 Garland Greever, op. cit., pp. 140–1.

78 Murray to Bowles, between 20 and 24 Dec. 1812: ibid., p. 141.

79 Bowles to Murray, 24 Dec. 1812: National Library of Scotland, John Murray Archive, MS 12604/1137.

80 Garland Greever, op. cit., pp. 142–3.

81 John Benett (1773–1852), a Wiltshire landowner and friend of Bowles. Benett's father and Bowles's wife were first cousins, both being grandchildren of Archbishop Wake.

82 Garland Greever, op. cit., pp. 143–4.

83 Robert Nares (1753–1829), formerly keeper of manuscripts at the British Museum, Archdeacon of Stafford and Vicar of St Mary's, Reading, until 1818.

84 Edward Adolphus, 11ᵗʰ Duke of Somerset (1775–1855).

85 Henry Richard Vassall Fox (1773–1840), 3ʳᵈ Baron Holland, stateman.

86 Lansdowne to Bowles, 5 Jan. 1813: William L. Clements Library, University of Michigan.

87 *Wiltshire Meeting on the Roman Catholic Claims; held at The Devizes, Jan. 27ᵗʰ, 1813* (London 1813), p. 1.

88 *SWJ*, no. 3953, 1 Feb. 1813.

89 Howley to Bowles, 6 Aug. 1813: Lambeth Palace Library, MS 3355, ff1–5.

90 Howley to Bowles, 13 Aug. 1813: ibid.

91 William Douglas (1769–1819), clergyman.

92 John Douglas (1721–1807), clergyman.

93 Germaine de Stael (1766–1817), political socialite.

94 P.W. Claydon, *Rogers and his Contemporaries* (London 1889),

vol. 1, pp. 135–6.

95 Maria Fairweather, *Madame de Stael* (London 2005), p. 418.

96 Ibid., p. 424.

97 Lansdowne to Bowles, Oct. 1813, William L. Clements Library, University of Michigan.

98 Maria Edgeworth (1767–1849), novelist.

99 Christina Colvin, ed., *Maria Edgeworth, Letters from England, 1813–1844* (London 1971), p. 96.

100 Garland Greever, op. cit., p. 102.

101 de Stael to Bowles, [Oct. 1813], ibid.

102 Lansdowne to Bowles, 2 Aug. 1814: William L. Clements Library, University of Michigan.

103 Garland Greever, op. cit., p. 103.

104 Ibid., pp. 106–7. For copies of further correspondence between Lady Lansdowne and Magdalene Bowles concerning the running of the school in Bremhill, see Garland Greever, op. cit., pp. 108–13.

105 *Digest of Returns to the Select Committee on the Education of the Poor . . . County of Wilts* (1818), p. 1017.

106 Thomas Moore, *The Works of Lord Byron with his Letters and Journals and his Life* (London 1832–3), vol. V, p. 165.

107 Bowles to Murray, 6 Dec. 1814: National Library of Scotland, John Murray Archive, MS 12604/1137.

108 Garland Greever, op. cit., p. 146.

109 Murray to Bowles [between 6 and 13 Dec, 1814]: ibid., p. 148.

110 *SWJ*, no. 4092, 28 Aug. 1815.

111 The whole hymn is printed in Gilfillan, op. cit., vol II, pp. 328–9.

112 William Peachey, Major-General 1813, Lt-General 1825.

113 Bowles to Southey, 11 Feb. 1815: The Carl H. Pforzheimer Collection of Shelley and His Circle, New York Public Library, Astor, Lenox and Tilden Foundations, Misc. 0375.

114 Garland Greever, op. cit., pp. 149–50.

115 Kathleen Coburn, ed., *The Notebooks of Samuel Taylor Coleridge* (London 1957), vol. 3 1808–1819, Text, f52, 4233, L125.

116 Richard Holmes, *Coleridge: Darker Reflections* (London 1998), p. 374.
117 Probably *The Fifth Booke of the Church* (1610) by Richard Field (1561–1616).
118 Wilts Cuttings, Cunnington vol. 4, p. 34 in the Wiltshire Archaeological and Natural History Society Library, Devizes.
119 Richard Holmes, op. cit., p. 377.
120 P.W. Claydon, op. cit., pp. 192–3.
121 Bowles to Murray, 30 May 1815: National Library of Scotland, John Murray Archive, MS 1260/1137.
122 Andrew Nicholson, ed., *The Letters of John Murray to Lord Byron* (Cambridge 2007), p. 197.
123 James Dallaway (1763–1834), topographer.
124 George Crabbe (1754–1832), clergyman and poet.
125 P.W. Claydon, op. cit., pp. 195–7.
126 Garland Greever, op. cit., p. 151.
127 Cecil Woolf, 'Some Uncollected Authors XVIII William Lisle Bowles, 1762–1850', *Book Collector*, vol. 7, 1958, p. 407.
128 Garland Greever, op. cit., p. 147.
129 John Britton, *The Auto-biography of John Britton . . .* (London 1850), Pt 1, p. 292.
130 William Shenstone (1714–1763), poet.
131 Timothy Mowl, *Historic Gardens of Wiltshire* (Stroud 2004), pp. 124–5.
132 St Bruno of Cologne (c. 1030–1101).
133 The *Gentleman's Magazine*, Sept. 1814, pp. 203–4.
134 Wilfred S. Dowden, ed., *The Journal of Thomas Moore* vol. 1 (Newark 1983), p. 33.
135 Nikolaus Pevsner, *The Buildings of England, Wiltshire* (Harmondsworth 1963), p. 127.
136 John Skinner (1772–1839), clergyman and antiquary.
137 Howard and Peter Coombs, *Journal of a Somerset Rector 1803–1834* (Weston-super-Mare 1987), p. 121.
138 Garland Greever, op. cit., p. 73.
139 Ibid., pp. 73–4.
140 A.M. Broadley and Walter Jerrold,

141 op. cit., p. 101.
141 Ibid., p. 114.
142 George Crabbe, *The Poetical Works of the Rev. George Crabbe: with his letters and journals, and his life* (London 1834), p. 270.
143 Doubtless George Howland Beaumont.
144 Bowles to Southey, 30 Dec. 1815: The Carl H. Pforzheimer Collection of Shelley and His Circle, New York Public Library, Astor, Lenox and Tilden Foundations, Misc. 03736.
145 Kathleen Coburn, op. cit., Notes, 4300,f63.
146 John William Cunningham (1780–1861), clergyman.
147 Garland Greever, op. cit., pp. 151–3.
148 Lady Lansdowne to Mrs Bowles [undated]: ibid., p. 110.
149 George Lavington (1684–1762), clergyman.
150 Bowles to Murray, 13 Feb. 1816: National Library of Scotland, John Murray Archive, MS 12604/1137.
151 The *Quarterly Review*.
152 William Godwin, *Lives of Edward and John Philips, Nephews and Pupils of Milton* (1815).
153 Bowles to Murray, 14 Mar. 1816: National Library of Scotland, John Murray Archive, MS 12604/1137.
154 Joseph Stenett (1663–1713), Baptist minister and hymn writer.
155 Garland Greever, op. cit., p. 116.
156 John Scott (1794–1871), journalist.
157 John Hamilton Reynolds (1796–1852), poet.
158 William Robert Spencer (1769–1834), poet and wit who moved in aristocratic circles.
159 William Hayley (1745–1820), poet.
160 John Wilson (1785–1854), author and 'Christopher North' of *Blackwood's Magazine*.
161 Edmund Spenser (c. 1552–99), poet.
162 John Milton (1608–74), poet.
163 Leonidas M. Jones, ed., *Selected Prose of John Hamilton Reynolds* (Cambridge, Massachusetts 1966), p. 50.
164 Ibid., pp. 51–2.

165 Garland Greever, op. cit., pp. 74–5.
166 *SWJ*, no. 4204, 27 Oct. 1817.
167 P.W. Clayden, op. cit., pp. 250–1.
168 Wilfred S. Dowden, ed., *The Letters of Thomas Moore 1793–1818* (Oxford 1964), vol. 1, p. 431.
169 Ronan Kelly, *Bard of Erin: The Life of Thomas Moore* (Dublin 2008), p. 316.
170 James Henry Leigh Hunt (1784–1859), essayist.
171 Leigh Hunt, *Lord Byron and Some of his Contemporaries with Recollections of the Author's Life and of his visit to Italy* (London 1828), vol. 1, p. 3.
172 Wilfred S. Dowden, op. cit., p. 442.
173 James Corry, an old friend of Thomas Moore from Ireland and later Clerk to the Irish Journals in the House of Commons.
174 Paul Methuen, later 1st Baron Methuen (1779–1839).
175 Wilfred S. Dowden, op. cit., p. 460.
176 Wilfred S. Dowden, ed., *The Journal of Thomas Moore* (Newark 1983), vol. 1, pp. 33–4.
177 Ibid., p. 36.
178 Stephen Woolriche, a surgeon friend of Thomas Moore.
179 Wilfred S. Dowden, *The Journal of Thomas Moore*, op. cit., p. 50.
180 *Wiltshire Archaeological and Natural History Society Magazine*, 24 (1889), p. 254.
181 Angelica Catalini (1782–1849), Italian opera singer.
182 Wilfred S. Dowden, *The Journal of Thomas Moore*, op. cit., p. 55.
183 Characters from Shakespeare's *The Tempest*.
184 *The Works of Mr Thomas Brown*, published early in the eighteenth century and a very secular work to find in a parson's library.
185 Wilfred S. Dowden, *The Journal of Thomas Moore*, op. cit., p. 57.
186 *SWJ*, no. 4252, 28 Sept. 1818.
187 The poet Samuel Rogers.
188 William Crowe (1745–1829), clergyman and poet, rector of Alton Barnes.
189 Philipp Melanchton (1497–1560), German theologian.

190 Wilfred S. Dowden, *The Journal of Thomas Moore*, op. cit., p. 67.
191 George Crabbe, *Life and Poems of the Rev. George Crabbe* (London 1834), vol. 1, pp. 262–3.
192 Wilfred S. Dowden, *The Journal of Thomas Moore*, op. cit., p. 104.
193 Almost certainly the family of William Macdonald, vicar of Bishop's Cannings and later Archdeacon of Wiltshire and a canon residentiary of Salisbury Cathedral.
194 Wilfred S. Dowden, *The Journal of Thomas Moore*, op. cit., p. 104.
195 Louisa Stuart Costello (1799–1870), artist and author.
196 Henry Hall Joy (1786–1840), barrister.
197 Michael Joy of Hartham Park near Biddestone and one of Bowles's fellow magistrates.
198 Wilfred S. Dowden, *The Journal of Thomas Moore*, op. cit., p. 104.
199 Henry Peter Brougham (1778–1868), later Lord Chancellor and Baron Brougham and Vaux.
200 Wilfred S. Dowden, *The Journal of Thomas Moore*, op. cit., pp. 82–3.
201 Ibid., p. 143.
202 Bowles to Brougham, 30 Dec. 1818: The Brougham Papers, University College London Library Services, Special Collections, MS. HB 32,140
203 *The Poetical Works of Milman, Bowles, Wilson, and Barry Cornwall* (Paris 1829), p. vi.
204 William Pole-Tylney-Long-Wellesley (1788–1857), later 4th Earl of Mornington.
205 A 'plumper' was a vote cast for one of the candidates only.
206 Lady Lansdowne to unknown, 30 June 1818: William L. Clements Library, University of Michigan.
207 The *Gentleman's Magazine*, vol. 88 (1818) pt 1, pp. 45–6.
208 W.L. Bowles, *The Parochial History of Bremhill in the County of Wilts*, op. cit., p. 170.
209 Christina Colvin, op. cit., pp. 97–8.
210 Hoare's gift to Magdalene and over

600 of the Buckler watercolours of Wiltshire churches are in the possession of the Wiltshire Archaeological and Natural History Society, Devizes.

211 Watercolour in the Library of the Wiltshire Archaeological and Natural History Society, Devizes.

212 John Britton, op. cit., p. 292.

213 Mary Anne (b. 1794), wife of Stephen Dark of Maiden Bradley.

214 Henry Dark (d. 1817), purchased the manor of Whitley c. 1794.

Chapter 4

1 Presumably Philip Melanchton (1497–1560), German Protestant reformer.

2 Thomas Campbell (1777–1844), poet.

3 Wilfred S. Dowden, ed., *The Journal of Thomas Moore* (Newark 1983), vol. I, p. 151.

4 Paul Methuen of Corsham House.

5 Doubtless 'A Landscape called Evening' and 'A Landscape representing dawn of morning' both by Claude Lorrain (1600–82) mentioned on pp. 35 and 43 of John Britton, *An Historical Account of Corsham House, in Wiltshire; The Seat of Paul Cobb Methuen, Esq, with a Catalogue of his Celebrated Collection of Pictures* (London 1806).

6 Wilfred S. Dowden, op. cit., p. 152.

7 *The Bath and Cheltenham Gazette*, vol. VII, no. 338, 24 March 1819.

8 Thomas Campbell (1777–1844), poet.

9 Wilfred S. Dowden, op. cit., pp. 152–3.

10 James Mackintosh (1765–1832), philosopher.

11 *Thoughts on the Increase of Crimes* was duly printed and published in Salisbury by Brodie and Dowding.

12 Wilfred S. Dowden, op. cit., p. 155.

13 *DNB*, vol. II, p. 978.

14 Garland Greever, *A Wiltshire Parson and his Friends: The Correspondence of William Lisle Bowles with Four

Hitherto Unidentified Reviews by Coleridge* (London 1926), p. 117.

15 Ibid., pp. 117–8.

16 Ibid., p. 119.

17 Wilfred S. Dowden, op. cit., p. 164.

18 Garland Greever, op. cit., p. 84.

19 Wilfred S. Dowden, op. cit., p. 168.

20 Ibid., p. 172.

21 John Dugdale Astley (1778–1842), landowner and later baronet.

22 For a full account of both the 1818 and 1819 county elections see Robert Moody, *Mr Benett of Wiltshire: the life of a County Member of Parliament 1773–1852* (East Knoyle 2005), pp. 53–118.

23 A.M. Broadley and Walter Jerrold, op. cit., pp. 237–8.

24 Ibid., p. 202.

25 Longleat House in Wiltshire, seat of the Marquis of Bath.

26 Lansdowne to Bowles, undated: William L. Clements Library, University of Michigan.

27 Lucilio Vanini (1585–1619), Italian free thinker.

28 Moore's first literary success was a metrical translation of *Anacreon* (1800), dedicated to the Prince of Wales.

29 A.M. Broadley and Walter Jerrold, op. cit., p. 241.

30 John Russell (1792–1878), statesman, later 1st Earl Russell.

31 Probably Wadham Locke (1780–1835), MP for Devizes.

32 Probably Philip Bury Duncan (1772–1863), keeper of the Ashmolean Museum, Oxford, and his brother John Shute Duncan, his predecessor as keeper of the Ashmolean Museum.

33 Moore's children.

34 The oratorio *Palestine* was the greatest work of William Crotch (1775–1847) and first performed in 1812.

35 Catherine Stephens (1794–1882), singer and actress, later Countess of Essex.

36 Probably his *A Sicilian Story, with Diego de Montilla and other poems*.

37 William Cobbett (1762–1835), politician.

38 Humorous skits written by Moore under the pseudonym Thomas Brown.

39 Lord John Russell, ed., *Memoirs Journal and Correspondence of Thomas Moore* (London 1860), pp. 261–2.

40 *The Quarterly Review*, vol. XXIII, no. XLVI, May & July 1820, pp. 400–34.

41 James Burnett, Lord Monboddo (1714–99), Scottish judge and writer.

42 Octavius Graham Gilchrist (1779–1823), antiquary.

43 Garland Greever, op. cit, pp. 119–21.

44 Bowles to Southey, 22 Oct. 1820: The Carl H. Pforzheimer Collection of Shelley and His Circle, New York Public Library, Astor, Lenox and Tilden Foundations, Misc 0374.

45 Bowles to Murray, 22 Oct. 1820: National Library of Scotland, John Murray Archive, MS 12604/1137.

46 Garland Greever, op. cit., p. 123.

47 Bowles to Murray, 22 Oct. 1820: ibid., pp. 121–3.

48 John Wilson (1758–1854), poet and author.

49 William Gifford (1756–1826), editor.

50 John Gibson Lockhart (1794–1854), biographer.

51 Bowles to Wilson, 30 Oct. 1821: Box/Folder B2/F12, Manuscripts Division, Department of Rare Books and Special Collections, Princeton University Library.

52 Theocritus, third century BC, Greek poet.

53 Bowles later regretted making these remarks about Gilchrist's station in life, see Jacob Johan van Rennes, *Bowles, Byron and the Pope Controversy* (New York 1966), p. 28. The author acknowledges the very considerable assistance he has received from this work in unravelling the complexities of the controversy.

54 Isaac D'Israeli (1766–1848), author.

55 *DNB*, vol. 7, p. 1223.

56 Andrew Nicholson, ed., *The Letters of John Murray to Lord Byron* (Cambridge 2007), p. 319.

57 Frederick Page, ed., *Byron Poetical Works* (London 1970), p. 108.

58 Andrew Nicholson, op. cit., p. 354.

59 Ibid., p. 403.

60 Ibid., p. 386.

61 Bowles to Murray, 6 Apr. 1821: National Library of Scotland, John Murray Archive, MS 12604/1137.

62 Wilfred S. Dowden, ed., *The Journal of Thomas Moore* (Newark 1984), vol. 2, 1821–1825, p. 443.

63 Martha Blount (1690–1762), friend of Alexander Pope.

64 A reference to Bowles's *The Invariable Principles of Poetry . . .* published in 1819.

65 Thomas Medwin, *Conversations of Lord Byron: noted during a residence with his Lordship at Pisa in the years 1821 and 1822* (London 1824), p. 299.

66 Leigh Hunt, *Lord Byron and Some of his Contemporaries with Recollections of the Author's Life and of his visit to Italy* (London 1828), vol. 1, pp. 178–9.

67 Jacob van Rennes, op. cit., pp. 46–7.

68 Thomas Medwin (1788–1869), biographer.

69 Thomas Medwin, op. cit., pp. 298–9.

70 Bowles to Murray, 15 Apr. 1821: National Library of Scotland, John Murray Archive, MS 12604/1137.

71 Bowles to Murray, 17 Apr. 1821: ibid.

72 James Mackintosh (1765–1832), philosopher.

73 Thomas Lawrence (1769–1830), portrait painter.

74 Bowles to Murray, 22 or 23 Apr. 1821: National Library of Scotland, John Murray Archive, MS 12604/1137.

75 George Isaac Huntingford (1748–1832), clergyman and later Warden of Winchester College.

76 The arms confirmed to Bowles's ancestor by the Heralds in their Visitation of Wiltshire in 1623 were 'Azure, between the horns of a crescent or, a sun argent'.

77   'rubbers' was a term used in bowls from *c.* 1600.

78   Andrew Nicholson, op. cit., p. 397.

79   Jacob van Rennes, op. cit., p. 64. The reader will find in this book a detailed account and analysis of all the arguments contained in many of the pamphlets published during the course of the controversy.

80   Andrew Nicholson, op. cit., p. 401.

81   Samuel Smiles, *A Publisher and his Friends: Memoir of John Murray* . . . (London 1891), vol. i, p. 421.

82   Mrs Anthony Crosse, 'Poet, Parson, and Pamphleteer', *Temple Bar* (1894), vol. 103, p. 28.

83   Leslie A. Marshant, ed., *Byron's Letters and Journals* (London 1978), vol. VIII, p. 207.

84   John Scott (1784–1821), journalist.

85   Bowles to Scott, 27 Dec. 1820: Huntingdon Library, Art Collections, and Botanical Gardens, San Marino, California, USA, MS HM24175.

86   The *Gentleman's Magazine*, vol. 91 (1821) pt i, p. 292.

87   Bowles to Nichols, 2 May 1821: Beinecke Rare Book and Manuscript Library, Yale University, USA.

88   Bowles to Nichols, undated: ibid.

89   William Hazlitt (1778–1830), essayist.

90   Jacob van Rennes, op. cit., p. 10.

91   William Hazlitt, *The Spirit of the Age or Contemporary Portraits*, E.D. Mackerness ed., (London 1969), pp. 121–2.

92   Abraham John Valpy (1787–1854), publisher and printer.

93   Mary Russell Mitford (1787–1855), novelist.

94   Sir William Elford, Bart (1749–1837), banker and politician.

95   A.G. L'Estrange, *Life of Mary Russell Mitford* (London 1870), vol. i, p. 363.

96   Jacob van Rennes, op. cit., pp. 11–12.

97   Rowland E. Prothero, ed., *Letters and Journals of Lord Byron* (London 1898–1901), vol. 6, pp. 86–7.

98   William Roscoe (1753–1831), historian.

99   Wilfred S. Dowden, op. cit., p. 767.

100 Ibid, p. 772.

101 Ibid., p. 835.

102 Henry Peter Brougham (1778–1868), later Lord Chancellor and Baron Brougham & Vaux.

103 Jeremy Bentham (1748–1832), writer.

104 Bowles to Hurst & Robinson, Jan 1826: Harvard University MS Eng. 505. 5.

105 The *Gentleman's Magazine*, vol. XCVI (1826), pt i, pp. 238–40.

106 Bowles to Hurst & Robinson, 8 Feb. 1825: Harvard University, MS 505. 5.

107 Thomas Frognall Dibdin (1776–1847), bibliographer.

108 Probably Charles Burton (1793–1866), theologian.

109 Jacob van Rennes, op. cit., pp. 13–14.

110 *The Poetical Works of Milman, Bowles, Wilson, and Barry Cornwall* (Paris 1829).

111 W.L. Bowles, *Scenes and Shadows of Days Departed* . . . (London 1835), p. 16.

112 *The Cambridge History of English and American Literature in 18 Volumes* (1907–21), VIII Southey p. 24. William Lisle Bowles (quoted in www.bartleby.com/221/0824. html).

113 *Devizes and Wiltshire Gazette* (hereafter *DWG*), no. 210, 6 Jan. 1820.

114 *SWJ*, no. 4140, 29 July 1816.

115 *The Poetical Works of Milman, Bowles, Wilson, and Barry Cornwall* (Paris 1829), p. vi.

116 W.L. Bowles, *The Parochial History of Bremhill in the County of Wilts* . . . (London 1828), pp. 22–3.

117 *A Calendar of Prisoners in the County Gaol of Fisherton – Anger, Devizes Prisons and Marlborough Bridewell; Salisbury Sessions April 16 1822*, p. 7.

118 *A Calendar of Prisioners for Trial at the Lent Assizes to be holden at the City of New Sarum 9 March 1822*, p. 10.

119 *DWG*, no. 357, 31 Oct. 1822.

120 Stephen MacCarthy, 3rd Earl Mountcashel (1792–1883).

121 W.L. Bowles, *A Word on Cathedral Oratorios, and Clergy-Magistrates,*

Addressed to Lord Mountcashel
(London 1830), pp. 31–2.

122 *DWG*, no. 229, 18 May 1820.
123 George Watson Taylor (d. 1841),
owner of Erlestoke estate and also
slave owner.
124 *SWJ*, 4322, 15 May 1820.
125 Lansdowne to Bowles, 10 Feb.
1820: William L. Clements Library,
University of Michigan.
126 *DWG*, no. 253, 2 Nov. 1820.
127 Henry Colburn (d. 1855), publisher.
128 Jack Simmons, ed., *Letters from
England by Robert Southey* (London
1951), p. 41.
129 William Pickering (1796–1854),
publisher.
130 *DWG*, no. 263, 11 Jan. 1821.
131 Lansdowne to Bowles, 23 Jan.
1821: William L. Clements Library,
University of Michigan.
132 *DWG*, 264, 18 Jan. 1821.
133 Charles Kemble (1775–1854), actor.
134 Bryan Waller Procter, op. cit., p. 131.
135 Thomas Phillipps (1792–1872),
antiquary.
136 Thomas Moore rather unkindly
describes Wansey as 'an odd sort
of ignorant old fellow, with a good
fortune, who has passed most of
his life in travelling', Wilfred S.
Dowden, ed., *The Journal of Thomas
Moore 1826–1830* (Newark 1986) vol.
3, p. 949.
137 Bowles to Phillipps, 8 Feb. 1821:
Bodleian Library, University of
Oxford, MS. Phillipps-Robinson, b.
108, fol. 135r.
138 Bowles to Phillipps, 11 Feb. 1821:
ibid., fol. 137r.
139 Ibid., MS. d. 68.
140 Bowles to Phillipps, Feb. 1821: ibid.,
c. 428, fol. 105v–106r.
141 John Nash (1752–1835), architect.
142 George Julius Poulett Scrope
(1797–1876), geologist and political
economist.
143 Bowles to Phillipps, Dec. 1821:
Bodleian Library, University of
Oxford, MS. Phillipps-Robinson b.
108, fol. 139r.
144 Colt Hoare's copy of Phillipps's

*Monumental Inscriptions in the
County of Wilts* can be seen in
the Library of the Wiltshire
Archaeological and Natural History
Society, Devizes.
145 Christina Colvin, ed., *Maria
Edgeworth: Letters from England
1813–1844* (London 1971), pp. 280–1.
146 William Jerdan (1782–1869),
journalist.
147 George Croly (1780–1860), author.
148 Alaric Alexander Watts (1797–1864),
poet and journalist.
149 Archdeacon Robert Nares, now
rector of Allhallows London Wall.
150 Bowles to Jerdan, 9 June 1822:
Huntingdon Library, Art Collections,
and Botanical Gardens, San Marino,
California, USA, MS HM 7311.
151 William Jerdan, *The Autobiography of
William Jerdan* (1852–3), vol. 1, n. 151.
152 Charles Lloyd (1775–1839), poet.
153 Francis Jeffrey (1773–1850), critic.
154 James Belcher (1781–1811), prize-
fighter.
155 Bowles to Phillipps, 17 June
1822:Bodleian Library, University of
Oxford, MS Phillipps-Robinson, c.
410, fol. 71r.
156 Bowles to Phillipps, 21 June 1822:
ibid., fol. 73v–74r.
157 Bowles to Phillipps, 22 June 1822:
ibid., fol. 75r.
158 *The Grave of the Last Saxon or Legend
of the Battle of Hastings.*
159 Bowles to Phillipps, 26 June 1822:
Bodleian Library, University of
Oxford, MS Phillipps-Robinson,
c. 410, fol. 77r.
160 *DWG*, no. 336, 13 June 1822.
161 Edward Dowden, ed., *The Correspon-
dence of Robert Southey with Caroline
Bowles* . . . (Dublin 1881), p. 26.
162 Garland Greever, op. cit., p. 40.
163 John Rutter (1796–1851), bookseller
and printer.
164 *SWJ*, no. 4440, 26 Aug. 1822.
165 *DWG*, no. 348, 29 Aug. 1822.
166 Bowles to Phillips, 17 Oct. 1822: The
Carl H. Pforzheimer Collection of
Shelley and His Circle, New York
Public Library, Astor, Lenox and

Tilden Foundations, Misc. 0377.
167 The purchaser was John Farquhar.
168 Letter in a copy of Britton's
Fonthill Abbey with prints, sketches
and other letters in Wiltshire
Archaeological and Natural History
Society Library, Devizes.
169 The *Gentleman's Magazine*, vol. XCII
pt 2 (1822), p. 102.
170 John Bowyer Nichols (1779–1863),
printer and antiquary.
171 John Nichols, *Historical Notices of
Fonthill Abbey Wilts with eleven plates
and fifteen embellishments* (London
1836), pp. 22–3.
172 William Bartlett (1809–1854),
topographical draughtsman.
173 This sketch is in the Library of
the Wiltshire Archaeological and
Natural History Society, Devizes.
174 Bowles to Phillips, 22 Oct. 1822:
The Carl H. Pforzheimer Collection
of Shelley and His Circle, New York
Public Library, Astor, Lenox and
Tilden Foundations, Misc. 0377.
175 James Ingram (1774–1850), Anglo-
Saxon scholar.
176 Bulkeley Bandinel (1761–1861),
librarian.
177 Philip Bliss (1787–1857), antiquary
and librarian.
178 W.L. Bowles, *The Parochial History
of Bremhill in the County of Wilts* . . .
(London 1828), p. xviii.
179 Daniel Lysons (1762–1834),
clergyman and topographer.
180 William Dugdale (1605–86), writer
and Garter King-of-Arms.
181 Bowles to Lysons, 28 Nov. 1822:
Seymour Adelman Collection, Bryn
Mawr College Library, Bryn Mawr,
USA.

Chapter 5

1 Thomas Kibble Hervey (1799–1859),
poet, critic and editor of *Friendship's
Offering* 1826–7.
2 Alaric Watts.
3 Bowles is referring to his *Two
Sonnets on the busts of Milton, in
Youth and Age at Stourhead.*

4 Doubtless the sculpture of sleeping
children in Lichfield Cathedral by
Francis Legatt Chantrey (1781–1841).
5 Bowles to Unknown, no date:
Box/Folder B2/F12, Manuscripts
Division, Department of Rare Books
and Special Collections, Princeton
University Library.
6 Archibald Constable (1774–1827),
publisher of the *Edinburgh Review.*
7 Wilfred S. Dowden, *The Journal of
Thomas Moore*, (Newark), vol. 2,
1821–1825, p. 638.
8 David Ricardo (1772–1823),
economist.
9 Wilfred S. Dowden, op. cit., p. 653.
10 Ibid., pp. 653–4.
11 Joanna Baillie (1762–1851), poetess.
12 Wilfred S. Dowden, op. cit., p. 703.
13 John Henry Hume (1796–1848),
clergyman.
14 'Verdi prati, op. 27' by George
Frederic Handel.
15 Wilfred S. Dowden, op. cit. pp. 687–8.
16 Henry Purcell's 'Mad Bess'.
17 Wilfred S. Dowden, op. cit., pp. 687–8.
18 William Stewart Rose (1775–1842),
poet.
19 Garland Greever, *A Wiltshire Parson
and his Friends: The Correspondence
of William Lisle Bowles together with
Four Hitherto Unidentified Reviews by
Coleridge* (London 1926), p. 47.
20 Wilfred S. Dowden, op. cit., p. 689.
21 Henry Edmund Goodridge (1797–
1864), architect.
22 *DWG*, no. 391, 11 Aug. 1823.
23 *Saxon Chronicle* (1823) edited by
James Ingram (1774–1850).
24 Bowles to Hurst & Robinson, 4 June
1823: Harvard University, MS Eng,
505. 5.
25 Ibid.
26 Ibid.
27 Bowles to Baillie, 4 July 1823:
The Royal College of Surgeons of
England.
28 Wilfred S. Dowden, op. cit, p. 619.
29 Bowles to Caroline Bowles, 4 Nov.
1823: Harvard University, MS Eng.
505.
30 *DWG*, no. 401, 23 Oct. 1823.

31 Wilfred S. Dowden, op. cit., p. 693.

32 The *Gentleman's Magazine*, vol. XCIV (1824), pt 1, p. 77.

33 *DWG*, no. 367, 9 Jan. 1823.

34 The *Gentleman's Magazine*, vol. XCIII (1823), pt 1, p. 73.

35 W.L. Bowles, *The Parochial History of Bremhill in the County of Wilts* . . . (London 1828), pp. 243–4. For further examples of Bowles's epitaphs see pp. 242–3.

36 These lines appear in Charles Noel Douglas, *Forty Thousand Quotations: Prose and Poetical* (New York 1917), p. 531.

37 Alaric Alfred Watts, *Alaric Alexander Watts, a Narrative of his Life, by his Son* (1884), vol. 1, pp. 191–2.

38 William Henry Fox Talbot (1800–77), pioneer of photography.

39 Fox-Talbot to Fielding, 25 Jan 1824: British Library from the Fox Talbot Museum/Lacock Abbey Collection Lacock, doc. no. 1154.

40 Francesco Petrarca (1304–74), poet.

41 Leonidas M. Jones, ed., *Selected Prose of John Hamilton Reynolds* (Cambridge, Massachusetts), p. 391.

42 George Gilfillan, *The Poetical Works of William Lisle Bowles . . . with Memoir, Critical Dissertation, and Explanatory Notes* (Edinburgh 1855), vol. II, p. xviii. On the title page to this work Gilfillan inexplicably describes Bowles as a Canon of St Paul's Cathedral.

43 Thomas Moore, *The Letters and Journals of Lord Byron with Notices of his Life In Four Volumes* (London 1830), p. 779.

44 Wilfred S. Dowden, op. cit., p. 728.

45 Christina Colvin, ed., *Maria Edgeworth: Letters from England 1813–1844* (London 1971), pp. 98–9.

46 General Peachey's first wife was Emma Francis who died in Madeira in 1809. The memorial stanzas by Bowles and Southey copied into her sister's album were composed following her death.

47 Edmund Burke (1729–97), statesman.

48 Wilfred S. Dowden, op. cit., p. 728.

49 A.M. Broadley and Walter Jerrold, *The Romance of a Elderly Poet: A hitherto unknown chapter in the life of George Crabbe revealed by ten years' correspondence with Elizabeth Charter 1815–1825* (London 1913), p. 269.

50 Wilfred S. Dowden, op. cit., p. 758.

51 Probably Henry Rowley Bishop (1786–1855), composer and director of Covent Garden and musical director of King's Theatre, Haymarket and conductor of oratorio concerts.

52 W.L. Bowles, *The Ark: a dramatic oratorio. Written expressly for musical effect* (Bath 1824).

53 This song was probably published in 1825 and not in 1822, the conjectural year of publication given in the British Library's Integrated Catalogue: Shelfmark H. 1421. (36).

54 George Thomas Smart (1776–1867), musician and orchestral conductor.

55 The *Musical Times*, 1 Nov. 1908, vol. 49, no. 789, p. 702.

56 Thomas Henry Sutton Sotheron Estcourt (1801–76), statesman.

57 *DWG*, no. 451, 26 Aug. 1824.

58 Wilfred S. Dowden, op. cit., p. 762.

59 Ibid., p. 767.

60 Ibid., p. 768.

61 Robert Cadell (1788–1849), publisher.

62 William Hayley (1745–1820), poet.

63 Presumably William Seward (1729–99), man of letters.

64 Alaric Alfred Watts, *A Narrative of his Life . . .* (London 1884), pp. 192–3.

65 Introduction to the edition of the sonnets published in 1837.

66 Uvedale Price (1747–1829), writer and 1st baronet.

67 P.W. Clayden, ed., *Rogers and his Contemporaries* (London 1889), vol. 1, pp. 387–8.

68 Perhaps Richard Bingham (1765–1858), a clergyman who was at Winchester with Bowles.

69 Probably Charles Lewis Phipps of Dilton Court (b. 1782).

70 Wilfred S. Dowden, op. cit., 771–2.

71 Lansdowne to Bowles, 28 Oct. 1824: William L. Clements Library, University of Michigan.

72 George Augustus, 11th Earl of Pembroke (1759–1827) and Catherine, Countess of Pembroke (1783–1856).

73 Sir Thomas Stamford Raffles (1781–1826), colonial governor.

74 Wilfred S. Dowden, op. cit., p. 772.

75 Bowles to Phillips, 2 Nov. 1824: Huntingdon Library, Art Collections, and Botanical Gardens, San Marino, California, USA, MS 11457.

76 Ex. info. Mr John Wells, Department of Manuscripts and University Archives, University of Cambridge.

77 Thomas Burgess (1756–1837), clergyman.

78 James Montgomery (1771–1854), poet.

79 Ernest de Selincourt, ed., The Letters of William and Dorothy Wordsworth: The Later Years (Oxford 1939), vol. 1, 1821–30, pp. 136–7.

80 DWG, no. 469, 30 Dec. 1824.

81 Wilfred S. Dowden, op. cit., p. 801.

82 Rene Huchon, George Crabbe and his Times 1754–1832: A Critical and Biographical Study (London 1907), p. 468.

83 Charles Robert Cockerell (1788–1863), architect.

84 Thomas Hood (1799–1845), poet.

85 Probably Ralph Gaby (1749–1829), formerly a solicitor in Calne.

86 Perhaps John Cole (1792–1848), bookseller and antiquary.

87 Bowles to Britton, 30 Jan. 1825: Wiltshire Archaeological and Natural History Society Library, Devizes, MS. 2602.

88 Bowles to Britton, 5 June 1825: ibid.

89 DWG, no. 533, 30 Mar. 1826.

90 An angel whose spear exposes deceit.

91 DWG, no. 534, 6 Apr. 1826.

92 William Lisle Bowles, Lessons in Criticism to William Roscoe, Esq . . . With Further Lessons in Criticism to a Quarterly Reviewer (London 1826),

pp. 157–8.

93 William Roscoe was the author of The Butterfly's Ball, published in 1808.

94 DWG, no. 540, 18 May 1826.

95 Charles Butler (1750–1832), lawyer and writer.

96 C.C. Southey, ed., The Life and Correspondence of Robert Southey in Six Volumes (London 1850) vol. V, pp. 206–7.

97 Thomas Ken (1637–1711), clergyman and Bishop of Bath & Wells.

98 Abraham Cowley (1618–67), poet.

99 Wilfred S. Dowden, op. cit., pp. 805–6.

100 Ibid., p. 819.

101 Ibid., p. 806.

102 Lansdowne to Bowles: University of Michigan, William L. Clements Library. In common with many of Lansdowne's letters to Bowles this letter is undated and so may have been written after Bowles had paid another visit to Cheltenham.

103 'Topographical Gatherings at Stourhead, 1825–1833' in Memoirs Illustrative of the History and Antiquities of Wiltshire and the City of Salisbury communicated to the Annual Meeting of the Archaeological Institute of Great Britain and Ireland, held at Salisbury, July, 1849 (London 1851), p. 22.

104 Ibid., p. 27.

105 George Baker (1781–1851), the Northamptonshire topographer.

106 Bowles to Nichols, 6 Aug. 1828: Huntington Library, Art Collections, and Botanical Gardens, San Marino, California, USA, MS 11489.

107 Bowles to Southey, 5 June 1825: ibid., MS SY 10.

108 Christian Friedrich Schwartz (1726–98), missionary.

109 DWG, no. 501, 18 Aug. 1825.

110 A group of wealthy men who met at the Bear Inn in Devizes with annual subscriptions and donations being applied to the schooling and clothing of poor boys in the neighbourhood.

111 DWG, no. 501, 18 Aug. 1825.

112 *DNB*, vol. 18, p. 1056.

113 John A. Hodgson, *An Uncollected Poem by William Lisle Bowles* pasted in a bound collection of Bowles's pamphlets in Wiltshire Archaeological and Natural History Society Library, Devizes.

114 Bowles to Unknown, 9 Oct. 1825: Box/Folder B2/F12, Manuscripts Division, Department of Rare Books and Special Collections, Princeton University Library.

115 Wilfred S. Dowden, *The Letters of Thomas Moore, Volume 2 1818–1847* (Oxford 1964), p. 540.

116 Edward Dowden, ed., *The Correspondence of Robert Southey with Caroline Bowles* . . . (Dublin 1881), p. 93.

117 Lord John Russell, ed., *Memoirs Journal and Correspondence of Thomas Moore* (London 1860), pp. 368–9.

118 The biography was very Irish in character, thus the reference to 'potatoe'.

119 Ronan Kelly, *Bard of Erin: The Life of Thomas Moore* (Dublin 2008), p. 420.

120 Mary Ransome, ed., *Wiltshire Returns to the Bishop's Visitation Queries 1783* Wiltshire Record Society (Devizes 1972), pp. 44–5.

121 W.L. Bowles, *The Parochial History of Bremhill*, op. cit., p. 202.

122 Wiltshire and Swindon Archives, Chippenham (hereafter WSA), 451/20.

123 William Lisle Bowles, *Lessons in Criticism* . . . op. cit., pp. ix–x.

124 Wilfred S. Dowden, *The Journal of Thomas Moore* (Newark 1986), vol. 3 1826–1830, p. 910.

125 Ibid., p. 911.

126 *DWG*, no. 538, 4 May 1826.

127 *The Gentleman's Magazine*, June 1850, pp. 675–6.

128 John Houlton (1773–1844), landowner.

129 Wilfred S. Dowden, op. cit., p. 933.

130 *Notes and Queries*, July 1914, p. 61.

131 Charles Bowles, *Modern Wilts: Hundred of Chalke* (Shaftesbury 1830), p. 147.

132 Peregrine Bingham (1753–1826), clergyman.

133 James Abercromby (1776–1858), statesman, later 1st Baron Dunfermline.

134 James Macdonald, 2nd Baronet (1784–1832).

135 Wilfred S. Dowden, op. cit., pp. 945–6.

136 Ibid., p. 946.

137 *DWG*, no. 544, 15 June 1826.

138 Wilfred S. Dowden, op. cit., p. 949.

139 Ibid., p. 950.

140 Ibid., p. 950.

141 Ibid., p. 951.

142 WSA, 451/15.

143 Wilfred S. Dowden, op. cit., p. 951.

144 Andrew Bain of Heffleton, Dorset (1767–1827).

145 Wilfred S. Dowden, op. cit., p. 953.

146 Ibid., p. 953.

147 George Bubb Dodington (1691–1762), Baron Melcombe.

148 Wadham Wyndham of Salisbury (d. 1843).

149 Wilfred S. Dowden, op. cit., p. 954.

150 Wilfred S. Dowden, op. cit., p. 955.

151 Alaric Alfred Watts, op. cit., vol. 1, p. 250.

152 Maria Caterina Caradori-Allan (1800–65), singer.

153 Thomas Reynolds, 1st Earl of Ducie (1776–1840).

154 Wilfred S. Dowden, op. cit., p. 962.

155 Harvard University, Houghton Library, bMS Eng 1276(9).

156 James ('Jemmy') Wood (1756–1836), eccentric Gloucester banker and miser.

157 Bowles to Sheridan, 2 Oct [1826]: Harvard University, Houghton Library, op. cit.

158 Bowles to Relfe, 12 Oct. 1826: Box/Folder B2/F12, Manuscripts Division, Department of Rare Books and Special Collections, Princeton University Library.

159 J.A. Chamberlain, *Maud Heath's Causeway* (Chippenham 1974), p. 33.

160 Ibid., p. 33.

161 J.E. Jackson, 'Maud Heath's Causey', *Wiltshire Archaeological and Natural History Society Magazine*, vol. 1

(1854), p. 257.

162 W. Lisle Bowles, *Scenes and Shadows of Days Departed* . . . (London 1837), pp. xxxvii–iii.

Chapter 6

1 An annual dinner held in Bath named after the Greek poet Anacreon, noted for his verses in praise of love and wine.

2 Bowles to Houlton, 15 Jan. 1827: Rice University, Fondren Library, Houston Texas, MS. 167.

3 Bowles to Houlton, 23 Jan. 1827: ibid.

4 John Britton's copy presented to him by Bowles is in the Library of the Wiltshire Archaeological and Natural History Society, Devizes.

5 This pamphlet, printed and sold in Calne by William Bailey, was either followed or preceded in 1827 by another version entitled *Some Observations on those stupendous monuments of antiquity Wansdike and Avebury in the County of Wilts*, also printed by Bailey in Calne.

6 Edward Duke (1779–1852), clergyman and antiquary.

7 *DWG*, no. 609, 13 Sept. 1827.

8 Ibid., no. 610, 20 Sept. 1827.

9 Ibid., no. 613, 11 Oct. 1827.

10 The *Gentleman's Magazine*, vol. XCVII (1827), pt 2, pp. 406–8.

11 Ibid., vol. XCVIII (1828), pt 2, pp. 314–5.

12 Ibid., pp. 491–3.

13 Ibid., vol. XCIX (1829), pt 1, p. 98.

14 Garland Greever, *A Wiltshire Parson and his Friends: The Correspondence of William Lisle Bowles together with Four Hitherto Unidentified Reviews by Coleridge* (London 1926), p. 112.

15 Ibid., p. 46.

16 Thomas Moore, *The Epicurean: A Tale* (London 1827).

17 Hugh Clapperton (1788–1827), African explorer.

18 Wilfred S. Dowden, *The Journal of Thomas Moore* (Newark 1986) vol. 3, p. 1052.

19 Ibid., p. 1070.

20 Perhaps Sir William Jones (1746–94), oriental scholar, whose poems were included in Chalmers's *Collection of the British Poets*.

21 Wilfred S. Dowden, op. cit., p. 1080.

22 John Bowyer Nichols (1779–1863), printer and antiquary.

23 The *Gentleman's Magazine*, of which Nichols was one of the editors.

24 Bowles to Nichols, 24 Apr. 1827: Harvard University, MS. Eng. 505. 5.

25 Bowles to Nichols, 26 May 1827: Box/Folder B2/F12, Manuscripts Division, Department of Rare Books and Special Collections, Princeton University Library.

26 Bowles to Nichols, 15 July 1827: ibid.

27 The Marquis of Lansdowne.

28 Lord Arundell of Wardour.

29 Bowles to Nichols, 30 Sept. 1827: Box/Folder B2/F12, Manuscripts Division, Department of Rare Books and Special Collections, Princeton University Library.

30 Bowles to Nichols, 13 [no month] 1827: ibid.

31 Samuel Bellin (1799–1894), engraver.

32 Bowles habitually misspelt in his letters the surname of Nichols and his son.

33 Bowles to Murray, 14 Oct. 1827: National Library of Scotland, John Murray Archive, MS 12604/1137.

34 Bowles to Nichols, 28 Dec. 1827: Harvard University, MS. Eng. 505. 5.

35 This copy is in the Library of the Wiltshire Archaeological and Natural History Society, Devizes.

36 *DWG*, no. 626, 10 Jan. 1828.

37 Rene Huchon, *George Crabbe and his Times 1754–1832: a Critical and Biographical Study* (London 1907), p. 462.

38 Garland Greever, op. cit., p. 75.

39 *DWG*, no. 625, 3 Jan 1828.

40 Ibid., no. 627, 17 Jan. 1828.

41 Rene Huchon, op. cit., pp. 462–3.

42 William Pleydell-Bouverie, Lord Folkestone, later 3rd Earl of Radnor, (1779–1869).

43 *SWJ*, no. 5556, 21 Jan. 1828.

44 *DWG*, no. 628, 24 Jan. 1828.

45 Probably George Heneage Walker Heneage (1799–1875), MP for Devizes 1838–57.

46 *DWG*, no. 629, 31 Jan. 1828.

47 Rene Huchon, op. cit., p. 463.

48 Bowles to Phipps, undated, WSA, 540/225.

49 Bowles to Mrs Lyson, 20 Feb. 1828: Seymour Adelman Collection, Bryn Mawr College Library, Bryn Mawr, USA.

50 W.L. Bowles, *A Voice from St Peter's and St Paul's; being a few plain words addressed respectfully to the Members of both Houses of Parliament on some late accusations against The Church* establishment . . . (London 1823), p. 67.

51 Lansdowne to Bowles, 6 Mar. 1827: William L. Clements Library, University of Michigan.

52 John Cam Hobhouse, later Baron Broughton de Gyfford.

53 William Spencer, 6th Duke of Devonshire (1790–1858).

54 George Child, 5th Earl of Jersey (1773–1859).

55 Johann Wolfgang von Goethe (1749–1832).

56 Wilfred S. Dowden, *The Letters of Thomas Moore Volume 2 1818–1847* (Oxford 1964), pp. 779–80.

57 Ibid., p. 780.

58 One of the copies in the Library of the Wiltshire Archaeological and Natural History Society in Devizes is inscribed 'Marchioness of Lansdowne from the author, a tribute of respect & esteem'.

59 W.L. Bowles, *The Parochial History of Bremhill in the County of Wilts* . . . (London 1828), pp. iii–iv.

60 William Stukeley (1687–1765), antiquary.

61 *DWG*, no. 1198, 27 Dec. 1838, letter from Bowles to the editor.

62 W.L. Bowles, *The Parochial History of Bremhill* . . . (London 1828), p. 241.

63 A slightly different version of this epitaph appears on p. 242 of *The Parochial History of Bremhill*.

64 The original sketch of this plan can be seen in the library of the Wiltshire Archaeological and Natural History Society, Devizes, Misc. 4. 6 . In pencil is written on it 'Dear Sir, You may proceed with engraving this plate as speedily as convenient, Yrs truly J B Nichols, To Mr Milne'.

65 W.L. Bowles, op. cit. pp. xvi–xviii.

66 Humphrey Davy (1778–1829), natural philosopher.

67 Dugald Stewart (1753–1828), philosopher.

68 W.L. Bowles, op. cit., p. 253.

69 John Wilson (1785–1864), author.

70 J. Lee Osborn, *Chippenham, An Ancient Saxon Town, its Surroundings and Associations* (Cirencester 1921), p. 26.

71 Bowles to Nichols, 6 Aug. 1828: Huntingdon Library, Art Collection, and Botanical Gardens, San Marino, California, USA, MS HM 11489.

72 Garland Greever, op. cit., pp. 76–8.

73 *Mirror of Literature, Amusement, and Instruction*, no. 326, 9 Aug. 1828.

74 *Blackwood's Magazine*, 24 August 1828, pp. 227–8.

75 Temple of the Muses.

76 Bowles to Murray, 3 Jan. 1828: National Library of Scotland, John Murray Archive, MS 12604/1137.

77 Bowles to Murray, 5 Feb. 1828: ibid.

78 Bowles to Murray, 12 Feb. 1828: ibid.

79 Bowles to Nichols, 23 Mar. 1828: Box/Folder B2/F12, Manuscripts Division, Department of Rare Books and Special Collections, Princeton University Library.

80 Mark Gillings and Joshua Pollard, *Avebury* (London 2004), p. 161.

81 *The Gentleman's Magazine*, vol. 33 (1850) New Series, p. 675.

82 Rodney Legg, *Stonehenge Antiquaries* (Milborne Port 1986), p. 148.

83 George James Welbore Agar Ellis (1797–1833), MP for Ludgershall, later 1st Baron Dover.

84 Garland Greever, op. cit., p. 76.

85 Ibid.

86 This sonnet can be seen on page 31 of the first volume of Gilfillan, op. cit.

87 Bowles to Murray, 21 Nov. 1828: National Library of Scotland, John Murray Archive, MS 12604/1137.

88 *The Omnipresence of the Deity* (1828) by Robert Montgomery (1807–55).

89 Bowles to Cruttwell, 3 Feb. 1829: The Carl H. Pforzheimer Collection of Shelley and His Circle, New York Public Library, Astor, Lenox and Tilden Foundations, Misc. 3913.

90 Bowles to Nichols, Dec. 1828: Box/Folder Bor. Brou/Bowles, Manuscripts Division, Department of Rare Books and Special Collections, Princeton University Library.

91 'Lord of the whirling wheels' meaning manufacturers.

92 Wm Lisle Bowles, *Days departed, or Banwell Hill . . .* (London 1829), 2nd ed. pp. 62–3.

93 A revised version of *Ellen Gray; or The Dead Maiden's Curse* entitled *The Tale of the Maid of Cornwall* was appended to the second edition. Ex info. John Price Antiquarian Books.

94 Bowles to Murray, 20 May 1829: National Library of Scotland, John Murray Archive, 12604/1137.

95 John Anthony Galignani (1796–1873) and William Galignani (1798–1882), booksellers and publishers.

96 Presumably John Gibson Lockhart, the biographer of Sir Walter Scott.

97 Bowles to Murray, 9 June 1829: National Library of Scotland, John Murray Archive, MS 12604/1137.

98 *Mirror of Literature, Amusement and Instruction*, no. 350, 3 Jan. 1829.

99 Bowles to Kennet, c. 1829: The Carl H. Pforzheimer Collection of Shelley and His Circle, New York Public Library, Astor, Lenox and Tilden Foundations, Misc 3392.

100 *The Poetical Works of Milman, Bowles, Wilson, and Barry Cornwall* (Paris 1829), p. vi.

101 The *Gentleman's Magazine*, vol. XCVIII (1828), pt 2, p. 482.

102 Benjamin Johnson (c. 1665–1742), actor.

103 Wilfred S. Dowden, *The Journal of Thomas Moore* (Newark 1986), vol. 3, p. 1152.

104 John Britton, *The Beauties of Wiltshire . . .* (London 1825), vol. iii, p. 169.

105 W.L. Bowles, op. cit.,pp. 154–6.

106 William L. Bowles, *Days Departed; or Banwell Hill, a lay of Severn Sea . . .* (London 1829), p. xxii.

107 John Skinner (1772–1839), clergyman and antiquary.

108 Stephen Hyde Cassan (1789–1841), clergyman and biographer.

109 Howard and Peter Coombs, *Journal of a Somerset Rector 1803–1834* (Weston-super-Mare 1987), p. 360.

110 Ibid., p. 7.

111 Ibid., p. 361.

112 The Bath printer and publisher.

113 Howard and Peter Coombs, op. cit., p. 362.

114 William Coxe (1748–1828), clergyman and historian.

115 Minute of Chapter held 14 Aug. 1828: Chapter Act Book, no. 23, 1813–1834 in the Library, Salisbury Cathedral.

116 *DWG*, no. 658, 21 Aug. 1828.

117 Report of the Commission to Inquire into the Revenues and Patronage of the Established Church in England and Wales, 16 June 1835.

118 W.L. Bowles, *A Few Words, most respectfully addressed to Lord Chancellor Brougham on the Misrepresentations, Exaggerations, and Falsehoods respecting the Property and Character of the Cathedral Clergy of the Church of England* (Salisbury 1831), pp. 11–12.

119 John Peniston (c. 1778–1848), surveyor and architect.

120 Mrs Hinxman is named in the Salisbury list of 'Nobility, Gentry and Clergy' in the Close in J. Pigot's *Commercial Directory* (1830).

121 Michael Cowan, ed., *The Letters of John Peniston, Salisbury Architect, Catholic, and Yeomanry Officer*

1823–1830, Wiltshire Record Society (Trowbridge 1996), vol. 50, p. 114.

122 *Salisbury: The Houses of the Close* (Royal Commission on the Historical Monuments of England), (London 1993), p. 129.

123 Ibid., p. 130.

124 *DWG*, no. 742, 1 Apr. 1830.

125 Peter Hall, *Picturesque Memorials of Salisbury* . . . (Salisbury 1834), after plate XVI.

126 This poem can be seen on pages 298–9 of the second volume of Gilfillan, op. cit.

127 *SWJ*, no. 3668, 29 Mar. 1830.

128 Joseph Skelton (fl. 1820–1850), engraver.

129 *Etchings of the Antiquities of Bristol from original sketches by Hugh O'Neil* (1825).

130 Bowles to Skelton, 9 Oct. 1828: Harvard University, MS Eng. 505.

131 The *Gentleman's Magazine*, vol. XCIX (1829), pt 1, p. 533.

132 Edward Moxon (1801–1858), publisher and verse writer.

133 Bowles to Moxon, 28 Dec. 1828: Harvard University, MS Eng. 505,

134 *DWG*, no. 676, 25 Dec. 1828.

135 Ibid., no. 678, 8 Jan. 1829.

136 Howley to Bowles, undated: Lambeth Palace Library, MSS 3355, ff. 1–5.

137 Moore's *Life of Byron*.

138 Probably Charles Hoyle, clergyman and vicar of Overton near Marlborough.

139 A man acting as attendant or servant. It is not known to whom Bowles was referring.

140 Lord John Russell, op. cit., pp. 480–1.

141 Mrs Bowles [Magdalene Bowles], *Summer Visits to Cottages in a Country Village with Observations on the Morals and Habits of the Inhabitants; and particularly in exemplifying the pernicious effects of Beer Houses* (London 1836), p. 30.

142 The Recollections of John Harding of his time as a chorister at Salisbury Cathedral, 1826–1832, in the *Hatcher Review*, 1980, no. 10, p. 19.

143 The poem is printed in Gilfillan, op. cit., vol. 1, pp. 259–60 and at the conclusion of an article on Salisbury Cathedral in the *Saturday Magazine*, 25 Oct. 1834, no. 148, p. 155.

144 *DNB*, vol XIV, p. 93.

145 Hugh Nicholas Pearson (1776–1854), clergyman.

146 John Fisher (1748–1825), Bishop of Salisbury 1807–25.

147 Philip Barrett, *Barchester: English Cathedral Life in the Nineteenth Century* (London 1993), p. 7.

148 Arthur Thomas Corfe (1773–1863), organist and composer.

149 Philip Barrett, op. cit., p. 164.

150 Dora H. Robertson, *Sarum Close: A History of the Life and Education of the Cathedral Choristers for 700 years* (London 1938), pp. 279–80.

151 A.T. Corfe, *A Collection of Anthems with a List of the Services used in the Cathedral Church of Salisbury* . . . (Salisbury 1852), p. 9.

152 Ibid., p. 154.

153 Wilfred S. Dowden, op. cit., p. 1201.

154 Bowles to unnamed, 11 July 1829: Harvard University MS Eng. 505.

155 *DWG*, no. 705, 16 July 1829.

156 The *Gentleman's Magazine*, vol. XCIX (1829), pt 2, pp. 489–90.

157 Ibid., vol. C (1830), pt 1, pp. 23–4.

158 Henry Alworth Merewether (1780–1864), lawyer and Town Clerk of London.

159 Bowles to Caroline Bowles, 30 Mar. 1830: Harvard University MS Eng. 505. 5.

160 Bowles to Phillipps, 30 Apr. 1830: Bodleian Library, University of Oxford, MS Phillipps-Robinson, c. 428.

161 Bowles to Hutchinson, 2 Jan. 1830: Northamptonshire Record Office, ref. D(CA)422/5.

162 W.L. Bowles, *A Word on Cathedral Oratorios and Clergy Magistrates* . . . (London 1830), p. 87.

163 Wiltshire Cuttings, vol. 22, p. 287 in Wiltshire Archaeological and Natural History Society Library, Devizes.

164 The *Gentleman's Magazine*, vol. C (1830), pt 1, p. 443.

165 This volume in now in the library of the Wiltshire Archaeological and Natural History Society, Devizes.

166 Bowles to Hutchinson, 2 July 1830: Northamptonshire Record Office, ref. D(CA)422/8.

167 Garland Greever, op. cit., pp. 50–1.

168 Wilfred S. Dowden, op. cit., p. 1336.

169 For a full account of the 'Battle of Pythouse' see Robert Moody, *Mr Benett of Wiltshire: the life of a county Member of Parliament 1773–1852* (East Knoyle 2005), pp. 181–204.

170 Howard and Peter Coombs, op. cit., p. 505.

171 Thomas Howard, 6th Earl of Suffolk & 9th Earl of Berkshire (1776–1851).

172 *DWG*, no. 762, 19 Aug. 1830.

173 Herbert Hawes (1766–1837), clergyman.

174 Bowles to Murray, 18 Jan. 1830: National Library of Scotland, John Murray Archive, MS 12604/1137.

175 Bowles to Murray, 5 Mar. 1830: ibid.

176 Bowles to Lockhart, 17 May 1830: National Library of Scotland, MS no. 929, folio 16.

177 Bowles to Nichols, 14 Mar. 1831: Harvard University, MS Eng. 505.

178 Edward Dowden, *The Correspondence of Robert Southey with Caroline Bowles . . .* (Dublin 1881), pp. 254.

179 Ibid., p. 252.

180 Garland Greever, op. cit., p. 52.

181 Probably Richard James Lane (1800–72), line-engraver and lithographer.

182 Bowles to Calcott, 8 Nov. 1829: Huntington Library, Art Collections, and Botanical Gardens, San Marino, California, USA, MS HM 11447.

183 W.L. Bowles, *The Life of Thomas Ken D.D. Deprived Bishop of Bath and Wells . . .* (London 1830), vol. 1, p. xiii.

184 Wilfred S. Dowden, *The Journal of Thomas Moore* (Newark 1987), vol. 5, pp. 1402–3.

185 Henry Bellenden Bulteel (1800–66), theologian.

186 Thomas Arne (1710–78), composer.

187 In its time one of the most successful of all English operas and first performed in 1762.

188 Bowles to D'Israeli, June 1832: Bodleian Library, University of Oxford, Dep. Hughenden G/I/97.

189 Offered for sale in 2008 by Peter Harrington, antiquarian bookseller.

190 Samuel Rogers, *Recollections of the table-talk of Samuel Rogers* (London 1856), pp. 258–9.

191 John Murray (1808–92), publisher.

192 Bowles to Murray, 29 June 1830: National Library of Scotland, John Murray Archive, MS 12604/1137.

193 Charlotte Sophia (1799–1837), daughter of Sir Walter Scott.

194 George Isaac Huntingford who in 1762 was admitted a scholar of Winchester College.

195 Bowles to Lockhart, 9 July 1832, National Library of Scotland, MS 929, folio 15.

196 Joseph Hunter (1783–1861), antiquary.

197 Joseph Hunter mss, British Library, Add. 36527, ff. 207–209.

198 Magdalene's *Characters and Incidents of Village Life mostly founded on fact . . . to which is added some account of the utility . . . of small clubs in country parishes* was published in 1831.

199 Bowles's sister, Amy, had married Sir Richard Williams, KCB as her second husband.

200 Caroline Bowles lived at Buckland.

201 Garland Greever, op. cit., p. 52.

202 Richard Fowler (1765–1863), physician.

203 Dr Fowler's wife, Ann, was the daughter of William Bowles of Heale near Salisbury, a distant cousin of Bowles.

204 Garland Greever, op. cit., pp. 54–5.

205 *SWJ*, no. 5696, 18 July 1831.

206 Henry Fielding (1707–54), novelist.

207 Both of the nearby asylums at Laverstoke and Fisherton had been established and were run by members of the Finch family.

208 Edward Dowden, op. cit., pp. 253–4.

209 A song said to have been written by Larry Grogan, the Wexford piper.

210 Wilfred S. Dowden, op. cit., p. 1423.

211 W. Lisle Bowles, *Scenes and Shadows of Days Departed* . . . (London 1837), pp. xix–xx.

212 Nathaniel Crewe (1633–1721), 3rd Baron Crew of Stene and Bishop of Durham.

213 William Cobbett (1762–1835), essayist and politician.

214 Rev. W.L. Bowles, *A Few Words most respectfully addressed to the Lord Chancellor Brougham* . . . (Salisbury 1831), pp. 51–3.

215 *Blackwood's Edinburgh Magazine*, Sept. 1831, pp. 475–6.

216 Probably John Gibson Lockhart, editor of the *Quarterly Review* 1825–53.

217 Bowles to Scrope, 7 Feb. [no year]: Harvard University, MS Eng. 505.

218 Caroline Augusta, wife of Viscount Valletort and daughter of Rear Admiral and Lady Elizabeth Feilding, Fox Talbot's mother.

219 Ela (d. 1261), widow of William Longspee and first abbess of Lacock.

220 The whole of the poem can be read in Gilfillan, op. cit., vol. 2, p. 305.

Chapter 7

1 Garland Greever, *A Wiltshire Parson and his Friends; The Correspondence of William Lisle Bowles with Four Hitherto Unidentified Reviews by Coleridge* (London 1926), p. 87.

2 Garland Greever, ibid., p. 79.

3 The suggestion was that Crabbe should not long remain a curate.

4 Bowles to Murray, Feb 1834?: National Library of Scotland, John Murray Archive, MS 12604/1137.

5 *DWG*, no. 848, 12 Apr. 1832.

6 Bowles to D'Israeli, 3 May 1832: Bodleian Library, University of Oxford, Dep. Hughenden G/I/101.

7 Bowles to D'Israeli, 20 May 1832: ibid., Hughenden G/I/98.

8 Philip Bliss (1787–1857), antiquary.

9 Garland Greever, op. cit., p. 136.

10 William Buckland (1784–1856), geologist.

11 Martin Joseph Routh (1755–1854), clergyman and editor.

12 Bowles to D'Israeli, 30 May 1832: Bodleian Library, University of Oxford, Dep. Hughenden G/I/196.

13 William Thomas, Earl of Kerry (1811–36).

14 Ingram to Bowles, 31 May 1832: Bodleian Library, op. cit., G/I/604.

15 D'Israeli's house in Buckinghamshire.

16 Bowles to D'Israeli, 1 June 1832: Bodleian Library, op. cit., G/I/197.

17 Ingram to unnamed, c. 10 July 1832: ibid., G/I/603.

18 George Henry Law (1761–1845), clergyman.

19 Wilfred S. Dowden, *The Journal of Thomas Moore* (Newark 1987), vol. 5, pp. 1630–1.

20 Julian Charles Young, *A Memoir of Charles Mayne Young, Tragedian, with Extracts from his Son's Journal* (London 1871), pp. 226–7.

21 W. Lisle Bowles, *Scenes and Shadows of Days Departed* . . . (London 1837), pp. xii–iii.

22 Ibid., pp. xxxi–ii.

23 Perhaps John Fitzgerald Pennie (1782–1848), writer.

24 Garland Greever, op. cit., pp. 55–6.

25 Edward Dowden, *The Correspondence of Robert Southey with Caroline Bowles* . . . (Dublin 1881), pp. 249–50.

26 Edward Williams (1746–1826), Welsh bard.

27 William Gifford, editor of the *Quarterly Review*.

28 Edward Dowden, op. cit., pp. 251–2.

29 Charles Grey, 2nd Earl Grey (1764–1845).

30 C.C. Southey, ed., *The Life and Correspondence of Robert Southey in Six Volumes* (London 1850) vol. VI, pp. 192–4.

31 Howley to Bowles, 18 Aug. 1832: Lambeth Palace Library, MSS 3355, ff. 1–5.

32 Garland Greever, op. cit., pp. 155–7.

33 Ela, Countess of Salisbury, the

founder of Lacock Abbey.

34 Bowles to Fox-Talbot, Sept 1832: British Library from the Fox Talbot Museum/Lacock Abbey Collection, Lacock, collection number LA32–040.

35 *DWG*, no. 869, 6 Sept. 1832.

36 Lansdowne to Bowles, undated: William L. Clements Library, University of Michigan.

37 Ibid.

38 Joseph Jekyll (d. 1837), politician.

39 *DWG*, no. 870, 13 Sept. 1832.

40 Wilfred S. Dowden, op. cit., p. 1487.

41 *DWG*, no. 871, 30 Sept. 1832.

42 Joseph Hunter mss, British Library, Add. 36527, ff. 207–9.

43 Wilfred S. Dowden, op. cit., p. 1490.

44 The master of the choristers' school and also the cathedral librarian.

45 Edward Kite, 'Wiltshire Topography [1659–1843] With some Notes on the late Sir Thomas Phillipps and his Historical Collections for the County', *Wiltshire Notes and Queries*, December 1908, p. 149.

46 Suzanne Eward, *Salisbury Cathedral Library*, (2004), p. 11.

47 P.M. Gough, G.H. Hickman & M.D. Slatter, *The Derry Hill Story: History Under Our Feet* (1979), p. 12.

48 *DWG*, no. 887, 10 Jan. 1833.

49 John Banim (1798–1842), novelist and poet.

50 *DWG*, no. 889, 24 Jan. 1833.

51 Peter King, 7th Baron of Ockham (1776–1833).

52 *DWG*, no. 910, 20 June 1833.

53 Robert Henry Henley, 2nd Baron Henley (1789–1841).

54 Bowles to Carrington, 11 May 1834: Harvard University, MS Eng. 505.

55 W.L. Bowles, *A Last and Summary Answer to the Question 'Of what use have been, and are, the English Cathedral Establishments'* . . . (London 1833), pp. 100–2.

56 John Allen (1771–1843), political and historical writer.

57 *DNB*, vol. I, p. 309.

58 Bowles to Allen, 4 June 1833, British Library.

59 *DWG*, no. 893, 21 Feb. 1833.

60 For a detailed account of the foundation of the priory at Monkton Farleigh, see *VCH Wilts*, vol. III, eds. R.B. Pugh and Elizabeth Crittall (1956), p. 262.

61 Joseph Hunter (1783–1861), antiquary.

62 WSA, 380/907.

63 Irvine Gray, 'James Dallaway, b. 1763, a Gloucestershire Antiquary and Writer', *Bristol and Gloucestershire Archaeological Society Transactions*, 1962, vol. LXXXI, p. 209.

64 *DWG*, no. 953, 17 Apr. 1834.

65 Wilfred S. Dowden, op. cit., p. 1550.

66 Ibid., pp.1550–1.

67 Mrs Andrew Crosse, Poet, Parson and Pamphleteer, *Temple Bar*, vol. 103, Sept. 1894, pp. 30–1.

68 *Blackwood's Edinburgh Magazine*, no. CCXII, Sept. 1833, vol. XXXIV, p. 312.

69 Bowles to Wilson, 3 Sept. 1833: Harvard University, MS Eng 505 and 505. 5.

70 Abraham Hayward (1801–84), essayist.

71 Bowles to Hayward, 10 Oct. 1833: Harry Ransom Humanities Research Center, The University of Texas at Austin.

72 Nicholas Lee Torre (1795–1868), writer and translator.

73 *DWG*, no. 954, 24 Apr. 1834.

74 The *Gentleman's Magazine*, vol. II, July 1834.

75 *DWG*, no. 963, 26 June 1834.

76 Wilfred S. Dowden, op. cit. p. 1611.

77 *DWG*, no. 966, 17 July 1834.

78 Bowles's sonnet appears in the thirty-two copies of the *Brief History* . . . that were printed separately from Hall's *Picturesque Memorials of Salisbury* . . . to which the *Brief History* . . . was prefixed.

79 Peter Hall (1803–49), clergyman and topographer.

80 Britton to Fox-Talbot, 26 July 1834: British Library from the Fox Talbot Museum/Lacock Abbey Collection Lacock, doc. no. 2965.

81 *The Times,* 13 Aug. 1834.
82 Mary de Vere Chamberlain, *Coleridge in Calne* in Wiltshire Archaeological and Natural History Society Library, Devizes, Box 344, MS 3361, p. 2.
83 Garland Greever, op. cit., p. 62.
84 Joseph Butler (1692–1752), clergyman.
85 Bowles to Southey, Sept. 1834: The Carl H. Pforzheimer Collection of Shelley and His Circle, New York Public Library, Astor, Lenox and Tilden Foundations, Misc. 0373.
86 Garland Greever, op. cit., p. 63.
87 John Gough Nichols (1806–73), printer and antiquary.
88 Bowles to Fox-Talbot, 1834: British Library from the Fox Talbot Museum/Lacock Abbey Collection Lacock, LA34-034.
89 Samuel Buck (1696–1779), draughtsman and engraver.
90 Bowles to Nichols, undated: University of Tennessee Special Collections Library, Dr Kenneth Curry Collection.
91 Wiltshire Archaeological and Natural History Society Library, Devizes, Wilts Cuttings, vol. 16, p. 184.
92 Hester Stanhope (1776–1839), eccentric.
93 Wilfred S. Dowden, op. cit., p. 1684.
94 Ibid.
95 Marie Louise Victoire, Duchess of Kent (1786–1861).
96 Wilfred S. Dowden, op. cit., p. 1691.
97 The *Gentleman's Magazine,* vol. III New Series (1835), p. 576.
98 Anna Maria Hall (1800–81), novelist.
99 Wiltshire Archaeological and Natural History Society Library, Devizes, Wilts Cuttings, vol. 16, p. 183.
100 *SWJ,* no. 59012, 17 Aug. 1835.
101 Ibid., no. 59013, 24 Aug. 1835.
102 Mrs Bowles, *Summer Visits to Cottages in a Country Village* (London 1836), pp. 52–4.
103 Bowles to Nichols, Sept. 1835: box/folder B2/F12, Manuscripts Division, Department of Rare Books

and Special Collections, Princeton University Library.
104 The *Gentleman's Magazine,* vol. IV New Series (1835), pt 2, p. 489.
105 *DWG,* no. 1028, 24 Sept. 1835.
106 Doubtless William Macdonald, by now a canon residentiary of Salisbury Cathedral.
107 Bowles to Estcourt, 21 Sept. 1835: Bath Public Library.
108 *DWG,* no. 1032, 22 Oct. 1835.
109 Almost certainly Charles Hoyle.
110 Sidney Smith (1771–1845), clergyman and writer.
111 Mountain in Greece revered as the abode of Apollo and the Muses.
112 Wilfred S. Dowden, op. cit., p. 1724.
113 Ibid.
114 *Fudges in England ; Being a Sequel to 'The Fudge Family in Paris'.*
115 Wilfred S. Dowden, op. cit., p. 1725.
116 Bowles to Nichols, 9 Nov. 1835: Harvard University, MS Eng. 505. 5.
117 Perhaps William West (1796?–1888), comedian and musical composer.
118 Wilfred S. Dowden, op. cit. p. 1727.
119 In 2007 a copy of this extract from *The Ark* was advertised for sale by Amazon.
120 Wilfred S. Dowden, op. cit., p. 1735.
121 Seat of Bowles's friend Michael Joy.
122 John Benett of Pythouse, President of the Wiltshire Society for the Encouragement of Agriculture.
123 Bowles to Scrope, 11 Dec. 1835: Harvard University MS Eng. 505.
124 *DWG,* no. 1039, 10 Dec. 1835.
125 Ibid.
126 The cartoons are now in the Victoria and Albert Museum.
127 Wilfred S. Dowden, op. cit., pp. 1738–9.
128 *DWG,* no. 1040, 17 Dec. 1835.
129 *SWJ,* no. 5930, 21 Dec. 1835.
130 *DWG,* no. 1042, 31 Dec. 1835.
131 Bowles to Scrope, 21 Dec. (?) 1835: National Library of Scotland, MS 929, folio 14.
132 William Petty (1623–87), political economist.
133 Bowles to Phillipps, 28 Dec. 1835: Bodleian Library, University of

Oxford, MS Phillipps-Robinson,b.
130, fol. 60r.

Chapter 8

1 John Dryden (1631–1700), poet.
2 *SWJ*, no. 5937, 8 Feb. 1836.
3 Ibid.
4 Susan Batt (d. 1843).
5 John Thomas Batt (1746–1831),
barrister.
6 Francesco Zuccarelli or Zuccherelli
(1702–88), painter.
7 George Matcham, *The History of
Modern Wilts, Hundred of Downton*
(London 1834), p. 62.
8 William Bates, *The Maclise Portrait-
Gallery of 'Illustrious Literary
Characters' with Memoirs . . .*
(London 1883), p. 362.
9 John Liston (*c.* 1776–1846), comic
actor.
10 Marie Taglioni (1804–44), ballerina.
11 Francis Jeffrey (1773–1850), Scottish
judge and editor and contributor to
the *Edinburgh Review*.
12 *Frazer's Magazine for Town and
Country*, 1836, vol. XIII, p. 300.
13 Fielding's pig-keeping parson.
14 A traditional Scottish song.
15 A traditional Jacobite song.
16 *Frazer's Magazine for Town and
Country*, op. cit., pp. 498–9.
17 Julian Charles Young, *A Memoir
of Charles Mayne Young, Tragedian,
with extracts from his Son's Journal*
(London 1871), p. 225.
18 John Britton, *The Auto-Biography of
John Britton . . .* (London 1850),
p. 293.
19 John Greenly (1778–1862),
clergyman.
20 Chapter Meeting, 9 March 1836:
Chapter Act Book no. 24, 1834–51.
21 Chapter Meeting, 6 Apr. 1836: ibid.
22 George Simpson (1792–1871),
printer and newspaper proprietor.
23 *SWJ*, no. 5966, 5 Sept. 1836.
24 *SWJ*, no. 5941, 7 Mar. 1836.
25 William Chillingworth (1602–44),
theologian.
26 William Osmond (*c.* 1790–1875),

sculptor and monumental mason.
27 *SWJ*, no. 5942, 14 Mar. 1836.
28 Richard Hooker (*c.* 1554–1600),
theologian.
29 John Jewell (1522–71), Bishop of
Salisbury.
30 *SWJ*, no. 5943, 31 Mar. 1836.
31 Wilfred S. Dowden, *The Journal of
Thomas Moore* (Newark 1988), vol. 5,
p. 1792.
32 *DWG*, no. 1059, 28 Apr. 1836.
33 *SWJ*, no. 5965, 29 Aug. 1836.
34 Wilfred S. Dowden, op. cit., p. 1800.
35 Wiltshire Archaeological and
Natural History Society Library,
Devizes, Wilts Cuttings, vol. 11, p.
130.
36 Nicholas Vansittart, Baron Bexley
(1766–1851), stateman.
37 *DWG*, no. 1067, 23 June 1836.
38 Ibid., no. 1069, 7 July 1836.
39 Hugh Charles, 7th Baron Clifford of
Chudleigh (1790–1858).
40 Wilfred S. Dowden, op. cit.,
pp. 1802–3.
41 Mary Wollstonecraft Shelley (1797–
1851), second wife of Percy Bysshe
Shelley.
42 Wilfred S. Dowden, *The Letters of
Thomas Moore* (Oxford 1964), vol. 1,
pp. 803–4.
43 Perhaps Sir William Parker, 7th
baronet, (b. 1770) the owner of a
moiety of an estate at West Hatch,
Semley, and of a property at nearby
Chicklade, both villages being not
far from Bowles's early home at
Donhead.
44 *SWJ*, no. 5962, 8 Aug. 1836.
45 Poem written by Moore and
published in 1817 that established
his fame.
46 Wilfred S. Dowden, *The Journal of
Thomas Moore*, op. cit, p. 1820.
47 Ibid., p. 1814.
48 *DWG*, no. 1079, 15 Sept. 1836.
49 R.E. Sandell, ed., *Abstracts of
Wiltshire Tithe Apportionments*,
Wiltshire Record Society (Devizes
1975), p. 60.
50 Ibid., p. 24.
51 Bowles to Murray, 25 Sept. 1836:

National Library of Scotland, John Murray Archive, MS 12604/1137.

52 Bowles to Southey, 30 Dec. 1836: Huntingdon Library, Art Collections and Botanical Gardens, San Marino, California USA, MS HM11484.

53 Garland Greever, *A Wiltshire Parson and his Friends: The Correspondence of William Lisle Bowles with Four Hitherto Unidentified Reviews by Coleridge* (London 1926), pp. 64–6.

54 The *Examiner*, no. 1508, 25 December 1836.

55 Osmund, Saint (d. 1099).

56 Bowles to the editor of the *Examiner*, 17 Jan. 1837: Box/Folder B1/F2, Manuscripts Division, Department of Rare Books and Special Collections, Princeton University Library.

57 *DWG*, no. 1095, 5 Jan. 1837.

58 Ibid., no. 1099, 2 Feb. 1837.

59 Samuel Best (1802–73), clergyman.

60 Wilfred S. Dowden, *The Letters of Thomas Moore* (Oxford 1964), vol. 2, pp. 807–8.

61 Bowles to unnamed, 7 Feb. 1837: Harvard University, MS Eng. 505.

62 *SWJ*, no. 5992, 6 Mar. 1837.

63 This printed poem, slightly amended in Bowles's handwriting, is held with the collection of Bowles MSS in Harvard University.

64 Henry Phillpotts (1778–1869), clergyman.

65 C.C. Southey, ed., *The Life & Correspondence of the late Robert Southey in six Volumes* (London 1850), vol. VI, p. 332.

66 Bowles to Southey, June 1837: Harvard University, MS Eng. 505. 5.

67 *Mirror of Literature, Amusement, and Instruction*, no. 854, 23 Sept. 1837.

68 John Britton, op. cit., p. 292.

69 Cecil Woolf in 'Some Uncollected Authors XVIII, William Lisle Bowles 1762–1850', *Book Collector* vol. 7, 1958, states on p. 288 that the first edition of *The Village Verse Book* or *The Little Villager's Verse Book* had eluded him.

70 *DWG*, no. 1110, 20 Apr. 1837.

71 Perhaps Isaac Watts (1674–1748), hymn-writer.

72 *SWJ*, no. 5875, 1 Dec. 1834.

73 *DWG*, no. 1010, 21 May 1835.

74 George Gilfillan, op. cit.,vol. 2, p. 241.

75 Julian Charles Young, op. cit., pp. 225–6.

76 Ibid.

77 Wilfred S. Dowden, *The Letters of Thomas Moore* (Oxford 1964), vol. 2, p. 825.

78 W.L. Bowles, *The Parochial History of Bremhill . . .* (London 1828), pp. 159–60.

79 Lansdowne to Bowles, 8 May 1837: William L. Clements Library, University of Michigan.

80 Salisbury Plain, which would have to be crossed in travelling from Salisbury to Bremhill.

81 Garland Greever, op. cit., p. 113.

82 Nikolaus Pevsner, *The Buildings of England: Wiltshire* (Harmondsworth 1963), p. 128.

83 Cecil Woolf, op. cit., p. 415.

84 Henry William Lamb. 2nd Viscount Melbourne (1779–1848), politician.

85 Charles Grant, Baron Glenelg (1778–1866), statesman.

86 *DWG*, no. 1136, 19 Oct. 1837.

87 Wilfred S. Dowden, *The Journal of Thomas Moore*, op. cit., pp. 1923–4.

88 Presumably the annotated Bible prepared by Richard Mant, Bishop of Down, Connor and Dromore and George D'Oyly in 1814.

89 Bowles to Scope, 30 Nov. 1837: Harvard University, MS Eng. 505.

90 Perhaps John Wiltshire (b. c. 1762) who matriculated Queen's College in 1779.

91 The Aldine dolphin and anchor – a favourite printer's device and one adopted by William Pickering.

92 The *Gentleman's Magazine*, Feb. 1836, vol V New Series, p. 180.

93 Bowles to Murray, 2 Feb. 1836: National Library of Scotland, John Murray Archive, MS 12604/1137.

94 Either Richard Westall (1765–1836), painter or his younger brother

William Westall (1781–1850), also a painter.

95 Murray to Bowles, 12 Feb. 1836: National Library of Scotland, John Murray Archive, MS 41910.

96 Bowles to Murray, 7 Mar. 1836: ibid., MS 12604/1137.

97 Probably James Bulcock, a London publisher.

98 Bowles to Pickering, 22 Feb. 1837: Harvard University, MS. Eng. 505. 5.

99 Isaak Walton (1593–1683), author.

100 On p. 172 of his *The Cartoons of Raphael – a series of discources . . .* (Salisbury 1838) Bowles mentions that of Ken's watch will 'descend to Sergeant Merewether, Ken's nearest relative'.

101 Bowles to Pickering, 23 Feb. 1837: Harvard University, MS Eng. 505. 5.

102 Garland Greever, op. cit., pp. 161–2.

103 Bowles to Pickering, 13 June 1837: Harvard University, MS Eng. 505. 5.

104 Probably *The Power, Wisdom and Goodness of God as manifested in the Creation* (1836), by William Buckland (1784–1856).

105 Bowles to Pickering, 17 June 1837: ibid.

106 The butler.

107 Constance Fox-Talbot to Fox-Talbot, 28 June 1837: British Library from the Fox Talbot Museum/Lacock Abbey Collection Lacock, doc. no. 3528.

108 Charles Mayne Young (1777–1856), actor.

109 Bowles to Pickering, 24 July 1837:Harvard University MS Eng. 505. 5.

110 Constance Fox-Talbot to Fox-Talbot, 28 July 1837: British Library from the Fox Talbot Museum/Lacock Abbey Collection Lacock, doc. no. 3543.

111 Bowles to Pickering, Aug. 1837: Harvard University MS Eng. 505. 5.

112 George Gilfillan, op. cit., vol. 1, pp. 27–8.

113 Charles Whittingham (1767–1840), printer.

114 A proof of *Scenes and Shadows* extensively amended by Bowles

is held at Harvard University. This shows that the title was originally intended to be *Melodies of Melancholy and Fancy from the Morning to the Evening of Life.*

115 William Humphries (1794–1865), engraver.

116 Garland Greever, op. cit., p. 163.

117 Bowles to Pickering, 16 Nov. 1837: Harvard University, MS Eng. 505. 5.

118 Bowles to Pickering, c. Nov. 1837: ibid.

119 William Cowper (1731–1800). poet.

120 *SWJ*, no. 6025, 30 Oct. 1837.

121 Alexander Pope's poem *Eloise to Abelard.*

122 The *Art Journal* (1856), p. 375.

123 A number of these letters are held by Keswick Museum and Art Gallery. In writing to Bulcock both Bowles and his wife sometimes address him as 'Bullcock' or 'Bullock' as well as 'Bulcock'.

124 Thomas Sternhold (d. 1549) and John Hopkins (d. 1570), versifiers of the psalms.

125 Bowles to Bulcock (sic), 16 Apr. 1836: Keswick Museum and Art Gallery.

126 Bowles to Bulcock (sic), 24 June 1836: ibid.

127 Magdalene Bowles to Bulcock, 25 Nov. 1836: ibid.

128 Bowles to Bulcock, 6 Mar. 1837: ibid.

129 John Pease (1799–1872), philanthropic Quaker and Member of Parliament.

130 Magdalene Bowles to Bulcock, 3 May 1837: Keswick Museum and Art Gallery.

131 Held at Keswick Museum and Art Gallery are Bowles's notebook containing some of the poems that appeared in *The Little Villager's Verse Book* and various drafts of the poems with corrections.

132 Wadham Wyndham (1773–1843), Member of Parliament.

133 Bowles to Bulcock, 23 December 1837: Keswick Museum and Art Gallery.

Chapter 9

1 WSA, 451/19.
2 William Erle (1793–1880), lawyer.
3 Henry Ellacombe (1790–1885), clergyman and writer.
4 Bowles to Ellacombe, 8 Feb. 1838: Harvard University, MS Eng. 505.
5 Bowles to Murray, 1 Jan. 1838: National Library of Scotland, John Murray Archive, MS 12604/1137.
6 Bowles to Murray, 28 Feb. 1838: ibid.
7 An engraving by A.W. Warren of Raphael's 'The Charge to Peter' was chosen as the frontispiece.
8 Bowles to Murray, 5 Mar. 1838: National Library of Scotland, John Murray Archive, MS 12604/1137.
9 Probably the Hon. Mary Fox, the adopted (and perhaps illegitimate) daughter of Henry Edward, Lord Holland.
10 Georgiana (d. 1853), 2nd wife of Lord John Russell.
11 Arthur Wellesley, 1st Duke of Wellingon (1769–1852).
12 Bowles to Murray, 28 Mar. 1838: National Library of Scotland, John Murray Archive, MS 12604/1137.
13 Printed copy of the letter in National Library of Scotland, ibid.
14 Bowles to Murray, 1 Apr. 1838: ibid.
15 Bowles to Murray, 13 Apr. 1838: ibid.
16 Bowles to Murray, 15 Apr. 1838: ibid.
17 Bowles to Murray, 18 Apr. 1838: ibid.
18 *SWJ*, no. 6040, 26 Feb. 1838.
19 Wilfred S. Dowden, *The Journal of Thomas Moore* (Newark 1988), vol. 5, p. 1961.
20 Garland Greever, *A Wiltshire Parson and his Friends: The Correspondence of William Lisle Bowles with Four Hitherto Unidentified Reviews by Coleridge* (London 1926), pp. 97–8.
21 Wilfred S. Dowden, op. cit., p. 1987.
22 Garland Greever, op. cit., p. 97.
23 *DWG*, no. 1179, 16 Aug. 1838.
24 *DWG*, no. 1163, 26 Apr. 1838.
25 Harriet Martineau (1802–76), writer.
26 A poem in the style of the Greek poet Pindar.

27 This was in the frontispiece to *Scenes and Shaddows of Days Departed* . . . published by Pickering in 1837.
28 Bowles to Pickering, 4 May 1838: Harvard University, MS Eng 505. 5.
29 Garland Greever, op. cit., pp. 163–4.
30 Bowles to Pickering, 9 May 1838: Harvard University, MS Eng. 505. 5.
31 Bowles to D'Israeli, 21 May 1838, Bodleian Library, University of Oxford, Dep. Hughenden,G/I/103a.
32 The author is indebted to Mr Colin Pedley for drawing his attention to the fact that this sonnet first appeared in *Felix Farley's Bristol Journal*. See his 'Two Uncollected Poems by William Lisle Bowles' in *Notes and Queries for Readers and Writers,Collectors and Libarians* (Oxford 1990), vol. CCXXXV, pp. 404–5.
33 *SWJ*, no. 6061, 23 July 1838.
34 The *Gentleman's Magazine*, July 1838, p. 44.
35 Garland Greever, op. cit., p. 69.
36 Sir Gabriel Goldney, Bart (1813–1900).
37 Mrs Andrew Crosse, Poet, Parson, and Pamphleteer, *Temple Bar*, vol. 103, Sept. 1894, p. 45.
38 Bowles to Wilson, 31 Aug. 1838: Harvard University, MS Eng. 505. 5.
39 James Henry Monk (1784–1856), clergyman.
40 *DWG*, no. 1182, 6 Sept. 1838.
41 Cecil Woolf, op. cit., p. 416.
42 Bowles to Murray, 25 [no month on letter] 1838: National Library of Scotland, op. cit.
43 Simon Magus was believed by an early Gnostic sect to be God in human form.
44 Garland Greever, op. cit., p. 164.
45 *DWG*, no. 1182, 6 Sept. 1838.
46 Chapter Meeting 10 Oct. 1838: Chapter Act Book no. 24, 1834–1851.
47 *DWG*, 1203, 31 Jan. 1839.
48 Cecil Woolf, 'Some Uncollected Authors XVIII, William Lisle Bowles 1762–1850', *Book Collector*, vol. 7, 1958, p. 416.
49 *DWG*, no. 1192, 15 Nov. 1838.

50 Ibid., no. 1193, 22 Nov. 1838.
51 Ibid., no. 1198, 27 Dec. 1838.
52 Wilfred S. Dowden, op. cit.,
    pp. 2028–9.
53 Simonides (550–460 BC), ancient
    Greek poet.
54 *SWJ*, no. 6085, 7 Jan. 1839.
55 James Stoughton Money (1814–52),
    later Money-Kyrle, clergyman.
56 *DWG*, no. 1199, 3 Jan. 1839.
57 Ibid.
58 Allen Mawer and F.M. Stenton, *The
    Place Names of Wiltshire* (Cambridge
    1939), p. 257.
59 *DWG*, no. 1201, 17 Jan. 1839 and
    SWJ, no. 6087, 21 Jan. 1839.
60 *SWJ*, no. 6088, 28 Jan. 1839.
61 Bowles to Murray, 20 Jan. 1839:
    National Library of Scotland, John
    Murray Archive, MS 12604/1137.
62 The author is grateful to Graham
    Hendy for making available to him
    the records of the attendance of
    all the residentary canons that he
    had extracted from the Chapter Act
    Books of Salisbury Cathedral.
63 Southey's *Hymn to the Penates*
    published in 1797.
64 Garland Greever, op. cit., pp. 34–5.
65 William Fisher (1800–74),
    clergyman.
66 Garland Greever, op. cit., pp. 35–6.
67 Ibid., p. 98.
68 John Edmund Reade (1800–70),
    novelist.
69 Bowles to Fox-Talbot, May 1839:
    British Library from the Fox Talbot
    Museum/Lacock Abbey Collection
    Lacock, doc. no. 03885.
70 Bowles to Fox-Talbot, Sept. 1839:
    ibid, doc. no. 3937.
71 Henry Alworth Merewether (1780–
    1864), lawyer.
72 Constance Fox-Talbot to Fox-Talbot,
    27 Sept. 1839: ibid., doc. no. 3595.
73 Augustus Welby Northmore
    Pugin (1812–52), architect and
    ecclesiologist.
74 *SWJ*, no. 6103, 6 May 1839.
75 Ibid., no. 6109, 17 June 1839.
76 An ancient city of Egypt and seat of
    the sun god Re.

77 Wilfred S. Dowden, op. cit., p. 2051.
78 Daughter of James Kenney (1779–
    1841), both of whom were staying
    with Moore.
79 Wilfred S. Dowden, op. cit., p. 2082.
80 *DWG*, no. 1229, 1 Aug. 1839.
81 Howard and Peter Coombs, *Journal
    of a Somerset Rector 1803–1834*
    (Weston-super-Mare 1987), p. 507.
82 John Scandrett Harford (1787–
    1866), biographer.
83 Bowles to Murray, 30 Dec. 1838:
    National Library of Scotland, John
    Murray Archive, 12604/1137.
84 Edward Denison (1801–54),
    clergyman.
85 Bowles to Murray, 2 Apr. 1839:
    National Library of Scotland, op. cit.
86 Bowles to Murray, 28 Apr. 1839:
    ibid.
87 Philip Henry, Viscount Mahon
    (1805–75), historian.
88 Bowles to Murray, 7 July 1839: ibid.
89 *SWJ*, no. 6139, 13 Jan. 1840.
90 *DWG*, no. 1278, 9 July 1840.
91 Magdalene Bowles to unnamed,
    24 June 1840: Bodleian Library,
    University of Oxford, Dep.
    Hughenden G/I/106.
92 Wilfred S. Dowden, *The Journal of
    Thomas Moore*, op. cit. p. 2161.
93 *DWG*, no. 1299, 3 Dec. 1840.
94 Edward Denison (1801–54),
    clergyman.
95 Walter Kerr Hamilton (1808–69),
    Bishop of Salisbury 1854–69.
96 Thomas Russell (176–1788), poet.
97 *Elegy, written at the Hot-Wells,
    Bristol, Addressed to the Revd William
    Howley.*
98 Thomas Russell had been at
    Winchester with both Howley
    and Bowles. Shortly after his
    death Howley edited *Sonnets and
    Miscellaneous Poems by the late
    Thomas Russell, Fellow of New College,
    Oxford.*
99 Howley to Bowles, 6 Dec. 1841:
    Lambeth Palace Library, MSS 3355,
    ff. 1–5.
100 G. Gilfillan, *The Poetical Works of
    William Lisle Bowles . . .* (Edinburgh

101 *DWG*, no. 1421, 6 Apr. 1843.

102 Bowles to Ellacombe, 12 Dec. 1843: Harvard University, MS Eng 505. 5.

103 WSA, 451/21.

104 John Britton, *The Auto-Biography of John Britton . . .* (London 1850), p. 373.

105 The last line of *Elegiac Stanzas Suggested by a Picture of Peele Castle in a Storm by Sir George Beamount* written by Wordsworth following the death of his brother John.

106 E. de Selincourt, ed., *The Letters of William and Dorothy Wordsworth, vol. viii, The Later Years, Part iv, 1840–1853*, 2nd edn, A.G. Hill (Oxford 1988), pp. 551–2.

107 Basil Montagu (1770–1851), legal and miscellaneous writer.

108 E. de Selincourt, op. cit., p. 610.

109 Julian Charles Young, op. cit., p. 230.

110 John Britton, op. cit., p. 373.

111 Either Daniel Ingram in St Anne's Street or Thomas Ingram in the Market Place.

112 Ambrose Tucker, *A Catalogue of Some Portraits and other Prints Having to do with the County of Wilts* (Salisbury 1908), p. 65.

113 John Britton, op. cit., p. 372.

114 Edward Thurlow, 2nd Baron Thurlow (1781–1829), poet.

115 Alaric Alfred Watts, *Alaric Watts, A Narrative of His Life* (London 1884), vol. I, pp. 140–1.

116 Arthur Houlton, 3rd son of John Houlton of Farleigh Castle.

117 Houlton to Jackson, 12 Apr. 1850: Rice University, Fondren Library, Houston, Texas, MS 167.

118 The memorial is on the east side of the south-eastern transept, now used as the virgers' vestry.

Index

Parochial History of Bremhill and of its reception, 207–9; the publication of *Days Departed; or Banwell Hill . . .* and correspondence with Murray, 215–17; visit to the bishop of Bath and Wells and Skinner's account, 220–1; his election as a residentiary canon of Salisbury Cathedral and an account of his duties and improvements to his canonry, 221–3; publication of his *A Word on Cathedral Oratorios . . .*, 232; publication of his life of Thomas Ken, correspondence with Murray and Nichols and its reception, 234–7; correspondence with Caroline Bowles, 240–1

1832–1835: he presses for an honorary degree to be awarded to Isaac D'Israeli, 249–51; publication of *St John in Patmos . . .*, 254; is visited by Joseph Hunter who describes his peculiarities, 259; satirical poem in response to his lines on the drinking spout at Derry Hill, 261; publication of his *Last . . . Answer to the Question 'Of what use . . . are the English Cathedral Establishments' . . .* and his subsequent correspondence with

the master of Dulwich College, 262–5; writes to *The Times* following the death of Coleridge, 271; publication of his history of Lacock Abbey, 273; visit of the bishop of Bath and Wells to Bremhill, 276–7; correspondence with John Gough Nichols, 277; a performance of his oratorio *The Ark*, 279–80; correspondence with George Scrope, 281–2

1836–1837: his nocturnal adventure in London, 285–8; publication of his works on the patronage of Deans and Chapters, 289–92; visits Clifton with Moore, 294–6; correspondence with Murray, 296–7; his letters to the *Examiner* on the question of the powers of deans and chapters, 299–301; his part in the erection of a monument to Maud Heath, 307–8; he receives a visit from the Prime Minister, 308; correspondence with Murray, 311–12; correspondence with John Mitford and William Pickering concerning his *Scenes and Shadows of Days Departed* and a visit by them to Bremhill, 314–7; correspondence with James Bulcock relating to a new publication, 320–3

1838–1850: he makes his

last will, 325; receives a visit from Samuel Rogers, 329–30; publication of *The Cartoons of Raphael . . .*, 333; publication of *A Final Defence of the Rights of Patronage of Deans and Chapters . . .*, 337; relates the finding of Roman coins at Derry Hill, 338–9; meets and writes to William Wordsworth, 341–3; visits Lacock Abbey, 344; correspondence with John Murray (2), 346–8; illness of, 349; the death of his wife and letter of condolence from Wordsworth, 352–3; resigns the living of Bremhill, 353; his last years and death, 354–5; his monument in Salisbury Cathedral, 356

Bowles, Rev. William Thomas (1736–86), 1, 3, 9, 48

Bowen, Rev. Mr, 65

Bowood: Lord Lansdowne writes to WLB about rock-work at, 56; Rogers's account of WLB's visit to, 73; WLB meets Madame de Stael at, 74; Maria Edgeworth's account of WLB's behaviour at, 102; theft of property from, 136; WLB opens new chapel at, 160; WLB amuses guests at dinner at, 266

Brabant, Dr, 79

Brackley, 1

Bradenham, 251

Brean, 1, 48, 253

Printed in the United Kingdom by
Lightning Source UK Ltd., Milton Keynes
142061UK00001B/43/P